Nor-tec Rifa!

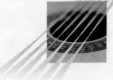

Currents in
Latin American
& Iberian Music

WALTER CLARK, SERIES EDITOR

Nor-tec Rifa!
Electronic Dance Music from Tijuana to the World
Alejandro L. Madrid

Nor-tec Rifa!

Electronic Dance Music
from Tijuana to the World

Alejandro L. Madrid

OXFORD

UNIVERSITY PRESS

2008

OXFORD
UNIVERSITY PRESS

Oxford University Press, Inc., publishes works that further
Oxford University's objective of excellence
in research, scholarship, and education.

Oxford   New York
Auckland   Cape Town   Dar es Salaam   Hong Kong   Karachi
Kuala Lumpur   Madrid   Melbourne   Mexico City   Nairobi
New Delhi   Shanghai   Taipei   Toronto

With offices in
Argentina   Austria   Brazil   Chile   Czech Republic   France   Greece
Guatemala   Hungary   Italy   Japan   Poland   Portugal   Singapore
South Korea   Switzerland   Thailand   Turkey   Ukraine   Vietnam

Copyright © 2008 by Oxford University Press, Inc.

Published by Oxford University Press, Inc.
198 Madison Avenue, New York, New York 10016

www.oup.com

Oxford is a registered trademark of Oxford University Press

Library of Congress Cataloging-in-Publication Data
Madrid-González, Alejandro L. (Alejandro Luis)
Nor-tec rifa! : electronic dance music from Tijuana to the world / Alejandro Madrid
p. cm. — (Currents in Latin American and Iberian Music series)
Includes bibliographical references (p.   ).
ISBN 978-0-19-532637-6; 978-0-19-534262-8 (pbk.)
1. Underground dance music—Mexico—Tijuana (Baja California)—History
and criticism.   2. Colectivo Nortec.   I. Title.
ML3540.5M33 2008
781.640972'23—dc22   2007030216

Recorded audio tracks (marked in text with 🔊)
are available online at www.oup.com/us/nortecrifa
Access with username Music4 and password Book2497

1 3 5 7 9 8 6 4 2

Printed in the United States of America
on acid-free paper

Aquí yacen tus pasos:
En el anonimato de las huellas
—José Emilio Pacheco, "Tradición"

Rifa ('ri·fa)
—v. tr.
    1. *Spanish slang:* to control or direct; to exercise dominating
       power, authority, or control
—v. intr.
    1. *Spanish slang:* to be excellent or superior
    2. *Spanish slang:* to be in total control or command

Acknowledgments

This project reflects the interest, support, and benevolence of many people. I wish to express my deep gratitude to Frances Aparicio, Arved Ashby, Harris Berger, Jan Fairley, Jane Florine, Talía Jiménez, Robin Moore, Deborah Paredez, Ronald Radano, Brenda Romero, Helena Simonett, and the anonymous reviewers at Oxford University Press for kindly reading and commenting on my manuscript or portions of it. Their insights and criticisms were extremely helpful, although I remind the reader that all polemics, oversights, and errors are my own. I am forever indebted to Margarita Mazo for sharing with me her ideas about "multiple identity" back when few musicologists were talking about such notions; although I do not embark on a discussion of multiple identity per se in this book, her intellectual camaraderie was very influential in the development of the theoretical framework that informs my work.

Numerous individuals with whom I have had contact have enriched this study in countless ways. I would like to thank the late Gerard Béhague, Sara Cohen, Ignacio Corona, Bernardo Íllari, Jill Lane, José Limón, René T. A. Lysloff, Susan McClary, Ana María Ochoa, José Antonio Robles Cahero, Leonora Saavedra, and Barry Shank for taking interest in my project as it unfolded. My deep appreciation also goes to Claudia Carretta, Miguel Hernández Montero, Kai Fikentscher, José Ignacio López (El Lazo Invisible), Ed Luna, Alejandro Magallanes, Georgina Rojas, Luis Rojo, Pepe Rojo, Rafa Saavedra, and Eréndira Torres for their help and encouragement at different stages of my research.

I would like to offer thanks to the current and former members of the Nortec Collective (Ramón Amezcua, Pedro Gabriel Beas, Sergio Brown, Octavio Castellanos, Ignacio Chávez Uranga, Fernando Corona, Iván Díaz Robledo, José Luis Martín, Roberto Mendoza, Pepe Mogt, Jorge Ruiz, Fritz Torres, and Jorge Verdín) for enthusiastically believing in this project from the beginning and for their patience and availability while the book was being written. Sincere gratitude is extended to DJ Zen from Sonic 360, to Omar Foglio and Sebastián Díaz from BulboTV, to Hans Fjellestad, and to David Harrington from the Kronos Quartet for selflessly sharing their work with me. I am particularly thankful to Raúl Cárdenas (Torolab), Iván Díaz Robledo (VJ Wero Palma), Octavio Hernández, José Luis Martín (VJ Mashaka), Pepe Mogt, Josh Norek from Nacional Records, Fritz Torres from Cha3, and Gerardo Yépiz (Acamonchi) for granting permission to use copyrighted music and images both in this book and on the Web site that accompanies it.

I am indebted to Alberto Vital and Elizabeth Colín Arroyo at Mexico's Secretaría de Relaciones Exteriores (Ministry of Foreign Affairs) and to Bruno Hernández Piché, former cultural attaché at the Mexican consulate in Chicago, for eagerly supporting my application for a Genaro Estrada Fellowship. This grant permitted me to spend the summer of 2004 at El Colegio de la Frontera Norte (COLEF) in Tijuana, conducting field and archival research. I would also like to offer thanks to José Manuel Valenzuela Arce and Fiamma Montezemolo, members of the Department of Cultural Studies at COLEF, for their help and encouragement during that period, and to Nancy Utley, Bricia Rivera, and Sandra Bello, the always-ready COLEF staff members whose assistance was priceless.

I wish to acknowledge Nicolas Shumway, former director of the Teresa Lozano Long Institute for Latin American Studies (LLILAS) of the University of Texas at Austin. A visiting scholar position at LLILAS allowed me to focus on writing the first chapters of this book. I would also like to thank Jennifer Mailloux, administrative assistant at LLILAS, and the staff at the Nettie Lee Benson Latin American Collection for their kind support and help during my tenure at the University of Texas.

My sincere gratitude is also expressed to my colleagues and former colleagues at the Latin American and Latino studies program of the University of Illinois at Chicago: Frances Aparicio, Chris Boyer, Ralph Cintrón, Nilda Flores, Elena González, Suzanne Oboler, Joel Palka, Amalia Pallares, Cristián Roa-de-la-Carrera, María de los Ángeles Torres, and Javier Villa-Flores; their outstanding scholarly support, friendship, and solidarity provided the perfect intellectual environment to finish writing this book. Also, when I was a visiting lecturer at the School of Music of Northwestern University, my research project kept moving forward thanks to Peter Webster, Linda

Austern, Inna Naroditskaya, and the gracious help of my research assistant, Rose Whitmore.

I am grateful to the staff at Oxford University Press for their support and guidance. Thanks in particular to Walter Clark, editor of the Currents in Latin American and Iberian Music series, to Norman Hirschy, to my superb editor, Suzanne Ryan, and to Christi Stanforth for their suggestions and for resolutely believing in my work.

Portions of this book have appeared in the following publications and appear here (in revised, adapted, and extended form) with permission of the original publishers:

Brief parts of chapters 1 and 7 originally appeared as "Navigating Ideologies in 'In-Between' Cultures: Signifying Practices in Nor-tec Music," *Latin American Music Review,* vol. 24, no. 2 (2003), © University of Texas Press, and have since been substantially revised and expanded.

Portions of chapters 3 and 4 appeared in "Imagining Modernity, Revising Tradition: Nor-tec Music in Tijuana and Other Borders," *Popular Music and Society,* vol. 28, no. 5 (2005), © Routledge.

"Dancing with Desire: Cultural Embodiment and Negotiation in Tijuana's Nor-tec Music and Dance," a shorter version of chapter 6, was published in *Popular Music,* vol. 25, no. 3 (2006), © Cambridge University Press.

Contents

List of Figures   xiii

List of Music Examples   xv

Introduction: Nor-tec and the Borders   3

ONE   Origins Revisited: Myth and Discourse
in the Nortec Collective   24

TWO   Tradition, Style, Nostalgia, and Kitsch   50

THREE   Getting the Word Around   87

FOUR   "Where's the Donkey Show, Mr. Mariachi?":
Reterritorializing TJ   114

FIVE   Producers, DJs, VJs, Fans, and the
Performance of Nor-tec   147

SIX   Dancing with Desire   169

SEVEN   Nor-tec and the Postnational Imagination   189

Notes   205

Bibliography   227

Index   243

Figures

Figure 1.1   Cover of *Música maestro* from
El Nuevo Sueño de la Gallina (1999)   37

Figure 1.2   Octavio Hernández and Pepe Mogt,
descriptive chart for "Poder Beat (Politics to the Bone)"   40

Figure 1.3   An example of Torolab's Sistema
Evolutivo de Binomios   42

Figure 2.1   Fritz Torres and Jorge Verdín's
"Nortec Bandido"   83

Figure 2.2   TV host Raúl Velasco, according to Acamonchi   84

Figure 2.3   Luis Donaldo Colosio, according to Acamonchi   85

Figure 3.1   Flyer used for the first concert of the
2003 La Leche tour   110

Figure 3.2   Flyer used for the first Miami night of the
2003 La Leche tour   111

Figure 3.3   Flyer used for the second Miami night of the
2003 La Leche tour   112

Figure 4.1   The Tijuana arch welcomes tourists to *La Revu* 116

Figure 4.2 Sign outside El Dandy del Sur, one of the Nortec Collective's favorite meeting places in Tijuana			117

Figure 4.3 Original city plat of Tijuana, according to Ricardo Orozco's 1889 model			118

Figure 4.4 Typical colonial Spanish city plat			119

Figure 4.5 Current map of Tijuana's Zona Centro			120

Figure 4.6 Promotional flyer for Nortec Live at Las Pulgas			125

Figure 4.7 Kin-Klé bar on the margins of Tijuana's downtown			130

Figure 4.8 Unicornio club on Tijuana's Avenida Revolución			131

Figure 5.1 Fan from Tijuana playing his part at the Nortec City performance			163

Figure 5.2 *El guachaman*			166

Figure 6.1 Ana and David dancing to the beat of Plankton Man's "Recinto portuario"			175

Figure 6.2 Dancing fans at the Echo			180

Figure 6.3 Doing the Robot to Nor-tec music at the Hot House			183

Figure 7.1 Tijuana, Tercera Nación exhibition along the walls of the Río Tijuana canal			190

Music Examples

Example 2.1 Basic rhythmic pattern of *cumbia norteña* as played by the *güiro*   59

Example 2.2 Terrestre, "El cereso," basic harmonic sequence   70

Example 2.3 "El cereso," trumpet sample   70

Example 2.4 "El cereso," bass line   71

Example 2.5 Bostich, "Polaris," rhythmic sequence manipulated with a vocoder   72

Example 2.6 "Polaris," rhythmic sequence without vocoder manipulation   73

Example 2.7 Fussible, "Infierno," basic bass line   75

Example 2.8 "Infierno," piano chord progression   75

Example 4.1 Hiperboreal, "Tijuana for Dummies," beginning section, first rhythmic interpretation   132

Example 4.2 "Tijuana for Dummies," beginning section, second rhythmic interpretation   133

Example 4.3 Polytemporal layering in Panóptica's "And L"   135

Example 4.4 Bostich, "Tijuana Bass," beginning
    melodic sequence   135

Example 4.5 "Tijuana Bass," beginning melodic sequence
    with added bass   136

Example 4.6 "Tijuana Bass," bimodal sequence   136

Nor-tec Rifa!

Introduction

Nor-tec and the Borders

As much as this is a book about a music culture and about the growth and transnational dissemination of a music scene, it is primarily a book about borders. It is an exploration of geographic and epistemological limits, their discursive stability, and their practical impermanence. In this book, I examine different understandings of the notions of border and boundary and the ways in which people deal with the contradictory circumstances of living in these geographic but also ideological and even mental spaces. My intention is to show how individuals in liminal circumstances continuously negotiate their identities, their pasts, their presents, and their imaginary futures, in the production, regulation, and consumption of cultural goods. Furthermore, I am interested in showing these types of negotiations as strategies that allow border communities to chart and navigate their everyday lives under the challenging pressures of globalization.

In this book, I am concerned with a variety of borders and boundaries. I deal with the geographic border between two nation-states, the United States of America and Mexico, and also look at individuals living in multicultural contexts as epistemological borders where different cultures and visions of the world meet. I investigate the boundaries between tradition and innovation as well as the borders between different musical genres, and I explore the thin line that separates the hip from the unsophisticated. In an attempt to move beyond simplistic dichotomies, I understand these borders as both limits and connecting tissue, as discontinuities and continuities, as margins and as centers. In short, I see borders as fluid give-

3

and-take areas where complexity, negotiation, and hybridity are everyday constants.

The Nor-tec scene is a prime example of the types of strategies necessary to chart and navigate these border zones. My analysis focuses on the relationship between this scene (including music, multimedia performances, distribution strategies, embodied culture, and networks of consumption and reception) and its social and cultural surroundings, including the desires and aspirations that make the music appealing to certain people. Thus, I take Nor-tec musicians, promoters, and fans as individuals whose actions are the results of their interactions with specifically liminal social, economic, cultural, and often psychological circumstances, but also, and most important, as individuals whose actions have an impact in that sociocultural world. Moreover, I do not attempt to arrive at the "true meaning" of this artistic manifestation or scene but rather to advance an informed interpretation and a viewpoint based on my experience of the music, the dance, the performances, and especially border and diasporic life. My analysis throughout the book should be read accordingly as a critical inquiry into border social life through music and performance.

What Is Nor-tec?

Like most hybrid manifestations, Nor-tec is a border site, a contact zone where distinctly different elements meet to produce a new form of expression. Thus, Nor-tec works as a perfect metaphor for the exploration of a large variety of issues of liminality and border life, from the stylistic and aesthetic to social, personal, and political boundaries. Nor-tec began in Tijuana in 1999 as a musical manifestation that sampled the sounds of traditional music from the north of Mexico (*norteña* music and *banda sinaloense* or *tambora*), transforming and reorganizing them with the help of the computer technology used in European and American electronic dance music (EDM). Hence, in the composite word Nor-tec, "Nor" stands for "north" and "tec" stands for "technology." The idea of Nor-tec as an articulation of local tradition from the north of Mexico through modern technology was quickly embraced by local video and installation artists and by graphic and fashion designers; this transformed it from a musical experiment into an aesthetic of hybridity. Such a crossbreed aesthetic has allowed these musicians and artists to express the complex fluidity between the "American" and the "Mexican," the "First" and the "Third" Worlds, the modern and the old, the cosmopolitan and the local, the center and the periphery, and the hip and the kitschy, as they experience it in their everyday lives at the Tijuana–San Diego border. Accordingly, Nor-tec is not only the manifestation of a border culture but also a border zone in itself, a place where these contradictions collide and are resolved in its production, consumption, distribution, and performance.

Although the terms "Nor-tec" and "Nortec" were used interchangeably when the music was first made public, they quickly came to identify different aspects of the same experience. While "Nortec" became a synonym for the activities, music, and art produced by the members of the Nortec Collective (a formal group of musicians and visual artists working as a team in exploring the possibilities of the hybrid aesthetic), "Nor-tec" became a label for the aesthetic itself. Throughout this book, I favor the use of the hyphenated version and use the nonhyphenated word only when referring to the collective or when quoting a printed source that spells it that way.

The founding members of the Nortec Collective were musicians and producers Ramón Amezcua (Bostich), Pedro Gabriel Beas (Hiperboreal), Ignacio Chávez Uranga (Plankton Man), Fernando Corona (Terrestre), Roberto Mendoza (Panóptica), Jorge Ruiz (Melo), and José Trinidad Morales (Pepe Mogt; Melo and Mogt were Fussible) and Jorge Verdín and Fritz Torres (members of Clorofila). The visual side of the collective was formed by Verdín and Torres (who also make up a team of graphic designers called Cha3), Sergio Brown (VJ CBrown), Octavio Castellanos (VJ TCR), Iván Díaz Robledo (VJ Wero Palma), José Luis Martín (VJ Mashaka), and Salvador Vázquez Ricalde (VJ Sal).[1] Since the early twenty-first century, Plankton Man, Terrestre, VJ CBrown, VJ Wero Palma, and VJ Sal have each left the collective after serious differences regarding management, distribution strategies, and even aesthetics. However, many of them, especially Plankton Man and Terrestre, have continued to cultivate a Nor-tec sound in their individual productions and collaborations. The work of many musicians, producers, disc jockeys (DJs), artists, and graphic designers who are not formal members of the collective but who have collaborated with it or embraced the aesthetic from time to time was also fundamental in the development of the scene. DJs and producers Daniel Rivera (DJ Tolo), Aníbal Silva (DJ Aníbal), Enrique Jiménez (Mr. Ejival), Álvaro Ruiz (Balboa), and graphic designers, visual artists, and performance artists Claudia Algara, Raúl Cárdenas (Torolab), Ángeles Moreno, and Gerardo Yépiz (Acamonchi) have produced music and visual art that has become essential to the Nor-tec experience.

Most Nor-tec artists and musicians are middle-class individuals in their thirties. With few exceptions, all of them are from Tijuana or have spent several years in the city. Melo was born in Chula Vista, California, but has lived all his life in Tijuana; Verdín was born in Los Angeles and lives in Pasadena, California, but was raised in Tijuana; Plankton Man is from Ensenada and currently lives in Los Angeles but resided in Tijuana for many years; Ángeles Moreno is from Mexico City and currently lives in Barcelona but also spent several years in Tijuana. They are all individuals whose life experiences make them carry the border within. Being from Mexico City, Balboa is the only musician affiliated with Nor-tec who has not lived in Tijuana.[2] Before the success of Nor-tec, many of these artists were part-time musicians. Although most of them had been involved in music for over 15 years (with the exception of Jorge Verdín, Fritz Torres, and Hiperboreal, whose concern with music had only been tangential as enthusiastic aficionados), in order to make a living they worked in a variety of nonmusic fields. Pepe Mogt was an engineer and used to work full time at a local *maquiladora,* a job he quit after Nor-tec. Panóptica spent some years proofreading articles and manuscripts at El Colegio de la Frontera Norte. Bostich was and still remains a full-time orthodontist. Fritz Torres and Jorge Verdín make their living as graphic designers. Hiperboreal was a student of Spanish literature. Plankton Man and Terrestre were already full-time musicians and had played in several progressive rock and electro-rock bands before joining the collective. The visual artists of the group are all professionals who have graduated with degrees in communication or filmmaking from local universities. Most of them hold on-and-off positions as adjunct professors at private and public colleges in order to supplement their income. They are all very active in the local artistic and intellectual scene as documentary makers, community workers, and organizers of cultural events. Although they had all collaborated on documentary and visual anthropology projects, they did not have much experience as video jockeys (VJs) before Nor-tec.

Who Listens to Nor-tec?

The first followers of Nor-tec were a group of music enthusiasts who belong to the same generation as the members of the collective. They are an extended group of friends and music lovers who have followed the careers of Pepe Mogt and Bostich for almost 15 years. The group is made of young middle-class professionals (architects, writers, poets, etc.) who call themselves *la familia* (the family) or *los culturosos* (the cultured ones) (due to their proclivity for cultural events). Still a loyal fan base, they were at the core of the first local crowd that embraced Nor-tec in the late 1990s. As the Nor-tec experiment gained international notoriety and forced national and international electronica (electronic dance music) fans and critics to look at Tijuana, younger and younger fans joined the scene.

An interesting process of distribution that moves along the boundary between the mainstream and the underground, often crossing back and forth, has been an important factor in shaping the Nor-tec international following. As the excitement about Nor-tec grew among international electronica fans, the Nor-tec scene diversified and acquired singular characteristics. The Internet was a fundamental aspect of the early, alternative distribution of Nor-tec, and it also played an essential role in the development of a transnational virtual community. From being a tool for the circulation and even the production of music, the Internet became an actual site where fans from Germany, Japan, Italy, and the United States could meet fans from Mexico and the rest of Latin America. These methods allowed for the widening and diversification of the Nor-tec fan base; the broad range of ethnic and class experiences among Nor-tec's transnational audiences often resulted in complex processes of reception and re-signification of the music. Thus, in the United States, the music began to be consumed by Anglos and Latinos alike, although it came to mean different things for the different communities that embraced it. In Mexico, after a few years of resistance, Mexico City fans finally gave in and succumbed to the sounds that had rocked the Tijuana scene since the late 1990s, a situation that puts in evidence the conflicting and complex relations between the center and the margins of the country.

Nor-tec and the International Underground Dance Music Scene

With some notable exceptions, the transnational audiences that have embraced Nor-tec are the middle-class youngsters that support electronica. Indeed, to fully appreciate Nor-tec within the phenomenon of globalization, we need to understand it as part of a larger musical tendency, electronic dance music (EDM). Furthermore, we should also understand Nor-tec as part of a distinct type of alternative EDM, underground dance music (UDM). Ethnomusicologist Kai Fikentscher defines UDM as a continuation of the 1970s disco phenomenon that, in response to dominant moral and aesthetic codes in contemporary American and European societies, "is cultivated outside the view of the general public eye."[3] The social spaces and institutions that allow the dissemination of UDM are DJs and producers, home studios, independent record labels, raves, discotheques, and clubs. In most cases, these spaces and institutions are run privately or semi-privately and, as sociologist Sarah Thornton observes, are defined in open rejection or even denigration of the mass media and the mainstream music industry.[4] As this book shows, Nor-tec is a type of "in-between" musical manifestation; it is a music style that continuously crosses back and forth over the borders between different UDM genres and a scene that, although self-defined as underground, finds ways to subtly cross the boundaries between the mainstream and the alternative via savvy distribution and consumption strategies.

Thus, against a large body of scholarship that approaches alternative music as resistance, I propose that alternative music often engages cultural and social constructs in complex ways that equally resist and reinforce aspects of hegemonic culture.

Just as the disco music scene was crucial in the development of UDM, another major influence in the late 1970s was the growing recognition of European electronic music by American underground musicians. The pioneering work with synthesizers, drum machines, and sequencers of bands like Kraftwerk and Depeche Mode was pivotal in the growth of an underground dance scene that also articulated the youngsters' futuristic imagination of modernity. As music critic Simon Reynolds suggests, "[E]lectronica's aura of non-humanity is part of a cultural obsession with a future conceived as either a utopia of aerodynamic technological pleasure or as a nightmare of control and automation."[5] This passion with technology is very important in the production process of UDM, which is based on sampling and the technological manipulation of sound as basic compositional techniques. As in hip-hop, UDM tracks generally use breaks sampled from older recordings as basic units to "make beats" or to build the track's rhythmic foundation (usually in 4/4 meter) or groove. Most often, harmonic motion in UDM tends to be rather simple; however, harmonies work as a base for the introduction of innovative timbres and textures, the elements in which electronic musicians and producers are really interested and where the complexity of the music lies.

EDM and UDM do not refer to single heterogeneous music styles or genres. There is a wide variety of EDM genres and styles, each of them defined by a combination of specific stylistic features, discourses of origin and authenticity, practices of distribution, and networks of consumption and reception that conform to distinct scenes. Among the most important are house, techno, ambient, intelligent dance music (IDM), drum'n'bass, breakbeat, and trance, each including a large variety of substyles. House is a genre developed in Chicago in the early 1980s. It is characterized by a 4/4 meter at 118–135 beats per minute (bpm) produced by a sampler or drum machine. It features musical acoustic elements from disco music, funk, and European synth pop. Acid house, hip house, jazz house, and garage are different house substyles associated with specific clubs or DJs; they are all dance-floor-oriented styles that favor the dancing body over the listening experience. Techno music was launched in Detroit, also in the early 1980s, and was quickly embraced by European (especially German) fans. Musically, techno features a quick 4/4 meter at 130–140 bpm, slightly faster than house; it stresses synthesized sounds and lessens the acoustic musical elements found in house. Substyles of techno include minimal techno, gabba, acid techno, and hardcore. Ambient is a style of down-tempo music developed in the late 1980s that deemphasizes the dancing body. It is based on experimentation with sound for the creation of music characterized by background sonic textures. IDM is also an experimental down-tempo style that rejects the dance floor but, contrary to ambient, aspires to be listened to instead of becoming part of the room's "decoration." Substyles of ambient and IDM include bleep'n'bass, braindance, chill out, lounge music, and trip hop. Drum'n'bass was developed in London and Bristol by DJs who mixed reggae bass lines with quick breaks sampled from hip-hop and funk. It is a vigorous dance style also referred to as jungle. Among the subgenres of drum'n'bass are drumfunk, 2step, clownstep, neurofunk, etc. They are all characterized by the presence of an intricate bass line, exploration of timbres in the lower registers, and fast tempi that range between 165 and 180 bpm. Breakbeat originated in the mid-1990s in London, Brighton, and Bristol. It is characterized by an irregular 4/4 meter with prominent use of syncopation and polyrhythm. Breakbeat tracks usually range from 115 to 150 bpm and emphasize breaks that relate it to African American musics, such as funk and soul. Among the subgenres of breakbeat we may include big beat, nu skool breaks, drill'n'bass, and brokenbeat. Trance is a genre of electronic dance music developed in Germany, Belgium, and the Netherlands in the early 1990s. It is characterized by its emphasis on melody and a 4/4 steady meter at 135–150 bpm. Stylistically, trance favors minor chord sequences and the use of synthesized sounds. Arguably, trance is the most popular genre of electronic dance music, having been embraced by the mainstream music industry. Such mainstream access has meant a dramatic stylistic shift that frequently includes the addition of vocals, a very rare element in other types of EDM. Subgenres of trance include acid trance, anthem trance, euro trance, progressive trance, and others.

Nor-tec shares many of the particularities of UDM genres: it is a type of home-produced, sample-based EDM, and it is also an underground manifestation that rejects the mainstream and makes use of alternative methods of distribution (although, as I show in chapter 3, Nor-tec musicians often find clever ways to use the mainstream for their own benefit). However, a mere taxonomical understanding of the notion of genre shows Nor-tec not necessarily as a genre itself. Nor-tec lacks the stylistic homogeneity of a genre; it is instead a heterogeneous music whose styles are as diverse as the number of musicians, producers, and DJs that compose it, mix it, and remix it. If anything, Nor-tec stands at the border of a number of different genres which are articulated differently by each member of the collective. Bostich seems to have developed the most personal and heterogeneous style among the Nor-tec producers. His is a unique, crude, and experimental down-tempo type of techno that often finds its groove with the use of cumbia-driven percussion rhythmic patterns ("Polaris," "Tijuana

Bass," "Unicornio," "Synthakon").[6] Fussible's Nor-tec goes from ambient
and IDM ("Ventilador," "Trip to Ensenada," "Zona N") to house ("El sonar
de mis tambores," "Casino Soul," "Odyssea") and even electro pop ("Tijuana Makes Me Happy"). The music of Hiperboreal is a curious mix of
down-tempo jazz house and progressive trance ("Loop eterno," "Kin-klé
futurista," "Dandy del Sur"). Panóptica prefers a type of minimal techno
("And L," "Revu Cruising," "She's in Fiestas") but also composes
drum'n'bass tracks ("El chivero de tepatoche") and IDM ("Aguasnegras
en dub," "Camposanto"). Clorofila's music ranges from ambient and
lounge ("Huatabampo 3 AM," "Cantamar '72") to electro funk ("Funky
Tamazula") and IDM ("Paseo moral"). The down-tempo sound of Terrestre stretches from a type of lounge or chill out ("California 70") and
ambient ("Secondary Theme Inspection") to jazz house ("Gran chapa-
rral") and even new age ("Maraka Man"). Finally, Plankton Man's music is
an interesting mixture of breakbeat ("Rancho tron," "Recinto portuario")
and neurofunk ("No hay volver," "No liazi jaz"). Even in the collective's
latest production, *Tijuana Sessions, Vol. 3* (2005), one is able to hear the
music crossing over a variety of genres and subgenres beyond the seemingly
superficial stylistic homogeneity of the tracks.

As observed in the variety of genres adopted by these musicians, it is
clear that there is no such thing as a distinct Nor-tec style. Nevertheless, as
in the case of house, techno, drum'n'bass, or any other prominent UDM
genre, the fact that the boundaries of Nor-tec are clearly and meticulously
defined by fans, critics, and marketing strategists in a continuous social
performance makes it clear that it is the articulation of ideas and experiences beyond the music's mere stylistic features that makes the music and
the scene meaningful. Thus, Nor-tec should be understood as a strategy
based on the social signification of an aesthetic idea rather than on an independently developed music style.

Defining the Field

The particularities of the Nor-tec scene, my intention to explore epistemological borders beside geographic boundaries, and the fact that I am an individual raised at the border (and have carried the border within myself as
I have moved to the north of the United States)—all have made it difficult
to define where the field began and where it ended. For practical reasons, I
could assume that I entered the field almost without realizing it, after attending a concert in Mexico City that featured Bostich and Fussible among
a variety of German acts in early 2000. Nor-tec was relatively new, and it
was the first time the project had been presented in Mexico City. Retro-
spectively, I realize that I immediately began to observe the event and ask

questions about it from an ethnographic perspective (What made people dance? What made them stop dancing? What was there in Nor-tec they did not like? What kind of cultural issues were at stake in their dancing or lack of dancing?). I began to gather printed materials about Nor-tec, but it was not until a year later that I started a more systematic research approach when I contacted the members of the collective for interviews. During the years 2003, 2004, and 2005, I was more actively conducting in situ field-work in Tijuana. I visited the city two times in 2003, spent the summer of 2004 there, and visited it once more, for the last time, in 2005. There, I befriended the members and former members of the collective as well as collaborators, fans, and detractors. I attended parties, witnessed recording and composition sessions, and enjoyed academic conversations about my project with local scholars. In the meantime, I realized that if I wanted to get a good picture of the Nor-tec phenomenon, I also needed to pay attention to its reception by fans and critics in the United States and Mexico City. I also recognized that the Nor-tec scene was different from other music scenes in that it did not have an actual meeting place. Even in Tijuana, Nor-tec was a nomadic scene that lacked fixed clubs and concert venues. I quickly understood that Nor-tec fans were not bounded by geographic location but were rather a transnational crowd whose meeting place was the Internet. Blogs, listservs, chat rooms, and cyber-lounges were the actual sites where Nor-tec fans got together to talk about the music, express their opinions about the musicians, discuss their favorite tracks, and state their fascination with the images produced by the Nor-tec video artists. It was also through these spaces that they shared pictures, videos, newly composed music, and DJ sets. The complex transnational and globalized web of distribution and consumption of Nor-tec forced me to develop an innovative type of virtual fieldwork I have called "cyber-fieldwork." Cyber-fieldwork recognizes the Internet as much more than a tool for communication or a space for the storage and retrieval of information; it acknowledges its importance as a virtual space where relationships are established, knowledge is produced, and cultural meaning is negotiated. For this, I became a member of several Internet-based listservs, groups, and chat rooms where I participated in and followed lively discussions about Nor-tec and electronic music. I also developed a systematic routine to check and keep track of a wide variety of fan blogs and kept an eye on several Internet-based channels of music distribution where fans circulate Nor-tec music free of charge.

After four years of traveling to Tijuana to interview fans, musicians, and event organizers; attending Nor-tec concerts in Mexico City, Los Angeles, and Chicago (in an attempt to account for the local, national, and transnational reception of Nor-tec); and mapping the Internet in search of

opinions, fans' cyber-journals, music, and artwork, I decided to put an end
to the fieldwork and cyber-fieldwork phases of the project at the release
party of *Tijuana Sessions, Vol. 3,* on 30 September 2005, in Tijuana. The
combination of fieldwork, cyber-fieldwork, archival research, and oral history would permit me to thoroughly chart about ten years of Tijuana's
electronic pop music scene, from 1995 to 2005. Understanding the history
of continuously changing musical tastes among *tijuanense* musicians and
fans throughout this time span allowed me to appreciate Nor-tec as a fleet-
ing moment, one that articulated the desire and cultural capital of young
middle-class border people according to the specific circumstances of that
particular time.

Doing Fieldwork at the Border

I spent the first 14 years of my life in Reynosa, Tamaulipas, at the U.S.–
Mexico border. Growing up there, I learned to come to terms with a series
of ideological discourses and everyday practices that would seem contradictory to most Mexicans from the center of the country. My mother used
to buy Mexican sweet bread at El Rey, a local store in Reynosa, and milk
at the Globe in McAllen, Texas. My sister took Mexican folk dance lessons at Reynosa's Cultural Center and celebrated her birthday parties at
McAllen's Skateland. My family used to get together at my grandfather's
place to enjoy his fabulous stories of being a rural school teacher during
Mexican president Lázaro Cárdenas's 1930s socialist educative reform, but
also celebrated New Year's at my uncle's in Brownsville, Texas. I used to
draw short cartoon strips based on the latest episodes of *The Incredible
Hulk* years before the show made its way to Mexican television in a dubbed
version. Equally happy watching *Captain Kangaroo* or Chabelo, Fat Albert
or *Odisea Burbujas,* but also local TV entertainers like Pipo or El Tío
Rodolfo, I felt at ease dealing with regional, U.S., or Mexican mainstream
popular cultures. As is true for many kids growing up at the border, the
lines separating these cultural experiences were indistinguishable for me.
Without a doubt, growing up at the northern Mexican border was an experience radically different from that of most Mexican kids of my generation. I was able to actively corroborate this when, after moving to Mexico
City in the early 1980s, I had to listen to all sorts of crazy stories about the
norteños' "lack of culture" while at the same time sensing the *chilangos'*
envy for my American jeans and tennis shoes.[7]

When I decided to travel to Tijuana for my first field trip in May 2003,
I was sure that my experience as a "border kid" would help me to dispel
the hypnotic American and Mexican stereotypes about the "sinful" and

"lawless" border. Nevertheless, by pure chance, I arrived in Tijuana like most U.S. tourists do, through San Diego via San Ysidro, and was immediately directed toward the infamous Avenida Revolución (*La Revu,* as locals call it)—and there they were, the strip clubs, the donkeys painted as zebras, the bars where the legal drinking age is 18, the drugstores where you can buy anything without a prescription. It was the same Tijuana that had been invented for U.S. tourists, the Tijuana celebrated in Manu Chau's infamous song: "Welcome to Tijuana / *Tequila, sexo, marihuana.*"

It was there that I realized that although my condition as a border kid did give me a few advantages, it also situated me in an ambiguous—although rather familiar—emic and etic position at once; I felt both an insider and an outsider.[8] I am from the border but I am not a *tijuanense.* I understand and have experienced life at the border, but I did not resolve its contradictions with the same means that have allowed people from Tijuana to develop a unique *tijuanense* culture. I am aware and can understand the sense of crisis experienced by *tijuanenses* as border citizens, but I am not completely able to decipher the particular codes developed by locals in order to sort through their everyday lives. Experiencing this dilemma was an important step in problematizing the radical separation between "us" and "other," the border that, according to cultural anthropologists Akhil Gupta and James Ferguson, informs contemporary politics of difference.[9] This problem found its way into a personal narrative style that continuously juxtaposes ethnographic sections written in the first person and present tense with interviews, historical narratives, analytical discussions, snippets of autobiography, and even literary recreations of historical events. Influenced by sociologist Pablo Vila's reflections on border ethnography, I developed this narrative style in an attempt to "shed light on the [complex] process of meaning construction involved in any research project."[10] In this type of process, the borders between self and other and the boundaries between insider and outsider disappear or are blurry at best.

By being constantly aware that I was both an insider and an outsider, I was able to chart the complexity of self/other relations at the border and understand the *tijuanenses'* seemingly contradictory relation with the alienating discourses of representation coming from both Mexico and the United States. Indeed, Tijuana is a unique border city. It is a place where individuals have appropriated the legends about their city and have made them into goods for consumption. The transformation of those myths into merchandise with exchange value empowers locals to question those discourses that attempt to write them as marginal and to eventually challenge the center/margin dichotomy.

Tijuana in the American
and Mexican Imagination

Tijuana, *aquí empieza la patria* (the motherland begins here).[11] Tijuana, the nearby hell. Tijuana, *ahí acaba la patria* (the motherland ends there). Tijuana, the happiest place on earth.[12] Tijuana, Tía Juana, T.J.[13] Myth, experience, discourse, representation, and identification, legend, reality, desire, and shame continuously intertwine to build the complex mythological web that surrounds Tijuana's symbolic past, present, and imaginary future. Mythology, whether Mexican or American, has always been central in the development of symbolic ideas about and images of Tijuana. Both Mexican and U.S. media have historically played a fundamental role in constructing Tijuana as a liminal site, the end of a nation where the slightest mistake of the Border Patrol is an opportunity to sneak illegal aliens or drugs into the United States; or, the end of a nation, the barbaric land where U.S. cultural imperialism threatens Mexican, Latin American, and Hispanic culture in every bar where you order your beer in Spanglish and pay with a mix of dollars and pesos. However, mythology is a complex process that creates contradictory images and infuses them with ambiguous and often multiple meanings according to the changing historical, cultural, and social circumstances that surround it. If people in the United States often identify Tijuana with immorality, perversion, and violence, they also see it as a land of emancipation from the moralistic restrictions of their own society; thus, the contradictions of U.S. moral and social codes make Tijuana into both an object of vilification and an object of desire. The case is not different when viewed from the center of Mexico, where people often see in Tijuana not only the limits of their own culture, but also the limitations of their economic and social system; for them, the northern border in its everyday relations with the United States represents both the margins of Mexican nationality and an access to American modernity that makes it an ambiguous depository of despicability and desire. Clearly, Tijuana is made into a physical as well as a moral liminal site in both U.S. and Mexican discourses.

This contradictory construction of Tijuana and the border feeds a series of myths and legends about border cities and citizens. Discourses developed both in Mexico and the United States have written Tijuana and the border as a passing zone, a mirage where impermanence and desire coexist, denying its citizens a culture of their own. Like the loops of electronic music, the continuous repetition of these discourses has performatively hypnotized those who receive them, creating a symbolic reality that is shared, although not necessarily appropriated in the same manner, by border and nonborder subjects. The performative character of myth actually makes the city and its citizens into what it states they are.

A quick glance at Tijuana's history reveals the intricate relationships among mythology, the construction of urban spaces, and the construction of local citizenship that have informed the development of the city. In 1848, as a result of the Mexican War and the negotiations that concluded with the Treaty of Guadalupe Hidalgo, the Valley of Tijuana, the southern tip of Alta California (the current American state of California), was separated from that territory and annexed to Baja California in order to become the new U.S.–Mexico border.[14] Thus, after its separation from the San Diego Valley and Alta California, for which the Valley of Tijuana remained a land for agriculture and grazing, Tijuana began to develop into an urban area. The gold rush and the economic boom of California during the second part of the nineteenth century played an important role in both the urban development of Tijuana and its mythical representation as "Sin City." The early urbanization of Tijuana, influenced by U.S. construction companies working in southern California and even in Mexican cities like Ensenada, was planned according to nineteenth-century U.S. models. This resulted in a city plat that greatly differs from those of older Mexican cities, which follow colonial Spanish urban conventions. On the other hand, the location of Tijuana, nearby yet beyond the limits of the United States, allowed its imaginary construction as the lawless other where those who benefited illegally from the gold rush and the Californian boom could hide.

Ironically, Tijuana, a place that owes its existence as part of Mexico to a desperate patriotic strategy to contain U.S. expansionism, remained largely isolated from the rest of the country. Thus, a shared geography and a common history compelled *tijuanenses* to strengthen their economic and cultural ties with San Diego. By the 1910s, the growing urbanization and economic power, as well as the increasing moralist restrictions of California, resulted in the slow development of nearby Tijuana as a permissive site, a hedonistic haven for the leisure of U.S. tourists. From the very beginning, tourism in Tijuana was an activity triggered and controlled by U.S. capital; casinos, hotels, bars, and brothels were built and boxing matches and horse races organized in order to satisfy U.S. demand and generate revenue for U.S. entrepreneurs. This situation only became more obvious when the U.S. Congress passed the Volstead Act in 1919, which prohibited the sale of alcoholic beverages nationally and increased the flow of California tourism and capital into Tijuana. Many more bars were opened (La Ballena, a famous saloon that claims to have the largest bar in the world, dates from this time), and beer and liquor factories were built in the city as a result of the new alcohol restrictions in the United States. The growth of Tijuana as a refuge for tourists provided fuel for the development of the city's dark legend in the imagination of the most radically moralist in the United States. For them, Tijuana became the quintessential other against which they could develop discourses of U.S. belonging: Tijuana as Old Mexico (against their own "Spanish" New Mexico), as a representation of Mexican exoticism; Tijuana as an open city, the source of evil and un-American immorality; Tijuana as a dialectically opposite site, "the place where Americans become savages."[15] In turn, this legend was appropriated by *tijuanenses* who, in an attempt to keep the flow of U.S. tourism and the benefits from this economy, made their city match the imaginary construction of U.S. demand in a never-ending simulacrum where myth and reality continuously inform each other. As such, the history of Tijuana appears as a continuous reinforcement of myth that reproduces its negative aspects while benefiting from them.

Indeed, it would be impossible to understand the complex identity of the Tijuana–San Diego border area without considering the symbiotic economic, social, and cultural interdependence—whether visible or invisible—between the two cities. The particular character of the culture nurtured by the Tijuana–San Diego border corresponds to Homi Bhabha's notion of "culture's in between," as the connecting tissue between larger hegemonic cultures.[16] As a society on the margins of American and Mexican mainstream cultures, both have constructed Tijuana as the other, a discourse reinforced by a series of myths developed to validate it. For the young Americans who yell "what happens in Mexico stays in Mexico" inside a bar on Avenida Revolución, or who look for the infamous donkey show along Coahuila Street (*La Coahuila*), Tijuana is the city where they can experience every excess forbidden in their country.

La cultura acaba donde empieza la carne asada (culture ends where grilled meat begins) states the infamous Mexico City saying attributed by vox populi to José Vasconcelos, the well-known minister of education in the early 1920s.[17] The sentence, validated via its association with the name of one of the "fathers" of twentieth-century Mexican national identity, encompasses the lack of respect felt toward *norteña* culture (where grilled meat is indeed a cornerstone of the local diet) by many Mexicans from central and southern Mexico. For them, who get their information about Tijuana via the news on the centralist Televisa or TVAzteca network channels, the northern city is a place of barbarians who kill each other by command of the Arellano Félix brothers and order their beers in English while a group of *norteño* or *banda* musicians play *narcocorridos* loudly in the background.[18]

Mythology, Simulacrum, and Desire

*Ya no se como implementar nuevas reglas en este lenguaje
diminutoy quiero que algún DJ de drum'n'bass remezcle mi vida*
[I do not know how to implement new rules in this diminutive
language and want a drum'n'bass DJ to remix my life]

—Mr. Ejival, "Un diseño para vivir"

Clearly, the development and deconstruction of myths and mythologies play a central role in my account of Nor-tec culture and border life. Semiologist Roland Barthes defines myth as a system of communication that articulates a semiotic chain at a specific moment in time.[19] Thus, a myth works like a Lacanian *point de caption;* it is a moment that fixes the meaning of a large number of uninterpreted signifiers at a specific time in a larger sequence of unlimited semiosis.[20] A myth is a narrative system that organizes and provides meaning to a collection of elements that would otherwise remain empty of signification. Therefore, a myth creates the identity of a given ideological field, controls its transmission, guides its utilization, and maps its distribution.

The history of and the everyday life in a place like Tijuana, with the continuous migrations that have shaped its culture, is marked by stereotypes from both Mexico and the United States (the donkeys painted as zebras) and work as a continuous reinforcement and reinvention of the myth. As sociologist Néstor García Canclini suggests, in a place like this, the notion of "simulacrum comes to be a fundamental category of the culture."[21] García Canclini's idea allows us to understand mythology itself as a type of simulacrum. Philosopher Jean Baudrillard defines simulacrum as an abstraction that "does not correspond to a territory, reference, or substance, but is generated by the models of something real without origin: the hyperreal."[22] In this kind of abstraction, reality is homologized with the models that simulate it by reconstituting reality through the bits and pieces of memory that make up a myth as an imaginary representation. Therefore, a myth, like a simulacrum, is a discourse that occupies the place of reality in the imagination of those who adopt it; this type of simulation actually questions the difference between the "real" and the "imaginary." However, as Baudrillard affirms, the development and re-signification of myths do not imply a false representation of reality or authenticity; they rather camouflage the fact that the "real" or the "authentic" no longer exist since they have been long replaced in a process of unlimited semiosis.[23]

Throughout this book, I analyze cultural processes, local stories, music and dancing styles, distribution strategies, changing urban landscapes, and the production of music tracks, mixes, and remixes as simulacra, as "free-floating" signifiers that, by being links in larger chains of continuous re-signification, override previous "realities" and find themselves detached from any referent in the "real world," as argued by ethnomusicologist Peter Manuel.[24] However, I am not interested in just exposing the lack of authenticity or the absence of originals that would grant essential meaning to a wide variety of cultural practices and manifestations in Tijuana. Instead, I am concerned with an ethnography of the global imagination that, as ethnomusicologist Veit Erlmann suggests, takes into account the changing measure of the real under globalization, an ethnography that "examine[s] why and in what way people's measures of the real, truthful, and authentic change and through which discursive and expressive genres and by which technological means they create a sense of certainty about the world they live in."[25] In short, I am not interested in the essentialist claims for authenticity behind the myths, discourses, or cultural practices surrounding the Nor-tec experience. Nor am I concerned with the absence of such an essence in any simulacrum. My interest is to find out how musicians, fans, and individuals involved in the Nor-tec scene negotiate the meaning of those myths and simulacra at specific moments in (their) (hi)story and how these signifying practices inform us of their desires and aspirations in a globalized scenario. It is in their everyday use and appropriation by regular folks that claims to authenticity become powerful tools of social and cultural mediation. I am interested in understanding how authenticity itself acquires meaning by articulating the past and the future according to an imagined global present.

The concept of desire, as employed by philosophers Slavoj Žižek, Gilles Deleuze, and Félix Guattari, is also fundamental in my critical apparatus. Deleuze and Guattari define desire as that which "produces [a] fantasy and produces itself by detaching itself from the object [of its desire]."[26] The urgency to satisfy a necessity or attain a given object is continuously reproduced as desire when the object destined to satisfy our need "is transformed once it is apprehended in the dialectics of demand."[27] In other words, desire is perpetually reproduced in an impossible circular economy between a subject and his/her object of desire because every time the object is attained, it is also transformed into something different; thus, desire is never satisfied and is always reproduced. These types of libidinal circular processes or libidinal economies are central conditions of a consumer society under capitalism. They are economies fueled by desires to obtain consumer goods or cultural artifacts, but also by aspirations for belonging.

Throughout the book, I argue that the desires and aspirations for modernity and cosmopolitanism of musicians and fans alike (their desires to be part of modern worldly communities that transcend their local every-

day lives) lie at the core of the Nor-tec experience. It is exactly this desire
to imagine themselves as part of an imagined modern, cosmopolitan, and
global community that Nor-tec's re-signification of tradition through technology exemplifies. As such, Nor-tec is an example of audiotopia as defined
by cultural theorist Josh Kun, a sonic space "of effective utopian longing
where several sites normally deemed incompatible are brought together, not
only in the space of a particular piece of music itself, but in the production
of social space and mapping of geographical space that music makes possible as well."[28] The development of musical practices is always informed
by contradictory desires to embrace and replace tradition, and, as ethnomusicologist Mark Slobin states, many of these circumstances are informed
by a complex interaction of local, transnational, and global economies,
cultural areas where "the global [exists] within the local and vice-versa."[29]
This situation results in the development of true "glocal" phenomena,
where local issues are reflected and negotiated in a global context and vice
versa.[30] Following this line of argumentation, ethnomusicologist Thomas
Turino suggests that cosmopolitan formations "are not specific to a single
or few neighboring locales, but situated in many sites which are not necessarily in geographical proximity; rather, they are connected by different
forms of media, contact, and interchanges."[31] Clearly, the cosmopolitan
aspirations and desires of local popular music scenes such as Nor-tec need
to be understood in relation to the global and translocal webs of music production, distribution, and consumption they articulate.

Modernity, Postmodernity, and Globalization

While the first draft of this book was taking shape, a few colleagues asked
me why I was using the idea of modernity as an object of desire if I was
dealing with a seemingly postmodern phenomenon. Although this worried
only a couple of my readers, I thought it was fair to address their concern
and explain my decision to largely avoid using the term postmodernity (although I use the notion of postmodernism a few times) throughout the book.

   Postmodernity is a term often used to refer to a general sense of "living through a period of marked disparity with the past,"[32] which makes us
aware of the unreliability of preexisting forms of knowledge and the teleology of history. According to this perspective, the postmodern period is
unique in that these epistemological uncertainties produce a sense of decentralization and confusion in the individuals living through it. According to this, postmodernity would be a condition resulting from the crisis of
Euro-American modernity as experienced by those individuals at the center
of these societies who suddenly feel that their taken-for-granted sociocultural
"universal" values and structures have begun to collapse. Postmodernism,

on the other hand, refers either to aesthetic or artistic movements that reflect upon this Euro-American condition or to the systematic approach to theorizing about this condition. Curiously, literary critic Fredric Jameson homologizes postmodernism with the condition of postmodernity, when he states that postmodernism is "not merely a cultural ideology or fantasy [but a] genuine historical and socio-economic reality."[33] Nevertheless, we should be quick to differentiate between an aesthetic or theoretical movement and a social, cultural, and economic condition. Furthermore, as sociologist Anthony Giddens suggests, the crisis of modernity that postmodernist theorists identify as postmodernity is actually a radical phase of modernity:

> [T]he break with providential views of history, the dissolution of foundationalism, together with the emergence of counterfactual future-oriented thought and the "emptying out" of progress by continuous change [are disjunctions that] should rather be seen as resulting from the self-clarification of modern thought. . . . We have not moved beyond modernity but are living precisely through a phase of its radicalization.[34]

This radicalized phase of modernity is characterized by an intense and highly revolutionized exchange of information and capital that links distant geographic localities, a phenomenon often referred to as globalization.

Globalization as a continuous process that brings the world closer and closer together can be traced back to the origins of the project of modernity and European imperialism.[35] This process of expansionism was accompanied by a clash of cultures and the development of hybrid artifacts, manifestations, and cultural formations. However, toward the end of the eighteenth century, with the technological achievements that triggered the industrial revolution, these processes of expansionism increased their speed (accompanied by large migrations, new communication tools, and new forms of accumulation and exchange of capital). Indeed, technology has played a fundamental role in the increasing pace and the advancement of globalization. Just as they were fundamental in the nineteenth century during the industrial revolution, new technological developments at the end of the twentieth century propelled the speed, reach, and character of these processes of expansion. No longer bounded by nation-states, the global flow of capital and the omnipresence of people via digital technology and virtual communication systems do make the current phase of globalization look like a different animal. However, a closer look at globalization as an ongoing process, vis-à-vis the industrial revolution and its social and cultural consequences, allows us to identify common traits as well as the capitalist and modernist logic behind it (e.g., globalization as a regulator for capitalist overproduction, which results in the invasion and dismantling of foreign local markets, plus its never-ending searching for new consumers and cheap raw materials and labor).

Ironically, and regardless of its representation as a premodern relic due to Euro-American civilization standards, the underdeveloped world plays a key role in understanding the true range and impact of the project of modernization and its accompanying process of globalization. Marginality and underdevelopment are intrinsic parts of the project of modernity as well as its crisis; they are, as ethnomusicologist Peter Manuel puts it, "a flip side to Enlightenment modernity."[36] This might be exemplified by the current migration of transnational corporations' *maquiladoras* and factories to underdeveloped countries in order to take advantage of the very economic imbalances that allow capital to be reproduced, including the labor of workers with few economic prospects willing to work for much less than what would be minimum wages in developed countries; this kind of underdeveloped labor is a commodity when consumed by the capitalist as it produces more value than it consumes. These corporate moves and the governmental policies that accompany them exacerbate a sense of crisis and the failure of the modern project—loss of jobs, the collapse of welfare and social security institutions, mass migration as a result of faulty neoliberal economic policies, and so on—in the very centers (namely, Europe and the United States) that officially celebrate it. In fact, the so-called crisis of modernity is only the realization by subjects at the center that the project itself is flawed.

Throughout this book, I understand globalization (and postmodernity) as an extension, intensification, and radicalization of the Western project of modernity. Globalization and postmodernity are phases where the contradictions of this project are made evident via the self-reflective character of modern thought. These phases discursively praise the emancipation of the individual, the individual's empowerment via an imagined access to equal consumption beyond the borders of the nation-state, and a sense of transnational democratization. Regardless of the celebratory tone of those for whom globalization stands as a scenario for individual equality and liberation, however, the increasing gap between the rich and the poor that globalization has witnessed throughout Latin America suggests that globalization has done nothing but further encourage the unequal distribution of wealth that characterizes capitalist expansion in modernity.

Like Giddens, I believe that "our" postmodern era of globalization is a radicalization of the condition of modernity. Furthermore, I also believe that, as cultural theorist Chela Sandoval affirms, the decentralization and uncertainty that characterize this radical phase of modernity have been experienced for centuries by individuals in postcolonial conditions in marginal areas, as in Latin America.[37] Such conditions have also historically required intellectuals on the margins to develop theories similar to postmodernism

in that they are concerned with the citizens' sense of decentralization and
the fragility of modern institutions such as the nation-state.[38] In dealing
with a cultural manifestation at both the geographic and epistemological
border between Latin America and the "First World," my work also keeps
crossing the borders between European/U.S. and Latin American academia.
However, I have decided to retain the idea of postmodernity as a radical
phase of modernity, thus I interpret the Nor-tec musicians' and fans' am-
bitions to be part of a cosmopolitan global community as desires for a
modern condition that modernity itself fails to provide, thus keeping those
aspirations alive.

I use the notion of reterritorialization, coined by Deleuze and Guattari
to describe the relationships among civilized modern societies, the residual
archaic forms that remain within them, and their citizens' desires for social
justice and cultural recognition,[39] as a tool to bring together the critical and
postcolonial theories that inform my interpretation of border culture and
the Nor-tec scene. I use the notion of reterritorialization within a framework of globalization and postcolonial theory to describe practices by
which marginal cultures gain new meaning in new territories but also how
these territories are re-signified in the process. In relation to Nor-tec music,
place, and performance, I see reterritorialization as a moment when the
cultural meaning of given spaces is changed (even for a brief period of time)
by their novel uses by a group of people different from those who use them
normally. This concept reclaims Deleuze and Guattari's interest in the desire of individuals and their relation to larger social institutions and rearticulates it in a postcolonial theoretical context.

Studying Nor-tec

As I have explained, this book handles Nor-tec culture through an interdisciplinary approach that draws from social, postcolonial, and critical
theories in combination with methodologies from musicology, ethnomusicology, history, cultural and performance studies, urban studies, and
border studies. As the idea of the book was growing, I was particularly
concerned with a graceful incorporation of music analysis into cultural critique. I wanted to avoid two frequent problems in music scholarship: first,
cultural theorists' lack of systematic discussion of sound and its structural
organization; and second, traditional musicologists' claim that music analysis could somehow unlock the "true" meaning of a musical work as if the
very analytical methods used to dissect it were not ideologically charged. I
needed to find a common ground between these two approaches and decided that such a place could be built by using music analysis to deconstruct
discourses of authenticity and by finding sonic metaphors that reflected

and illustrated specific theoretical discussions. In both cases, I started by analyzing music using my ears and memory as guiding instruments: first, to trace the relationship of specific music samples to traditional and popular Mexican music; and second, to find stylistic ambiguities that could be taken as similes of social and cultural disjunctures. Only after aurally finding these elements did I sit down to produce notated versions of them. In other words, the notated examples found throughout the book are translations of my understanding of the music; and, to be more specific, they are translations of my interpretations of the elements I found most intriguing in the music. They are not meant to be thorough and accurate representations, descriptions, or even prescriptive guides to reproduce the music.

My cultural study of Nor-tec and liminality explores the intersection of individual choice and hegemonic discourses on ethnicity, class, desire, and difference in the construction and negotiation of individual and collective identities in liminal contexts and under conditions of globalization. I am interested in studying these processes without losing their dynamic qualities. For that reason, I developed a model that, based on the concept of identity as a pluralistic and heterogeneous phenomenon, incorporates current notions of mythology, multiple identity, transculturation, libidinal economies, simulacrum, and performativity into a design that emphasizes choice as a fundamental aspect of hegemonic construction.

The book focuses on four interrelated themes:

1. The construction of identity and the negotiation of discourses of marginality in multi-ideological contexts as expressed and constituted by audiences, dancing fans, musicians, promoters, and artists in the performance of Nor-tec.
2. Nor-tec's rearticulation of tradition within larger processes of modernization as a strategy for the reevaluation of clichéd discourses of authenticity.
3. The distribution and commodification of Nor-tec as a process that both challenges and reproduces the culture industry, taking into account the local and global implications of such a process.
4. The consumption of Nor-tec and its contradictory role in the development of postnational music and dance scenes—such as the creation of translocal and virtual communities that use technology to move beyond traditional concepts of time, space, and location.

Throughout the book, I see Nor-tec as a strategy invented to come in and out of the web created by the multi-ideological conditions of both radicalized modernity and postcoloniality. At a moment in American history when the fear of the "edge of national identity" has launched a conservative crusade about "closing the border," transnational cultural phenomena like Nor-tec are ideal forms for studying and understanding the complex and contradictory state of "marginal" cultures under conditions of globalization.

1

Origins Revisited

Myth and Discourse
in the Nortec Collective

It is 31 May 1999. A few friends gather at the house of Pedro Gabriel Beas (Hiperboreal) in Playas de Tijuana. Hiperboreal's birthday is the excuse for getting together, drinking a few beers, sharing the latest gossip about the *culturosa* (artistic and cultural) scene of Tijuana, and listening to some music.[1] Pepe Mogt from Fussible brings a CD "fresh from the oven" that includes three recently composed tracks, one apiece by Ramón Amezcua (Bostich), Roberto Mendoza (Panóptica), and Fussible (Jorge Ruiz [Melo] and Mogt himself). A few hours into the party, someone raises the question on everyone's mind: *¿Cuándo van a poner el CD?* (When are you going to play the CD?). Everyone stops talking and a mantle of silence covers the living room as Pepe Mogt approaches the sound system, introduces the CD, and the loudspeakers spit out the remarkably unique sounds of Bostich's "Polaris," Fussible's "Ventilador," and Panóptica's "And L." Although everyone is excited and responds enthusiastically to this new music, no one could have imagined that in less than two years it would grab the attention of the national and international press and recording industry and put Tijuana at the forefront of the EDM movement in Latin America.

Every historical narrative needs a myth of origin in order to validate its claims to authenticity, and the history of the Nortec Collective, as short as it may be, is no exception. The story of Hiperboreal's birthday party as the locus for the informal presentation of the Nor-tec sound to the artistic community of Tijuana is fundamental in the development of the Nortec Collective's myth of origin. This myth plays an important role in the con-

24

firmation of a coherent collective identity and in the establishment of the aesthetic goals that have maintained the core of the collective even under the pressures of the music industry and its globalized market and distribution channels. Indeed, an exploration of the myth of origin of the Nortec Collective and its original cultural and social contexts is fundamental to understanding Nor-tec's aesthetic and artistic strategy as a simulacrum. If, as Josh Kun suggests, music might work as audiotopia, then deconstructing Nor-tec's myth of origin will help us in perceiving this music as one such space, where desires and identities are projected and negotiated, and also in discovering the ways in which it embodies cultural or subcultural capital for a variety of communities north and south of the U.S.–Mexico border.

The official version of the development of the Nor-tec aesthetic and the foundation of the Nortec Collective, as it has been printed and reproduced in dozens of magazines, fanzines, and cyber-fanzines around the world and on the Internet, offers an easily digested narrative. In 1999, in an effort to develop a "new musical sound," Pepe Mogt, a longtime proponent of electronic music in Tijuana, called for the creation of a musical style that would fuse the sounds of the traditional music from the north of Mexico, *conjunto norteño* (accordion, *tarola* [snare drum], *bajo sexto* [a type of twelve-string bass guitar]) and *banda* (tuba, trumpet, clarinet, *tarola*), with the compositional principles of EDM (juxtapositions of sound blocks and loops; combinations of breaks, samplings, and synthesizers; and computer manipulation). Mogt visited a studio in Tijuana, got a disc with sounds from recordings of *banda* and *norteña* music, and proceeded to convince his friends to take them and make new tracks "with the only requirement of maintaining the groove of traditional [*norteña*] music."[2] Two weeks after Mogt's invitation, Bostich finished "Polaris," a piece that would quickly become a hit in the club scene of Tijuana and would gain him the honorary title of Godfather of Nor-tec. The presentation of Fussible, Bostich, and Panóptica's first Nor-tec tracks at Hiperboreal's birthday party finally convinced Hiperboreal himself, Fernando Corona (Terrestre), Ignacio Chávez Uranga (Plankton Man), and Fritz Torres and Jorge Verdín from Cha3 and Clorofila, to join their experimental efforts. Hiperboreal affirms that the idea was risky and presented plenty of possibilities for experimentation.[3]

However, the simplified synthetic version of the story offered to fans and media alike by the members of the collective partially contradicts the individuals' narratives. A detailed consideration of such contradictions in relation to the official discourse presented to the media and the local specificities in which this discourse was produced, distributed, and consumed offers many opportunities to reflect on the social, economic, and cultural conditions of *tijuanenses*' border life. According to Pepe Mogt, it was at a family party that he had the idea of using rhythmic patterns sampled from *norteña* and *banda* percussion as the foundation for a type of electronic music that would have a "local" flavor:

> Jorge [Ruiz] "Melo" and I went to my sister's party. Obviously, my family hired a *norteño* group, and we ended up sitting right by the stage. We were there, enjoying the party but I was already listening to those *norteño* sounds with new ears. Listening to the instruments, especially the percussion, the drum set . . . and I thought that it might be possible to integrate them into electronic music because they sounded very interesting. You know, when it is live, the sound is really huge and that motivated me to try to experiment and create something new, especially because it is a sound that has always been in Tijuana but I had never really paid attention to it. So I told Jorge and he was like: "*¡N'ombre!* [No, man!] How do you think we are gonna mix *norteño*? That's the very last thing we are gonna mix!" That's why I call him the first Nor-tec dissident. Jorge's attitude was that of most musicians.[4]

On the other hand, Hiperboreal states that it was at a party celebrating the presentation of *El Nuevo Sueño de la Gallina,* a local magazine created by Cha3, the name of the team of graphic designers Fritz Torres and Jorge Verdín, that the Nor-tec idea was born. The magazine included a CD titled *Música maestro,* whose aesthetic vision combined:

> a few local electronic music projects and some *norteño* musicians. It was at this celebration of Baco, in the heat of discussing music and drinking wine, that the first ideas about fusing these two entities [electronic and *norteña* music] were born. It was that evening, at that idealistic moment, that the concept arose to experiment musically with those different sonic worlds in a more integrated fashion. That is, the conversation was about unifying the worlds of electronica and regional folk, both of which are undeniable elements of our lives. We continued drinking amidst jokes and shabby comments about what a crazy idea it was. However, that day would be marked as the date of birth of what we currently know as Nortec.[5]

Although somewhat contradictory, Mogt and Hiperboreal's accounts have been repeatedly reproduced by the media and as a result have become indispensable elements in the imaginary of the Nortec Collective. Indeed, the basic components for the creation of an appealing modern urban legend are easily dissected from the two stories: an individual reinterpretation of a local tradition as a source of authenticity; a negative response that seems to miss the novelty of the proposal and should be overcome (rejection and "dissidence"); and the very notion of the idea being "crazy," even beyond the boundaries of the permissible allowed by the aesthetic searches of contemporary local artists.[6] Furthermore, the fact that the two accounts occur in different locations and social scenes—a family versus an intellectual, artistic setting—as their places of origin is only a symptom that refers to a contested negotiation hidden behind the predigested official version of the birth of Nor-tec. Such negotiation suggests different motivations, desires, aspirations, and expectations that are ultimately reflected in a variety of musical styles, strategies of regulation and distribution, and artistic alliances.

In this chapter, I trace the history of electronic music in Tijuana in an attempt to understand the Nor-tec myth of origin as a historical contingency that gave meaning to a series of cultural manifestations and artistic pursuits in that city at the end of the 1990s. I am interested in showing the individual and collective aspirations implicit in the production and consumption of Nor-tec, and in investigating how memory is performed and how imaginaries of tradition and modernity are articulated in Nor-tec's myth of origin. What do these narratives and their contradictions reveal about power relations and struggles among producers, distributors, and consumers in Tijuana? In order to thoroughly tackle these questions and grasp the importance of the narrative of Hiperboreal's birthday party as an ideological intervention, it is necessary to explore the local artistic and electronic music scenes of Tijuana in their relation to broader, global, alternative artistic and music scenes.

Tracing Steps I (Tijuas Mix):
From Techno Pop to Electronic Dance Music

Tijuana's strategic position as a border city and its proximity to San Diego and Los Angeles, California, has inevitably had a strong influence on the development of its economic and cultural circuits. The continuous presence of U.S. tourists strolling up and down *La Revu* in search of bars, gambling houses, discotheques, and the "authentic" Mexico of Mexican curio shops has traditionally provided *tijuanenses* with their most important source of income. As Olivia Ruiz notes, tourism has not only been Tijuana's most important engine for economic growth but actually its very raison d'être.[7] From the infamous Agua Caliente casino to the iconic Jai Alai building, the development of musical practices could not completely escape the performative power of this economic force. Musicians and music entrepreneurs from Tijuana have historically articulated the demands of tourists coming from the north. Concerts organized in the 1980s and 1990s at the Hipódromo de Agua Caliente or at clubs like the Iguanas allowed underage California teenagers[8] to hear live bands like the Ramones, Nirvana, Red Hot Chili Peppers, Jane's Addiction, or Pearl Jam as well as to escape the alcohol restrictions of the U.S. government. They also gave local musicians firsthand access to the latest U.S. musical trends well before they were heard in Mexico City. This situation has given Tijuana musicians a strategic edge over their peers in the center of the country, making the border one of the main points of entry for musical and cultural trends associated with U.S. modernity. The fact that many musicians from Tijuana learned their craft while performing for crowds of teenagers requesting the latest hits from the U.S. charts has also allowed them to assimilate this music. They have simultaneously developed transcultural musical styles that make their way into Mexican and U.S. urban centers. The success of *tijuanenses* like Javier Bátiz, Los Dug Dugs, and Tijuana 5 (leaders of the so-called *onda chicana*) in Mexico City at the end of the1960s[9] or Tijuana-raised Carlos Santana's accomplishments in the United States are good examples of these processes, developments where center and periphery labels are clearly problematic.

Musicians in Tijuana have been practicing electronic music for more than two decades. Their interest was born as an outgrowth of Tijuana's long-standing rock tradition; the *tijuanenses*' interest in electronic music appeared in the late 1970s and early 1980s at the intersection of this local rock scene and a growing involvement with new pop music trends. Indeed, most of Tijuana's early electro-oriented bands followed progressive rock, new wave, and techno pop and played covers of U.S., British, and German bands such as Rush, San Francisco Tuxedomoon, Ultravox, Depeche Mode, and Kraftwerk. Tijuana's proximity to California has been fundamental in the development of the city's electronic music scene. It allowed many young middle-class *tijuanenses* to attend U.S. high schools and granted them not only access to equipment and recordings unattainable in Mexico but also created the possibility of getting together with U.S. teenagers to form amateur bands. Radio stations such as San Diego's KCR and 91X and Los Angeles's KROQ also played a key role in this process, keeping electronic U.S. and European music flowing into the ears of Tijuana's youngsters. It is important to take such conditions into consideration since they permitted Tijuana's electronic music to survive and prosper. On the other hand, the early interest in electronic music on the part of Mexico City bands like Vía Lactea, the High Fidelity Orchestra, or Sincronía in the early 1980s succumbed to a lack of information, deficient channels of communication with foreign music scenes, a scarcity of state-of-the-art equipment, and, as a consequence, a general inability to develop loyal audiences.[10]

However, in the mid-1980s, a radical shift took place among Tijuana's electronic musicians and fans. As Tijuana chronicler Rafa Saavedra affirms, "1985 is what I call 'ground zero' for alternative culture in Tijuana because that's when bands began playing their own music and stopped doing just covers."[11] This shift coincided with the commercialization and increasing dominance of MIDI (musical instrument digital interface) technology in U.S. music production (equipment and technology to which middle-class *tijua-*

nense bands had relatively easy access) and with the underground development of La Movida Española (the alternative pop movement in Spain) with
its proliferation of provocative electronic bands such as Aviador Dro, Alaska
y Los Pegamoides, and Muzak. Although some of the most commercial
bands of La Movida (Radio Futura, Nacha Pop, Los Hombres G, Mecano,
etc.) were central in the later development of the media-supported Rock en
Español (or Rock en tu Idioma) movement in Mexico City during the late
1980s, it was the more futuristic, avant-garde, and underground aspect of
the movement that influenced the development of Tijuana's early electronic
music scene. By 1985, Rafa Saavedra and Ramón Amezcua were active
members of the Red Organizada de Mutantes (R.O.M.), Aviador Dro's
fan club, which was quickly transformed into a transnational information and music exchange network, giving young *tijuanenses* access to the
latest Spanish and European electronic music trends. However, despite
the Spanish connection, early Tijuana electronic musicians still favored
English lyrics. The mid-1980s also witnessed the growing presence of radio
shows in Tijuana devoted to local rock and electronic music manifestations. Estereo Frontera 102.5 and Radio Tecnológico 88.7 are especially
noteworthy. It was Radio Tecnológico which allowed Saavedra to share his
latest discoveries of European electronic and techno pop with a keen generation of young *tijuanenses* through his hosting of a prominent show titled
Sintonía Pop.[12]

Some of the pioneering *tijuanense* electronic projects were established
under the influence of music coming through both U.S. radio and R.O.M.
(via Saavedra and his radio show). They included Avant Garde, Skyland,
Vandana, Synthesis (later known as Artefacto or Artefakto), Pepe Mogt's
Fetiche, and Ramón Amezcua's Bostich. The musical styles adopted by
these bands, from techno and electro pop to progressive rock and dance
music, are a testament to the great variety of electronic trends to which *tijuanenses* were exposed by the mid-1980s. Bostich and Artefacto were the
most successful projects as they were able to record LPs for commercial
labels and break into the national electronic music circuit, being continuously invited to play in Guadalajara, Monterrey, and Mexico City. In 1988,
after spending a few years composing electronic music for a local contemporary dance company, Ramón Amezcua created Bostich, his alter ego,
under the direct influence of the Swiss electronic band Yello.[13] Bostich
began exploring the possibilities of his synthesizers and developed a rough-
edged ambient techno style for the dance floor. He quickly gained the respect of the electronic music scene of the center of the country and recorded
two albums: *Tiempo d'Afrodita* (1992), a compilation of experimental contemporary music and techno, and *Elektronische* (1994), an album of house

and trance. Already by 1993, Bostich's was a familiar name at the most prominent rave parties in the country.

Synthesis was formed in 1985 by Javier Modelevsky (El Bola), Jorge Ruiz (Melo), and Roberto Mendoza. During their earlier years, the trio developed an electro pop sound that survived until their first recording. This was an LP titled *Synthesis* (1988), produced once the band had changed its name to Artefacto. In 1991, after El Bola left the trio, a more radical transformation took place; Pepe Mogt, the former Fetiche, joined the band and, under his pragmatic influence, the trio changed its name once again to Artefakto.[14] This change was accompanied by a newly acquired taste for the darker and strenuous sounds of the industrial music practiced by Throbbing Gristle, Ministry, and Fear Factory. Artefakto's interest in industrial music owes much not only to these groups' influence but also to Melo's taste for heavy metal, which he had played as a rebellious teenager in San Diego, California.[15] In the 1990s, Artefakto became one of the most significant electronic bands in the Mexican underground. It landed a deal with Opción Sónica, a well-established independent label from Mexico City, and produced three albums, *Des-construcción* (1993), *Tierra eléctrica* (1995), and *Interruptor* (1997). The first one, which featured mixes by Sascha Konietzko from the German band KMFDM, was distributed in Europe through licensing with the German label Zoth Ommog. With *Tierra eléctrica* and *Interruptor*, Artefakto consolidated the industrial sound the group had explored in its first recording; however, *Interruptor* already points toward an electro dance sound that is starting to move away from the obscure and heavy style of the group's early project.

In the meantime, at the end of the 1990s, while Artefakto enhanced its position in the national scene and attempted an important breakthrough into the international electronic music scene, a number of interesting and varied electronic music projects were developing in Tijuana and the neighboring city of Ensenada. Bands like Nona Delichas and Othli combined elements from gothic and progressive rock with electronic sounds; Loopdrop and Aquadelfín based their ambient sound on a strong acoustic foundation combined with electronic instruments and computer processing; Minuit and Telephone attempted a retro return to techno pop; and Ford Proco and Tovar presented new all-electronic experimental music projects. Sonios, a band from Ensenada, developed an acid jazz sound and collaborated with writer and radio host Enrique Jiménez (Ejival) and graphic designer and musician Rubén Tamayo (Fax) in the creation of the Tijuana-based label Static Discos. In the interim, an incipient underground electronic dance music scene began to gain supporters due to the diligent work of disc jockeys like Daniel Rivera (DJ Tolo), Max Llanes (DJ Max), and Jesús Santana

(DJ Chuy); and organizers such as Ricky Martínez de Castro, Luis Tucker, and Susan Monsalve; and the creation of a few dance music clubs (Café Eléctrico, Techno Club, Half-Way House, and Mezzanine), music labels such as Tlahuila Records, and organizations like the Tijuana House Club, Naza, and Orbit. As is the case with many independently developed music scenes, most of these clubs, labels, and promotional organizations were partly owned or managed by the musicians themselves.

Although I have focused on the continuities of the rock, industrial, and electronic dance music traditions in Tijuana, this account should not be read as a historicist narrative. It should be noted that every stylistic change and adoption of a new musical trend in Tijuana has been a local response to the changing global music industry. In other words, the history of Tijuana's changing music scene puts in evidence a truly glocal phenomenon. Nevertheless, the allure of the border, as both an object of desire and an epitome of "the forbidden," has sometimes resulted in attempts to explain Tijuana's music scenes solely in terms of what seem to be specific local questions, overlooking the complex interaction between local and global issues in these border manifestations. In these terms, an interpretation of the changes in Tijuana's industrial and electronic music scene as a continuation or rejection of local traditions, or as a critique of local urban conditions, as Susana Asensio once suggested, would lose sight of this music as a manifestation where local individuals articulate and negotiate the desire for otherness of the global music industry.[16] In fact, the industrial and postindustrial music from Tijuana (such as Artefakto's) articulates disillusionment with an increasingly global capitalist system whose contradictory nature—the need to maintain unequal economic conditions in order to produce wealth—is put in evidence, experienced, and negotiated on a daily basis by individuals at the U.S.–Mexico border.

Keeping such a worldwide vision is fundamental for the interpretation of cultural phenomena in Tijuana. It is clear that the early development of an electronic music scene in Tijuana owed much to its connection and active interaction with similar music scenes beyond the realm of the Mexican nation-state. Bostich's appropriation of musical styles such as techno, house, trance, and drum'n'bass; Artefakto's adoption of an industrial, post-punk image; the traces of progressive rock, techno pop, and acid jazz found in Nona Delichas, Sonios, Loopdrop, and Minuit; and the development of an underground dance music scene are evidence of artistic forms that express a desire encoded in the styles and practices of an "eminently cosmopolitan music" that, according to Michel Gaillot, "would be that of the commons of the world."[17] In these cases, styles and practices appear to be screens upon which desires for modernity, cosmopolitanism, and cultural identification are projected, rearticulated, and transformed into cultural capital. If the desire for modernity and cosmopolitanism of these young *tijuanenses* is not fulfilled by a centralized Mexican libidinal economy that discursively pushes them to the intellectual periphery, then these adopted musical styles become audiotopic sites with which to identify themselves.

The exploration of these musical styles in Tijuana did not take place in a cultural vacuum but articulated a larger phenomenon: the crisis of the rock scene and the worldwide development of a so-called post-rock aesthetic.[18] If, due to increasing commodification by large corporations, the "death of rock" had been announced by music critics for almost two decades,[19] the development of alternative means of music distribution in the 1990s made many commentators believe that rock was indeed dead and that the future of popular music was with genres that emphasized individual practices of production and distribution. In Mexico, the commercial success of Rock en tu Idioma (Rock in Your Language) in the 1990s, backed by Televisa, the largest TV network in Latin America, kept the lure of rock alive throughout the decade. However, as Rock en tu Idioma (clearly coerced by corporate power) increasingly lost its edge as a tool for youths' social contestation, as piracy caused the local recording industry to collapse, and as electronica (as well as genres such as hip-hop and rap) gained international acceptance, it was only a matter of time before do-it-yourself electronic music scenes made their appearance in Mexico. Musicians from Tijuana, taking advantage of their easy access to novel music and technology, quickly developed a scene that responded to the new economic and cultural trends. By aligning themselves with such progressive aesthetic projects, *tijuanenses* attempted to recognize themselves as part of the transnational processes that were changing the face of mainstream popular music worldwide. Enrique, a local fan of electronic music states, "[T]he pioneers of Tijuana's electronica (including the current members of the Nortec Collective) made the city into an important avant-garde site not only for Mexico but for other countries as well."[20] Melo's experience while playing at a festival of electronic music in Barcelona further acknowledges the desire for cosmopolitanism that informs the scene: "I remember I felt *bien fregón* [really cool] because [the audience] was 100% European, and they wouldn't stop dancing."[21] For Enrique and Melo, as for many other fans and musicians, the imagined global techno, pop, and electronic communities, with their futuristic rhetoric and aesthetics, are sites that enunciate these musicians' and fans' desire for cosmopolitanism and modernity; belonging to these sites by adopting their musical stylistic features provides them with a cultural capital that allows them to transcend the limitations of their local community.

Tracing Steps II (Sueño sur Mix):
The Question of a Frame for Reception

Que puedo ver / que no haya visto ya / Que puedo oír /
que no me haga esta vez / desconfiar / sospechar
[What could I see / that I have not seen yet / What could I hear /
that this time would not make me / distrust / suspect]

— Hiperboreal, "Sueño sur," *Música maestro* (1999)

For a myth to be successfully embraced by a community, it needs to speak to the particular aspirations of the members of that community, and it should be able to validate and provide meaning to a series of events that would otherwise remain unconnected. A myth should be able to provide a site for individual and collective libidinal recognition. Pepe Mogt's narrative about his sister's party and Hiperboreal's account of the presentation of *El Nuevo Sueño de la Gallina* provide two sides of a multifaceted story, one that engages a confrontation among foreign discourses of representation, locals' search for originality, and a confrontation with tradition and heritage on the part of several musicians and visual artists from Tijuana.

In the mid-1990s, the changing scenery of rock music in Tijuana began to reflect the crisis being experienced by the international rock industry and leaned toward the genre that many thought would replace it, electronic dance music. In 1996, the members of Artefakto formulated a new project called Fussible in order to escape the dark, industrial style of their band. Early Fussible was a project of dance music, mostly techno, house, and breakbeat, that severed the band's ties to industrial rock and punk and reflected the changing tastes in the electronic music scene of Tijuana. Following this trend, Roberto Mendoza, the singer of the band, opened Café Eléctrico, a club where he and his wife, DJ Bulma, spun breakbeat; they also created Noarte, an organization devoted to the promotion of electronic music through fanzines and parties. Pepe Mogt, who joined DJ Tolo to open the Techno Club to play techno and house, elaborates on this stylistic shift:

> In 1997 we decided to put all our eggs into the Fussible basket 'cause we were tired of Artefakto . . . our musical tastes had changed. We opened our electronic music dance clubs and it was a very strong influence 'cause that was Fussible's thing [dance music] . . . but we were sending our demos and nothing was happening with the labels. In 1998 we stopped doing music altogether 'cause we were *agüitados* [burnt out]. There were no new ideas and it was not clear what the next move should be. . . . the only solution seemed to be to produce music independently, to forget the companies and do it ourselves.[22]

Roberto Mendoza (Panóptica) further explains the situation:

> [W]e changed our name to Fussible and began doing electronic dance
> music. But there was a moment where we hit a wall; we didn't know what
> to do musically. We were frustrated and couldn't do anything to satisfy our-
> selves. Pepe and I began talking about how sometimes you can identify a
> sound belonging to a specific geographic location. . . . We asked ourselves
> how to produce a sound that could be identified as Mexican . . . although,
> we were not thinking about a regional sound. So, we stopped doing music
> for over a year, we didn't rehearse and would just get together to talk and
> think about these issues.[23]

Roberto Mendoza eventually left the band to pursue his one-man project,
Panóptica, while Pepe Mogt and Melo kept working together and produced
Fono, Fussible's first CD, in 1999. A close reading of Fussible's strategies
of self-representation to promote the band and its CD and an examination
of the musical style developed by the band in this recording show another
revealing discrepancy among the narratives of origin of the members of the
Nortec Collective: Fussible's preference for cosmopolitan musical styles
versus Panóptica's statement that their concern was to create a "Mexican"
sound. This helps us to understand the frame for reception—the system of
references shared collectively that allows similar processes of reception
among different individuals from the same community—that informed the
aesthetics of artists and musicians in Tijuana at the time. Most important,
it reveals the retroactive construction of myth in order to account for that
so-called frame for reception.[24]

In September 1999, Rafa Saavedra reviewed Fussible's *Fono* in the following terms:

> [Fussible's] music moves towards funk rhythms and big beats. . . . Fussible
> plays with influences from Black music (soul, reggae, and dub) bringing
> them back to their terrain. Think about the Chemical Brothers with a Mo-
> town sensibility or the hip hop that could be made in Mexico if we had a
> bit of techno culture. . . . [These elements] place Fussible at the top of the
> "Next Big Thing" list.[25]

In 1999, the year the Nor-tec project was launched, Pepe Mogt described
Fussible's music as "based on more rhythmic music patterns and in the
combination of styles like funk, reggae, etc. . . . There is more groove in
Fussible [than in Artefakto]";[26] Mogt spoke without referring to the Nor-
tec aesthetic nor to any attempt to search for a localized Tijuana or Mexican sound. The style of Fussible in *Fono*, from the funky bass and driving
drum set à la James Brown in "Slap da Bass" to the trance-like effects and
minimal repetition of "Trippy Boy," from the robotic remnants of their
postindustrial past in "Milenio" to the hip-hop rhyming of MC Chris and
the scratches of DJ Who in "Orgánica," reveals an open-minded eclecticism
that, in relation to Mexico's musical traditions, points outward rather than

inward. Fussible's desire for musical change is clear in the tracks of *Fono*, as the lyrics of "Milenio" confirm: "*Consigo el reflejo / de esa voz / camino en el tiempo / ecléctica / el rojo dice: / 'Vuelve' / . . . volver a nacer* [I find the reflection / of that voice / I walk in time / eclectic / the red color says: / 'Come back' / . . . to be born all over again]." However, the "reflection" and the "voice" found by Fussible in this recording point toward the United States and Europe and not necessarily toward the local musical practices of Mexico or Tijuana. Certainly, if Fussible were considered to be the "next big thing" in 1999, it was because of its relation to the sounds, rhythms, and genres of the First World music market, the *tijuanenses'* nostalgia for modernity ("if we had a bit of techno culture") that *Fono*'s sonic world fulfilled, and not because of the improbable and kitschy rhythmic patterns of local *cumbia grupera* and *banda sinaloense* that their soon-to-be-born Nor-tec aesthetic would deliver.

Two important questions arise from the seeming contradiction between Fussible's cosmopolitan musical practices and Panóptica's assertion that the band was preoccupied with creating an identifiable "local" sound. What is this frame for reception that Panóptica seems to incorporate into his narrative? If we acknowledge that any frame for reception is not an inevitable teleological stage but rather a complex construction that reveals desires, concerns, dreams, representations, and aspects of self-identification, what are the power relations at stake in the production and consumption of such a frame for reception?

Que puedo ver / que no haya visto ya / Que puedo oír / que no me haga esta vez / desconfiar / sospechar [What could I see / that I have not seen yet / What could I hear /that this time would not make me / distrust / suspect]." The lyrics of Hiperboreal's "Sueño sur" reflect a general dissatisfaction with the status quo of visual arts and music in Tijuana at the time the song appeared in *Música maestro*, the CD that accompanied Cha3's fanzine *El Nuevo Sueño de la Gallina* in 1999. If Hiperboreal's lyrics are a cry of frustration, they are also a lingering modernist call for originality and authenticity, a call for that which would not make us "distrust [or] suspect." This modernist creed rests at the foundation of the so-called frame for reception mentioned earlier. It is this desire for originality and change, the necessity to deal with their condition as peripheral subjects, and the increasing interest in kitsch of many artists around the globe that pushed artists in Tijuana to search for elements of artistic identification in the sounds and images of local popular culture. *El Nuevo Sueño de la Gallina* was the third issue of *Cha3*, a fanzine that took its name from Cha3, the team of Jorge Verdín and Fritz Torres. The idea of the fanzine was to bring together the work of writers and artists from Tijuana who, due to the precarious channels of art distribution in the city, worked in relative isolation. Torres explains:

We invited friends, who we knew were doing *curado* [cool] stuff in their houses without anybody knowing of it, to participate in this fanzine. It was a forum to show what we were doing. Sometimes we had articles by a friend and would ask someone else to do the graphic art for it . . . sometimes up to 20 guys would have a hand on a single piece. . . . it was truly a collaborative effort. . . . For the third issue we wanted to expand the idea to music and asked several friends who had musical projects to send us their material. . . . the idea was to do a compilation, we did not attempt to follow a homogeneous style. Again, the idea was to make it work like a forum . . . or rather, like a memory album of what was happening in Tijuana at that time. So, we started inviting *raza* [people],[27] Pepe Mogt, Ramón Bostich [*sic*], Pedro from Hiperboreal, and also asked friends who were playing *norteña* music. All of a sudden, without planning it, we ended up with a CD that contained electronica and *norteña*, it wasn't a fusion but they were there together, side by side. . . . Even the cover! It was a picture of electronic music equipment and an accordion.[28]

The fanzine contained articles on electronica, rock, lounge music (and its symbol, Juan García Esquivel), Mexican popular culture, and narco-culture (the lifestyle of drug dealers) by writers from Tijuana, Ensenada, and Germany, which were illustrated in a postmodernist, collage-like fashion. It incorporated comics, photography, bizarre graphics, kitschy montages, and avant-garde computer-manipulated images by designers from Tijuana, San Diego, and Los Angeles. The content of the CD, titled *Música maestro,* was no less eclectic; it included electronic music by Bostich, Fussible, Hiperboreal, Monnithor (Pepe Mogt and Bostich), Aquadelfín, and Clorofila (Fritz Torres and Jorge Verdín); *norteña* music by Mario Kumara y Sultán del Norte, Mariux (Mario Lagsbartt, who was also the sound engineer for the project); and a special appearance by *norteña* superstar band Los Tucanes de Tijuana. The collage-like style of the art conveyed the aesthetic behind the juxtaposition of diverse musical manifestations; the mortar that kept the bricks of such a heterogeneous musical construction together was a poignant sense of humor that recycled retro and kitschy items from Mexican popular culture, including everything from images of the masked *lucha libre* wrestler El Santo to samples of the 1970s TV comedians Los Polivoces, from 1950s mambo to 1960s rock 'n' roll and contemporary tacky popular wedding music. The result is a straightforward continuous track that freely moves from electronica to *norteña* and back through a series of sonic bridges made up of hilarious soap opera recreations, silly TV samples, and nostalgic old songs. The central ingredients for the Nor-tec experience were already present in the waggish sounds and images of Cha3's multidisciplinary project: a desire to articulate the modern in the sounds of electronica, a reevaluation of tradition in the form

Figure 1.1   Cover of *Música maestro* from *El Nuevo Sueño de la Gallina* (1999), © Cha3. Used by permission

of popular *norteña* music, and a sense of identification with nostalgia and kitsch.

The musical collage presented in *El Nuevo Sueño de la Gallina* was just one of the earliest and most visible examples of the sort of postmodernist rearticulation of the local and the global that *tijuanense* artists were eager to explore by the end of the 1990s; it was, however, neither the first nor the only one. In 1997, Octavio Hernández, a Tijuana artist, received a commission from InSite, an important San Diego–based cultural institution in charge of funding binational art projects and border-based art interventions. Hernández's project was titled *Zoosónico* and consisted of a sonic landscape of the San Diego–Tijuana border made out of sound samples recorded in both countries. Hernández chose to record sounds from the Tijuana–San Ysidro crossing point, public announcements inside the San Diego–San Ysidro trolley, out-of-tune street musicians, beggars, TV samples of soap operas and U.S. and Mexican politicians, street evangelical preachers, *tarola* players of *norteña* music, and the noise of moving street traffic. For the final part of his project, Hernández brought his massive amount of samples to Pepe Mogt's studio in order for Mogt to put them together in an organized fashion. Mogt describes the encounter:

> The project itself was very interesting but the way it was going to be put on CD was rather boring. I felt that it wasn't going to be what Octavio [Hernández] wanted. . . . Okay, it may have worked for the [InSite] commission but I wanted to stretch the idea and do more with it. So, I told

him "Let's respect your project and leave parts of your soundscapes," but I put them into a synthesizer to control the patches. . . . Let's imagine we had a rhythm from a tire repair workshop, what I did was to convert it into electronic signals that generated volts and certain sounds that were in sync with the urban rhythm. Then, I recorded several of those sounds in that fashion and showed them to Octavio . . . and the CD came out and he was very happy with his project, *Zoosónico,* and so was I with my role in it.[29]

The result is a bilingual and bicultural sound collage that juxtaposes the soundscapes of two seemingly irreconcilable worlds, the modernity of San Diego and the alleged chaos of Tijuana, in a manner that emphasizes their similarities. The chaos of modernity in San Diego and the modernity of Tijuana's chaos are effectively represented in Hernández and Mogt's game of sonic mirrors, a true *speculum musicae* that puts face to face the verbal diarrhea of U.S. and Mexican politicians, the strident sounds of the San Diego trolley and those of the Tijuana *maquiladoras,* the drama of the *mojado* (illegal) immigrant and the U.S. factory manager's need of cheap labor. These are all sounds from the border that could indistinctly come from the northern or the southern side of the fence but that accurately portray the sonic landscape. The fluid character of sound is reflected in the bilingual titles of the tracks that make *Zoosónico: Ruidos y sonidos en la frontera de dos mundos* (1998), the CD produced by Hernández along with Mogt. In "Trance Frontera," "Evangelio's Danza," "Drama Drum," "Maquila Dub," and "Lunatic Trova," the hybrid and flexible character of border language with its combination of Spanish words and English grammar is matched by the multiplicity of meanings and locations of sounds. Mogt's organization of Hernández's samples, arranged as an abstract sonic mosaic that gracefully and almost imperceptibly moves from the trolley to the *maquiladora* and from the street evangelist to the *merolico* (street vendor), is a powerful representation of the smoothness of cultural, economic, and human movement at the border.

A good example of the sonic result of this exercise is "Poder Beat (Politics to the Bone)," a track that seamlessly moves from samples of speeches by former neoliberal Mexican president Carlos Salinas de Gortari and postmodernist revolutionary icon Subcomandante Marcos to their English translations read by a U.S. anchorman (see figure 1.2). [◉ **Track 1**] The result is a sonic fabric that makes sense only when the borders between the apparently contradictory worlds presented are blurred and the listener is able to witness a larger picture. Here, an interpretation is possible only in the listener's experience of the dialogic exchange produced in the constant and complementary interactions of all of the samples. This track shows that Mogt and Hernández's project is also a critical assessment of the discourses that pretend to describe the region according to reductionist dichotomies, such as order versus chaos, development versus underdevelopment, or civilization versus barbarianism. In the ingenious sonic representation created by Hernández and Mogt, the boundary between those notions—and those "noises"—just like the cultural and economic border between Tijuana and San Diego, is cleverly contested and amusingly rearticulated.

El Nuevo Sueño de la Gallina and *Zoosónico* are just two instances of the type of artistic exploration that characterize the Tijuana frame for reception that would be amplified by the arrival of the Nor-tec aesthetic. Even closer to the hybrid Nor-tec ideal were the work of Tijuana-based architect, designer, and installation artist Raúl Cárdenas (Torolab) and the incipient electronic music of former Sonios keyboardist Fernando Corona (Terrestre). In 1999, Torolab was developing a method for artistic and creative hybridization called Sistema Evolutivo de Binomios (Evolving Binomial System). Torolab's idea was to take two unrelated concepts and combine them, making them develop into a single organism. He explains his initial interest in creating dystopian architectural hybrids in the following terms: "I would take pictures of different architecture typologies in Tijuana and San Diego and combine them to create images of things that do not exist in reality but that you could still recognize . . . as if saying: 'I have seen this somewhere else,' even though it does not exist."[30]

Torolab's system allowed him to create imaginary heterogeneous cultural icons based on the collage-like juxtaposition of up to 17 pictures. In each case, the resulting image was used as the foundation for the creation of a new set of images based on the same constructive principle. Through a system that combines the spirit of an artisan's craftsmanship with a type of perfunctory reproduction, Torolab managed to clearly show that cultural fusions are temporally frozen moments within larger processes of unlimited semiosis or simulacra; they are cultural remixes in which meaning is continuously reconstituted as new representations come to replace old ones in the arena of symbolic signification.

Torolab's Sistema Evolutivo de Binomios articulates the modernist desire for renovation and originality expressed in Fussible's "Milenio" and Hiperboreal's "Sueño sur" and infuses it with the postmodernist preoccupation with hybridization that the projects of Cha3 and Octavio Hernández share with Terrestre, Fernando Corona's alter ego. *Que puedo ver / que no haya visto ya / Que puedo oír / que no me haga esta vez / desconfiar / sospechar.* Hiperboreal's desire "to see what has not already been seen" also informs Corona's musical dive into the sounds of a large variety of local traditions, from indigenous music from the north of Mexico to Brazilian samba and bossa nova, to develop the hybrid musical aesthetic of his project, entitled Terrestre (Earthly). The very term Terrestre defined Corona's new music; here, the former acid house and rock jazz musician attempted

Time	Sound Event	Text	Translation
0	Fade in loop 1 (6 times)	"Y si algo es la cárcel es el no cambio." Sub-comandante Marcos	If there is a jail it is the [condition of] no change
0:15	Loop 2 (3 times)	"Poder no tiene edad, es para todos." Male voice	Power has no age, it is for everyone
0:18	Marching troops in permanent loop until the tracks' end		
0:30	Loop 1 (7 times)	"Y si algo es la cárcel . . ."	
0:47	Loop 2(4 times) New, simultaneous loop	"Poder no tiene edad . . ." "Esta guerra por justicia de un ejército formado por miles de indígenas." Sub-comandante Marcos	This is the just war of an army made up of thousands of indigenous people
0:57	New voice sample	"This is such an [inaudible] war. It's an army made up of thousands of indigenous people. Badly [inaudible], badly trained, badly moved, badly [inaudible] disciplined. And maybe some of the challenges [inaudible] challenge free trade." American anchorman	
1:04	Loop 1 (6 times)	"Y si algo es la cárcel . . ."	
1:10	New voice sample	"Esperamos pues, de toda la sociedad." Sub-comandante Marcos	Thus, we hope all of society
1:12	New voice sample	"We hope Mexican society will [inaudible]. Because the forces that lead to this movement are just. You can argue about the methods we choose but not the causes." American anchorman	
1:20	Loop 2 (3 times)	"Poder no tiene edad . . ."	
1:28	Synthesized sound in crescendo		

Time	Description	Spanish	English
1:34	Loop 1 (7 times) New, simultaneous voice sample	"Y si algo es la cárcel ..." "The Zapatistas sent the army ..." Female voice	
1:39	New voice sample	"Tomando en cuenta el sentimiento y la opinión de la nación, y por las propias convicciones del Presidente de la República, con toda responsabilidad he tomado la decisión ..." President Salinas de Gortari	Taking into account the pulse and opinion of the Nation, as well as the very convictions of the President of the Republic, with all responsibility I have made the decision . . ."
1:51	Loop 2 (4 times)	"Poder no tiene edad ..."	
1:53	New voice sample	"I have made the decision to cease fire in Chiapas. The army will guarantee the order and tranquility of the citizens." American anchorman	
2:09	New loop (3 times)	"Estuve precisamente en Margaritas, estuve en Ocosingo, estuve en Altamirano, estuve en Comitán." Male voice	I was precisely in Margaritas, I was in Ocosingo, I was in Altamirano, I was in Comitán"
2:23	Loop 2 (3 times)	"Poder no tiene edad ..."	
2:36	All loops fade out with the exception of loop 2		
2:35	Mexican folk song sample by itself	"Yo quiero, cuerito viejo/ morirme aquí en tu suelo/ bajo la luz del cielo/ que un día me vio nacer"	I want, my dear old skin/ to die here in your soil/ under the light of the sky/ that once witnessed my birth
2:42	Computer manipulation. Filters.		

Figure 1.2 Octavio Hernández and Pepe Mogt, descriptive chart for "Poder Beat (Politics to the Bone)," from *Zoosónico: Ruidos y sonidos en la frontera de dos mundos* (1998)

Figure 1.3   An example of Torolab's Sistema Evolutivo de Binomios, this is one of the covers for the CD *Bostich + Fussible: Nortec Remixes* (2000), © Raúl Cárdenas. Used by permission

to move away from the U.S. and European musical styles played by Sonios into a more localized and "earthly" or "organic" sound (as opposed to an international and mostly synthesized sound) based on samples from traditional and ethnically marked musics. The musician describes this aesthetic shift:

> I always liked the combination of acoustics with electronics, the organic and the digital . . . those kinds of contrasts. Before Nor-tec I was experimenting with electronica and ethnic sounds from the north of Mexico. In fact, just a few weeks before I found out about Nor-tec I was beginning to sample vinyls of mambo, *danzón,* and *banda sinaloense.* When I got the invitation to collaborate with Nor-tec I was surprised that they [Fussible, Bostich, and Panóptica] were working on something very similar to what I was looking for. So, I decided to participate in their project, which would

later become the Collective. We were all on the same search for our own sound . . . and what could be better than doing that collectively? Why regional music? Because those are our everyday sounds, what we hear on the streets, on TV, etc. We asked ourselves to take these elements and make them into something new. It was a matter of looking back to our immediate surroundings and experimenting with those local sounds instead of continuing imitating foreign trends.[31]

Terrestre's statement clearly expresses the desire for the renovation and reevaluation of popular culture that informs the work and discourse of Cha3 and Octavio Hernández, but introduces a new key element: an anxiety about influence and an ambivalence toward foreign models ("experimenting with those local sounds instead of continuing imitating foreign trends"). Terrestre's self-accepted anxiety is fundamental to understanding the ideological web that informs the frame for reception articulated by Nortec. The recognition of the ambiguous relation to foreign models, both as objects of desire and as sources of an ethnic reification, speaks to the contradictory discourses that informed the artistic manifestations of Tijuana artists in the late 1990s.

The presence of Nor-tec antecedents like the projects of Cha3, Octavio Hernández, Torolab, and Terrestre clearly establishes the aspirations of an important portion of the artistic community in Tijuana at the end of the 1990s: renovation, originality, cosmopolitanism as well as a reevaluation of local traditions and popular culture as claims for authenticity within larger processes of globalization. Indeed, one of the most important aspects of the Nor-tec project is its ability to combine these interests into a single, unified strategy and to provide meaning for a wide variety of local endeavors. Nor-tec manifests the complex relations among modernity, tradition, otherness, and self-identity as rearticulated in the imaginary of *tijuanense* artists. In fact, the discourse surrounding Nor-tec's origins exposes the conciliatory nature of the Nor-tec project. Hiperboreal's account of the presentation of *El Nuevo Sueño de la Gallina* as a site for the development of the Nor-tec idea and Panóptica's retroactive conciliatory narrative articulate the late 1990s Tijuana cultural frame for reception. These trends were "floating signifiers" that acquired a coherent global significance after being articulated by the Nor-tec project. It was this early catholicizing impulse of the Nor-tec idea and the openness of the Nortec Collective which allowed it to become a tacit alliance that permitted the work of a wide variety of local musicians and visual artists to gain international exposure and thus local recognition and validation.

Regardless of the common aesthetic trends shared by the different artistic projects that preceded Nor-tec, a careful analysis of Torolab, Hernández, and Terrestre's shows that what I have called a *tijuanense* frame for reception of the late 1990s should not be interpreted as the last achieve-ment in a goal-oriented idealist teleology. Rather, we might view it as a cul-tural construction contingent upon a series of power relations at play in the local articulation of the production, distribution, and consumption of a globalized economy of desire. Nor-tec should not be viewed as the sole re-sult of a local reconsideration of tradition and heritage but as a complex process that negotiated a place among global, national, and transnational discourses of representation, authenticity, ethnicity, and otherness; local sites of identification, class, race, nationality, and imaginaries of cosmo-politanism; and center, periphery, hegemony, and marginality. The contin-gency of the so-called frame for reception is evident in the development of the notion of a "new sound" that permeates Artefakto's transformation into Fussible and Panóptica, Terrestre's post-Sonios musical searches, and Hiperboreal's infatuation with experimentation. In every case, the search for originality is the result of the appropriation of a modernist creed that, combined with the pressures of popular culture's impermanence, produces a desire for renovation (*camino en el tiempo / ecléctica / el rojo dice: / "Vuelve"/ . . . volver a nacer*). However, the longing to produce a "new sound" is not only the result of embracing a globalized modernist cos-mopolitanism, but also the contradictory consequence of the desiring ma-chine that the mainstream puts in operation to counterbalance the crisis that globalization itself triggers in formerly centered subjects. On the one hand, globalization provides an optimistic discourse of cosmopolitanism and iden-tification that naïvely promises to lead toward the fulfillment of *tijuanenses'* desires and aspirations. On the other hand, the pressures of globalized cap-ital and the crisis it prompts within formerly autonomous centers of power force individuals to react endogenously, searching for sites of identification in the seeming security of locality and heritage. This reaction reinforces discourses about difference and otherness, and in turn forces marginal sub-jects to reactivate the desiring machine of ethnic identification. As such, the search for a new sound that a modernist belief in progress instills in marginal subjects (such as these *tijuanense* artists) could only be achieved through the incorporation of the elements that mark those marginal sub-jects as different.

As Pepe Mogt explains, the rejection by European and U.S. labels ("we were sending our demos and nothing was happening with the labels") played a fundamental role in Artefakto's and Fussible's reinvention in the late 1990s. Mogt states that the typical response from these labels was to invite "us to make [our music] more pop or put vocals on. The European labels thought it was too old and unoriginal, because in Europe, you know, there are 300 guys doing breakbeats. The problem is that we were trying to sound just like them."[32] These labels did not reject Fussible's music on the basis of its musical quality but rather because it did not sound the way it was "supposed" to sound. This music sounded too much like the European bands' and, according to the implicit logic, a Mexican band should not sound European. Clearly, a "European type of non-European music" would not be appealing to European audiences, as they expect those cultural productions to display a distinguishable marker of otherness. Mexican bands and their European counterparts, as well as the label owners from both regions, joined in the common effort of constructing their own musical identities and exploiting their respective handles on the discourses of race and ethnicity. As my genealogy shows, Pepe Mogt's early descriptions of the Fussible project made no reference to the Nor-tec project. It was only after the European labels positioned Mogt and his music within a discourse of difference that clearly set him apart as the other that he stepped in the direction of Nor-tec and used local sounds. Pushed into a corner where the music he was composing did not have a place, Mogt chose to strategically position himself within the European discourse of difference and, from that position, to develop a musical style that would give him a card to play within music marketing networks. Indeed, Mogt's move was successful, the "Mexican sounds" paid off, as proved by James Lien's review of *The Tijuana Sessions, Vol. 1*, the collective's first commercial CD: "with underground practitioners like Fussible, Plasma [*sic*] and Modula 3 [*sic*] paving a new path for Nortec, one can only hope there will be even more indigenous Mexican sounds and influences permeating the party."[33]

The interconnection of local, national, transnational, and global circumstances is also at stake in the development of the electronic music scene in Tijuana, which embraced Nor-tec and contributed to its early success. Indeed, it was the global crisis of rock and the development of a post-rock discourse in the late 1990s which opened the door for electronic dance music to be considered "the music of the future."[34] The easy availability of music technology and the creation of more democratic networks of distribution resulted in more direct access to music. This trend favored the activities of local do-it-yourself crews (DJs, music producers, concert organizers, etc.) such as those active in Tijuana at the end of the 1990s. As I mentioned earlier, it was the local articulation of these global circumstances in the work and activities of DJs like Tolo, Max, and Chuy; radio hosts and music critics like Rafa Saavedra and Enrique Jiménez (Mr. Ejival); and concert organizers like Ricky Martínez de Castro, Luis Tucker, and Susan Monsalve which paved the road for the success of Nor-tec after 1999.

In summary, Nor-tec should not be interpreted as the product of a naïvely optimistic regeneration of hope and pride in border culture. Instead, it is the border condition itself which should be problematized in relation to the global discourses that inform its representation. It is the contradictory

economic, social, and cultural conditions created by the global expansion
of capitalism, and the global libidinal economy which spark the desires for
modernity and cosmopolitanism in border citizens. Nor-tec is a prime example of the complex ways in which hegemony is both contested and reproduced, challenged and reinforced. This music is part of individuals'
continuous negotiation of their place within alienating discourses of difference and all-embracing discourses of globalization, between their discursively ascribed marginal condition and their actual marginality within
the nation-state. Ironically, this same marginality gives them access to an
otherwise denied modernity.

A Name Is Just a Name? (Nor-tec Mix): Naming as Representation of Myth

Chatting in a hotel room a few blocks from Sunset Boulevard in Los Angeles, California, Bostich shares with me a handful of stories from his twenty-
year-old life as an underground musician. Anecdotes from his parallel life
as a family man and professional orthodontist embellish a narrative that
continuously shifts back and forth between totems of art and popular electronic music, like Karlheinz Stockhausen, Steve Reich, and Kraftwerk, and
local heroes of Tijuana's music scene, such as Javier Bátiz, Vandana, and
the teachers at the Escuela de Música of the local Casa de la Cultura (where
Bostich studied piano, cello, and composition). Bostich's conversation constantly crosses borders, from his role as a father to his place as a celebrated
underground musician, from the mainstream to the underground, from
highbrow to lowbrow culture, from Mexico to the United States, and from
Mexico City to Tijuana and San Diego. Inevitably, his recollections lead
him to the foundation of Nor-tec in 1999, and he emphatically states: "Nobody can say that Nor-tec started as a single event. Nor-tec is not the idea
Pepe got at his sister's party, or 'Polaris,' or even the name [Nor-tec] suggested by Panóptica. In fact, Nor-tec is the combination of those three
things."[35] Undeniably, the myth of origin represented in Pepe Mogt's narrative and the craze caused by "Polaris" are two important reasons behind
the local success of Nor-tec. However, in the semantic possibilities that surround it, a name is never just a name; Panóptica's fortunate suggestion to
call it Nor-tec is worth analyzing.

Nor-tec as a musical style is the result of the *tijuanenses'* negotiation of
the contradictory circumstances of living at the U.S.–Mexico border, the
boundary between the First and the Third World, the line that separates
modernity and the dreams about modernity. Nor-tec is a music that rearetic-
ulates the issues that surround Tijuana's culture. The hyphenated term "Nor-
tec" was originally coined by Panóptica as a fusion of the words *norteño*

and *tecnología* (technology). The term was not meant to be a permanent one but rather a temporary label for an experiment in fusion whose success was not foreseen at that early stage. However, the neologism stuck since it was catchy and easy to remember, and electronic music fans from Tijuana quickly made it their own, canceling any possibility for the musicians to change it later. Tellingly, the fans' appropriation of the term resulted in a reinterpretation of its meaning; while "Nor" still stood for *norteño*, "tec" came to stand for *tecno* (techno) music. This appropriation soon made its way back into Nor-tec mythology, and the musicians' narratives were adapted to account for the semantic change. Thus, Nor-tec became the liminal site for a once improbable encounter of two distinctly different dance scenes—*norteño* and underground dance—as opposed to the discursive reinterpretation of northern traditions through technology, which was implied in the original semantics of Panóptica's hybrid term.

It is revealing that the musicians shifted from the hyphenated neologism Nor-tec to the seemingly more fluid, nonhyphenated presentation "Nortec" after their first production, the *Nor-tec Sampler* (1999).[36] According to H. Ned Seelye and Jacqueline Howell Wasiliewski, multicultural groups adopt hyphenated identities to position themselves within the diversity of their social and cultural context.[37] This theoretical formulation is adequate to interpret Nor-tec as a movement only in relation to its hyphenated name, but it is inadequate if we consider that the Nortec Collective recognizes itself as a hybrid. More than a terminological dispute, the hyphenated versus hybrid identities imply a competition of perspectives regarding the coexistence of different cultures versus the fusion that the term hybridity conveys.

The hybrid character of the term emphasizes the transcultural nature of Mogt and Ruiz's idea, a notion that, in the audience's re-signification, attempts to reconcile the young *tijuanenses*' desire for modernity with a musical tradition often associated with rural people and considered to be unsophisticated. It is in this conciliatory process that tradition is rewritten according to the present and rearticulated in relation to the future. The sampling of *norteña* music originates in a desire to authenticate current musical practices in their relation to the past, and results in music that rewrites that past, thereby reconstituting tradition in a performative way. The sampling creates a prism that allows us to observe tradition and at the same time transforms our perception of that tradition. The liminal character of Nor-tec articulates processes of transculturation that subjects at the border collectively experience. The musicians' recognition of such liminality simultaneously announces and negotiates their places within a multi-ideological context. Furthermore, the term Nor-tec reflects the creation of a myth. The coinage of the term and its semantic changes speak to the origins of the Nor-tec movement. Nor-tec is thus both a metaphorical and an actual borderline where two worlds (or representations of those worlds) meet; the term itself becomes an epistemological gate for moving from one world to the other. As such, the new word is a myth or a simulacrum since it works at the level of a metalanguage; it refers to something beyond the meanings of the words it hybridizes; it is the articulation, at a specific moment in time, of that process of hybridization. The discourses embedded in the words *norteño* and techno (or technology) find a seemingly contradictory site of negotiation in the terms Nor-tec and Nortec; they not only conceal previously used terminology but also the discourses of coexistence or hybridization that the new terms imply. Nor-tec or Nortec are simulacra inasmuch as they are specific sites where the semantic meanings of two different terms find a moment of reconciliation and (as Torolab would argue with his Sistema Evolutivo de Binomios) develop into a single organism.

Members of the Nortec Collective are aware of the distinct political implications of the two terms and play with them to distinguish themselves from those who embrace the aesthetics of *norteña*-electronica fusion but have chosen to leave the collective. Melo states, "Nor-tec the sound is one thing and Nortec the Collective is another thing. There are artists like Terrestre or Plankton Man who were included in *The Tijuana Sessions, Vol. 1,* and still work with the sound [aesthetic]. But we [Bostich, Clorofila, Fussible, Hiperboreal, Panóptica, VJ CBrown, VJ Tavo, and VJ Mashaka] are the Collective, that's the only difference."[38] Thus, the more fluid Nortec becomes in the musicians' imagination a site of identification and belonging while the hyphenated Nor-tec remains an open site for coexisting with those who embrace a similar aesthetic project. Clearly, the resemanticization of the words Nor-tec and Nortec reflects the power relations within the collective and the appropriation and consumption of its aesthetic project. The complex dialogic process of cultural signification is accurately expressed in the performative acts of naming and renaming the project as part of a symbolic mythology.

"When Are You Going to Play the CD?": Myth, Simulacrum, and Discourse

A historic and cultural contextualization of Hiperboreal's 1999 birthday party situates it as part of larger, if discontinuous, cultural and social processes. The participants' anticipation regarding the new music of Fussible, Bostich, and Panóptica—expressed in their contained but anxious request, "When are you going to play the CD?"—as well as their enthusiastic response to it should be interpreted in the light of desires for originality and cosmopolitanism. They likewise encourage the interaction of local artists with larger discourses of representation and global processes of marketing and distribution. The Nor-tec CD that the partygoers anxiously awaited was the materialization of many of the ideas that had circulated among the *culturosos tijuanenses* in the late 1990s. The mythology of Nor-tec, exemplified in the accounts of its origins by Hiperboreal, Pepe Mogt, and Panóptica, developed into a discourse that opened doors for the recognition of a wide variety of intellectual and artistic endeavors. Pepe Mogt's playing of the CD at Hiperboreal's birthday party allowed these narratives to enter the level of myth. In this case, the myth not only names a site for the projection of aesthetic desires and intellectual preoccupations but also performatively writes the memory of the creation of such site. Thus, the Nor-tec myth of origin acts as a simulacrum by reconstituting reality through the bits and pieces of memory that make up the myth itself as an imaginary representation.

"When are you going to play the CD?" "Even the cover! It was a picture of electronic music equipment and an accordion."[39] "¡N'ombre! How do you think we're gonna mix *norteño?*"[40] "We asked ourselves how to produce a sound that could be identified as Mexican . . . although, we were not thinking about a regional sound,"[41] "the hip hop that could be made in Mexico if we had a bit of techno culture,"[42] "[it was] in the heat of discussing music and drinking wine, that the first ideas about fusing these two entities [electronic and *norteña* music] were born."[43] These phrases, gathered through fieldwork, cyber-fieldwork, and archival research, are all bits of memory that constitute the discourse of the Nor-tec myth. They are discursive slips that inform us of the contradictions, desires, and anxieties at stake in the construction of a local site of cultural identification. As Bostich states: "Nobody can say that Nor-tec started as a single event. Nor-tec is not the idea Pepe got at his sister's party, or 'Polaris,' or even the name suggested by Panóptica."[44] Nor-tec is the contingent amalgamation of many events, ideas, and practices that provide it with complex and shifting cultural meanings throughout its processes of production, distribution, and consumption.

2

Tradition, Style, Nostalgia, and Kitsch

I am sitting inside Mariscos Mazatlán, a well-known seafood restaurant in Tijuana, interviewing Ursula, an upper-middle-class (from the La Mesa neighborhood) Nor-tec fan in her early 30s. Ursula has been one of my most enthusiastic informants: I met her on the Internet through a mutual friend before my first field trip to Tijuana, and she was fundamental in facilitating lodging arrangements for my first two trips to the city and for one of my field trips to Los Angeles. The friendship we have developed allows her to speak more openly about her feelings regarding the Nor-tec scene and its music. Our conversation touches upon her first encounter with the scene, her continuous interest in Nor-tec music and visual art, and her own past as a *culturosa,* from which she eventually shifted away for a more profitable occupation working at one of the companies of a nationally notorious businessman who lives in Tijuana. At some point in our dialogue, I ask her to tell me about the kinds of music she likes besides Nor-tec; her answer is significant: "I like almost all types of music but curiously I hate *norteña*. I just don't like that."[1]

Ursula's comment points at the contradictions that inform the rearticulation of *norteña* traditions as performed by the local Nor-tec scene in its search for modernity and cosmopolitanism. She is not alone in her disdain for *norteña* and *banda* music. A number of statements by members of the Nortec Collective and by Nor-tec followers indicate that a type of kitsch and camp sensibility was indispensable in the development of the hybrid Nor-tec aesthetic. When I asked Jorge Ruiz (Melo) about his hesitance to quickly embrace Pepe Mogt's Nor-tec experiment, he shortly replied: "I was afraid it was going to be too folksy . . . *de a tiro corrientón* [way too vulgar]."[2] Heriberto Yépez, one of Tijuana's most prominent young writers, reflected on this issue: "At the beginning I did not like these guys [the members of the Nortec Collective] because I [was] sure they used to judge this music [*norteño* and *banda*] as music from the *maquiladoras, naco* music. But I could not avoid [being won] over by their pieces."[3] Among electronic music fans, the feeling against traditional *norteña* music is similar. Bruno Ruiz, a journalist and blogger, posted the following text on his blog:

> I do not like any of that. Nor *gruperos,* nor *corridos,* nor any of that. That's why I do not really like the Nortec thing, because they want to remix the techno thing with the *norteña* thing. They use these *sombrerudos* [guys with big hats] in their logos and, in a way, even machine guns and marihuana-type shirts, and that is like honoring the *narco* lifestyle.[4]

Even among younger Nor-tec fans, the typical lack of interest in *norteña* and *banda* music that characterizes young middle-class *tijuanenses* is evident, as Alex acknowledges: "I never really [listen to] *banda,* although I can distinguish the [*banda*] snare drum and its groove in Nor-tec."[5]

The relationship between Nor-tec and tradition is worth analyzing. The contradictory and complex character of this relationship is acknowledged by music producers, visual artists, and Nor-tec fans both in their claims for authenticity and in the generalized disdain for the actual sources of that "authenticity" among young, upper-middle-class *tijuanenses* (the local audiences of Nor-tec). Nor-tec articulates three clearly differentiated musical traditions from the north of Mexico or, to put it more correctly, traditions appropriated for decades by Mexican northerners: *norteña, banda sinaloense,* and *onda grupera.* Each of these traditions has been historically identified with the lower classes, the unsophisticated countryside, and, particularly in the cases of *banda* and *norteña,* with older generations. In other words, echoing Yépez's criticism, these traditions were for many decades considered *naco* music[6] by young middle-class *tijuanenses,* an opinion that reflected the generalized disdain toward *norteño* culture among many Mexicans throughout the rest of the country.

The purpose of this chapter is to identify the aesthetic criteria behind Nor-tec's appropriation of *norteña, banda,* and *grupera* traditions. Which issues of class, race, ethnicity, and nationality are at stake in such an appropriation? What do particular artistic and musical styles tell us about the glocal desires that have informed the development of the Nor-tec scene? How does the hybrid music style of Nor-tec actually allow for the transformation of key dichotomies privileged in the colonial imagination? In short, how does Nor-tec's contemporary rearticulation of *norteña* traditions challenge conventional assumptions about the very notions of tradition and cosmopolitanism, heritage and modernity, center and periphery? In order to answer these questions, I explore the histories of *norteña, banda,* and *grupero* musics and their identification as markers of specific social, cultural, and generational groups. I also trace the use of samples from these traditions to understand the development of individual musical styles by different Nor-tec artists. Finally, I explore the contradictory relation between Nor-tec fans and musicians and the *norteña* traditions as a type of articulation that re-signifies *de a tiro corrientón* or "unsophisticated" manifestations as kitsch artifacts.

Regional Mexican Mix I:
Tradition and Local Identities

Conventionally, tradition has been homologized with cultural heritage, the transmission of beliefs and knowledge from one generation to the next. According to this characterization, tradition is that which links human beings to their past, to their "essence," and validates the "authenticity" of their acts in the present. Indeed, in this primordialist perspective of tradition, there is no distinction between the past and the present inasmuch as individuals consider inherited modes of behavior to be part of their own natures. Nevertheless, this essentialist understanding of tradition has been critiqued by scholars who consider traditions to be inventions or constructions developed in order to validate present cultural, political, and economic projects with the aura of authenticity of the past.[7] Accordingly, "tradition should not be interpreted as the static legacy of the past but rather as a model for the dynamic reinterpretation of the present."[8] A contemporary approach to tradition should take into account not the place or location claimed by any given tradition but rather the actual information it provides for the definition and refinement of cultural identities according to specific power struggles in the present. Thus, in order to respond to the questions at stake in Nor-tec's modernist articulation of popular *norteña* musics, it is necessary to perform a genealogy of these traditions in accordance with the idea that traditions are the "foil for exploring the contested subjectivities involved in producing and/or occupying space."[9]

As a kid growing up in Reynosa, Tamaulipas, at the Texas border in northeastern Mexico during the 1970s, I was surrounded by the *fara-fara* sound[10] of *norteña* and *conjunto* bands like Los Alegres de Terán, Los Cadetes de Linares, Eulalio González (Piporro), Ramón Ayala and Cornelio Reyna (Los Relámpagos del Norte), and Leonardo "Flaco" Jiménez. This was my grandfather's favorite music, and it was usually part of the musical repertoire at family gatherings. Listening to this music, at that time still largely absent from the centralized Mexican media, and discussing the lyrics of the songs and *corridos*—deliberations that went as far as to speculate about the towns and even neighborhoods mentioned or implied by the lyrics—was a way to clearly establish our identity as *norteños* and to culturally separate ourselves from Mexicans from the center of the country. For my grandfather and his generation, *norteña* music was clearly a marker of northeastern identity, one that should not be confused with that represented by northwestern *banda* music. I learned this the hard way when, knowing that my grandfather was an admirer of the Mexican revolutionary hero Pancho Villa, I gave him a birthday present that consisted of a recording of *corridos* about Villa performed by Antonio Aguilar in *banda* style; understandably, the gift remained unopened in my grandfather's music room for years. However, even though *norteña* music was still considered a trademark of northeastern identity, it was the "Mexicanized" cumbia of Rigo Tovar y su Costa Azul, the mellow ballads of Los Ángeles Negros, and American rock which accompanied my friends' dancing at our school parties in the late 1970s. In fact, the local younger generation, eager to find its own personality, rebelled against the music of their elders in two ways: upper-middle-class youngsters shifted toward rock and preferred to listen to American radio stations, while lower- and lower-middle-class youths tended to embrace one of the most representative Latin American popular music trends at the end of the twentieth century, *onda grupera* (ensemble or group trend).

Although clearly three different musical traditions, the histories of *norteña, banda,* and *onda grupera* are complex, interconnected, and share a very important common feature: they are not only hybrid music genres embraced on both sides of the U.S.–Mexico border but are also truly transnational traditions in their sources and development. The undifferentiated way they have been portrayed by Mexican and Latino media from the mid-1990s on, under the label *onda norteña,* or regional Mexican music, has only contributed to the non-*norteño* public's confusion regarding the stylistic differences among them, as well as the different social strata to which they originally appealed.[11] The goal of this genealogy is to clearly acknowledge the particular social, economic, and cultural experiences that make each of these traditions a unique transnational phenomenon, to keep track of the continuous processes of intertextuality that have characterized their expansion, and to show the simulacrum-like nature of tradition as exemplified in the processes of unlimited semiosis that have informed their development.

Tracing Steps III: *Banda Sinaloense*

The tradition of *banda* music in the northwestern Mexican state of Sinaloa goes back to the mid-nineteenth century and the presence of military bands that, instead of restricting themselves to their military unit, performed in a wide variety of venues.[12] According to Héctor Olea, *la tambora* (the name locals give to *banda* ensembles) was a constant presence in the social life of nineteenth-century Mazatlán, from the carnival to open-air concerts.[13] However, as Helena Simonett argues, it was only after the 1910 Mexican revolution that a characteristic regional *banda sinaloense* style was developed with the increasing standardization of the ensemble lineup (three clarinets, two trumpets, two trombones with valves, two *charchetas* [sax horns], *bajo de pecho* [upright-bell tuba], *tarola* [snare drum], and *tambora* [double-headed bass drum]) and its repertoire (regional *sones*, waltzes, and *corridos* [ballads]).[14] However, the standardization of the ensemble did not mean a fossilization of the *banda* tradition. In fact, the survival of *banda* music until today is due to the musicians' ability to adapt to a rapidly changing musical environment and to adopt the musical trends preferred by their audiences. Furthermore, *banda* music was never made into an "official" Mexican music tradition (unlike mariachi or *son jarocho*), and thus was never required to remain faithful to a unique source of authenticity to become a tourist attraction; as Simonett states, the economic survival of *banda* musicians "depends very much on their being flexible and innovative."[15] This has required musicians to be able to incorporate elements from a wide variety of musical genres into their repertoires and adapt them to their instrumental setting.

The history of Banda El Recodo, arguably the most influential *banda sinaloense* of the twentieth century (founded by Cruz Lizárraga in 1938 and still touring worldwide under the direction of his sons), accounts for the many changes and the transnational success that *banda* music experienced throughout the twentieth century. The early repertoire of the group was rooted in traditional instrumental Sinaloan music, especially *corridos*. Aspiring to perform at elite dance events, however, the band quickly began to incorporate the repertoire favored by middle- and upper-class urban audiences (swing, boleros, and mambos).[16] By the end of the 1950s, Banda El Recodo was part of La Caravana Corona, a traveling company that included some of the most famous singers and musicians of the country. Their participation in the troupe opened to them the doors of Mexico City's Teatro Blanquita (a leading theater devoted to popular music and political satire) and eventually led to contracts to perform at Los Angeles's Million Dollar Theater, well known for booking the Mexican music stars of the 1950s.[17] Responding to their growing national and international success, the band developed a musical style characterized by powerful melodies in parallel motion played in an alternate or combined fashion by clarinets and trumpets, punctuating harmonies provided by the *charchetas* and the trombones, a driving and often virtuosic counterpoint played by the tuba, the embellished rolls of the *tarola,* especially at cadences and the end of phrases, and the juxtaposition of solo and tutti sections. Accused of having departed from traditional *banda sinaloense* practices, the sound of El Recodo was criticized by many *banda* musicians who remained in Sinaloa; these musicians were particularly bitter over El Recodo's increasingly frequent appearances as an accompanying ensemble for some of Mexico's leading *ranchera* singers, among them José Alfredo Jiménez and Lola Beltrán. The popularity of Afro-Cuban bands first, in the 1950s, and cumbia groups later, in the 1960s, had a strong influence on the most commercially oriented Sinaloan bands, which, like El Recodo, experimented with mambo, *guaracha, danzón,* and cumbia without losing the distinctly Sinaloan style that I have described above.[18] By the 1970s, the public's request for singers eventually led the band to hire a vocalist as part of its lineup, a practice that quickly became common among commercial *bandas.*

Regardless of the international recognition achieved by bands like El Recodo, and although Mexican stars like singer-actor Antonio Aguilar and *ranchera* icon Lucha Villa recorded with *bandas* in the 1970s and 1980s, the genre was still considered by most Mexicans, especially those from central and south Mexico, as a marker of unsophisticated, lowbrow folk culture, and it remained largely absent from the country's mainstream media. It was not until the late 1980s and early 1990s that, supported by the economic power of an increasing immigrant community in the United States from western and northwestern Mexico, an amazing transnational resurgence of *banda* began. This revival, initially supported by the local music industries of Los Angeles and Guadalajara, was accompanied by important instrumental changes, including the incorporation of electric bass and keyboard, which led to the development of technobanda. Banda Machos, Banda Vallarta Show, and Banda Maguey were among the bands that helped to revitalize the genre by incorporating fast rhythms, elaborate *vaquero* (cowboy) outfits, and energetic choreographies that emphasized the important exchange of energy between the stage and the dance floor.[19] Central to the commercial success of technobanda was the *quebradita* dance craze that accompanied it. *Quebradita* (little break) combines elements from country-western, flamenco, and Brazilian *lambada* into a vigorous, fast-rhythm dance characterized by the "back-bending contortion the female dancing partner makes as the male swings her toward the floor."[20] In the 1990s, the U.S. Latino music industry and the mainstream Mexican media capitalized on the transnational *banda* phenomenon. For the first time, *banda* music, musicians, and fans were granted access to primetime mainstream shows like Raúl Velasco's *Siempre en Domingo* and recognition through the Billboard Latin Music Awards, the Latin Grammy, as well as specially created prizes, such as the Premio Furia Musical.

Tracing Steps IV: *Norteña* Music

If *sinaloenses* took *banda* as a marker of northwestern Mexican identity, *norteña*—which historically had developed in parallel to *banda*—was embraced by *neoloenoeses* and *tamaulipecos* as a musical site for northeastern Mexican identity.[21] *Norteña* is the musical twin sister of Texan-Mexican *conjunto*. Both northeastern traditions have mutually influenced the other as they have become, over the last century, the favorite musics of families whose members live on both sides of the Rio Grande. Both *norteño* and *conjunto* have folk-based rural origins and share a standard instrumentation that includes the button accordion, *bajo sexto, tololoche* (double bass, which has often been replaced, especially in *conjunto* music, by the electric bass since the mid-1950s), and *redova* (a homemade drum that was largely replaced by the drum set or *tarola* and cowbell since the 1950s). Ramiro Burr states that *norteño* and *conjunto* are nearly identical styles except that "*norteño* singers typically exhibit a more pronounced Mexican accent and a pinched, nasal quality, the polka backbeat tend[s] to be less pronounced than in Tejano music, and *norteño* accordionists generally len[d] more subtlety to their riffs."[22]

As Manuel Peña and Cathy Ragland discuss, the economic boom at the end of the nineteenth century of the northeastern Mexican city of Monterrey, with its trade ties to border Mexican towns like Reynosa, Matamoros, and Piedras Negras and to small American cities like San Antonio and Laredo, was fundamental in the development and dissemination of *norteña* and *conjunto* music throughout the Mexican Northeast and the American Southwest.[23] As the undisputed economic and cultural metropolis of the area toward the end of the nineteenth century, Monterrey became a magnet for immigrants from rural Mexican areas as well as European settlers, mostly Germans, Czechs, and Poles, who came to work on the railroad lines from central Texas to northern Mexico, stayed in the area, and created breweries and steel-making businesses. In fact, throughout the twentieth century, the economic success of Monterrey was exemplified by its metallurgic and brewing industries. Musicologists and music historians have largely agreed that the introduction of the accordion and European dances such as the *polca* (polka), *redova* (redowa), and *chotís* (schottische) to the region dates from that period. Monterrey was not the only Mexican city to embrace these dances, however; as Manuel Peña points out, these dances prevailed in Mexico due to the pressures to Europeanize the country.[24] I would argue that the widespread success of these dances in Mexico was also informed by the filtering of the Mexican elite's desire for cosmopolitanism (at the time represented by European culture) through the lower strata of Mexican society. At any rate, by the 1890s and 1900s, the newly introduced music traditions were quickly embraced by already established music ensembles such as military bands, *orquestas típicas* (string ensembles), and *tamborileros* (groups formed by clarinets and a homemade drum called *tambora de rancho*). As Cathy Ragland states, it was common for these ensembles to play European dance styles like polkas, redowas, and schottisches, along with favorite local genres such as the *corrido* or *huapango*.[25]

By the 1890s, one- and two-row button accordions accompanied by *bajo sexto* and *tambora de rancho* were common musical features in Mexican weddings and *funciones* (three- to four-day-long celebrations that included music and dance performances known as *bailes de regalo*) along the border.[26] Due to the instrument's affordability and the low cost of hiring one or two musicians instead of a large band, the accordion became the instrument of choice for these kinds of musical activities on both sides of the border by the beginning of the twentieth century.[27] It was during this time that Narciso Martínez, Pedro Ayala, and Bruno "El Azote" Villarreal, three of the most influential musicians in the history of *norteño* and *conjunto* music, were born; they represent the link between the music traditions alive at the border in the 1910s and the first commercial recordings (made by American labels such as Decca and Bluebird Records in the late 1920s) of what came to be known as *norteño* music. In the 1930s, these musicians established the basic instrumental lineup (accordion as the lead instrument and *bajo sexto* supplying the rhythm and bass line) and repertoire (a combination of the lyric-oriented *corridos, canciones rancheras,* and *huapangos* along with instrumental *polcas, chotises,* and *redovas*) for the nascent *norteño* and *conjunto* traditions.

The development of a typical *norteño/conjunto* style, which emphasized a more syncopated melodic line,[28] quickly set this tradition apart from the German and Czech polka bands that, to this day, still exist in central Texas. The consolidation of this Mexican/Mexican-American sound took place after World War II, when Chicano recording companies filled the vacuum left by the departure of major labels (like RCA's Bluebird and Columbia's Decca) from the borderlands.[29] Thus, many local independent labels were created in the Texas Rio Grande Valley. Among them, Falcón Records and Ideal Records achieved a modest commercial success that allowed a number of local musicians to have their music heard throughout the borderlands. This *norteño/conjunto* musical style could be characterized by that of the award-winning band Los Alegres de Terán, a rather folksy, nasalized singing style complemented by a higher-pitched voice in close harmony (usually a third above), the addition of a *tololoche,* and the melodic embellishments of the accordion at the beginning and end of vocal phrases and in the instrumental introductions and interludes of most songs.[30]

However, although a characteristic Mexican/Mexican-American style developed as a hybrid of Mexican, border, and European traditions, it did not become a static, fossilized musical practice. *Norteño* and *conjunto* traditions kept changing as the economic conditions of their audiences on both sides of the border were continuously transformed by migration, racial discrimination, illegal trafficking, and influences from other genres popularized by the U.S. and Mexican media throughout the 1950s and 1960s. For example, the increase of goods and drug smuggling as a subaltern economic activity at the U.S.–Mexico border was reflected in the development of the *corrido de contrabando* (smuggling ballad) first and the *narcocorrido* (drug ballad) later. The Colombian cumbia craze that reached Mexico in the 1950s and 1960s, headed by groups like Sonora Dinamita and appropriated by Mexican ensembles such as Mike Laure y sus Cometas, resulted in yet another hybrid genre, the *cumbia norteña* or Tex-Mex cumbia, which quickly gained a place among the older repertoires of *norteño* and *conjunto* musicians. These types of cumbias differ from their Colombian predecessors in that they are often rhythmically simpler (see example 2.1) and usually substitute the brass instrumentation of *sonoras* (big-band type of brass ensembles) with accordion. Since the early 1990s, the continuous interbreeding of *norteño* and *conjunto* with other musical traditions (mostly *banda, cumbia, onda grupera,* and *balada pop*) has resulted in further changes in the instrumental composition of *norteño* and *conjunto* bands, including larger ensembles, such as Los Tigres del Norte and Los Tucanes de Tijuana. This growth also coincided with a growing presence of Mexican immigrant culture in both American and Mexican media. Such a powerful economic presence had an impact on the increasing change of attitude from both the Latino music scene in the United States and Mexican media toward *conjunto* and *norteña* music. As a result of this shift, long-standing *norteña* bands like Los Tigres del Norte began to share the stage and radio and TV airwaves with Latino rock stars like Maná, Afro-Caribbean combos like Juan Luis Guerra y 4.40, and pop stars like Ricky Martin and to attract a new, heterogeneous, and all-inclusive Latino music market.

Tracing Steps V: *Onda Grupera*

The musical developments and transnational economic successes experienced by the *banda* and *norteña* traditions since the late 1980s need to be

Example 2.1   Basic rhythmic
pattern of *cumbia norteña* as
played by the *güiro*

interpreted alongside the development of another massive music phenomenon across the U.S.–Mexico border, the so-called *onda grupera*. The development of *la onda grupera* owes much to the slow but continuously
growing success of cumbia in Mexico during the 1950s and 1960s. By the
1960s, Mexican groups like Mike Laure y sus Cometas, Sonora Santanera,
and Chelo y su Conjunto had largely replaced the big bands of Afro-
Caribbean music (mambo and cha-cha-chá) that dominated the popular
music scene in central Mexico up until the 1950s. However, as Olvera, Torres, Cruz, and Rodríguez explain, the Mexican appropriation of cumbia
came with a number of instrumental and stylistic modifications to the
Colombian genre; noticeably, the polyrhythmic practices of traditional
cumbia were replaced by the typical and simpler *güiro* rhythmic pattern
that characterizes today's *cumbia norteña* (example 2.1), the substitution
of the accordion by the electric organ or the synthesizer, and the introduction of the drum set and *güiro* as the instrumental basis of the percussion
section.[31] These modifications gave birth to the *cumbia tropical,* a genre
that, as I mentioned earlier, eventually filtered into the *norteña* and *conjunto* repertoires to become *cumbia norteña.*

The first bands to explore the type of musical sound that came to be
known as *grupero* appeared in Mexico toward the end of the 1960s and
in the early 1970s. Groups like Los Freddy's, Los Babys, and Los Flamers
began their professional careers doing covers of U.S. and British rock bands
but eventually developed a more personal repertoire that incorporated elements from the *balada pop* tradition (itself an outcome of the 1930s, 1940s
and 1950s bolero tradition) and the *cumbia tropical,* most noticeably, the
use of lyrical romantic melodies and cumbia rhythms. Music critic Toño
Carrizosa suggests that this shift in repertoire responded not only to the
exploration of individual creativity, but also to the economic pressures of
the local music market.[32] For many of these bands, it was very difficult to
access a mainstream media that tended to demonize rock (especially after
the moralist backlash against the Avándaro Festival in 1971)[33] and to promote instead *balada pop* singers like José José, Julio Iglesias, and Camilo
Sesto. For many Mexican rock bands, a way to make a living performing
music was to appeal to a market that offered steadier work. The answer
was to play at *bailes de pueblo* (dances in towns and smaller villages in the

countryside) for the lower classes, who had been exposed to and had embraced cumbia since the 1960s due to the increasing presence of *bailes
sonideros*.[34] The incorporation of cumbia into these bands' sound was
clearly a response to the demands of this market.

Arguably, the first superstar band of the *grupero* tradition was formed
in Houston, Texas, in 1972 by Rigoberto Tovar García (Rigo Tovar), a
Mexican immigrant from the northeastern border city of Matamoros. The
huge success of Rigo Tovar y su Costa Azul, with its trademark keyboard-
driven cumbias and a hybrid music style that combined *cumbia tropical*,
rock, *ranchera*, and *balada pop*, dominated the music scene in the 1970s
and early 1980s. Tovar's group, along with foreign bands which entered the
Mexican and Mexican-American markets at that time (non-cumbia groups
like the Chilean Los Ángeles Negros, the Peruvian Los Pasteles Verdes, and
the Venezuelan Los Terrícolas, among others), witnessed the transformation
of the *grupero* trend from a local phenomenon into a true transnational
music movement, with the establishment of an economically powerful music
industry on both sides of the U.S.–Mexico border. Rigo Tovar's record sales
and massive concerts, largely attended by the lower classes, prepared the
industry for the truly gigantic events of bands like Los Bukis, Los Teme-
rarios, and Bronco, whose fan base, although still rooted in the lower classes,
was able to transcend class barriers with the support of the Mexican and
Latino media in the 1990s.

Bronco, a band formed in 1978 that exploded on the *grupero* scene
in 1990, deserves to be mentioned separately as it is a perfect example of
the complex intertextuality that informs the current musical production as
well as the practices of representation of *grupero*, *norteño*, and *banda* music
by the Mexican and Latino mainstream media. Originally a *norteño* group
that followed the musical and costume style of Los Tigres del Norte (such
as stylized versions of the Tamaulipas *cuera*, the traditional northeastern
clothing), Bronco slowly developed a new type of *norteña* fusion when, in
the mid-1980s, it began to integrate musical influences from Los Bukis, Los
Ángeles Negros, and even rock bands like the Beatles and developed a repertoire that included *norteñas*, *corridos*, *rancheras*, cumbias, and romantic
ballads. Indeed, Bronco became one of the most successful bands in the history of Mexican music, receiving 11 Discos de Oro (the Mexican recording
industry's award for bestselling recordings) for a single album (*Salvaje y
tierno*, 1991), appearing on the highly popular Mexican soap opera *Dos
mujeres, un camino* (1993)—itself a transnational hit that starred Puerto
Rican actor Erik Estrada as a Chicano truck driver in Mexico—having a
Las Vegas street named after it, playing worldwide tours throughout the
Americas and Spain, and selling out Azteca Stadium to its 115,000 capac-
ity for the band's 1997 farewell concert in Mexico City.[35] The new musical

fusion that characterized *gruperos* in the 1990s is also revealed in the work of Selena and Los Dinos as well as La Mafia, two of the most successful Mexican-American *grupero* bands, which incorporated elements from the mainstream American and Latino music industries into their sound (from reggae to disco to the pop sound of the Pretenders).

Regional Mexican Mix II:
The Simulacrum of Authenticity

Undeniably, with minimal support from the mainstream Mexican media and the Latino music industry before the mid-1990s, the *grupero* trend became a unique transnational phenomenon. However, transnational corporations like Televisa, Telemundo, and Univision were eager to benefit from the movement's huge economic profits and, as a result, began to support the bands, giving them access to their TV and radio shows, signing them for their own labels (such as Televisa's Musivisa), and launching their own marketing campaigns through magazines like *Furia Musical*.[36] Such strategies resulted in generic marketing labels like *onda grupera*, or regional Mexican music, which grouped together every music style remotely associated with the north of Mexico (in the case of Mexican media) or everything Mexican (in the case of the Latino music industry in the United States) into an almost undifferentiated mass where boundaries between traditions were blurry at best. Thus, *conjunto, banda, norteña, gruperos,* and some types of cumbia were all lumped together in the pages of *Furia Musical* or on TV shows like *El Show de Johnny Canales*.[37]

Clearly, the development of *banda, norteña,* and *onda grupera* illustrates the contingency of the processes of appropriation, signification, and identification behind the claims for authenticity of any tradition. In fact, a critical look at the histories of these traditions challenges their own claims for authenticity. As observed in my genealogy, current and past practices in *banda* and *norteña* music are the result of historical processes of globalization, cultural colonialism, and local musicians' active practices of negotiation with the pressures of hegemonic cultures. Although most Mexicans (including northerners) have historically identified *banda* and *norteña* with specific geographic locations, both music traditions are hybrids that, taking European genres as points of departure, developed into unique genres according to the desires for cosmopolitanism of audiences and musicians alike. The appropriation of European polkas, schottisches, and redowas in nineteenth-century Mexico; the incorporation of *corrido, huapango, ranchera,* mambo, cha-cha-chá, bolero, cumbia, and *balada pop* throughout the twentieth century; and the development of *narcocorrido, quebradita,* and technobanda trends are all responses to a combination of collective

desires for cosmopolitanism and the need to address the musical demands
that those desires prompted in the audiences. *Banda, norteña,* and *onda
grupera* as traditions are certainly simulacra where every stylistic novelty
negotiates the role of an idyllic past according to desires in the present.
Here, the authenticity of tradition is produced through miniature cells of
memory, making it into a hyperreality that continuously replaces and re-
signifies authenticity in an attempt to rescue the very principle of authenticity. Thus, the development of *cumbia norteña* and its incorporation into
the traditional repertoire of *norteña* music (therefore making it into an
"authentic" example of *norteña* music) was the result of rearticulating
tradition according to the desires represented in the working classes' acceptance of Colombian cumbia in the 1960s in the same way in which the
quebradita craze was a consequence of Mexican and Mexican-American
banda and *norteño* fans incorporating dance movements from rock and
roll, cumbia, flamenco, *lambada,* and *ballet folklórico* into traditional
Mexican *polca* and *chotís* dance steps.[38] These are clear examples of musical practices in constant flux in which current cultural meanings are discursively validated in the "authenticity" of tradition as they change and
transform themselves. An exploration of how *tijuanenses* have appropriated these musics and produced their own authenticities will allow us to
better understand the contested subjectivities involved in "producing and
occupying spaces" in the context of a multicultural society of migrants
such as Tijuana.

"La Casa de Toda la Gente [Everybody's Home]"

*Si vienes a Tijuana, a los quince días de haber llegado es tan
tuya como de los otros*
[If you come to Tijuana, after fifteen days of your arrival, the
city will be as yours as it is the others']

—Hiperboreal

During my second field trip to Tijuana, I met an older *tijuanense* middle-
class couple who were related to a friend of my parents. They were glad
that I was working on a book about music from their city and invited me
to have dinner at their home. The meal was nothing out of the ordinary:
vegetable soup, grilled fish, and rice. As we were talking after dinner, I
asked what they thought was Tijuana's most traditional dish. The couple
looked at each other and answered without hesitation: "Chinese food, of
course!" First, I found their answer sort of amusing; but later, as I thought
about it over and over, I realized that it was not only a tacit recognition of
local culture as the result of fluid processes of hybridization but also a

powerful statement about the role of migration and the foreign in the development of a local culture.[39]

Tijuana's population growth, from 16,486 in 1940 to more than a million in the 1990s, has been mostly dependent on its place as a staging ground for Mexican migrants (especially from Mexico City and the states of Oaxaca, Puebla, and Michoacán) and immigrants heading for the United States.[40] Since the 1960s, the establishment of *maquiladoras* has made it a magnet for unemployed Mexicans from other, poorer regions of the country, and Tijuana's geographic position as a border town has attracted immigrants not only from Mexico, but also from Central America, South America, and even Asia. Some of these people wait for their chance to enter the United States, while many others have decided to settle on the Mexican side of the border. The migration and social mobility of these groups of people, their everyday interrelations in the city, and their need to develop ties of identification have played important roles in constituting the hybrid culture that characterizes Tijuana. Under these circumstances, processes of appropriation and transculturation are everyday phenomena that shape local culture by re-signifying the symbolic practices of old and new *tijuanenses* according to their current living conditions.

To encounter countless examples of these types of cultural simulacra, one need do no more than to walk a few blocks along the infamous Avenida Revolución. The presence of the stereotypical donkeys painted as zebras or the *jaladores* who speak English with a specially cultivated accent that sounds "more Mexican than a Mexican would sound" could not be better examples of simulacra than an advertisement board placed on top of a Mexican curio shop that might go unnoticed to the uneducated eye.[41] The picture shows the 1950s Spanish actor Armando Calvo dressed as a Mexican *charro* (cowboy from central Mexico) under a caption that proudly announces "Museo de la Charrería." The layers of irony do not end in the fact that Calvo was neither Mexican nor a *charro* (throughout his acting career, Calvo became known for his roles as an elegant urban playboy) but also the *charros* represent a stereotypical icon of central and western Mexican identity that has historically little relation to Tijuana and the north of the country. Just like the Chinese restaurants that locals consider typically *tijuanenses,* the zebras, the strong accent of the *jaladores,* and the authentically Mexican *charro* are all simulacra that allow for the establishment of a cultural space that just "fifteen days after your arrival," as Hiperboreal affirms, "will be as yours as it is the others'."

Migration and social mobility have also played vital roles in the national and transnational dissemination of *banda, norteña,* and *onda grupera,* in the stylistic changes experienced by each of these traditions, and in their adoption as Tijuana's musical icons. As I have shown, neither *banda* nor *norteña* are originally musical traditions from Tijuana. *Norteña* music was slowly embraced along the U.S.–Mexico border throughout the twentieth century, eventually reaching northwestern Mexico as larger immigrant waves made Tijuana into their gateway to southern California. The presence of *banda* music in Tijuana responds to a similar trend, the increasing presence of large immigrant communities from Sinaloa and Sonora on both sides of the U.S.–Mexico border. Indeed, the 1990s *banda* and technobanda craze that gave this music access to the Latino entertainment industry in the United States and to the Mexican mainstream media bows to the transnational presence of these communities along the Pacific coast from the Los Angeles area down to Michoacán in western Mexico. Thus, at the end of the twentieth century, Tijuana and the American Southwest became the meeting point where these two distinctly different musical traditions met *onda grupera,* which, as a transnational musical phenomenon that owed its success to Mexican and Mexican-American audiences alike, had also been increasing its presence in the area for a long time. The musical hybrids produced by this encounter reflect a number of instrumental and stylistic changes among *norteña, banda,* and *grupero* ensembles; these include the incorporation of the button accordion into the *banda* and *grupero* lineups, the creation of crossover genres such as *cumbia norteña* and *quebradita,* the technobanda phenomenon, the increasing size of *norteño* groups (from three up to six musicians in some cases), and the adoption of audience-engaging performance strategies (which include colorful costumes, complex in-sync choreographies, and even rock star–like behavior by leading vocalists). The adoption of these migrant musical genres by a city of migrants par excellence like Tijuana has allowed for these kinds of transcultural developments to take place in a simulacrum-like fashion: the continuous borrowing of musical materials, performance practices, technology, and the sharing of distribution channels among these traditions means a permanent re-signification of each of them not only in relation to the elements borrowed from one another but also in relation to the desires promoted by the music industry and the pressures of its transnational market.

Consequently, the discourse that makes *banda, norteña,* and their hybrids into authentic *tijuanense* musical traditions responds to a local concern that, as Ronald Radano and Philip Bohlman state, "lends itself to a complex of metaphors about origins and their inalterability."[42] Indeed, as my genealogy has shown, there is nothing "authentic" in the history of these traditions inasmuch as they are not ineluctably bound to a given group or place. Accordingly, the processes of their re-signification in Tijuana make them into simulacra that, like the zebras, the Spanish *charro,* and the accent of the *jaladores,* allow people to meaningfully produce and occupy space. Authenticity itself lies in the appropriation that creates those sites of identification. In Tijuana, authenticity lives in the simulacra that make the city "everybody's home."

"It Is and It Is Not":
Sound and Authenticity in Nor-tec Music

As I noted in chapter 1, Pepe Mogt's call to experiment with the rhythmic patterns, sounds, and timbres of *norteño* and *banda* music as the source for an "authentic" Tijuana sound of electronic music was a savvy response to his experience with transnational music markets and their expectations of Mexican or Latin American musicians. Needless to say, the perspective of the Nortec Collective articulates larger discourses about tradition, authenticity, and music from the north of Mexico. However, while the musicians' claim to search for a local sound in the sonic elements that surround them in their city expresses an essentialist notion of authenticity, their distinct musical styles suggest that they are complex exercises in double or multiple codings which "mobilize two or more plains or fields of idiomatic reference in any given work."[43] Therefore, what might seem a straightforward acceptance of the rules imposed by the transnational music markets to exoticize the other is in fact a multilayered fabric that is at the same time an exercise in strategic essentialism, a challenge to hegemonic practices of representation, and an ironic commentary on the deafness of a music industry that is prepared to hear anything it wishes to hear as long as it is disguised under the appropriate aesthetic discourse.

One of the first aspects that interested me about the Nor-tec phenomenon was the different receptions it got from international audiences and from local *norteño* and *banda* fans. While the international electronic music community immediately accepted the hybrid credo of the Nortec Collective and commended the "indigenous Mexican sounds and influences permeating the [Nor-tec] party,"[44] the reaction among Mexican audiences familiar with *norteña* and *banda* was mixed. Hiperboreal reports that "some people would tell us 'I can't really hear it, ¿dónde está la tambora?' [where is the tambora?]."[45] Although I heard similar comments during my fieldwork, I also witnessed unexpected responses from unexpected people at unexpected places. At a Nor-tec performance in Los Angeles, I asked a middle-aged Mexican immigrant from Sinaloa if he liked the music, and he plainly answered: "I am not used to this modern music but I like it because it reminds me of my hometown."[46] Undeniably, Nor-tec is different from other examples of electronic music that borrow from local folk or popular traditions. While the Indian bhangra-house of Joi Bangla, the Argentinean techno tango of Gotan Project and Bajo Fondo, the Algerian sound of Khaled, or

B-Tribe's flamenco-house would normally sample or imitate complete melodic or harmonic sequences from bhangra, tango, raï, or flamenco songs, loop them, and add a beat, the members of the Nortec Collective generally have avoided quoting *norteña* or *banda* songs, and do it only occasionally for dramatic effect. Instead, they prefer to use very small fragments of *tarola* rolls and brass, woodwind, and accordion sounds that are utterly unrecognizable out of their original musical context. As Hiperboreal explains:

> [A] very important part [of Nor-tec] is to decontextualize, to change, and to put *tambora* and *norteña* music in a different place. . . . we could have made *tambora* music with the computer, keeping its structure, but we would not be offering anything new. . . . But the *tambora* is right there, *cabrón* [dude], it's just that it is manipulated. A lot of people read about Nor-tec and thought we were going to sound like a *tambora* or *norteña* song. . . . that's what is surprising, it is and it is not.[47]

Furthermore, most of the samples used by the members of the Nortec Collective in their tracks do not come from existing commercial recordings of *norteña* or *banda* music, but rather from a CD of samples put together and passed among Tijuana producers by Pepe Mogt in 1999 (although later, some producers also sampled street musicians and sometimes even their own playing). The CD is made from the outtakes from the recording sessions of three songs, Lorenzo Santamaría's well-known *balada romántica* "Para que no me olvides" in a *banda sinaloense* arrangement, the classic *banda* song "El sauce y la palma," and a newly composed *corrido norteño* that is difficult to identify. The CD features mostly individual *tarola* and *güiro* parts, short samples of *banda* harmonic instrumental bridges, solo trumpet and clarinet ornamental runs, accordion improvisatory sequences, a few *bajo sexto* strummings, and even false starts and conversations among the musicians. It is also important to note that the different samples in the CD are not organized as individual tracks but were rather recorded continuously one after the other in a single track, thus leaving Nor-tec producers with complete freedom in deciding how to fragment the raw musical elements at hand. As observed, Pepe Mogt's CD of samples is already made out of the fragmented pieces of a musical puzzle difficult to be put together; thus, the very essence of the discourse of authenticity is lost at the beginning of the process of Nor-tec production because there is no "original" to be copied. Accordingly, a *norteña* and *banda* fan would have a more difficult time trying to find *norteña* music in Nor-tec than a tango fan would have trying to find tango in the music of Bajo Fondo or Gotan Project.

For most hip-hop producers, a fundamental aspect of developing a sense of authenticity rests in a process that Joseph G. Schloss calls "digging in the crates" (searching for rare records from which to sample).[48] However, as DJ Tolo expresses, "*norteña* or *sinaloense* were not musics that we collected . . . at least that was neither my case nor Ramon's [Bostich] . . . nor for any of the other guys who have done this [Nor-tec]."⁴⁹ Thus, for Nor-tec producers, who do not engage in the practice of searching, gathering, and collecting rare *norteña* and *banda* recordings to extract their source material, the development of authenticity through sampling is found somewhere else. Here, the cry of the *norteño* fan ("*¿Dónde está la tambora?*") could be reformulated as "*¿Dónde está lo auténtico?* [Where is the authentic?]." The members and former members of the Nortec Collective would decisively argue that it is in the sounds and timbres of *norteña* and *banda* music, and not necessarily in the recognizable melodies or the classic recordings, that such authenticity is found. However, *tarola* rolls are also typical in Brazilian zabumba and samba ensembles and in Jewish klezmer, just as the timbre of the button accordion characterizes Colombian vallenato, and the oompah-oompah driving lines of tubas also identify band music in Central Europe and Serbia. Clearly, if timbre and sound themselves are not markers of any particular ethnic identity (especially when dealing with international audiences), the question remains, how is it that elements as elusive as timbre and sound could be made into sources of authenticity by Nor-tec? In addressing similar essentialist claims on identity and authenticity, Stuart Hall suggests that what is at stake when analyzing these discourses "is not the rediscovery of [roots] but what they as cultural resources allow a people to produce."⁵⁰ Therefore, since Nor-tec's claims for authenticity are the sounds and timbres themselves, it is important to explore what different producers do with those sounds, what musical styles result from their electronic and technological manipulations, in order to understand how their music articulates their particular desires for a modern, cosmopolitan identity and rearticulates tradition and authenticity in the process.

The Nor-tec Sound: Imagining Modernity, Transforming Tradition

"Recinto portuario" by Plankton Man is divided into two clearly different sections that work as metaphors for the type of re-signification that tradition goes through when articulated by Nor-tec. The track opens with a syncopated synthesizer loop over an electric piano riff and a funky *tarola* pattern; on top of this sonic layer, the fragmented voice of a sampled *norteña* street musician states: *Yo me llamo Teodoro Pacheco / yo me dedico a la música* [My name is Teodoro Pacheco / I dedicate myself to music]. The music continues to unfold with the incorporation of scratching sounds and a driving bass line as the sentence is sporadically repeated and new fragmented phrases added, *Yo toco la tarola* [I play the snare drum]. Finally, at the end of the first section, as a sample of a street trumpetist plays a traditional *banda* tune, the spoken text is presented in its entirety *¿A qué se dedica usted?* [What do you dedicate yourself to?] asks a female voice, to which Teodoro responds, *Yo me dedico a la música desde hace cuarenta años* [I have dedicated myself to music for forty years]. The phrase is immediately looped, becoming more and more distorted as quick, jerky vinyl scratches and electronic sounds overpower it, providing the music with a modernist aura while moving right into the second part of the track. Here, the whole atmosphere changes, becoming even more fragmented and syncopated. The main melodic material is developed out of a fragment from the traditional trumpet melody played at the end of the first section, which is presented in quick, virtuosic scratch-like bursts that resemble battling in DJ turntablism. At this point, a process of continuous incorporation starts, where the synthesizer riffs of the first section slowly reappear to accompany the brass material. At the end of a climax where all of the loops appear simultaneously, the repeated *tarola* pattern is left alone as background accompaniment for a second presentation of the traditional tune, which brings the track to an end.

Plankton Man's track works as a perfect metaphor for the process of modernist transformation that traditional *banda* music undergoes when rearticulated in Nor-tec. The first section of the tracks offers an account of tradition and authenticity represented in the musical quotation of the traditional *banda* tune and the *banda* musician who stresses that he has dedicated himself to music for forty years. The brief bridge between the two sections acts as the cathartic moment when tradition and authenticity (both the popular tune and Teodoro's speech) are technologically manipulated through computer filters, distortion, and vinyl scratches, creating the modernist aural mirage that dominates the second section of the track. Mark Katz's idea that sampling is "most fundamentally an art of *transformation*"[51] is crucial in understanding the meaning of the different musical styles developed by the members and former members of the Nortec Collective in relation to the notions of tradition, authenticity, and cosmopolitanism. Nor-tec follows the basic construction principles of mainstream electronic popular music, mainly the extensive repetition, juxtaposition, and simultaneous presentation of loops and blocks of sonic material; the use of samples; the computer manipulation and organization of sounds with MPC 4000s or through computer software like Live and Cube Base and filters such as Acid, Mutator, D-Pole, and Sherman; and the incorporation of artificially produced sounds made with analog synthesizers such as the Roland JD 800, drum machines like the TR 606, and oscillators. Typically, the process of composition starts with a session of experimentation at the analog synthesizer. At this point, the musicians' goal is to find an interesting timbre that could be used as general background texture or even to develop a grabbing bass line and a "groove"; it is a matter of making beats. Once that foundation is established, they proceed to incorporate the *norteño* sounds stored in their computers; usually, they are *tarola, bombo* (low-pitched drum), and *güiro* fragments and brief melodic accordion, tuba, and brass sequences taken from Pepe's CD, which, depending on the musicians' taste, might or might not be electronically manipulated. This is a process of trial and error where musicians explore a wide variety of possible combinations: unaltered samples with electronically modified samples, unaltered samples with drum machine beats, modified samples with synthesizer pads, etc. Their goal is to create loops with driving bass lines and catchy rhythmic or melodic sequences that could be the basis for larger music tracks.

Notwithstanding the basic similarities in the process of composition among members and former members of the Nortec Collective, there is not a homogeneous method to deal with the sounds from *norteña* traditions. Samples of *banda* and *norteña* are clear and appear largely unprocessed in many tracks by Clorofila, Terrestre, and Plankton Man, but they are much more subtle (if not imperceptible) in the music of Fussible and Panóptica. A different approach is followed by Hiperboreal and Bostich, who often reinvent the sounds and the *norteña* and *banda* ensembles themselves, making them into virtual musical cyborgs. Furthermore, while the type of technological transformation through which a sample goes depends on the producer, the type of samples used also varies among them. Clorofila favors the use of relatively long brass and accordion bridges—which, regardless of their length, remain anonymous sections from often unrecognizable tracks—and conversations among musicians taken from the CD of samples gathered by Pepe Mogt (as in "El animal," "Huatabampo 3 AM," or "Paseo moral"). Plankton Man prefers to use his own samples of street musicians both talking and playing and to quote brief fragments of popular songs and the speech of local MCs (as in "Recinto portuario," "Rancho Tron," or "Don Valiente"). In order to show the different possibilities of expression found in the use of these samples, I take the work of three distinctly different Nor-tec projects (Terrestre, Bostich, and Fussible) and analyze the features that characterize their individual styles.

Terrestre's music has undergone a noticeable process of stylistic development from the early Nor-tec tracks on *Nor-tec Sampler* (1999) to the more minimal sounds of his solo album *Secondary Inspection* (2004). He acknowledges this stylistic change when he states, "at the beginning my tracks were structured like songs but now I work with fewer elements and have changed the structure of the pieces to make them more continuous."[52] In "Maraka Man," [🔊 Track 2] one of his earliest Nor-tec tracks, Terrestre

Example 2.2
Terrestre, "El cereso,"
basic harmonic
sequence

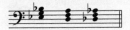

combines *tarola,* tuba, and *tambora* samples taken from Pepe's CD with flutes, drums, rattles, and chanting from the Huichol traditions of western Mexico, developing a conspicuous style where lounge and down-tempo styles intersect with an almost new age aesthetic. Regardless of the mysticism at the core of "Maraka Man," the more salient features in this piece already seem to point toward the distinct Nor-tec style of Terrestre's later tracks. An example of Terrestre's early Nor-tec style is "El cereso,"[53] a piece where the reconstruction of tradition takes place in the unfulfilled expectations of the listener. "El cereso" [⬥ **Track 3**] opens with a *tarola* roll accompanied by a low *tambora* playing a 3/4 to 6/8 hemiola rhythmic pattern that sets the mood for the wrong stylistic expectation, a *ranchera* song in *norteño* style. Instead, Terrestre quickly introduces a chromatic harmonic sequence (example 2.2) in vibrato with the electric piano over a 4/4 rhythmic pattern played by the *tarola* and accented by the *tambora.*

A sampled trumpet is introduced to accompany the *tarola* roll in the cadence at the end of the first four-measure cycle, leading into a second cycle dominated by a synthesizer pedal over which a percussive counterpoint between electronic sounds and a granulated *banda* sample unfolds. About two minutes into the song, a brief sample of a full *banda* trumpet section (example 2.3) triggers the compelling bass line (example 2.4) that characterizes the middle portion of the track.

Here, the electric piano's harmonic sequence and the bass line accompany a synthesizer melody while a complex but transparent rhythmic counterpoint is developed with the interplay of *güiro, tarola* rolls, electronic sounds, and short processed *banda* samples. The choices of electric piano, synthesizer, and a driving, Santana-sounding bass line in "El cereso" result in the characteristic retro quality that distinguishes Terrestre's early tracks ("Plan con maña" and "California 70"), a style that is further emphasized in the Deodato-like solo electric piano improvisation riffs in

Example 2.3   "El cereso," trumpet sample

Trumpets

Example 2.4   "El cereso," bass line

"Tepache Jam" and in the introduction of samba percussion in "Norteño de Janeiro" and "El palomar." An important feature of this early style (and possibly a stylistic leftover from Terrestre's past as a rock musician) is the presence of manifest melodic statements, especially in the middle sections of these pieces, which tend to be organized in loose ternary (ABA) forms. This is particularly evident in "El lado oscuro de mi compadre" and "Norteño de Janeiro," where the middle sections are clearly set apart from the introductory and final parts by using melodic material and instrumental samples that do not appear in the rest of the tracks.

The contrapuntal approach to music texture in Terrestre's tracks eventually made its way into Murcof, Fernando Corona's second one-man music project. In fact, with its samplings of music by Ärvo Part and a pointillistic approach to timbre and pitch looping ("Martes"), Murcof transforms the new age quality of "Maraka Man" into an IDM (intelligent dance music) style devoid of the "ethnic" sounds of Terrestre. This project quickly gained Corona the international recognition of the most uncompromising electronic music connoisseurs and influenced the style of the music he made as Terrestre. This change is noticeable in the tracks he composed for the Mexican feature film *Nicotina* (2003). Here, Terrestre's Nor-tec style becomes cruder and less refined, avoiding the Brazilian chill-out mood of earlier tracks as well as their ternary formal principle and developing pieces based on a larger selection of cumbia bass lines and *bajo sexto, banda* horn, and *tarola* samples in combination with computer-generated and electronic sounds (as in "Absynthe" and "Calladita se ve más chula"). However, the influences of the music produced under the alter ego of Murcof is already evident in Terrestre's concern with the organization of pitches and timbres, especially in tracks like "Broncota"—which starts with the sounds of *banda* and ends with long string harmonies and clarinet lines—and "Nico y Tina," a straightforward Murcof-style track characterized by piano melodies and long clarinet pedals over a cello line. This hybrid between the lounge style of early Terrestre and the concern with detailed pitch and timbre organization of Murcof finds its best synthesis in the heterogeneous style of Terrestre's latest production. In *Secondary Inspection*, Terrestre completely abandons the use of *banda* and *norteña* samples (with the only exception of a processed accordion attack that lasts less than a second and appears in "Vaqueros del ayer") other than percussive sounds from the *güiro, tarola, tambora,* congas, and cowbell, which are further fragmented (no popular rhythmic patterns such as cumbia are used or quoted throughout the CD), processed, and combined with noises, and computer-processed and synthesized sounds to create a fine pointillistic minimal texture. The contrapuntal quality of early Terrestre remains a constitutive stylistic element in these tracks, yet the slow-moving looped melodic sequences that characterize them are more reminiscent of the new age aesthetic of "Maraka Man" than the chill-out character of "El palomar." Indeed, in *Secondary Inspection,* the absence of brass, accordion, or *bajo sexto* samples and the further fragmentation of an already decontextualized set of percussion samples make it impossible to recognize these sounds as markers of any particular ethnic identity, making these tracks much more abstract than Terrestre's contributions to the *Nor-tec Sampler, The Tijuana Sessions, Vol. 1* (2001), and *Plankton Man vs. Terrestre* (2002).

If the Nor-tec music of Terrestre has gone through important stylistic changes that have slowly obscured the ethnic references to *banda* and *norteña,* the style of Bostich has been more homogeneous throughout his involvement with Nor-tec. Considered the Godfather of Nortec by producers and fans alike, Bostich's early Nor-tec music clearly established the aesthetic concerns that have characterized his style: an interest in the electronic exploration, fragmentation, transformation, and reconstitution of *tarola* rhythmic patterns and tuba sounds and timbres, and their combinatorial possibilities. Bostich's first Nor-tec track, "Polaris," bridges the musician's early influences from 1980s and 1990s electro-pop and his newly acquired curiosity with the timbre of *banda sinaloense* and *norteña.* The piece opens with three measures of a synthesizer-based rhythmic pattern over a retro-sounding drum-machine sequence that appears to be more an homage to the Cure than an exploration of *banda* and *norteña* sounds. Nevertheless, Bostich quickly forgets his past and moves on to a distinctly compelling electronic rhythmic sequence (example 2.5) over a *tarola-* and cymbal-based rhythmic pattern that, for many fans, defined the Nor-tec project back in 1999.

This electronic sequence is in fact a modified *tarola* roll taken from Pepe Mogt's collection of samples and processed through a vocoder.[54] The actual sample, without electronic manipulation, appears a few seconds later

Example 2.5   Bostich, "Polaris," rhythmic sequence manipulated with a vocoder

Example 2.6   "Polaris," rhythmic sequence without vocoder manipulation

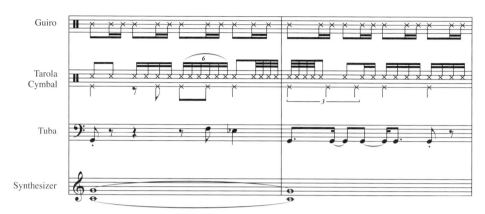

over a *güiro* playing the traditional *cumbia norteña* rhythmic pattern, accompanying the pungently syncopated tuba loop that is the track's trademark (example 2.6). The track progresses as Bostich masterfully combines and juxtaposes these sequences, gradually building up to a powerful climax where all of the loops are presented simultaneously.

The organic principle that underlies "Polaris" is clear upon a detailed analysis of the track and its constitutive loops. Not only is the vocoder sequence in example 2.5 a transformation of the *tarola* roll that permeates the piece, but the rhythmic pattern of the other prevailing loop in the piece, the tuba sequence, is fashioned after the rhythmic pattern of the cymbal that accompanies that same *tarola* roll. Thus, every musical element in the track (with the exception of the cumbia rhythmic pattern and the synthesizer-based introduction) is built out of the same *tarola* sample. This style of organic computer-generated composition, based on the collage-like organization of layers of sounds and loops, resembles more the cubist edifices of classical modernist composers rather than *norteña* or other styles of Mexican regional music.

In his later tracks, Bostich developed a more austere and rough musical style that takes as its point of departure the type of musical fragmentation that characterizes "Polaris." This style, which became Bostich's musical trademark and has been characterized by his fans as "very German,"[55] is based on the same collage-like organization of his first Nor-tec track but tends to avoid its organic principle of music development in his desire to acquire a broader timbric palette that would allow him to construct virtual *banda* ensembles on his laptop. This approach is evident in Bostich's "Rumba," "Tengo la voz," and remix of Julieta Venegas's "Sería felíz," where a wide variety of highly fragmented *tarola* rolls, *banda sinaloense* percussion samples, and deep tuba sounds are combined with vocoder effects and held together by pervasive conga- and *bombo norteño*–based beats. The sonic result of this assortment is a modernistic *banda sinaloense* that never existed, a cyber-*banda* that is real only due to Live, the software used by Bostich to put its constitutive fragments together. In "Autobanda," Bostich follows a process of continuous accumulation of loops that triggers in the listener a curious sense of nostalgia with the seeming recollection of the sounds of a *banda* to which they have never listened.[56] First, a typical *norteño* bass line appears filtered over a disjointed rhythm produced by combining a drum machine with a *tarola* sample taken from Pepe's CD. Immediately after, an unprocessed *bajo sexto* plays a series of staccato chords and introduces a synthesizer pad that frames the presentation of the main percussion rhythmic sequence (itself a virtual *tarola* cut and pasted from *tambora* and cumbia snare drum rolls and *norteña* bass drum samples). Although most of the sounds that characterize Bostich's "Autobanda" belong to *banda, norteña,* or cumbia ensembles, their fragmentation and decontextualization—as well as the fact that in the end they belong to ensembles that play different types of music—create in the listener an aural effect that resembles the visual effect of Torolab's Sistema Evolutivo de Binomios; it is as if one "had seen [or heard] this somewhere else even though it does not exist."[57] Both Bostich's music and Torolab's images are viratualities that do not refer to any particular reality; as Hiperboreal puts it, "that is what is surprising, it is and it is not [*tambora*]."[58]

While Terrestre uses *banda* and *norteña* samples as elements of color within larger chill-out or IDM styles that point toward cosmopolitan music audiences, and Bostich decontextualizes them in order to develop virtual music machines that somehow trigger a sense of nostalgia ("I like it because it reminds me of my hometown"), Fussible uses them to make beats upon which a more dance style is developed. Fussible's music is a type of Latin house style that does not show a prominence of Mexican sounds, with the exception of a few early tracks ("No One over 21" and "Odyssea") in which the *quebradita* bass line and the basic *güiro* rhythmic pattern of *cumbia norteña* are evident. Jorge Ruiz (Melo) acknowledges this when he states, "we were always criticized for that, they would say that Fussible wasn't Nor-tec. . . . 'Ventilador' does not sound like Nor-tec because Fussible was never too obvious, we never used loops just the way they were."[59] Indeed, although the first Nor-tec tracks of Fussible were abstract and difficult to dance to, Melo and Pepe Mogt soon developed a Latin house style that would characterize the project and link them to the big-beat sound they were searching for in *Fono,* their pre–Nor-tec recording. Such a style is best represented by the bouncy bass lines, driving bongos and congas, and retro synthesized strings in tracks like "Odyssea," "Casino Soul," "El

Example 2.7   Fussible, "Infierno," basic bass line

sonar de mis tambores," [⊗ **Track 4**] "Allegretto per signora," and early versions of "Infierno" (later released as "Bar Infierno" in *Tijuana Sessions, Vol. 3* [2005]). [⊗ **Track 5**]

The long process of composition of "Infierno" makes it an ideal piece to trace the use of samples and effects in relation to the changing aesthetics that affected the Nor-tec project between the releases of the two *Tijuana Sessions* albums, in 1999 and 2005, respectively. Pepe Mogt acknowledges that the first element of the track he composed was the bass line: "because it was a Nor-tec track I had to come up with a *guapachoso* [flavorful, festive] little bass line."[60] Following Fussible's usual composition process, Pepe developed this bass line through a time-consuming process of experimentation with the sounds and timbre of an analog synthesizer (example 2.7).

The first version of the track introduces this bass line after 40 seconds of a looping sequence made out of *bombo norteño* and cymbal, keeping the pulse and a processed vocal melody on the upper register. Soon after, a simple but timbrically rich chord progression played by the piano appears (example 2.8). The process of making this loop denotes Fussible's attention to detail. Every individual pitch in this chord sequence was recorded independently with a Steinway concert piano in order to be faithful to the acoustic sound of the instrument. Following this, Pepe built the chords and the harmonic progression in his studio by working with the sounds themselves; he affirms that he "didn't want to use a synthesizer because the piano sound would have been awful, [he] wanted to hear the *maderita* [sound of the wooden piano keys]."[61] Once the sequence was put together, and in order to avoid excessive computer memory usage, Pepe proceeded to record it as a regular loop.

Example 2.8   "Infierno," piano chord progression

In contrast to other members and former members of the Nortec Collective, Pepe does not use Live or Cube Base to work out the final versions of his tracks. Instead, he uses these softwares only to prepare a first draft; the final assemblage takes place in an MPC 4000 that allows him to be extra careful with details and to introduce subtle variations that make the final product more attractive and less repetitive. In "Infierno," this is reflected in the constant changes in the chordal progression and the bass line, which show small, almost imperceptible rhythmic variations every eight measures. Thus, the bass line sometimes appears on the beats and sometimes in syncopation, as shown in example 2.7. The final result is a house track that lacks any reference to *norteña* or *banda* music. This is one of those typical Fussible pieces that, as Melo suggested, fans would have a hard time recognizing as Nor-tec. This early version of "Infierno," like "Casino Soul" or "Allegretto per signora," is the kind of track one would hear in any club, disco, or rave around the world without necessarily labeling it as "ethnic sounding." Nevertheless, Pepe's claims for authenticity rely on the use of *tambora* and *bombo norteño* sounds—however unrecognizable they might be—in the basic looped beat of the track.

I had a chance to visit and interview Pepe Mogt in his Playas de Tijuana studio when he was working on a more refined, "Nor-tec–sounding" version of "Infierno." He acknowledged that the track worked nicely when he played it in non-Latino clubs in Los Angeles or Chicago, but that in order to include it in the *Tijuana Sessions, Vol. 3,* he needed to make it sound more Nor-tec.[62] It is important to compare the two versions of this track since such an analysis informs us exactly what it is that Pepe considers Nor-tec—beyond his own discourse—how more general nostalgia and retro aesthetics filter into his Nor-tec style, and what these aesthetics tell us about his own desire for modernity and cosmopolitanism. When I arrived in his studio, Pepe was working with the MPC 4000; he was trying to find a way to combine the piano chord progression in the early version of "Infierno" with a newly recorded sample of the same harmonic sequence played by a *vihuela* (a small five-string Mexican rhythm guitar played in mariachi bands). He was manipulating the *vihuela* sequence by lowering its pitch, changing its *rasgueo* pattern, and slowing it down, while constantly checking if the result matched the existing piano loop. Whenever he encountered an interesting combination he went ahead and incorporated the sound of synthesized strings (most typically in Fussible, this part of the process corresponded to Melo before he quit the project in 2003), which he said "is a very old sound, *del año de la canica* [from the hoary past], but that's the idea."[63]

Evidently, reworking "Infierno" meant not only getting it closer to the listeners' expectations of what Nor-tec ought to be, but also coming to terms with an apparent contradiction in Pepe Mogt's discourse and music style, namely, the rejection of synthesized sounds in the piano harmonic progression in an attempt to find a more authentic sound, while also using synthesized strings in a seemingly retro move. "Bar Infierno," the final version of the piece that appears in *Tijuana Sessions, Vol. 3*, emphasizes these contradictions. [🔊 **Track 6**] Overall, the track is flooded with both ethnic analog sounds (*vihuela* strumming, accordion melodies, cumbia *güiro* rhythmic patterns) and retro-sounding elements (string pads, cheesy girl choruses) that do not appear in the first versions of the track that Pepe played in clubs throughout the United States, Latin America, and Europe before the album was released. Clearly, Fussible's articulation of tradition, as is evident in the overall style of the project as well as in the particular details at stake in the composition of "Infierno" and "Bar Infierno," shows the savvy work of musicians in a continuous process of adaptation. In Fussible's style, tradition becomes an excuse that validates the musicians' search for cosmopolitanism and modernity in the beats of a hip dancing style like house. At the same time, Fussible challenges the assumptions of Orientalist discourses by erasing ethnic references in its music style while emphasizing them in its discourse. Thus, Pepe's speech about finding authenticity in local music is received with open arms by audiences and critics alike while his style dares them to find those ethnic markers in the music itself (as in Fussible's house style) or plainly mocks the Orientalist expectations of those audiences by returning to an excessive amalgamation of *norteño* and retro sounds that is cheesier than the expected kitschy sounds of *norteño* and *banda* (as in Fussible's tracks for *Tijuana Sessions, Vol. 3*).

The heterogeneous use of *norteña* and *banda* samples in the music of Terrestre, Bostich, and Fussible, as well as the music styles created by these producers using these samples as an excuse, confirms Stuart Hall's suggestion: the musicians' discovery of these sounds does not imply a sudden recognition of or an encounter with their "roots," but rather an excuse to develop cosmopolitan identities in a globalized music market. The music styles produced by these musicians show that through recurring exercises in double or even multiple coding, they are able to address the expectations of a wide variety of audiences and articulate them in music styles that, on close scrutiny, inform us of the musicians' own desires for modernity and cosmopolitanism. Thus, the importance of the lounge, IDM, and house music styles developed by Terrestre and Fussible is not that they might look back at their cultural roots, as their discourse would make us believe, but that they identify the specific niches in which these artists want to fit within the international cosmopolitan community of electronic music. Clearly, Bostich's deconstructed virtual *norteño* and *banda* ensembles also point toward a relation with tradition in terms of current desires for modernity. In Bostich's music, the decontextualized sounds of *banda* and *norteña* are the bits of memory of a musical simulacrum that for Nor-tec fans acquires cultural significance not in what they perceive as *naco* or *de a tiro corrientón banda* music, but rather in their illusion of a modern, sophisticated, "very German" style. In any case, if seen within the larger history of hybridization that informs *norteña, banda,* and *grupero* musics, the development of Nor-tec music styles acquires significance as a further process of continuous re-signification, one that takes into account the current pressures that globalization places on musicians and fans alike. Indeed the process of hybridity tied to or confronted by that of globalization collapses into an infinity of microprocesses of cultural change throughout history, as if paradoxically globalization announced a post-hybrid perspective. In this sense, Nor-tec music is as hybrid as traditional Mexican music, rock, jazz, electronica, or any other type of music. As observed in these analyses, the cultural marker that points to the differential uniqueness of the movement, while not being depleted of meaning, seems to rather perform a self-conscious political move and a simultaneous marketing strategy.

De a tiro corrientón:
Kitsch, *Naco,* Retro, and Nor-tec

When I visited Pepe Mogt in his studio, I was determined to find out specific details about his process of composition. I was particularly interested in understanding what makes a good Nor-tec groove in terms of music style. From previous interviews with Nor-tec producers and other electronic musicians, I had learned that the most crucial element in making a groovy loop is the bass line. With this piece of information, I asked Pepe to show me how he composed the catchy bass line for "Infierno." I mentioned earlier that he plainly answered that "because it was a Nor-tec track [he] had to come up with a *guapachoso* little bass line."[64] As simple as this answer might be, it is also enlightening as it clearly establishes that for Pepe there seems to be an inevitable link between Nor-tec and the slippery notion of *guapachoso.* The term *guapachoso* could be loosely translated as flavorful, tasty, or festive, but its cultural meaning goes far beyond a literal translation, especially when using it to describe music. Not all festive or tasty music can be designated as *guapachosa.* In Mexico, the term *música guapachosa* is often used interchangeably with *música tropical* (music from the tropics) to label musics with a certain degree of Afro-Caribbean or Afro-Colombian influence. However, the term is rarely used to actually describe classic Afro-Cuban genres like mambo or cha-cha-chá, or Puerto Rican and Dominican salsa and merengue musics. Instead, it is largely used to refer to early

Colombian and Mexican cumbia combos like Sonora Dinamita and Sonora Santanera, *grupero* bands like Chico Ché y la Crisis and Rigo Tovar y su Costa Azul, and local salsa artists like Pepe Arévalo y sus Mulatos. Certainly, in Mexico, the term *música guapachosa* seems to apply to the Mexican appropriation of those Afro-Caribbean and Afro-Colombian genres and carries the lower-class stigma of those who embraced them in the 1960s and 1970s. For middle-class rock and electronica musicians and fans, *música guapachosa*, with its references to the working and lower classes, is exactly the type of music to which Melo was referring when he mentioned being afraid that Pepe Mogt's Nor-tec idea was going to result in a *de a tiro corrientón* music style.

Interestingly, very few people would consider classic *banda* and *norteña* music to be examples of *música guapachosa* (following this logic, traces of this in *norteña* and *banda* repertoires appear only with the development of *cumbia norteña* and later with *quebradita* and the hybrid style of 1990s bands like Bronco and Los Tucanes de Tijuana). Nevertheless, the long-standing association of these musics with rural, lowbrow, and unsophisticated culture establishes a link between them and *música guapachosa* in the imagination of those middle-class individuals who assess it as semi-outsiders. Indeed, as the members of the Nortec Collective claim in their discourse of authenticity, *norteña* and *banda* music, as well as the *guapachosa* music of *gruperos*, has always been an important part of their soundscape in Tijuana, even if only to identify themselves against it. As the music of their grandparents and parents, and as the music of the large population of migrants from central Mexico, *norteña*, *banda*, and *grupero* musics have always been in their lives as part of most family and social settings. Their early desire to break away from these musics, and their alignment with transnational trends like industrial music, techno, and drum'n'bass, seem to be typical reactions against a local tradition that arguably lacked the sophistication to which they aspired. In short, it was a music tradition that could not fulfill these young musicians' desires for modernity and cosmopolitanism. However, seen under the light of what these musics represented for these musicians, their generation, and their social class, their final acceptance in Nor-tec needs to be interpreted as part of a trend where the music once considered to be cheesy, *naco*, and *corrientona* is observed and reinterpreted from a kitschy angle, with new eyes through which the undesirable past is re-signified in accordance with the possibilities it gives these musicians to fulfill their own desires. Undoubtedly, kitsch aesthetics lay at the core of Nor-tec's electronic re-signification of *norteño*, *banda*, and *grupero* traditions. It is necessary to consider those aesthetics within the liminal social and cultural context of the U.S.–Mexico border in order to grasp the significance of Nor-tec as a middle-class youth culture.

Although the notion of kitsch has changed considerably in the last century, it has always been associated with the domain of "bad taste." According to Matei Calinescu, the term is used to brand failed presumptuous artistic manifestations and art created to satisfy the ideals of beauty of the middle classes.[65] Theodor Adorno, Max Horkheimer, and Walter Benjamin used the notion of kitsch art in a negative manner, in order to identify mass-produced art (a parody of catharsis) in opposition to the aura of uniqueness of what they considered to be "genuine" works of art.[66] However, a new sensibility that embraced the very artificiality rejected by Adorno, Horkheimer, and Benjamin slowly developed throughout the second half of the twentieth century. Susan Sontag suggests that such a sensibility (which she calls "camp"), encouraged by democracy, free markets, and practices of commercialization in the literary and visual arts, promotes the cultivation of bad taste, extravagance, and artificiality.[67] As a result of the aesthetic validation provided by such a sensibility, cultural manifestations that elitist criteria would consider in "bad taste" are reevaluated as kitsch. These types of re-significations do not respond to changes in the actual objects being observed but rather to a change of attitude in the observer. In the case of *banda*, *norteña*, and *grupera* music, Nor-tec works as an aesthetic sensibility that allows those middle classes from Tijuana who pursued their desires for modernity in the global sounds and forms of jazz, rock, pop, and electronica to stop hearing those local musics as vulgar, *naca, de a tiro corrientona,* or *guapachosa* and begin to consider them kitsch.

Although the kitsch reevaluation of *norteña, banda,* and *grupera* music is already at work in the fragmentation, decontextualization, and transformation of cumbia rhythmic patterns and *banda* sounds in early pieces like "El cereso," "Polaris," "No One over 21," and "Infierno," it is in the tracks of *Tijuana Sessions, Vol. 3,* that the workings of such a kitschy aesthetic are more evident. After the release of the album, the *New York Times* published a review that praised it in the following terms: "Mexican regional music is the best-selling Latin music in the United States. But Nortec Collective's music gives the old sounds some long-term insurance: it makes them cool."[68] Clearly, the *New York Times* description of the Nor-tec re-signification of *norteña* and *banda* musics understands it as a phenomenon where the unhip is made hip once it is revisited from a kitsch perspective. However, the kitschiness of *Tijuana Sessions, Vol. 3,* goes beyond a mere re-signification of uncool *norteña* and *banda* sounds. The use of cheesy musical elements borrowed from 1970s commercial popular music also aligns the album with a type of retro aesthetic where nostalgia and kitsch together develop a site that needs to be interpreted through the eyes of irony. Thus, the electric guitar accompaniment, à la James Brown in "Funky

Tamazula," the corny, OTI-sounding[69] choruses in "Don Loope" and "Dandy del Sur," the Juan Torres–like sound[70] of the electric organ in "Olvídela compa," the synthesized strings in "Bar Infierno," the homage to Mario and Fernando Almada in "Almada,"[71] the clear references to the classic *narcocorrido* (drug ballad) "Contrabando y traición" by Los Tigres del Norte in the lyrics of "Colorado,"[72] and the overall sense of an almost baroque excess—too many cultural references, sounds, and things happening at the same time—throughout the album make it into an inside joke about living in Tijuana in the 1970s. This, and the fact that "the album was planned as a coherent unit from beginning to end,"[73] including a few transitional passages from track to track, remind the listener of the sense of humor of the early Cha3-produced album *Música maestro* (1999).

Indeed, the humor, irony, nostalgia, and kitsch of early Cha3 productions are elements and ideas that played a fundamental role in the development of the Nor-tec aesthetic. This is clear not only in the music but also in the images, graphics, and visuals that accompany the Nor-tec experience. Fritz Torres and Jorge Verdín, the creative forces behind the music of Clorofila and the graphics of Cha3, began collaborating first as graphic designers and later as musicians in the mid-1990s when they discovered each other's interest in images and sounds from everyday Mexican popular culture. Since Cha3's pioneering graphic style illustrates the covers of the albums *Nor-tec Sampler* and *Tijuana Sessions, Vol. 1,* one of my fieldwork priorities was to meet and interview this team of designers. After several telephonic mis-encounters, I was able to get hold of Fritz Torres, who gave me directions to the Varita de Nardo alley, where his office is located in the first floor of the EQ Studios building, a space where a wide variety of music is recorded and produced. In the images of Torres and Verdín, there is an amount of irony not found in the work of the video artists of the collective: T-shirts that show the word *culero* (asshole) below the image of a Mexican policeman, and cartoon characters that make fun of and dearticulate discourses about *norteño* men, their appearance, and occupations, by overemphasizing stereotypical features (long moustaches, cowboy hats, and the AK-47 guns preferred by drug lords' hitmen). Torres clearly argues that Cha3's work is based upon recovering the kitsch from Tijuana's everyday urban landscape; according to him, it was their interest in kitsch that led them to a reevaluation of the so-called *narcochic* aesthetic. Torres describes the process of creation undergone by himself and Verdín in the following terms: "what we did first was to take the essence of drug dealing culture, . . . because when we tried to find the most identifiable elements [from *norteña* culture], not so much in a local but in a global context . . . well . . . those were the more valuable ones: how they [drug lords] dress . . . Versace-imitation shirts, hats, boots."[74] Verdín explains his working relationship with Torres and their mutual interest in *norteño* kitsch:

> When I first met Fritz I did not like his work. I thought it wasn't cool. But later I found out that he was into collecting old Tijuana postcards and that he liked the music of Juan Torres. . . . when he invited me to collaborate in *El Sueño de la Gallina* I brought some Juan Torres' music, and everyone was like "*¡Este pendejo!*" [what a moron!]. But Fritz's reaction was "*Está curado* [it is cool], that's what my grandfather likes!" . . . So I realized that Fritz and I shared a taste for Mexican kitsch . . . and much of *música norteña* is very kitsch . . . well, sometimes it goes well beyond kitsch. . . . and then you have the *narcochic* style, the toilet seats made of gold, and there is the style of *norteña* and *banda* music flyers and posters. . . . well we thought that had to be part of the [Nor-tec] show.[75]

The notion of *narcochic* is essential in understanding the cultural value in Nor-tec's kitschy appropriation of *norteño* cultural icons. According to Fritz Torres, U.S. auction houses coined the term *narcochic* to identify objects and belongings recovered from captured drug lords (statues of themselves and their relatives, chains, earrings, and even toilet seats made of gold, etc.).[76] The materials used in these objects (gold, diamonds, emeralds, silver, and exotic animals' fur) give them a very high exchange value; however, the bad taste and eccentricity of the items made them difficult to sale at high-class auction houses. Torres argues that the classification of these items under the label *narcochic* allowed them to move from the realm of *naco* to that of art and, therefore, allowed the possibility for them to be sold for large amounts of money, disregarding their previous association with drug dealers.

Based on the relation between cultural artifacts and consumers, Celeste Olalquiaga suggests three different degrees of kitsch: "in first-degree kitsch, the relationship between object and user is immediate, one of genuine belief."[77] This type of kitsch is not recognized as such by those who consume it, but rather it is identified as such by outsiders. Second-degree kitsch is intentionally done as kitsch by borrowing and capitalizing "on an acquired taste for tackiness."[78] In third-degree kitsch, cultural manifestations are "invested with either a new or foreign set of meanings, generating hybrid products."[79] Olalquiaga states that the issue at stake in third-degree kitsch is an empowerment that comes from appropriating this tradition from "outside" in an attempt to adapt it to the expressive needs of the artist.[80] Nor-tec's would be an example of third-degree kitsch since it searches for a reevaluation of *norteña* traditions, takes its "inherent" tackiness, and provides it with a meaning beyond *naco* and *corrientón;* as the *New York Times* proposes, it makes it cool.

Figure 2.1   Fritz Torres and Jorge Verdín's "Nortec Bandido," as the image was called by *Time,* is a caricature based upon stereotypes of *norteña* culture, © Cha3. Used by permission

When members of the Nor-tec culture identify the irony and the humor in the sounds and the images of the Nor-tec musicians and artists, they create a new social and cultural order that re-signifies those sounds and those images as theirs, beyond the meaning codified in them by the dominant culture. One can observe an example of this practice in the work of Gerardo Yépiz (Acamonchi), a frequent collaborator of the Nortec Collective. Acamonchi's graffito of Raúl Velasco[81] exemplifies Nor-tec's scornful disdain of hegemonic Mexican media culture (figure 2.2). The sense of irony in the work of Acamonchi articulates the type of empowerment that Olalquiaga associates with third-degree kitsch. Acamonchi's version of Luis Donaldo Colosio (the PRI presidential candidate who was assassinated while campaigning in Lomas Taurinas, a Tijuana neighborhood, in 1994) over the caption *Regresaré* (I'll be back) ridicules the centralized official PRI speeches that have made him into a sort of lost savior of Mexico's political life (figure 2.3).

Nor-tec's ability to reappropriate cultural icons from foreign discourses in exercises of third-degree kitsch is clear to the eye in the graphics of Cha3 and Acamonchi. That type of articulation is also evident to the ear in the Nor-tec remixes of "El sinaloense" commissioned by the Kronos Quartet for *Nuevo* (2002). The album was planned over a period of seven years by David Harrington (first violin and leader of the Kronos Quartet) as a musical project that would celebrate:

> a distinctive sound, a distinctive approach to life and culture that an outsider like me and like the other members of Kronos, would be able to experience. I'm not claiming that this is the world of Mexican music, what

Figure 2.2   TV host Raúl Velasco, according to Acamonchi.
Image courtesy of Gerardo Yépiz/acamonchi.com

it is for us is what we've learned so far, it's a way of celebrating this amazing approach to life that we learned about.[82]

Nuevo is a collection of mostly popular Mexican music (the exception
being a string quartet and percussion arrangement of Silvestre Revueltas's
Sensemayá) arranged for string quartet and includes songs by the iconic
"king" of lounge, Juan García Esquivel, music by Roberto Gómez Bolaños
(Chespirito) for the 1970s hit TV show *El chavo del 8,* a collaboration with
superstar Mexican rock band Café Tacuba, and a few other selections. It
was decided that the album's first track would be the classic *banda* song
"El sinaloense" arranged for string quartet by the Argentinean composer
Osvaldo Olijov. Harrington states that he wanted a section of the album

REGRESARE

Figure 2.3   Luis Donaldo Colosio,
according to Acamonchi. Image courtesy
of Gerardo Yépiz/acamonchi.com

to be sampled and after hearing the *Nor-tec Sampler,* he decided to contact Bostich, Plankton Man, and Terrestre to commission remixes of "El sinaloense" and close the album with one of them. Harrington remembers:

> I wanted to create this kind of circular experience, and that's why "El sinaloense" is sampled at the very end of the album and it become something very different from what it started out as. I've noticed that that's how music works for me—it starts in one place and pretty soon becomes something else. It seems like Nor-tec takes elements from Tijuana and creates an entirely different experience using those building blocks that exist right there and I find that really inspiring.[83]

In order to make their remixes, Bostich, Plankton Man, and Terrestre received recordings of the individual parts of the string quartet version with no specific instruction on what to do. Following the Nor-tec aesthetic, the musicians combined *norteña* and *banda* samples, computer manipulation, and turntablist scratching with the sounds of the string quartet. Their final remixes are complete melodic and rhythmic transformations not only of the Kronos Quartet version, but also of the original song itself. With the exception of Bostich's remix, which is basically the Kronos Quartet version of "El sinaloense" with an added beat, the song is unrecognizable in the frenetic scratching sounds of Plankton Man's remix and in the gentle sounds of Terrestre's lounge version.

Plankton Man calls his final version of "El sinaloense" "a remix of a remix."[84] Truly, the process of remixing the string quartet arrangement of a *banda* piece illustrates the simulacrum-like quality of Nor-tec and emphasizes its quality as a third-degree kitsch phenomenon that provides the musicians with the power to reappropriate cultural icons. Kronos Quartet's *Nuevo* is an example of second-degree kitsch, a neo-kitsch inspired by the tackiness of *banda, El chavo del 8,* and Juan García Esquivel's music, but one that "lacks the devotional relation" present among actual *banda* and Juan García Esquivel's music, and *El chavo del 8* TV shows, and their Mexican audiences. Notwithstanding its noble intentions to experience the other's lifestyle, the Kronos Quartet's version is a representation that takes over reality, a commodity that, in its self-consciousness, fails to grasp the cultural meaning at stake in those manifestations. As Olalquiaga argues for third-degree kitsch, the Nor-tec remixes of "El sinaloense," with their reincorporations of *banda* and *norteña* sounds under the aesthetic umbrella of electronic music and the desire for modernization of the Nor-tec musicians, work as a meeting point between different cultures,[85] a site where processes of transculturation take place, a space for Nor-tec musicians and fans to imagine themselves as cosmopolitan individuals.

As Stuart Hall proposes, meaning only has effect when it is articulated in practice; therefore, the moment of "decoding" a cultural artifact is as determinant as the moment of "encoding" it.[86] It is through their shared ability to decode an event that a group enacts its collective identity and contests hegemony's ability to legitimate social and cultural order. When members of the Nor-tec culture identify the irony and the humor in the sounds and images of the Nor-tec musicians and artists, they create a new social and cultural order that re-signifies those sounds and those images as theirs, beyond the meaning codified in them by the dominant culture. Thus, Nor-tec is a moment where memory loses its connection to teleology, showing that the essentialist source of any discourse of difference has no meaning by itself but acquires it in the constant rearticulation and reassemblage. Nor-tec reconstitutes a memory that does not exist; such performative action is evident in the sounds and images where the artist's desire becomes the instruction for the reconfiguration of an "authentic" genetic code. Nor-tec artists make their artistic product into sonic and visual metaphors for how their desire for modernity symbolically reconfigures a place into a nostalgic memory of the past but mostly into a performed memory of the future.

3

Getting the Word Around

On a sunny summer afternoon, walking through the halls of a crowded mall in Tijuana's Zona Río, I decide to enter a record store and check on the musical preferences of the local middle-class customers. After a few minutes of observing clients and checking the musical selections on the shelves, I look for assistance: "Do you have any Nor-tec CDs?" I ask the manager. "What kind?" he timidly answers, unsure of whether I am asking for a specific band or a musical genre; to this, confused, I respond: "Well . . . Nor-tec." He directs me toward a section at the back of the store and tells me: "There are many over there." I go to that area only to find a great variety of *norteña* CDs by Tigres del Norte, Cadetes de Linares, and Piporro.

This experience led me to ask myself the reasons that I could find Nor-tec music at New York's Tower Records and meet Nor-tec fans in places like Columbus, Ohio, and Xalapa, Veracruz, but could not find Nor-tec CDs in a record store aimed at middle-class kids from Tijuana. Also intriguing was the fact that the record store manager had no idea about the kind of music to which I was referring. Undoubtedly, this experience shows that, besides the processes of production and consumption, the process of distribution is fundamental in shaping the identity of any cultural project. The dynamic interactions among these three processes defines them continuously and reciprocally. In the case of Nor-tec, my apparently contradictory experience with the record store manager is an index of the unusual process of distribution that has made Nor-tec into a transnational phenomenon of glocal character, thus developing a scene that articulates the global by strategically using conventional channels of distribution while largely avoiding the mainstream's pressures for commodification. Pepe Mogt states that one of the aspects that he finds so interesting about the Nor-tec phenomenon is that all of a sudden there were DJs in Italy and France spinning Nor-tec beats. Such a statement seems to contradict his own discourse about the necessity of living and experiencing Tijuana and the border in order to understand the essence of Nor-tec.[1] This slip in Mogt's discourse, which puts in evidence the complex relationship between local and global issues, is intimately related to the contradictions I witnessed regarding the music's local and global reception during my fieldwork. The Nor-tec scene is articulated through information networks that are at once global, alternative, and in many ways marginal in nature. This chapter explores the different distribution strategies adopted by members of the Nortec Collective. By exploring the translocal and virtual characteristics of these strategies and their articulation of underground as well as mainstream networks, I show that the development of a Nor-tec scene does not necessarily take place in specific places or sites, but rather through the unlocalized consumption of cultural artifacts, products, and ideas. Finally, a discussion of the use of Nor-tec in the marketing strategies of transnational companies illustrates the complex ways in which regulation and distribution intersect with issues of race and ethnicity among Latinos in the United States.

"I Want to Put This Out Myself": Underground Strategies in the Age of Digital Reproduction I

The launching of Nor-tec at the end of the 1990s coincided with a critical moment in the music industry, a period when the mainstream music market came to be dominated by five transnational companies—BMG, EMI, Sony, Warner, and Universal—often referred to as the "majors." This resulted in a shift in the relationship between the global power of these majors and the local, regional, or even national networks established by independent music companies (indies). As George Yúdice argues, under such circumstances, the indies were limited to discovering new talent and promoting it at a local level before a major would take it over and market it globally, thus denying the indies profit.[2] This situation had an important impact on music production since the strategies of the majors favored the production and marketing of a few music hits that would quickly return their investment instead of the promotion of several albums that would slowly return their investment over a longer period of time.[3] The inability of many indies to cope with the seemingly unchallenged power of the majors provoked their disappearance; however, the increasing availability of new technology also opened unforeseen avenues for the survival of those independent projects willing to accommodate to new market conditions. Cheaper music production software and the Internet became fundamental tools both in the indies' strategies to resist the monopoly of the majors and in the musicians' struggles to avoid having their artistic freedom co-opted. The increasing importance of EDM for independent and local music markets at the end of the 1990s is strongly connected to the ability of this music scene to take advantage of new technologies of production and distribution. The Nor-tec musicians' understanding of emerging virtual markets was fundamental in Nor-tec's global underground success.

Prior to 1999, when the Nor-tec project materialized, Pepe Mogt and the members of Artefakto had a long and bittersweet history of unfulfilled promises with record labels in Mexico, Germany, and the United States. Although they changed the band's name to Fussible and turned toward EDM, their distribution strategy remained the same throughout that period: to find an international or national label that would back them, validate them, and market their music. Fussible's lack of success in finding an international label interested in its first CD, *Fono*, marked the end of that approach. As Pepe Mogt says, the production of the first Nor-tec tracks was accompanied by a new strategy:

> [Composing "Ventilador"] was like finding a new excuse to keep making music. But *la onda* [the thing] was "this is what I want to do, this is what I have been searching for for so long," it wasn't any more like "I'll bring this to a label and put CDs out there." No, it was more like "I want to put this out myself, I want to produce it and put it out." I was no longer interested in the labels.[4]

Mogt's relative lack of success in grabbing the attention of an international label with Artefakto and the first Fussible CD made him aware that, with Nor-tec, he had to follow a different approach. His response was to adapt the do-it-yourself character of his production process to the distribution of the final product. Such a move allowed him not only to attain a high level of marketing control, but in the end also helped him to develop the unique glocal character of the Nor-tec scene. Although this new strategy was the result of responding to specific problems as the collective faced them and not a predetermined plan, the musicians' international success as self-promoters converted them into icons of "progressive marketing" for the Mexican business magazine *Expansión*. In 2001, the magazine dedicated an article to the collective in an issue devoted to "Los monstruos de la mercadotecnia [The Monsters of Marketing Techniques]."[5]

The first step in the new distribution process consisted of establishing an independent label that would make the first Nor-tec tracks available to the public. The label, Mil Records (One Thousand Records), was named after the collective's decision to press 1,000 copies of the *Nor-tec Sampler* (1999) for local distribution. Its creation was accompanied by the posting of an Internet Web site where the aesthetics of the collective were explained and the music was also downloadable. Word of mouth and an extended friendship network were fundamental for the early dissemination of the music. The *Nor-tec Sampler* was distributed free of charge among friends, fans, and radio DJs in Tijuana, San Diego, and Los Angeles. The idea was to develop a loyal fan base that incorporated audiences from Tijuana and southern California. Pepe Mogt explains this process:

> When we started the Nor-tec thing I was in charge of promoting the sound, so I began sending Real Audio of the tracks we were making. It was free for people to listen to and download. I used to send massive e-mails with the files. . . . We owe everything to the Internet. Having Mil Records and the Fussible Web site, where you could get the videos and watch the live concerts, also helped with the promotion and even got people in Europe interested [in our music].[6]

Developing a transnational fan base was a crucial move since it recognized that success in a border city like Tijuana could only be achieved by recognizing the transnational character of the city's economy and its people. Soon after the first presentations, individual members of the collective made use of Napster and other new Internet distribution networks to make mp3 versions of their tracks available free of charge to a large global audience. As the music began to make its way around the world, a number of local artists and writers (many of them members of a long-standing group of friends and supporters of Tijuana arts who called themselves *los culturosos*) began to write articles about their city's "next big thing." These articles appeared in local, national, and even international magazines, fanzines, and newspapers and created an underground media splash that slowly filtered into the mainstream. Shortly, influential magazines such as *Time* were publishing articles about Nor-tec, despite the fact that, as Bostich affirms, the music was still commercially unavailable.[7]

The charm of the underground played a fundamental role in the constitution of Nor-tec. Clearly, the rejection of mainstream media and industry, as well as the allure of an "alternative movement," was a plus for the fans who first downloaded the sound files. It is in this light that we can understand Nor-tec as part of the larger phenomenon of UDM. In 1936, Walter Benjamin proposed that the advent of mass mechanical reproduction presupposed the disappearance of the work of art's uniqueness or aura.[8] The shortcomings and contradictions of Benjamin's argument are somewhat put in evidence when dealing with postcolonial, non–Western European cultural artifacts, as Ángel Quintero Rivera implies in his account of the international success of Caribbean music due to—among other causes—mechanical reproduction.[9] One might even suggest that Benjamin's theory would be irrelevant in a "postmodern" age, with the practice of electronic repetition rising to the level of a new art in computer- and sample-based popular music. However, the arrival of digital technologies allowed artists to work around the channels of mass distribution, lent power to underground strategies, and infused their product with an aura of uniqueness often absent in mainstream commercial artifacts. Underground fans are attracted to musics like Nor-tec because they identify an aura of distinctiveness in music that tends to avoid mainstream channels of production and distribution. Belonging to an underground scene makes these fans feel part of an exclusive and select group. In this world, giving the music away or making the tracks available to be downloaded for free, a strategy most mainstream labels would consider foolish, is very important. These practices and strategies invoke a reevaluation of the idea of aura and shed light on how we should think about Benjamin's theory when avant-garde and antiestablishment art, perceived as authentic and grounded in a new type of cyber-community, use electronic and digital mass reproduction and distribution as the basis for contesting and taking advantage of commercialism. Jorge Ruiz (Melo) explains:

> We gave the music away for free. . . . we asked fans to pirate the CDs and many people were angry at us for that . . . because we would just tell them "buy the CD, burn it and give it to all your friends." If you don't do that nobody would listen to your music . . . not to mention the economic marginalization of electronica in Mexico. . . . you know, people do not have money to buy the CD. That's why we were not against piracy.[10]

Rubén Tamayo (Fax), a Tijuana-based electronica musician and one of the founders of the local indie Static Discos, stresses the importance of these types of strategies for the success of independent labels:

> E-mail and the mp3 are the two most important tools for our music. A lot of people, especially the big companies, complain and say it's a crime [to pirate a CD]. But for the indies it is an honor to have a CD bootlegged. . . . The big companies cry the most, but for me as an independent it is all right if someone buys a 100-peso CD and someone else burns it. You know, globalization helps for those kinds of things. . . . it *chinga* [screws] many others, but it helps for that [the distribution of alternative music].[11]

As Melo and Fax suggest, for the independent musicians of the Nortec Collective, who usually own their labels, what is really at stake is getting their music to as many people as possible. Mil Records, as we have seen, was primarily designed as a tool for the distribution of their music and not as a commercial venture. The logic behind this plan was that the wide circulation of the music would eventually lead audiences to request the presence of the collective in live concerts. It was as live musicians that the members of the collective believed they were going to make money. The rapid growth of the crowds attending their events reveals the success of their strategy.

Partying in Tijuana I (Nor-tec Mix)

Quiero bailar / hasta el día llegar
[I want to dance / until daybreak]
—Klansoff y Solariz, "Sabrosonix," *Electro congal* (2002)

By the end of the 1990s, Tijuana had slowly developed a small EDM scene. The efforts of Daniel Rivera (DJ Tolo), César Fernández (DJ Horse), Luis Tucker, Ricky Martínez de Castro, and Gabriel Castillo were fundamental to the creation of an electronic music club scene whose members were also willing to travel outside Tijuana and attend events organized on the beaches of Rosarito (a few miles to the south). These types of raves and club parties were the first sites where members of the collective presented their work and gave away copies of the *Nor-tec Sampler*. Although small crowds of no more than 50 people attended the first presentations, the presence of a unique and well-defined local project solidified the efforts of Rivera, Tucker, Fernández, Martínez de Castro, and Castillo around a common goal. Nor-tec helped to develop this small scene into a huge underground phenomenon that extended to neighboring cities. Pepe Mogt explains:

> I believe what made Nor-tec work out in our own homeland, not only in Tijuana, but also in Mexicali, Tecate, Ensenada, I mean, the whole northern area [of Baja California], was that it invoked a shared feeling among the people attending the parties, a feeling of identification, an identity that was somewhat lost, an identity that sometimes we ourselves had rejected out of our own prejudices.[12]

The partnering of the Nortec Collective with local promoters was one of mutual benefit. Not only did it allow members to take advantage of an already established network that quickly disseminated the new sound among electronica fans, but it also worked as the perfect style to galvanize the scene and make it grow beyond the promoters' imaginations. As Tijuana-based journalist Karina Paredes states, "[P]eople who were not used to attending these [types of] parties (which were frequented by Goths and techno fans) became more interested in joining them, until they became hybrid gatherings."[13] Nor-tec and its cosmopolitan re-signification of local traditions became the unifying element to fuse a number of fragmented local electronica crowds into a cohesive scene beyond the city's boundaries.

The first events that testified to the success of the collective's grassroots distribution strategy were a series of rave-like parties called Sabrosonic. Organized by DJ Tolo, DJ Max, and Ricardo Martínez de Castro (Ricky) and held at the Festival Plaza Hotel in Rosarito, Sabrosonic was the name given to a series of monthly beach parties that featured mainly live Nor-tec acts alongside resident and guest DJs from Tijuana, San Diego, and Ensenada. During the months preceding the first Sabrosonic party in November 1999, the collective participated in a series of events to present the *Nor-tec Sampler* and a Nor-tec vinyl for DJs mixed by DJ Tolo, *The Spaced TJ Dub* (1999). The first examples of Nor-tec graphic art had been shown at an event in Ensenada, and a number of influential local writers and intellectuals (including Luis Humberto Crosthwaite, Rafa Saavedra, and José Manuel Valenzuela Arce) published a special article on Nor-tec in *Mosaico*, the cultural supplement to *Frontera*, one of the most influential local newspapers. When the first Sabrosonic party took place on 13 November 1999, fans were already aware of the new music trend. Martínez de Castro explains the advertising campaign for the event:

> I was in charge of entertainment at the Festival Plaza Hotel, so I had access to the hotel's budget for promotion. We had commercial contracts with local newspapers like *Zeta* and *Frontera*, and later with cultural magazines like *Lumbre*, so all of a sudden you started seeing something that had never happened in Tijuana, the venues began advertising these events. . . . Some people came because of the advertisements, but many more found [out] about them through flyers and other media.[14]

For the advertisement of this event, the collective combined underground flyer distribution and fanzine publicity with mainstream advertising and a novel use of Internet resources. The Web site of DJ Tolo's Tijuana House Club devoted an area to Sabrosonic, featuring streaming music loops by Bostich, Fussible, and Terrestre, as well as high-quality flyers designed for the events by Ángeles Moreno. This type of hybrid advertising strategy became the norm for Nor-tec events.

By the end of 1999, word of Nor-tec as a new musical phenomenon reached the intellectual and artistic circles of Mexico City. This resulted in two events that had lasting effects on the music's reception beyond Tijuana. First, tracks by Fussible ("Mona B" remixed by the Japanese DJ Matsuoka) and Bostich ("Polaris") were selected for play during the new millennium celebration at Mexico City's Zócalo. Second, two other Nor-tec tracks ("La rom u rosa" and "Sabrosa" by Fussible and Bostich, respectively) were chosen as background music for the Mexican pavilion at the 2000 Hannover Expo in Germany.[15] The significance of these events rests not only in the recognition of Nor-tec outside of Tijuana but also in the fact that such recognition came in the form of an almost official legitimization that likened it to a symbol of national, cosmopolitan modernity for the twenty-first century. It was also important that both events made Nor-tec accessible to audiences different from that targeted by the musicians' underground strategy. Just as the TV broadcast of the Zócalo millennium celebration brought Nor-tec to the living rooms of a large national audience, the presence of the music in Hannover exposed the collective's work to an elite international audience at which they were not directly aiming in their early strategy. Both events put in evidence the workings of a distribution and regulation campaign that juxtaposed the local, the national, and the global, as well as the underground and the mainstream, in unforeseen ways.

A year after launching the Nor-tec project, as its sound was making its way beyond the Tijuana area and even beyond Mexico, the members of the collective prepared their anniversary party. The location was Luis Tucker's Sol Café in Rosarito. The idea seemed perfect since Tucker had continuously supported the collective's efforts by organizing smaller events at his Pueblo Café Baja, a club located inside one of Tijuana's architectural landmarks, the Jai Alai building. Ricky remembers the occasion:

> I used part of the marketing budget of Sol Café to promote the event. We had a huge number of very well-designed flyers. . . . [Laughing] I remember once I ran into Pedro [Hiperboreal] and he was all excited, like a teenager, because they had used flyers to spell the word "Nortec" on the wall [the border fence], and you could see it clearly from the highway. The promotion was very good, I remember going to downtown clubs . . . really ordinary clubs, and finding [Nor-tec] flyers on my car's windshield afterwards, it happened several times over a couple of weeks. Besides, we also used radio, newspapers, [the] Internet, and for the first time we got a crowd of over 1,000. That's when it hit me, "this has already exploded." For the first time 1,000 people in an electronic music event; we had never seen anything like that in Baja [California]. After that everything changed, not only for Nor-tec but for everyone. A new type of promotion and a new kind of event had arrived.[16]

The turnout for the anniversary party was much larger than expected. The presence of more than 1,200 fans from Ensenada, Tijuana, Rosarito, and Mexicali marked the beginning of a new era of massive parties in the region.[17] Going from playing for crowds of 50 to crowds of 1,200 fans in less than a year confirmed the success of the innovative combination of underground, mainstream, and Internet marketing in developing and shaping a translocal scene.

As I have shown in chapter 1, EDM in Tijuana has an important pre–Nor-tec history, which established a network of clubs and crowds that Nor-tec would later exploit. Nevertheless, it was Nor-tec with its double articulation of local desires for cosmopolitanism and the mainstream's desires for exotic otherness that became the perfect excuse to bring together a multiplicity of individual efforts. This double-edged articulation stimulated an exponential growth of electronica fans locally and drew the attention of the electronic dance mainstream toward the corner of the world that symbolizes the end of Latin America.

The Outside Gaze: Partying in and beyond Tijuana

By the end of 1999, Nor-tec's hybrid process of distribution was beginning to give results on an international level. In Japan, DJ Matsuoka had remixed a track by Fussible, and Terrestre's "El lado oscuro de mi compadre" had been included in a compilation edited by Cross Records that would later be available in the United States via the indie Shadow Records. The Nor-tec sound was moving widely, and it quickly made its way into the offices of several majors' marketing directors. Nevertheless, it was Kim Buie, senior executive at Chris Blackwell's mainstream indie label Palm Pictures, who after listening to the *Nor-tec Sampler* and witnessing the crowd at Rosarito's Sol Café party, signed the collective to a long-term pressing and distribution deal: "It's a whole community of kids that have put a new spin on electronic music. I went to Nortec nights in Rosarito twice, and there were at least 1,000 kids there who came to just hang out and dance."[18]

Panóptica states that, if there were "a key moment for us to make the leap from a local to an internationally known group, it was the Nortec City party."[19] To accompany the release of *The Tijuana Sessions, Vol. 1* (2001), the extended, revised, and more commercial version of the *Nor-tec Sampler* pressed by Palm Pictures, the collective organized Nortec City at Tijuana's Jai Alai building. In Nortec City, the underground marketing strategy of the members of the collective was complemented by an international marketing strategy designed by the public relations office at Palm Pictures. The outcome was the most massive EDM event in Tijuana up to that moment. Pepe Mogt recalls:

> It was impressive to see 2,000 dancing fans and 200 crew members working to put the event together. . . . there were photography exhibitions, installation artists, video jockeys, and DJs. Palm Pictures invited *Time Magazine*, the *New York Times*, the *LA Times*. It was the largest press coverage ever for a party in Tijuana.[20]

As Panóptica suggests, the mainstream awareness of Nor-tec owes much to the fact that the local fans responded to the collective's call and filled the Jai Alai building for Nortec City: "having the media witnessing the fans' reception of our music was what created the boom."[21]

Although the collective and its individual members had already played at international venues like New York City's Latin Alternative Music Conference and London's Club Cargo, and they had been invited to perform at the first Tecnogeist Festival in Mexico City, it was the impact of the Nor-tec City party that attracted the international UDM community to the new Tijuana sound. At the 2001 Coachella Valley Music and Arts Festival, the collective was featured along with electronica stars, like the Chemical Brothers, the Orb, Fatboy Slim, and St. Germain, and new and original underground projects, like DJ Dara, Squarepusher, and Photek. For American electronica fans and practitioners, Coachella was the event that materialized the Nor-tec experience; finally, Nor-tec became more than the sounds found on the Internet and the parties described in the *Village Voice* and the *New York Times*.

If playing at the Coachella Fest finally made the American electronica mainstream aware of the Nortec Collective, sharing the billing with Aphex Twin, Jazzanova, EDM-pioneering DJs like Frankie Knuckles and Jeff Mills, and even avant-garde legends like Terry Riley at Barcelona's 2001 Sónar Festival enabled the collective to reach a different audience. The Sónar Festival is advertised as a site for experimental and forward-looking electronic music. Certainly, the festival carries an aura of prestige among followers of underground and less commercial electronica projects. The invitation for Nor-tec to perform at the Sónar was achieved by means different than those that gained them access to one of the most prestigious alternative music festivals in the American Southwest, the Coachella festival. While Nor-tec's participation at Coachella resulted from an aggressive campaign designed by Palm Pictures to promote *The Tijuana Sessions, Vol. 1,* among young American audiences, Nor-tec at the Sónar was the result of the collective's own networking. Panóptica states that, in order to attend the 2000 edition of the Sónar, meet people, and make connections, he had to save money and pay for the trip himself. It was as a result of this trip that the organizers of the festival extended an invitation to the collective for the 2001 edition.[22]

To be part of the experimentalism and progressiveness of festivals like Sónar was important for Nor-tec since Pepe Mogt intended to keep the collective an alternative endeavor. Maintaining their own promotional networking independent from Palm Pictures' efforts and their links with less commercial crowds was important for the collective to balance their label's more conventional marketing. Being associated with the underground gave the Nortec Collective a certain aura of prestige, yet being able to appeal to more commercially oriented audiences helped them to become icons of successful cosmopolitanism for local fans in Tijuana and southern California.

Nor-tec's ability to be recognized by the mainstream while keeping its underground base was crucial in shaping the character of its scene.

It was their underground aura that interested the organizers of the
Canadian Mutek Festival in the Nortec Collective when the festival decided to expand its activities to Latin America in 2003. That year, as part
of the festival, the collective offered concerts in Mexico City, Guadalajara,
and Tijuana. It was Nor-tec's simultaneous underground and commercial
appeal that made it central in Mutek's campaign "to bring together independent and experimental electronica labels from Canada, the United States,
and Mexico [in an attempt] to establish new distribution channels."[23] According to Alain Mongeau, founder of the festival, Mutek was born as an
initiative that intended to promote innovative, independent, local projects
and scenes in order to help them consolidate and connect with other international scenes; accordingly, Mongeau states, "electronica could participate positively in globalization."[24] It was Nor-tec's development of a very
particular hybrid and fragmented scene, one that was local and global at
once, one that appealed to the underground but also strategically engaged
the mainstream, that attracted the organizers of Mutek. Undoubtedly, the
success and prestige of Nor-tec helped Mutek in securing a reliable audience and the collaboration of other independent groups and alternative
cultural spaces in its first Mexican incursion.

For the Nortec Collective, participating in this dual marketing strategy
was important not only because it gave them greater exposure, but also because it allowed them to be selective when choosing concert venues. Such
selectivity permits an artist to have an important degree of control over
shaping an audience and a scene. In the case of Nor-tec, as I have shown,
the gaze of the international electronica community, with its desire for otherness and its validating cosmopolitanism, played a crucial role in the glocal
development of such an aura.

Virtual Nor-tec Scenes

The rapid exchange of information and digitalized cultural artifacts such
as music through globalization has had a great impact in the formation of
communities and scenes. Fans of globally distributed music, visual arts,
movies, TV shows, or even specific practices (like playing video games) do
not necessarily get to interact face to face. However, the same cyber-flow
that allows them to have immediate access to the latest tracks, videos,
movies, or video games also brings them information regarding the types
of people who consume those cultural artifacts. In her study of the video
game "Dance Dance Revolution," Joanna Demers argues that Internet sites

have allowed video gamers not only to converse about the game, but also
to discuss "broader topics such as musical and sartorial taste, gender, sexuality, politics, and friendship . . . to maintain a sense of community."[25]
These Internet networks are fundamental to the dissemination of music,
ideas about music, and the kinds of identification developed around certain
music, the music's "scene."

In the case of Nor-tec, Internet blogs, listservs, chat rooms, e-mail lists,
and virtual forums developed from the very beginning and in many cases
were the channels that allowed the early dissemination of the music. Clearly,
as the music gained acceptance beyond Tijuana, this network quickly expanded. The first Internet sites where Nor-tec music was made available
were set up by the members of the collective; they consisted of both individual sites and others devoted to the collective. Nor-tec musicians also took
advantage of Internet networks already established by electronica practitioners; noteworthy is their use of DJ Tolo's Tijuana House Club e-mail list
and listserv, which allowed them to quickly spread their sound and to engage local fans. Soon after, two Web groups were founded specifically to
discuss Nor-tec tracks, parties, and dance scenes and to share pictures of the
musicians performing around the world. One of the groups was created by
Palm Pictures, but it quickly became autonomous from the label as the tone
and direction of the discussion were decided by the fans posting messages.
The second group, although independent from the beginning, managed to
outlive Palm Pictures' group; its members were still actively posting messages about concerts and events in mid-2006.[26] The members of these two
cyber-communities included people from Tijuana, Mexicali, San Diego,
Seattle, Los Angeles, Mexico City, and San Luis Potosí, ranging from ages
17 to 36.

Besides e-mail lists, listservs, Web sites, and sound-file-sharing sites,
the blog, a new type of Internet site developed at the end of the 1990s, became an important communication tool for the cyber-community of Nor-
tec followers. A blog is a type of electronic diary on which the owner posts
texts that are frequently updated; they are archived in reverse chronological
order. There are a great variety of blogs; many are kept as simple collec-
tions of personal commentaries on daily events. Others are communication-
oriented projects providing an alternative to mass media, and yet others
represent more complex literary exercises. One of the most important
cyber-communities that supported the Nortec Collective was a group of
bloggers called the Tijuana Bloguita Front (TJBF). This project was initiated
by Rafa Saavedra and the *culturosos,* but quickly grew to include members
living all over Mexico, the United States, and even Sweden. Each member
of the TJBF maintains his/her own personal blog and is allowed to post for
the main group's blog, which is linked to the personal sites of over 100

members. In turn, each individual blog offers links to sites and blogs owned by nonmembers of the TJBF, which exponentially increases the number of individuals linked to the cyber-community.[27] Although the TJBF was not specifically developed to support Nor-tec, a few members of the Nortec Collective participated in the blog project from the beginning (Hiperboreal and his former collaborator Claudia Algara and video jockeys CBrown, Mashaka, and TCR), and many of the bloggers were fans of their music. Indeed, following the history of group and individual posts gives us a chance to witness not only the growing interest in Nor-tec in and beyond Tijuana, but also to learn of the heated discussions about local tradition that the release of the collective's first tracks generated among *tijuanense* intellectuals. Interestingly, while blogs might be used to establish a sense of community among individuals living thousands of miles apart (as seen in the case of the Nor-tec Web fan groups and listservs), the Tijuana Bloguita Front, originally created by persons living in the same city, suggests the fragmented character of the Nor-tec cyber-scene even on a local level. There were individuals who, although having the opportunity of face-to-face interaction in the area, still privileged the development of a cyber-community.

In 2003, a new and promising type of blog network developed, MySpace. The system offers independent bands and musicians the ability to freely promote their music and have immediate access to fan feedback from all over the world. MySpace, based on the idea of a global cyber-community, became one of the most popular English-language Web sites in less than three years. Prior to the release of *Tijuana Sessions, Vol. 3* (2005), the Nor-tec Collective's new American indie label, Nacional Records, uploaded a MySpace blog for the group.[28] With more than 23,000 visits in less than a year, the Nortec Collective's MySpace blog became an important part of the record's distribution strategy. The eclecticism of a cyber-community like MySpace, its easy access, the ability of users to transfer music, video, and images to other profiles, and the possibility of adding public comments to anyone else's postings made the site a very useful tool. For the researcher, it also confirms the heterogeneous nature of the Nor-tec fan base, which is more obvious on MySpace than on a local site like that of the TJBF. Fans from small places where the collective has never performed can imagine themselves as part of a global community. Furthermore, these blogs give fans the illusion that they are actually in direct contact with their favorite musicians.[29]

This type of audience fragmentation is partly a result of the virtual marketing strategy favored by the collective. This explains why most middle-class *tijuanense* youngsters would know about Nor-tec despite the fact that I could not find the collective's CD at a local record store in Tijuana's middle-class Zona Río district. Being able to largely control the process of distribution allowed the Nortec Collective to shape its scene in a manner beneficial to the collective; a large virtual local scene that has access to Nortec via the Internet would eventually lead not only to larger live audiences but also to a huge number of consumers willing to pay for the latest tracks and other merchandise available online.

Local and International Labels

Signing a record contract with Palm Pictures was crucial in the internationalization of the Nortec Collective. As part of the deal, Palm Pictures acquired the rights to commercialize the tracks included in *The Tijuana Sessions,* volume 1, while the musicians received royalties from the album's sales and remained free to sign individual contracts with other labels. Thus, Panóptica signed a contract with the British label Certificate 18 to distribute *Panóptica* (2001) and *The Tijuana Remixes* (2002);[30] Fussible closed a deal with the British label Sonic 360 to release two individual CDs of remixes, *Odyssea* (2002) and *No One over 21* (2004); and Plankton Man had an LP, *4-Zeenaloas* (2001), released by Bleep Records. At the same time, the collective planned to use its own label, Mil Records, to produce and release a series of *mano-a-mano* recordings, each one alternating tracks by two different members. Due to unforeseen production and management problems, only two of those projects ever materialized, *Bostich + Fussible: Nortec Remixes* (2000) was released by Mil Records, and *Plankton Man vs. Terrestre* (2002) was released by Provider Recordings.[31]

The freedom to license their music was also important in reaching new audiences and in bringing extra money to the members of the collective. Thus, Nor-tec began to appear as incidental music on TV and radio shows, from Mexico's *Hora Nacional* (a weekly radio show played every Sunday evening by all Mexican radio stations) to a variety of shows on the popular U.S. cable network MTV. As the Nor-tec sound began to be identified as the next "cool" Latin American music, its tracks began to be used in movies and eventually video games. When John Leguizamo wanted to portray the hip sound of New York's club scene and the preferred newest music among young Latinos for his HBO directorial debut, *Undefeated* (2003), he selected Panóptica's "And L" and Fussible's "Casino Soul." The success of Nor-tec among Mexico City artists and intellectuals can be witnessed in the growing use of the collective's music in mainstream films that include *Por la libre* (2000), *Vivir mata* (2001), *Rosario Tijeras* (2005), and *La mujer de mi hermano* (2006). The hiring of Terrestre to compose the soundtrack for the all-star-cast Mexican movie *Nicotina* (2003) was also a result of Nortec's growing reputation among Mexico City artists. Even more profitable than the use of their tracks as incidental film music was the licensing of Nor-tec music for TV commercials and video games. Tracks by Bostich, Clorofila, and Fussible were used for commercials of Volvo, Nissan, Dell, and Sky Blue vodka and were featured in the popular video games FIFA 2005 and FIFA 2006 for PlayStation and Xbox. For many fans, associating the Nor-tec sound with a variety of fashionable transnational commodities has reinforced it as a symbolic gateway into the world of a hip, global, cosmopolitan community.

The aura of cosmopolitanism that came with Palm Pictures' mainstream marketing and Chris Blackwell's (the owner of the label) former connection to prestigious musicians such as Bob Marley also served to gain the collective a new status in Mexico. At the same time, the members' freedom to negotiate their licenses and individually establish commercial agreements with other labels allowed the collective to overcome Palm Pictures' unpredicted marketing shortcomings. Especially problematic were the audience to whom Palm Pictures targeted Nor-tec (middle- and upper-class Anglo-American kids) and the slow work of the label's subsidiaries in Europe and Latin America. Both circumstances would have limited the exposure of Nor-tec to Latin American and Latino audiences at a crucial moment in the development of a transnational scene, but the collective's underground networking, the marketing and distribution channels of their individual labels, and the members' ability to widely license their music kept the Nor-tec sound and the desire for cosmopolitanism associated with it flowing into those markets. Jorge Ruiz (Melo) explains some of the problems they had with their label:

> We had more dissemination power than the record company and it should be the other way around, right? When you want to sell a record you have to promote it, but when Palm Pictures realized that we did not require a professional marketing team because we ourselves were perfectly doing that, *le tiraron hueva* [they procrastinated]. We developed a huge campaign. For example, we would be invited to play in Colombia . . . and a lot of press would be there for us, and we would ask them: "What's up with the CD?" and they would say "No, we do not have it here, it hasn't been released here." So, how could that be possible? . . . It was very strange, we were always ahead of the label. It was always like that. When we went to Paris for the first time the CD was already out, but the distribution was so bad that it was like it wasn't out yet. . . . [The guys at] Palm didn't really do their job; they sort of put themselves out of the game. They sold what they could sell, but the success was really ours. . . . We started getting licenses . . . and the people at Palm were like "What's up with these guys? How are they doing it?" They were unable to take advantage of the circumstances.[32]

Although the support of Palm Pictures was very important in gaining the recognition of the mainstream, it is clear that there were serious problems trying to match the collective's underground marketing approach and the more conventional marketing strategies of the label. This situation generated a great deal of confusion between the musicians and the executives at Palm Pictures especially, as Melo suggests, since the label was not able to commercially benefit from the collective's alternative strategies.

Ponerse las Pilas: Waiting for the Second CD

During the summer of 2003, when I traveled to Tijuana to do fieldwork for the first time, the problems between Palm Pictures and the Nortec Collective had reached a critical moment. Two years had gone by since the release of *The Tijuana Sessions, Vol. 1,* and although the musicians had composed enough music to fill a second volume in the series, Palm Pictures was not hurrying the production of the new CD. At the time, this impasse was interpreted by many Tijuana-based electronica musicians, music critics, and fans as a sign of Nor-tec's demise. One of my first questions to the members of the collective concerned the release of the highly expected album *The Tijuana Sessions, Vol. 2.* The answer I received was always the same and remained the same for the next two years: "All the tracks are ready; it will come out within a few months." In the end, *The Tijuana Sessions, Vol. 2,* was never produced by Palm Pictures. The next CD of the Nortec Collective was not released until 2005 by Nacional Records under the title *Tijuana Sessions, Vol. 3.* The title of the CD jokingly plays with the fact that it took such a long time to be released that the collective might as well just have forgotten about volume 2 altogether. Jennifer Mañón, coordinator of the La Leche tour for Sonic 360, witnessed the promotion problems between Palm Pictures and the Nortec Collective during this tense period:

> It was pretty amazing because we did this big tour basically promoting their [Palm Pictures'] artists all summer in a major way and they did not acknowledge [it]. Which is kind of sick. . . . we're not selling albums off of it . . . maybe Fussible albums. [I don't see] why their record label is not doing anything. It's a shame.[33]

Mil Records' 2002 limited edition of the CD *Tijuana Beat Shop* was a direct response to the problems of distribution that the collective was facing after the release of *The Tijuana Sessions, Vol. 1. Tijuana Beat Shop* is a 74-minute-long continuous mix of Nor-tec tracks put together by DJ Aníbal, a native of Mexico City who had opened several parties for the collective. DJ Aníbal explains that his idea was to "edit and shorten tracks from the great amount of Nor-tec material available . . . to make a very entertaining mix."[34] One thousand copies of the CD were pressed and freely distributed among the fans at the Tijuana Beat Shop party, which was held at the Cortijo San José in Playas de Tijuana on 23 November 2002. Although the CD contains new versions of some of the tracks released on *The Tijuana Sessions, Vol. 1*, most of the music is compositions that the collective had been playing live for over two years but which were commercially unavailable. The issue at stake in the production and distribution of this recording is the musicians' disillusionment with the lack of distribution of their music. Pepe Mogt explains:

> *Tijuana Beat Shop* came about as a kind of protest against the national labels, which sometimes prevent the distribution of music. . . . Many of these tracks were released in other countries but were never available here [in Mexico], and if they ever got here you had to order them and it was very difficult to get them. . . . [Since Aníbal had already mixed and put together the CD] the idea was to give it away and forget about the labels. It was like "let's give it away and avoid having to wait until *The Tijuana Sessions* [*Vol. 2*]." No, we didn't care. We had the CD and we gave it away, that's what we did at the party; they [the fans] were getting in and one by one we gave them a copy of the CD. . . . the CD is not available for sale because the labels do not grant us permission to sell it. So, that's why we had the idea of giving it away.[35]

Although Pepe Mogt mentions only his frustration with the Mexican labels in charge of distributing the collective's music in Mexico, it is clear that Palm Pictures' delay in releasing *The Tijuana Sessions, Vol. 2*, was also on his mind when conceiving the production and distribution of *Tijuana Beat Shop*. Many of the tracks included on the CD were to be on the never-released Palm Pictures album and the label held the rights to the music; giving it away meant not only the advertising of the music itself but also a kind of declaration of independence from the label within the boundaries of their legal agreement.

Pepe Mogt's dissatisfaction with Palm Pictures' distribution strategies and the delay of the Nortec Collective's second CD was also evident during our first face-to-face interview in 2003. We met at his home studio in Playas de Tijuana a few days after he had been invited to play at the release party of Apple's iPod in Los Angeles. He was very excited about the possibilities of the new piece of equipment and its ability to record and play thousands of songs in mp3 format. For Pepe, the iPod represented the industry's acceptance that downloading music over the Internet, the collective's preferred distribution strategy, was the way of the future:

> For example, now that I was invited to play at the iPod party I had to convert my tracks into mp3s. I was feeling a bit lazy about it, so I just went into Kazaa and downloaded my own songs from other people. Of course, when you realize that a lot of people have them you go like "what's going

on?" But just imagine if I was going to sue the 2,000 guys who had the tracks . . . of course not! I mean, they are promoting us. When I go to Mexico City and find people who have burned the CD and ask me to sign it I am like "what's up? You have already burned the songs and the CD is not even out yet!" It's cool this is happening. I believe this is going to revolutionize the music industry. . . . Maybe at Palm *deben ponerse las pilas* [they should get their act together] and think about the future and a way to benefit as we do.[36]

Pepe Mogt's accusation that Palm Pictures *debe ponerse las pilas* is a clear reference to the contradictions between the collective's successful do-it-yourself distribution strategy and what he saw as the label's lack of commitment to fully promoting their music. However, such contradictions also inform us of the ways in which independent projects can take advantage of technology in a globalized scenario to empower themselves and to overcome the imbalances embedded in traditional label-artist relationships. Such a strategy moves beyond traditional resistance-compliance dichotomies and shows that power relations imply complex give-and-take acts of negotiation through which, as Pepe Mogt argues, it is hoped that both sides can benefit.

Managers and the Idea of "Selling Out"

Regardless of the collective's differences with Palm Pictures and the continuing use of underground distribution strategies, signing a contract with the label meant a more professional approach to the marketing of their product, at least in the United States and Europe. Such a move was accompanied by the necessary signing of managers to take care of the growing demand for live shows. This professionalization, however beneficial, was also harmful as it unwittingly emphasized the differences within the collective regarding the type of relationship the group wanted to have with the mainstream. Such problems eventually led to Terrestre and Plankton Man splitting from the collective in 2001.

Tomás Cookman, the owner of Fuerte Marketing and Cookman International (companies dedicated to reaching out to the Latino community and to the promotion of Latino artists in the United States), found out about Nor-tec through e-mails and local fanzines and finally heard the music through a Palm Pictures executive.[37] Although Cookman did not specialize in electronica, he was immediately interested in having the Nortec Collective join his management roster. The collective benefited from yet another deal that gave them enough freedom to keep finding gigs through their own underground networks while accessing more reputable venues through Cookman. This arrangement was especially helpful economically since a well-established manager like Cookman could get better concert rates than those the collective would normally get through their own contacts. However, although Cookman was able to negotiate higher rates when dealing with bigger music impresarios in the United States and Europe, those same rates would prove too high for most of the independent and alternative venues that had previously supported the collective. The ability to arrange concerts without having to solely rely on Cookman was also fundamental in continuing to have a degree of control over shaping the Nor-tec scene and the collective's identity.

The selection of Cookman as the collective's manager created a problem since Terrestre and Plankton Man had chosen different managers; it divided the collective into two blocs. At the beginning, the two factions within the collective were able to sort through the troubles created by the situation, but it soon became clear that they had very different ideas about how to market the group and manage its relation to the mainstream. Plankton Man recalls the moment:

> There were many who wanted to be in charge of the collective. The problems began there. Who was going to organize *las tocadas* [the gigs]? Who decided who played where? A fair distribution of *tocadas* in a collective is the most difficult thing in the world![38]

Plankton Man believes that the major problems among the members of the collective arose out of a power struggle to exercise control within the group. Clearly, this aspect played a major role in his and Terrestre's split from the collective. Nevertheless, the problem was a reflection of a larger struggle to maintain the identity of the collective as a project linked to the underground.

Pepe Mogt is more lengthy and specific about the particular events that led to Terrestre and Plankton Man abandoning the Nortec Collective:

> There were decisions they [Terrestre and Plankton Man] wanted to make. For example, they wanted to play in a certain festival and we did not agree. . . . There was money; the company would say: "OK, we'll give you a tour support budget, but it is for all the members of the collective to pay it back." So, let's say there was a chance to open a concert for Manu Chau in New York . . . with Caifanes and Manu Chau. . . . they [Terrestre and Plankton Man] would say: "we want to go and we want the tour-support money for that," and I would say, "Why? OK, use the money but not to open for Manu Chau. Use it to go to an electronica festival. I don't know . . . if you want something more commercial then go and open for Björk or play with Jazzanova." . . . We [Hiperboreal, Panóptica, Clorofila, Bostich, and Fussible] have a very clear idea of what Nor-tec is . . . although we even had discussions with Ramón [Bostich], we had problems with him about remixes I wouldn't make for certain commercial bands. I mean,

if Enrique Iglesias asks me for a remix I won't do it, just because I don't like his music. I mean, I am not a sellout; I have a very clear idea of what I want to do.[39]

Pepe Mogt's comments reflect his desire to keep Nor-tec associated with the electronic music scene and avoid it being perceived as pop music, especially in relation to those artists he considers to be too commercial. Clearly, the idea of the underground and the notion of selling out are at the core of what he identifies as the problem with Terrestre and Plankton Man's marketing strategy.

The anxiety about selling out is not unique to electronica musicians. The concern with the abandonment of one's ideals and giving in to commercial trends has accompanied the development of progressive music manifestations at least since the nineteenth century. However, the complex relationship between artists and the mass media at the turn of the twenty-first century makes loyalties more difficult to maintain. While staying away from commercial pop singers backed by the big music corporations, like Enrique Iglesias, seems like an obvious choice, rejecting Manu Chau and Julieta Venegas (the problem between Bostich and the collective to which Mogt refers came about when Bostich made a remix for Mexican pop singer Julieta Venegas) is more difficult to understand. Notwithstanding their recent commercial success, neither Manu Chau nor Julieta Venegas could seriously be considered corporate creations. Even in their most commercial productions, one still finds Chau and Venegas concerned with many of the same social and gender issues that interested them when they were members of underground bands like Mano Negra and Tijuana No. What has changed is their relationship to the mainstream music industry, as they have found ways to compromise and use aspects of that industry to pursue their own interests. Pepe Mogt's disregard for Chau's and Venegas's music shows that the very notions of "mainstream" and "underground" are complex constructions and that acts that lie in between can easily fall on one side or the other, depending on the listener's perspective. Clearly, the line separating Nor-tec from the mainstream proved to be too thin and difficult to identify even for members of the collective. The complex negotiations needed to keep the difficult balance between these two different worlds and even between the different degrees of commercialism and avant-gardism within each of these worlds are what led to Terrestre and Plankton Man's split from the collective. In the end, although the separation weakened the group by taking away two very talented members, it also allowed the members to continue having a certain amount of control over the shaping of the collective's identity. At the same time, once separated from the group, Terrestre's and Plankton Man's own takes on the Nor-tec aesthetic brought a welcome stylistic diversity to the scene.

"To Be Part of This Cool Thing":
Beer, Latino Markets, and Nor-tec

During my first field trip to Tijuana and the southern California area, I was surprised to find that the two largest events in which the Nortec Collective was participating that summer, the La Leche tour and the Noche de Pasión concert in Los Angeles, were sponsored by two giant brands in the American beer market, Heineken and Budweiser. What surprised me the most was not that there were beer companies sponsoring the events but rather that Corona, probably Mexico's most famous import product, was not one of them. I would later find out that, as Margaret Dorsey states, Grupo Modelo, the maker of Corona, has been partly owned by Budweiser since 2001, and the growing involvement of Budweiser with Latino media was part of an aggressive "ethnic marketing" campaign to reach out to the growing Latino (especially Mexican-American) community in the United States.[40] This campaign challenged Budweiser and Miller, the two dominant beer brands in the United States, at a crucial moment when the growing economic power of the Mexican-American community was becoming more and more apparent to the mainstream. However, Budweiser and Miller were not the only beer brands interested in tapping into the consumption power of the Latino community: Heineken was also eager to share the profits. Budweiser and Heineken recognized the importance of music in shaping identity groups and made Latin American and Latino musics into fundamental tools in trying to win over these markets; Nor-tec, the hippest Latino sound, had to play a role in their strategies. Although Budweiser and Heineken shared a common goal, their approach to the Latino music market differed greatly and resulted in varying degrees of success of their events.

Trying to capitalize on two of the young Latino community's passions, *rock en español* and soccer, Budweiser organized Noche de Pasión at a Los Angeles warehouse on 17 May 2003. The event combined a one-day-long indoor soccer tournament with an equally long marathon of live rock bands that reached its climax with the presentation of the famous Argentinean group Los Enanitos Verdes at midnight. Following Los Enanitos Verdes, the Nortec Collective closed the event with a brief, half-hour-long set. Noticeably, the crowd went down from a couple of thousand to a little over a hundred when Los Enanitos Verdes left the stage and the Nortec Collective began its performance. This unlikely situation was the result of the Budweiser marketing team not being particularly perceptive of the differences in musical taste within the Latino community. Programming Nortec among other music acts in style among young Latinos seemed like a perfect idea, but the Budweiser marketing team did not realize that, although electronic music has a following among young Latinos, it is not necessarily the same kind of crowd that attends *rock en español* concerts. The marketing team's ignorance of the nuances that characterize different Latino music communities made the inclusion of the Nortec Collective in Noche de Pasión insignificant.

Heineken's approach to the Latino market was quite different from Budweiser's. Instead of organizing an event and developing an audience for it, Heineken preferred to tag along with Sonic 360's La Leche tour, a project specifically aimed at Latino electronica audiences and managed by a group of people well acquainted with these crowds and their preferred musics. Jennifer Mañón, the event coordinator for Sonic 360, explains:

> Heineken was interested in doing a whole tour and so we talked with them for a really long time. [It was all] dependent on what markets they wanted to reach out to and if we were interested in putting La Leche there. We expressed our interest and said "here are some markets we think are good. What do you guys want to do?" It was like that. But it was the major Latino markets, definitely. . . . They get to push their products at the parties. They usually do some discount for Heineken. . . . the main reason they want to do it [sponsor the tour] is to be associated with the brand and with the music that we were putting on—Nor-tec music. But they just wanted to be a part of this cool thing going on, and they knew we were underground and were really doing things in a different way and reaching out to people who were not just *rockeros,* Latino *rockeros,* but kind of a hip, in crowd.[41]

The key to the success of Heineken's collaboration with La Leche was that the beer's marketing team allowed the event coordinators of Sonic 360 to deal with the particularities of the Latino electronica market. Sonic 360's 2003 La Leche tour was not the label's first attempt at exploring Latino markets; the 2002 La Leche tour had actually included Tijuana's Don Loope, a club owned by Hiperboreal, as one of their venues. Not surprisingly, well aware of the particular musical tastes of the Latino community, the marketing team at Sonic 360 avoided mixing *rock en español* and electronica crowds. Having the Mexican rock-electronica band Kinky also on their roster, the label could have easily committed the mistake of scheduling them alongside Nor-tec during the La Leche tour; nevertheless, it is clear that theirs was a conscious decision to avoid combining rock and electronica crowds.

Although their knowledge of the heterogeneity within the Latino community allowed Sonic 360 to organize more successful events than Budweiser's naïve homogeneous approach, the ethnic overtones of their promotion strategy did not go unchallenged. The most evident problem arose when organizing Nor-tec events in Miami. Jennifer Mañón explains:

In Miami, we had a tricky time, they're so conservative. . . . it's Cubans, they're known for that. One comment we got was for a Terrestre flyer which said "traditional Mexican samples fused with electronic music" in the description. They were always trying to give us advice on how to better promote the parties; and they said, "first of all, the flyer looks way too Mexican," and if it says "Mexican" forget it. They said "you should take the word Mexican off the flyer." And I was like, "Thank you." Sometimes I was really insulted by what people actually thought about the idea of how to reach other people and that we should change our image to make people happy.[42]

What Mañón unexpectedly experienced were the ethnic and class tensions between two of the largest Latino communities in the United States, Cubans and Mexicans, who have chosen to identify with different sides of their Latin American heritage. As Silvia Pedraza-Bailey explains, the social structure and class distinctions from prerevolutionary Cuba were replicated after the great 1950s Cuban migration to the United States.[43] Thus, the most economically influential portion of the Cuban-American community in Florida is formed by the so-called Golden Exiles, the *criollo* (creole) elite from prerevolutionary Cuba who migrated to the United States in the early years of the Cuban revolution. This Golden Exile group came to dominate important economic and political arenas in Miami, including the entertainment industry. Part of the community's economic and political success was achieved by taking advantage of the class and family relations that had formed the core of the social structure in prerevolutionary Cuba. The greater part of the 1960s and 1970s mass Cuban migration was upper- and middle-class whites; blacks represented only 4 percent of the Cuban-American community before the Marielito migration of 1980.[44] This demographic situation led to the portrayal of Cubans as "white" by non-Latino whites in the United States.[45] And truly, with notable exceptions (like Celia Cruz) and responding to the logic of the social hierarchy being replicated, the most prominent Cubans in the United States have tended to be white rather than black. On the other hand, Mexican Americans have preferred to take Indian and *mestizo* iconography as sources of cultural identification. The importance of the Aztlán myth in Chicano culture and the ubiquitous presence of mariachi as a symbol of Mexican-American identity are just two examples of this inclination. It is also important to notice that, in contrast to the Cuban experience from the 1960s and 1970s, the Mexican migration to the United States has largely come from the working classes. The Cuban-American desire to differentiate their community from other Latin American migrant experiences (especially the Mexican migration) is also related to their struggle to identify themselves as political refugees rather than as migrants in search of jobs. As I show in chapter 6,

Figure 3.1   Flyer used for the first concert of the 2003 La Leche tour.

in relation to music and dance practices, the cultural traditions and icons from each of these communities have understandably come to be marked by class associations; such a situation has helped to deepen the ethnic and class gap between the Cuban and Mexican communities in the United States.

Sonic 360's first Nor-tec concert during the 2003 La Leche tour was scheduled in Houston on 5 May. The concert featured Fussible and was advertised with a series of flyers that depicted a brown-skinned girl wearing a seemingly Mexican hat (see figure 3.1). The same image would be later used on a variety of flyers for different nights during the tour but, as Mañón pointed out, it became a problem with the Cuban community in Miami. According to Mañón's statement, it was in response to the community's pressure that Sonic 360 decided to slightly change the flyer's image for the first Miami concert on 18 June. The change consisted of lightening the skin color of the girl depicted on the flyer to appease the racial concerns of the Cuban Americans from Miami (see figure 3.2).

Figure 3.2   Flyer used for the first Miami night of the 2003 La Leche tour

Since the pressures to modify the flyer continued for the second event in Miami, the La Leche crew decided to eliminate most of the racial and ethnic references to Mexican ethnicity and culture (the girl's darker skin color and the Mexican hat) in favor of a Spanish look, emphasizing European racial and ethnic features (white skin and the somewhat stylized clothing, haircut, and makeup). The only references to Mexico in the new flyer appeared in the description of Terrestre's musical project (*samples mexicanos tradicionales* [traditional Mexican samples]), in small writing below the largest text, indicating the name and date of the event (see figure 3.3). The preeminence of visual over the written content in the design of these types of music flyers ensured that the Mexican elements (otherwise seminal in the marketing of Nor-tec) occupied a lesser place than the markers of European-derived *criollismo* with which many Cuban Americans would rather identify themselves.

Figure 3.3   Flyer used for the second Miami night of the 2003 La Leche tour

An important aspect in the marketing and distribution of consumer goods lies in the identification of the consumer's desires or, in more radical instances, the creation of desiring machines in an effort to link the product to that desire. Clearly, Budweiser and Heineken chose Nor-tec in an effort to identify their reach-out-to-young-Latinos campaigns with the cosmopolitanism and modernity that this music represented. Budweiser's marketing campaign failed to recognize not only the large ethnic, racial, and cultural differences within the Latino community but also the subtle differences in musical taste within specific ethnic or demographic groups. On the other hand, Heineken's reliance on Sonic 360's grassroots strategists not only allowed the company to be more sensitive to these differences but, most important, enabled it to respond expediently to the challenges of confronting them. It was this sensibility or lack of sensibility toward their aimed markets that defined Budweiser's and Heineken's attempts to link themselves to Nor-tec or, as Jennifer Mañón stated, "to be part of this cool thing."

Underground Strategies in the Age of Digital Reproduction II

If, according to Walter Benjamin, the outcome of implementing processes of mechanical reproduction is the end of the work of art's uniqueness, processes of digital reproduction and distribution allow for the renewal of a sense of aura in the consumer's imagination. In contrast to Benjamin's idea of the aura as the result of the artist's unique intervention during the process of creation, in this new experience the sense of uniqueness is intimately connected to the processes of antiestablishment reproduction and consumption. Thus, it is the audience's nostalgia for an aura, for authenticity, grassroots community, and a rejection of commercial marketing and commercial products, and the audience's desire to be part of something unique which provides the grounds for the restitution of aura itself.[46] Under these circumstances, it is important to understand what audiences find unique about artistic manifestations.

In the case of Nor-tec, it was the lure of the underground that attracted people, making them feel as if they were part of a unique musical experience, one that rejected commercial corporate power. The continuous presence of alternate distribution networks was beneficial not only because it allowed the musicians to overcome the shortcomings of its collective-label agreement, but also because it reinforced the image of Nor-tec as an underground endeavor that at least partially rejected corporate commercialization. Certainly, Pepe Mogt's struggle to determine at which concert venues the collective should appear forced Terrestre and Plankton Man to quit the group; however, as detrimental as this was for the collective's unity, such a strategy empowered him and the group. It gave them power over the collective's representation and therefore an important degree of control over shaping the Nor-tec scene by tapping into their audience's nostalgia for an aura.

4

"Where's the Donkey Show, Mr. Mariachi?"

Reterritorializing TJ

Guillermo Fadanelli has described Tijuana by borrowing imagery from some of its most recurrent mythology:

> [In Tijuana] you have a feeling that everyone is going to leave anytime, that everyone is going to emigrate into the desert or move to a different border. Even the Zona del Río, with its claims for modernity, looks like scenery, like an ephemeral montage, a location where an infinite number of movies and simulacra will be shot, but nothing will happen because in reality everyone is an actor, not by choice but by infection, because they recognize themselves in the middle of a territory with no history or future, a territory where everything is movement and continuous flux.[1]

In order to show Tijuana as a site where myth and reality often overlap, I propose to interpret Fadanelli's description as a mixture of reality, discourse, imagination, and desire. The imagery of Tijuana as "nobody's land," as a place where individuals reinvent themselves through acts of simulation, is inextricably linked to the complex social dynamics of tourism, migration, and the border economy that have shaped the city's urban landscape. However, a few fundamental questions rest disguised amid Fadanelli's collection of border stereotypes. For instance, where does myth end and reality begin? How does myth shape reality? Myths are cultural constructions, and their meanings are produced in the passing from the realm of the "real" to that of the "symbolic." Indeed, it is this fundamental step which allocates to myths their character as performative enunciations and allows them to act as simulacra that question the difference between reality and imagination. A typical example of such mythology made into a simulacrum in Tijuana is the infamous donkey show, which allegedly features a couple of prostitutes having sex with a donkey.[2] As a discourse, the donkey show occupies a place in the U.S. imagination of Tijuana; for U.S. tourists or visitors, that is the "real" Tijuana and, although *tijuanenses* often insist that "there's no such thing as a donkey show," it becomes an object of desire that triggers many tourists' exploration of *La Coahuila* whenever they visit the city.[3]

The purpose of this chapter is to show local cultural practices that appropriate the city and its mythology in novel ways that empower local individuals. First, I trace the issue of impermanence in the city's architectural history as a point of departure to explain the continuous re-signification of the city's urban landscapes by *tijuanenses*. Then, I explore the relationships among musicians, fans, and the changing urban landscape of their city, including concert venues, clubs, bars, and dancing locales. Finally, I use Nor-tec music and videos as metaphors for the ambiguity of cultural meaning and discourse in a city like Tijuana. My goal is to show that Nor-tec and Nor-tec–related expressive culture offer young *tijuanenses* alternative ways to territorialize and reterritorialize public spaces as well as hegemonic discourses of race, class, morality, and belonging in Tijuana.

Impermanence and Change in the City

It is important to take into account the discursive level of mythology and simulacra that I have explained above, as it is at this level that Nor-tec articulates a process of cultural reterritorialization of the mythical representations of Tijuana. Néstor García Canclini describes reterritorialization as a process by which individuals contest, reconfigure, and re-signify forms of identity organization.[4] Thus, reterritorialization in a cultural context refers to the appropriation of hegemonic symbols and discourses and their reconfiguration according to the specific needs and values of contesting individuals or communities. In Tijuana, Nor-tec has appropriated the myths and stereotypes about the city, turning them into goods for consumption, merchandise with exchange value which permits *tijuanenses* to question alienating discourses from within. In this form, Nor-tec culture works as an institution that challenges the dominant discourses of national and local identity and, therefore, notions of center and periphery. Nor-tec music, based on the characteristic loops of electronic music, exemplifies a symbolic sonic reterritorialization of Tijuana; as such, it becomes a strategy aimed at repossessing ideological discourses, an artistic tactic symbolized in the reclamation of the physical and sonic sites of performance.

Figure 4.1   The Tijuana arch welcomes tourists to *La Revu*. Photo by the
author

My interest in Nor-tec leads me to make an appointment to meet Pedro
Gabriel Beas (Hiperboreal) and Pepe Mogt at El Dandy del Sur, one of their
favorite bars, just a block away from *La Revu*. My conversation with
Hiperboreal freely flows among beers and *carnita* (a salty, sauce-drenched,
dry beef snack I have seen nowhere in Mexico besides Tijuana). We speak
about everything but soccer, which he confesses to hate; the topics of our
conversation range from music to literature, from architecture to the Internet, from food to the Filipino women who drink at a nearby table.

Notwithstanding the variety of subjects discussed, there appears to be
a constant, recurring idea that permeates them: Hiperboreal seems obsessed
with preserving the past and registering it in history. After complaining
about the decision of the city government to erect an arch at the entrance

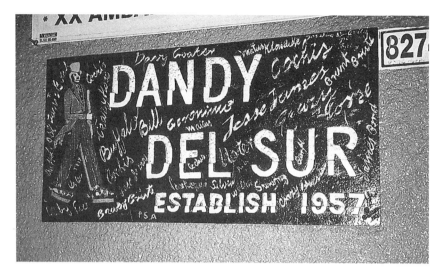

Figure 4.2 Sign outside El Dandy del Sur, one of the Nortec Collective's favorite meeting places in Tijuana. Photo by the author

of *La Revu,* an arch that seems to stand as a witness to the presence of tourists along the infamous avenue, Hiperboreal explodes: "this arch breaks with the architectural harmony of the city . . . because, in the middle of all this apparent chaos, there is harmony."[5] Immediately, our conversation focuses on the slow disappearance of the spaces that have witnessed the growth of the Nor-tec phenomenon—bars and clubs like El Dandy del Sur and La Estrella occupy a preponderant place. According to Hiperboreal, these meeting places, bars, clubs, and concert venues, where the initial concept of Nor-tec was shaped, have been slowly disappearing. In order to preserve their memory, in an attempt to prevent them from being forgotten, he has embarked on a photographic project to celebrate their existence.

A few days after our meeting, I found out that Hiperboreal himself had been the owner of one of these clubs, the Don Loope. This was a place located in an annex of the Jai Alai building, which had previously been occupied by Ricky Martínez de Castro's Pueblo Café Baja. Don Loope was open for a few months and then disappeared, but not without having plugged Tijuana into the international music stream by hosting Sonic 360's La Leche tour in 2002. After Don Loope closed, a new place—Centro Bar—opened in the same location, another club devoted to electronic music that quickly closed its doors after apparent financial disagreements with the management of the Jai Alai building. Reterritorialization and tradition are the notions that dominate both Hiperboreal's discourse and the power

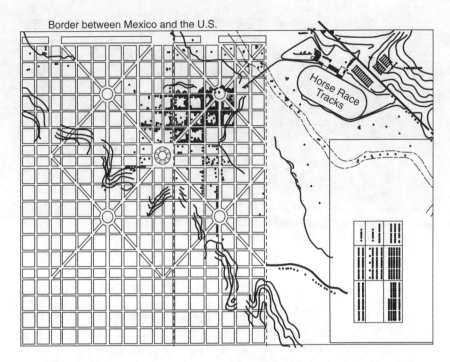

Border between Mexico and the U.S.

Figure 4.3   Original city plat of Tijuana, according to Ricardo Orozco's 1889 model

struggles behind the impermanence of the spaces that the electronic music scene seems to win for itself in Tijuana.

Impermanence is the only constant in the architectural reinvention of Tijuana. As I mentioned in the introduction, the original plat of the city shows the influence of nineteenth-century American and European models in designs that feature central squares in which a number of horizontal and vertical streets as well as two diagonal avenues converge. These diagonal avenues are the more salient feature that differentiates the modern European and U.S. models from the colonial Spanish urban practice, which was based mostly on parallel vertical and horizontal streets. However, the current configuration of Tijuana greatly differs from the original model. With a few exceptions, like the Avenida Argüelles, most diagonal avenues have been replaced with new buildings. This practice, which deemphasizes a sense of urban history in favor of a more practical approach to architecture, signals an aesthetic of ephemerality that owes much to the U.S. modernist obsession with change, renovation, and rejuvenation and its notion of things being disposable.

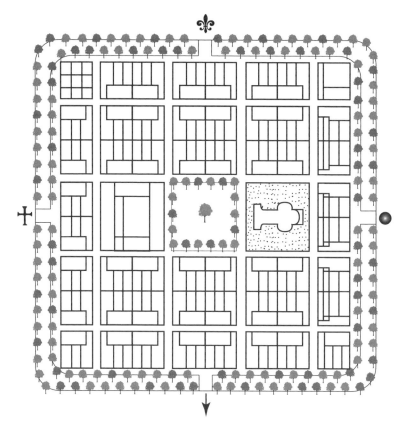

Figure 4.4 Typical colonial Spanish city plat

Tijuana, like its California siblings, is a city where the old is valued only when it is reconstructed in relation to the new. In a city where the oldest "historical" buildings date from the 1920s, impermanence accounts for a lifestyle in which the political exists in the intersection between modernity and tradition, heritage and innovation, and agency and hegemony. Such aesthetics of ephemerality have an effect on the citizens and individuals who relate to their urban landscape in an attempt to imbue it with symbolic meaning. The constant disappearance of these urban spaces forces individuals to be on a continuous search for locations that could symbolize their social and cultural belonging. However, many times, individuals plainly reject hegemonic attempts to resymbolize their sites of identification. One such example is the change of management of the Jai Alai building with the consequential attempt to change its name to El Foro in 2004. In part, such an attempt reflects the fact that the building no longer

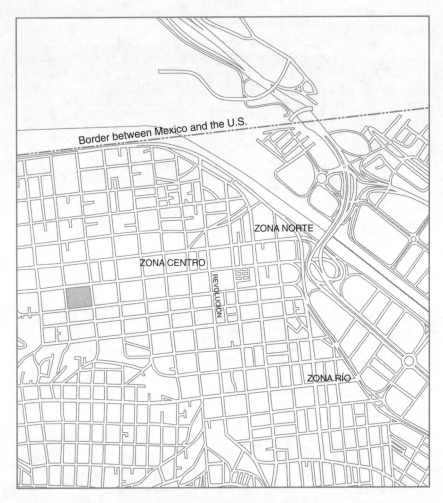

Figure 4.5   Current map of Tijuana's Zona Centro

holds jai alai matches and has been used for a long time as a music concert venue—including some of the most important Nor-tec parties—and as
a music forum, as the new name suggests. The response of Jazzanova, a
Nor-tec fan from Tijuana who maintains an electronic blog, illustrates the
reticence of young *tijuanenses* to stop using a name that has already been
appropriated and acquired important value as part of their cultural capital: "Oh really? To hell with all of you. I will never call it El Foro. For me
it will never stop being the Jai Alai."[6]

Hiperboreal's anxiety of ephemerality translates into a project that
attempts to freeze in time specific symbolic moments of Tijuana's changing
urban landscape (the memory of specific spaces at the moment they acquired

significance for the identity of the Nortec Collective). This is a strategy informed by nostalgia, an effort to possess the memory of urban spaces whose continuously changing cultural meaning makes them slip through our fingers. Jazzanova's response to the change of name of the Jai Alai building is an example of this nostalgia. Still, other *tijuanenses'* exercises of cultural reterritorialization are aimed not at trying to possess an impermanent moment in time, but rather at temporarily repossessing urban spaces and practices that have been made taboo by hegemonic discourses of differentiation. Exploring these exercises presents a larger and more complete picture of how individuals are able to negotiate the symbolization of the urban spaces in which they live.

Partying in Tijuana II (*Culturosa* City Mix)

I heard [the Nortec Collective] live for the first time at the *No Cover* magazine anniversary party. I was just 18 and wanted to go to the raves and see everything I'd seen in the flyers. I went to this little party at Don Loope. . . . I had read *un chorro* [a lot] about Don Loope and was hungry for all of that. I went there and everything I had read became real. So I said "*este es el rollo* [this is it], I'll come back and spend all of my time here." And it was just like that, they changed [Don Loope's] name to Centro Bar, or whatever, but I kept going as long as the *nortecos* kept playing.[7]

For Alex, a middle-class Nor-tec fan in his early 20s, Nor-tec parties are *el rollo* (the thing to do). He was underage when the Nor-tec boom hit Tijuana in 1999 and 2000 and, being unable to attend the large parties at the Jai Alai building, Las Pulgas, and Don Loope, he had to settle for witnessing the compelling phenomenon from afar. He learned from word of mouth about the parties where hot dog and *chicharrón* (fried pork skin) vendors shared an area inside the Jai Alai building, just a few feet from where DJs spun their vinyls of techno, dub, and house. He read in local fanzines and international media about the art installations and video projects that, sharing the spotlight with the bouncy rhythms of Nor-tec, denounced the working conditions at local *maquilas*.[8] He downloaded every single Nor-tec track he could find on the Internet. Through reading about Nortec City and Nortec Live at Las Pulgas, and by enjoying the kitschy artwork of these parties' promotional flyers, Nor-tec became an object of desire for Alex. Thus, when he was finally allowed to attend the events, Nor-tec parties became a site for identification, *el rollo* that linked his everyday life as a coffee shop manager with the globalism and cosmopolitanism (the "coolness") of a local music that had managed to break into the international EDM scene. Alex also states that, as long as Nor-tec was played, he would make the location occupied by Centro Bar (regardless of its name) the place to "spend all of his time." Such a statement—which resonates with Jazzanova's rejection of the Jai Alai building's new name by suggesting that the name is not important as long as the location is reterritorialized by the fans and musicians—emphasizes the power of the Nor-tec scene to resymbolize actual urban places in Tijuana and to become a screen upon which individuals' desire for cosmopolitanism and dreams of globalism could be projected and reconfigured.

As is evident from Alex's comments, partying is more than a simple, gratifying social experience. Partying allows for individuals not only to interact and establish social relations with people who share similar musical tastes, but also to participate in a process of nonrepressive sublimation, a collective *relajo* (relaxing, amusing activity) that ascribes new personal, social, and political meanings to urban spaces seemingly conquered by hegemony.[9] Questioned about the use of spaces by local party advocates, Gabriel Castillo, a local event organizer for Orbit, states that for him it is very special that "a place could be transformed into something it was not meant for; it is truly impressive how the fans' vibe could change that."[10] Indeed, the collective *relajo* of EDM parties works in a carnivalesque way (in a Bakhtinian sense); it creates a site of tolerable ephemeral social disorder where the territorial claims of hegemony in the urban landscape of Tijuana can be contested and the party areas temporally reterritorialized by musicians, dancing fans, and partygoers.[11]

In Tijuana, fans proudly remember two of Nor-tec's most noticeable acts of reterritorialization, the actual takeover of two of the city's landmarks, the "historical" Jai Alai building (with Nortec City) and the traditional *norteño* bar Las Pulgas (with Nortec Live at Las Pulgas). On 3 March 2001, Nortec City, a party for the presentation of the Nortec Collective's first commercial recording, *The Tijuana Sessions, Vol. 1,* was organized at the Jai Alai building. On that occasion, the old building located on Avenida Revolución, a symbol of the city's ambiguous relation to tourism and one of Tijuana's most famous stereotypes, was transformed by over 2,000 Nortec dancing fans into a site for the performance of identity in terms of tradition and modernity.

Playing an electronic keyboard, El Guapachoso Vengador (the Festive Avenger), a musician masked like a popular Mexican wrestler, welcomes fans to the party with the rhythms and sounds of cumbia music. On the sidewalk, as part of the *relajo*, a *jalador,* one of *La Revu*'s most ubiquitous characters, persuades fans to take the "Free Calafia Visual Trip," a free roundtrip from Tijuana's downtown to the Zona Río. Inside the vehicle, as the trip takes place, a TV shows continuous footage from three local projects that celebrate the urban landscape of Tijuana: Iván Díaz Robledo's

video for Hiperboreal's "Tijuana for Dummies," Itzel Martínez del Canizo's *Super Nortec,* and Martínez and Huicho Martín's *Salón de baile La
Estrella.* Inside the Jai Alai, in the lobby of the building, the thrilled fans
find food and clothing vendors as well as an exhibition of Nor-tec visual
art by Cha3, Gerardo Yépiz (Acamonchi), Gaby Núñez (Verdegaby), and
Germán Araujo, among others. Nortec City is the event where the happy
communion between Nor-tec sound and Nor-tec visuals first takes place.
Here, in front of a large audience of U.S. journalists—attracted by the fuss
generated by the collective's "cyber-word-of-mouth" distribution strategy
and Palm Pictures' public relations team—who are eager to register the
"unlikely" event, a team of visual artists join the grooves and loops of Nor-
tec music and the jumpy movements of the faithful dancing fans. For the
first time, the urban images of Tijuana bounce over large screens, accompanying the spatial and corporeal reterritorialization performed by musicians and dancing fans with a discursive visual appropriation of both corny
stereotypes of Tijuana like *La mona* or the arch and urban graffiti and the
images of local cumbia and *quebradita* dancers.

The glocal character of Nor-tec was clearly articulated in Nortec City.
There, the local reterritorialization performed by musicians, dancing fans,
and visual artists as a reevaluation of spaces and discourses about Tijuana
was projected onto a global screen in the U.S., Mexican, and European
newspapers, Web sites, and magazines, which defined the event as a party
that showed "the city in Technicolor."[12] If Nortec City inaugurated a new
relationship among the Nor-tec sound, the dancing fans, and the urban images of Tijuana, Nortec Live at Las Pulgas marked an equally important
moment in the process of local urban reterritorialization triggered by the
Nor-tec scene.

On 20 March 2002, Las Pulgas, the largest *norteña* and *banda* music
dancing hall in Tijuana, opened its doors to a type of music unfamiliar to
most of its customers. Las Pulgas, a bar and dance hall where all types of
norteña, banda, and cumbia music coexist in a large building divided into
four areas, is considered to be the most important live music venue of its
type in Tijuana. Here, before an audience of 3,000 dancing fans, the Nor-
tec sound successfully reterritorialized El Salón Vaquero, one of the areas
of the traditional dance hall. In order to adapt the locale to the needs of an
EDM event, the central area of the hall was emptied of tables and chairs,
creating an ad hoc space for the large dancing crowd to freely move
around. The Nortec Collective, accustomed to working with more restricted budgets, took perfect advantage of the extraordinary technical
facilities at Las Pulgas. Thrilled with the technical possibilities of such resources (20 monitors to keep track of and regulate the flow of sound and
images at their disposal), the collective presented an extraordinary show

where a novel performance practice (all members of the collective on stage at the same time) was combined with an increasingly complex use of visual resources.

The graphic designers in charge of promoting the event also took advantage of the advertising strategies of Las Pulgas and other traditional *norteña* and *banda* venues. Jorge Verdín from Clorofila and Cha3 explains:

> When we played at Las Pulgas I decided to copy one of those [*norteña* and *banda* concert] posters, using as many types of fonts as possible and manipulating the picture of the original musicians—I added . . . long moustaches and sunglasses. It was almost a given, if the location was Las Pulgas, then the vocabulary of the poster had to have something to do with that place.[13]

Verdín borrowed from the style of popular promotional flyers for *norteño*, *banda,* cumbia, and *grupero* musicians. This type of flyer, with its hectic and heterogeneous use of colors and wide variety of fonts and images, is typically glued on public walls and is aimed at lower- and lower-middle-class individuals, the usual attendees at these events. Verdín's flyer was posted, along with those of the usual Las Pulgas performers, outside the dance hall and on a billboard above the building. However, the collective also followed the standard promotional practices of EDM parties (individual leaflets distributed among friends, Internet advertisements, and word of mouth through Web lists and blogs), making the promotional strategy of the party a hybrid one, a combination of do-it-yourself electronic music scene tactics and more traditional advertisement approaches.

José Manuel Valenzuela Arce recognizes the relevance of Nortec Live at Las Pulgas as an event that temporally "colonized this traditional outpost," a party where "the sounds of accordion, *polcas,* and *narcocorridos* along with the sights of *sombrero-* and boot-wearing *vaqueros* [cowboys] were replaced by the sound[s] of nortec and their fans."[14] As Valenzuela Arce argues, the party at Las Pulgas was an important instance of Nor-tec's power of agency; however, such an event is much more complex than a simple act of colonization. I suggest that the strategic use of *banda* and *norteña* music sounds, the hybrid character of the advertisement campaign, and the combination of *norteño* clothing (*tejano*-style hats) and rave paraphernalia (dyed hair, baggy pants, piercings, trendy tennis shoes, and even bare-chested boys) among the partygoers exemplify an act of transformation and hybridization rather than a replacement of cultural practices. The sounds of accordions, *polcas, banda* brass, and *narcocorridos* were not replaced by the loops of Nor-tec but technologically transformed by them. More than an act of colonization, Nortec Live at Las Pulgas was an operation of reterritorialization that allowed for processes of negotiation to take

Figure 4.6   Promotional flyer for Nortec Live at Las Pulgas, © Cha3. Used by permission

place. Just like the hybrid character of the advertising campaigns mediated among established mainstream practices and underground strategies, and just as the style adopted by Verdín in the flyers took into account the graphic tradition associated with Las Pulgas, the night of the party became a moment for two different crowds (the Nor-tec fans at Salón Vaquero and the typical customers of the bar in the other three areas) to find a common site to ephemerally experience each other's lifestyle.

Nortec City and Nortec Live at Las Pulgas were sites that allowed the interaction and transformation of cultural practices and music scenes instead of the replacement of one by the other. Thus, partying in Tijuana's Nor-tec style, as exemplified in these two events and as described earlier in Alex's comments, allows individuals to temporally experience a *relajo* that challenges the hegemonic order, creates sites for identification, and, at the same time, articulates tradition as an important aspect in the processes of reterritorialization that develop new urban meanings for young *tijuanenses*. These acts do not only happen in the actual taking over of physical sites like the Jai Alai building or Las Pulgas, they also occur in everyday urban practices that contest a variety of discourses about specific areas of the city as markers of class and ethnicity for its citizens. Acts of cultural reterritorialization may translate into discursive actions as much as direct-action events do.

"Beers for 5 Bucks and Girls for 20": Race, Class, and the "Immoral Promenade" in Tijuana

A sequence of synthesized sounds playing in counterpoint against a crude, unprocessed sample of *banda* music opens "Paseo moral [Moral Promenade]," one of Clorofila's most cryptic titles and intriguing tracks. Here, the style of Clorofila's music, with its juxtaposition of recognizable *banda* samples and synthesized loops, is obscured by the clapping and whistling of a cheerful audience and an MC stating "*Pareces pollito que necesita maíz, cabrón* [You look like a little chicken that needs corn, dude]" and "*El amor es tan largo y la vida es tan corta* [Love is so long and life is so short]." Its strange title, the unusually long *banda* sample used as the basic motivic loop, and the extended sections of spoken dialogue (certainly odd for a piece of dance music) make "Paseo moral" into a rarity among Nortec tracks. Indeed, "Paseo moral" is more than a regular dance piece, it is a musical commentary on the leisure activities of the *culturosos*, the group of middle-class visual artists, poets, writers, and cultural entrepreneurs who supported the activities of the Nortec Collective from the very beginning.[15] Rafa Saavedra explains that this group of friends gets together every weekend to party the night away:

Nights of electrolux at Centro Bar, [nights of] drunkenness that start at El Turístico and end in the classic *paseo inmoral* [immoral promenade]. From the Espop to the Voodo House to 80s nostalgia at the Porkys. From visiting Cervecería Tijuana to dancing at La Estrella, from our ephemeral pass through the Avalon to our assiduous presence at El Zacazonapan. . . . Pure perdition pals.[16]

The lively exchanges between the MC and the audience and the distinctly *banda* sound in Clorofila's "Paseo moral," typical of clubs like La Estrella, are an attempt to recreate their atmosphere. However, the modernist techniques of computer manipulation, electronic musical organization, and minimalist repetition of the looped *banda* fragment transform this atmosphere into a new and almost surreal experience. "Paseo moral" is a simulacrum; it is the sound of the re-signification that takes place when the *culturosos* appropriate these bars through their weekly *paseo inmoral*. The shift from *paseo inmoral* to "Paseo moral" in Clorofila's track not only reflects the imaginary recreation of spaces that takes place in the urban experience of middle-class *tijuanenses,* it also articulates important ideas about the relationships among class and ethnicity and taboo, permissibility, morality, and immorality that permeate the traditional symbolization of urban spaces in Tijuana.

While the bars, clubs, and discotheques located on Avenida Revolución have been traditionally associated with U.S. tourism, and thus symbolically signified from the outside as part of Tijuana's "black legend," the places visited by Tijuana's *culturosos* tend not to be located on *La Revu* but a few blocks away from the infamous avenue, and they respond to a different, more local discourse of representation. Sergio Brown (VJ CBrown) states:

You may notice that all the bars we frequent are on the periphery of *La Revu*. It is quite *saico* [psychotic] because all of these little bars, El Dandy del Sur, La Estrella, although relatively near *La Revu*, are sort of alternative; *gringos* won't come here because *La Revu* is a very vertical thing and [when they visit Tijuana] they just walk up and down that street. We have practiced our own thing in these places and they are part of our history.[17]

If the bars and clubs on Avenida Revolución have been traditionally symbolized as immoral by the same U.S. mythology that makes Tijuana into the embodiment of evil otherness, the bars and clubs that form part of the *culturosos*' promenade have been characterized as immoral by discourses that respond to local ethnic and social class frictions. For the upper and upper-middle classes of Tijuana, the bars in the Zona Centro, with their *ficheras*,[18] prostitutes, working-class customers, and even "deviant" sexual practices (as in the case of Kin-Klé's predominantly homosexual and transsexual clientele) represent the prohibited sites of the other.

In Tijuana, as in many parts of the north of Mexico, discourses on racial difference are often disguised as part of larger discourses of class and social difference. Here, the elites tend to either be white or aspire to whiteness, and such desire is evident in the othering of the *mestizo* immigrants from southern Mexico and the local working class.[19] The ascription of morality and immorality and the delimitation of the permissible and the forbidden in downtown Tijuana are all processes that outline a strategy of discursive class—and, ultimately, ethnic and racial—differentiation. Writing the places frequented by these working-class individuals as immoral is a powerful tool to keep traditional social hierarchies beyond the official pro-immigration discourses for which Tijuana is famous (*Tijuana, una ciudad que nos abraza a todos* [Tijuana, a city that embraces us all]).[20] Tellingly, the upper classes' traditional representation of the local other as "immoral by association"—due to their preference for immoral places—borrows the mechanisms of racial, ethnic, and national differentiation that American discourses have used to write Tijuana as the other. The irony of such a strategy shows that, contrary to American representations of Tijuana as a homogeneous other, a complex web of power relations informs social, ethnic, and racial relations at a local level. As a result of these local discourses of differentiation, a significant urban area in downtown Tijuana is written as immoral and forbidden. The *culturosos'* weekly promenade throughout this area is a social *relajo* that represents a carnivalesque subversion of the discourses that write it as immoral. In fact, calling their weekly escapade a *paseo inmoral* is a deliberate irony that makes fun of the codes of morality that inform these sites with social meaning for Tijuana's upper classes. In this context, Clorofila's Nor-tec transformation of this promenade into "Paseo moral" is indeed a way to register the ephemeral reversal of codes of morality and permissibility that takes place in the *culturosos'* experience of these urban spaces.

Clorofila's "Paseo moral" is not the only Nor-tec track that offers a musical chronicle of such reterritorialization; this collective experience is also celebrated in Plankton Man's "Nordic Beat" and "4 Zeenaloas." Throughout these two tracks, as Clorofila does in "Paseo moral," Plankton Man inserts samples of an MC and *banda* music recorded live through an entire night at a local club. The result is a campy collage where the fragmented sounds, recomposed, rearranged, and reorganized according to the beats and grooves of EDM, give life to a bizarre environment where imaginary cumbia and *quebradita* dancers are replaced by wild house and techno fans.

The momentary character of the process of symbolic reterritorialization that takes place in the *paseo inmoral* resonates with Hiperboreal's anxiety of ephemerality regarding the slow disappearance and transformation of specific urban spaces in Tijuana. In both cases, the reterritorialization and re-signification of sites occur quickly and are temporary. Hiperboreal's project to photograph the bars where the concept of Nor-tec was shaped "before they disappear," Clorofila's musical celebration of the *culturosos'* transient urban appropriation through the *paseo inmoral,* and Plankton Man's kitschy reconfiguration of one of these bars into a modernist event are attempts to preserve the memory of these re-significations. Such desire also informs the continuous obsession of several members of the Nortec Collective with these clubs and bars. It is no coincidence that a large number of Nor-tec tracks are named after existing or long-gone legendary bars, clubs, and dance halls. Fussible's "Bar Infierno," Bostich's "Unicornio," and Hiperboreal's "Kin-Klé futurista" are a few examples of this. Every one of these tracks pays homage to lower-class bars in Tijuana's Zona Centro where, according to Pepe Mogt, "you could get beers for 5 bucks and girls for 20."[21]

Kin-Klé was a gay and transexual bar in a marginal area of the Zona Centro; located a few blocks away from *La Coahuila* and effectively hidden from most American tourists, the bar remained a refuge for lower-class homosexuals from Tijuana until it was closed in 2004. Clearly, electronic music targets a different social class than the usual clientele of bars like Kin-Klé, and such a contradiction is articulated in the sonic reappropriation performed by Nor-tec music. This opposition is more evident in Fussible's "Bar Infierno" since, in order to fully grasp the symbolic implications of the title's meaning, the listener does not only need to be well acquainted with Tijuana's working-class bar scene, but also with the history of electronic and U.S. dance music. First released in 1976, the Trammps' *Disco Inferno,* an LP which included a hit track by that title, is considered a classic of the 1970s U.S. disco scene. Thus, by referring to both the local bar and the international disco track, Fussible's "Bar Infierno" deliberately articulates two contrasting scenes: on the one hand, the *ficheras* who, "for 20 bucks," would dance cumbias with you at the Infierno; on the other hand, the upper-middle- and high-class dance scenes that developed in Mexico after the appropriation of American disco music in the 1970s. The house style of Fussible's "Bar Infierno," itself an outgrowth of disco music, is a witness to the conceptual reterritorialization that takes place in this music.[22] In the driving bass line, repetitive melody, and graceful harmonies of Fussible's music, the working-class Infierno becomes an upper-middle-class disco club much in the same way that the *culturosos' paseo inmoral* resymbolizes the clubs they visit.

Arguably, there is no better track to analyze the complex relationships among morality, immorality, representation, myth, and the continuous processes of reterritorialization that inform Tijuana's urban spaces than Bostich's "Unicornio." Unicornio was a club whose main clientele, as most

Figure 4.7 Kin-Klé bar on the margins of Tijuana's downtown. Photo by the author

businesses located on *La Revu,* were U.S. tourists. In 1979, the club appeared in *La ilegal,* a popular movie that told the story of a woman (played by Mexican soap opera star Lucía Méndez) who, on her way to illegally sneak into the United States, goes through the immigrant's clichéd "Tijuana rite of passage," where the city represents the first stop in a downward spiral of degradation that ends only when the immigrant decides to return to Mexico.[23] Although the club does not appear in the film for more than five minutes, it does play a crucial role in confronting Méndez's character, a naïve Mexican woman, with the "corrupt" life of the U.S.–Mexico border. After this movie, the Unicornio became Lucía Méndez's bar in the memory of a whole generation of *tijuanenses*. Thus, the Unicornio was discursively transformed from a location of immorality in the U.S. construction of otherness (as a place of excess for U.S. tourists and visitors) to a location of local immorality where the southern immigrant is made into the other. At the same time, the Unicornio's representation as a major step in the mechanism of corruption that destroys the "integrity" and "candor" of the young Mexican woman played by Méndez, speaks about the anxiety experienced by the center of Mexico when dealing with the margins of the nation-state.

Indeed, the transformation of virtuosic *tarola* rolls into mushy modernist sounds through a vocoder and the presence of what seems to be the quotation of an unprocessed *banda* sample in Bostich's "Unicornio" work as clever metaphors for the continuous processes of re-signification that make the bar meaningful for contemporary *tijuanenses*. In reality, the seemingly unprocessed *banda* sample is actually a "virtual *banda*" made by Bostich in his computer through the juxtaposition of different fragments of brass, accordion, percussion, and vocal samples. Here, Bostich's music

Figure 4.8   Unicornio club on Tijuana's Avenida Revolución. Photo by the author

could be interpreted as a commentary on the way in which the Unicornio
has been resymbolized by a series of discursive exercises that claim validity
through their rearticulation of discourses of immorality and place in Tijuana. As a result of these processes, the discourse of immorality is no
longer authentic but a mirage which is fragmented and resymbolized by
everyday practices of the city and its urban spaces, of which the *culturosos'*
paseo inmoral is a perfect example.

The Sounds of Nor-tec's Reterritorialization

If Clorofila's "Paseo moral" and Plankton Man's "Nordic Beat" and "4
Zeenaloas" are musical records of the type of reterritorialization that
occurs in practices such as the *culturosos' paseo inmoral,* and if Bostich's
"Unicornio" works as a metaphor for the complexities and inconsistencies
that inform the development of discourses of representation in the city, we
could attempt an interpretation of Nor-tec musical style as a reterritorialization of stereotypes about Tijuana. Hiperboreal's "Tijuana for Dummies"
is a good example of such an attempt to reterritorialize the city and its
physical and virtual spaces. Hiperboreal's music is a hallucinating aural
mirage, the result of a polyrhythm created by the superimposition of loops
accentuating different parts of the measure, welcoming the listener into a
musical landscape that seems familiar initially, but soon confuses the listener's rhythmic expectations. The absence of a prominent downbeat during the first eight measures of the piece forces the listener to cognitively
interpret that rhythmic sequence of bongos and cowbell in order to find
rhythmic stability throughout the section. The presence of a prominently
loud attack on the high bongo guides the listener to take it as the downbeat

Example 4.1   Hiperboreal, "Tijuana for Dummies," beginning section, first
rhythmic interpretation

Example 4.2   "Tijuana for Dummies," beginning section, second rhythmic interpretation

and to interpret the cowbell timeline as an off-the-beat event (a rhythmic feature typical in most *norteña* music). The rhythmic imprecision of the triplet in the melody of the synthesizer only adds an extra element of uncertainty to the passage (example 4.1).

However, the entrance of a clear cumbia rhythmic pattern played by the *güiro*, as well as a new rhythmic emphasis provided by the congas in measure 9, reverse our rhythmic interpretation of the introductory passage. In fact, the high bongo plays on an offbeat while the cowbell simply marks the beat. These new elements force us to reinterpret completely the opening eight measures of the piece (example 4.2). Therefore, the text at the beginning of the piece ("This is Tijuana . . . coming") does not intend anything but to point out that our expectations of Tijuana will not be fulfilled because the city is not what we presume it to be.

The deceptive character of Tijuana is also apparent in the disorienting first version of Panóptica's "And L." Panóptica's track first appeared in *Nor-tec Sampler* (1999) and later, in a revised and remixed version, in *The Tijuana Sessions, Vol. 1* (2001). There are significant differences between the two versions. The first version is rougher and presents a few elements of noise that most producers would try to get rid of, while the second one, prepared for Palm Pictures' commercial CD, is shorter, cleaner, and avoids many of the technical haziness that made the first version unique—and much better, in my opinion. In a few words, the track released on the commercial recording was a domesticated version of the more poignant and challenging track independently released earlier. Curiously, it is in the material extirpated from *The Tijuana Sessions, Vol. 1,* in the noises that were cleaned out of that version of "And L" that the most interesting challenges to the predictability of traditional electronica styles surface. The track opens with a typical techno convention, a straightforward, looped rhythmic pattern of synthesized sounds in a 4/4 measure at 124 bpm. As in "Tijuana for Dummies," the absence of a clear downbeat forces the listener to hear the first two sounds as an upbeat leading to the beginning of the next measure. The entrance of a vocoder loop at a slower tempo (approximately 93 bpm, although the high level of reverberation keeps the listener from clearly identifying the beat or even the grouping) in measure 5 only makes the rhythmic quality of the piece more unstable. Ironically, it is with the entrance of a series of background noises grouped in a loop at 93 bpm (a loop that, by moving at a different speed, clearly upsets the metric flow of the first loop) that the rhythmic quality of that first loop is clarified.

Unsurprisingly, the polytempo created by the superimposition of loops moving at different speeds generates disorientation in the listener. Nevertheless, Panóptica succeeds in synchronizing the downbeats by grouping each rhythmic pattern in a different metric signature: the beginning of every 4/4 measure at 124 bpm coincides with the beginning of every 3/4 measure at 93 bpm (example 4.3).[24] This all takes place during the first minute of the track, creating a sense of metric and rhythmic instability far greater than the one experienced in Hiperboreal's "Tijuana for Dummies" and quite uncommon for EDM—whose main concern is to clearly establish a beat for dancers to start moving.

The musical ambiguities in "And L" were so strong that the track was considered unfit for commercial distribution and was completely restructured for its release in *The Tijuana Sessions, Vol. 1.* The background noises were entirely eliminated from the track, and any trace of rhythmic uncertainty was erased by refiltering the vocoder line (thus, eliminating the excessive reverb that disturbed the understanding of the rhythmic pattern) and by making it fit the 4/4 rhythmic flow of the main rhythmic loop played by the synthesizer. This exercise of "normalization" performed on Panóptica's track in order to make it appealing to the U.S. mainstream media—it literally made it fit the norm of more conventional EDM—shows the anxiety that deviations and challenges to formulaic structures and clichéd views produces in the music industry.

"Tijuana Bass" [🔊 **Track 7**] is one of the most representative tracks of Bostich's rough and uncompromising Nor-tec style. The title of Bostich's piece is in itself a local reevaluation of the infamous Tijuana Brass, one of

Example 4.3 Polytemporal
layering in Panóptica's "And L"

the most influential bands in creating a musical stereotype of Tijuana for U.S. audiences. If Herb Alpert and the Tijuana Brass were fundamental in creating an association between the name of Tijuana and the sound of the trumpet, Bostich's playful paraphrase seems to announce "Tijuana Bass" as a musical reinterpretation that confronts the stereotype by acknowledging it first and dearticulating it later. "Tijuana Bass" is indeed brass music, but one of sharp and angular contours; it is a piece that deceives the ear, the expectations, and thus the stereotypes of Tijuana at every musical corner. Catchy trumpet melodies over driving hand clapping, snare drumming, and conga rhythms lead the listener toward awkward moments of harmonic travesty: our ears inform us we are in no man's land, a musical space that can be identified neither harmonically nor melodically.

The music starts with a trumpet phrase repeating over an up-beat that is accentuated by clapping hands. The melodic sequence is a three-note chromatic motif that emphasizes A as a tonal center through duration, melodic stress, direction, and the surrounding context (the G sharp seems to play the role of a leading tone; see example 4.4). However, the entrance of the tuba in measure 4, playing a G natural instead of the expected A, forces us to reevaluate the melodic context and our imaginary harmonic framework. Indeed, the G natural that appears only briefly at the beginning of the melodic gesture is what controls the harmonic structure of the composition (example 4.5). Another loud tuba playing the typical accompaniment pattern of a cumbia on a G major triad emphasizes it as a harmonic

Example 4.4 Bostich, "Tijuana Bass," beginning melodic sequence

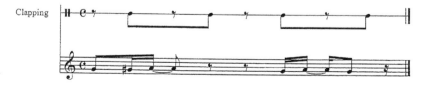

Example 4.5 "Tijuana Bass," beginning melodic sequence with added bass

center. At last, we seem to be certain of our place in the music; however, the entrance of the main melodic motif in G minor a few measures later proves that we should not take our sonic surroundings for granted, especially at the climax of the piece, when Bostich combines the G major tuba bass line with the G minor trumpet melody (example 4.6).

Tijuana, like the melodic, harmonic, and polymodal practices of Bostich and the disorienting polytempos and polyrhythms of Panóptica and Hiperboreal, betrays our eye and our ear. For this reason, in these musicians' tracks we find synthesizers and vocoders when we expect accordions, and *chirimías* (hornpipes or whistles of indigenous origin virtually recreated by Bostich from samples of a jazz flute player for the end of "Tijuana Bass") when we anticipate tubas; the human voice is processed and manipulated to the point of making words and texts, the elements that give it its human character, impossible to recognize. This music works as a metaphor that shows that Tijuana cannot be understood through the representations that stereotype it; Tijuana should be understood through the mirage of modernity that it creates in those who try to write it as marginal. There is no Tijuana; Tijuana is what is coming, a city that lives in the imagination, where it establishes its modernity and its future. Nor-tec is a virtuality that, paraphrasing Barbara Kirshenblatt-Gimblett, rewrites Tijuana, its traditions, and its stereotypes according to current experiences in order to validate the present.[25]

Example 4.6 "Tijuana Bass," bimodal sequence

Tijuana through After Effects

Hiperboreal, Panóptica, and Bostich's musical reterritorializations, Clorofila and Plankton Man's musical metaphors of the *culturosos*' ephemeral resymbolization of "immoral" spaces, and Hiperboreal's desire to preserve the memory of locales and spaces as historical archives that register the dents Nor-tec gives to hegemonic culture in Tijuana are all also reflected in the work of the visual artists that belong to the collective. The visual artists' work is also an attempt to re-signify the city spaces they frequent in their everyday lives. Curiously, it was at the Nortec City party, the event where the collective appropriated one of the most unequivocal symbols of the mythical, "forbidden" Tijuana (the Jai Alai building), that the visuals of Sergio Brown (VJ CBrown), Octavio Castellanos (VJ TCR), Iván Díaz Robledo (VJ Wero Palma, also known as VJ Piniaman), José Luis Martín (VJ Mashaka), and Salvador Vázquez Ricalde (VJ Sal) joined the sounds of Bostich, Panóptica, Fussible, Clorofila, Hiperboreal, Terrestre, and Plankton Man and consciously reclaimed the city, its spaces, and its images as the collective's own.[26]

During my fieldwork in Tijuana, I met VJ CBrown, VJ TCR, VJ Wero Palma, VJ Mashaka, and VJ Sal many times on both sides of the San Diego–Tijuana border. CBrown and TCR have been professors of graphic design and literature at the Universidad Iberoamericana and the Universidad Autónoma de Baja California (UABC), while VJ Mashaka is pursuing a degree in communications. VJ Wero Palma is a former punk singer with a degree in communications, and VJ Sal is a filmmaker and promoter, the founder of Tijuana's independent film festival, IAF. This group of friends had collaborated in several school and independent projects, and Mashaka, Wero Palma, and Sal had already mixed live images in music concerts before joining the Nortec Collective. Our conversations' points of departure were the principles taken by these video artists to visually translate the musical aesthetic of Nor-tec and the role of these visuals in the collective's live performance. By the time the Nor-tec boom hit the local scene, these video artists had all participated in different collective projects that reflected on the cultural significance of popular urban spaces in Tijuana. Their collection of visual material was large, ranging from videos and images of bars, dance halls, and buildings in downtown Tijuana, including urban stereotypes of the city, such as *La mona* and *el bordo,* to videos of local *quinceañera* parties and street musicians and prostitutes walking up and down *La Coahuila* in search of possible clients.[27] When asked to collaborate with the collective, these video artists returned to their archives of images with the idea of transforming and re-signifying them through computer manipulation in an attempt to visually articulate modernity and tradition in a manner similar to the ideal of Nor-tec music. Thus, through the use of computer software like After Effects, Photoshop, Illustrator, and Free Hand, the images of Tijuana were filtered, distorted, vectorized, flattened, and fragmented into unrecognizable subjects to be freely rearranged in the live visual mix of a Nor-tec performance. Thus, street *banda* or *norteña* musicians were reduced to their attire or their more iconic characteristics—the hat, the accordion, the *tololoche* (double bass), the boots, the tuba, the trumpet—and these in turn were made into bright objects of luminescent modernity through digital manipulation and their organization into visual loops that move in sync with the music. In these sequences, the fragile houses in the dells that surround Tijuana and the graffiti that embellish the edges of the buildings' roofs in downtown are transformed into complex, hallucinating constructions and hypermodern figures: Tijuana's desire for modernity embodied in Nor-tec.

CBrown gives the visual Nor-tec crusade a clearly avant-garde twist in his unabashed attempt to place the margins of Tijuana in the center stage of the Nor-tec visual experience. CBrown and I meet at El Tiburón, a bar located in front of the Jai Alai building, a few steps from *La Revu*. There, with the musical background of Ricardo Arjona and Marco Antonio Solís loudly coming out of a CD player, CBrown tells me all about his collaboration with the collective at the Nortec City party. He states that the city is the true star in the hypnotic visual loops of Nor-tec. He is aware that most Nor-tec party attendees belong to a social class that makes them foreigners to some of the poorest neighborhoods and areas of the city (places they do not visit in their everyday use of the city), and therefore he decided to use this opportunity to confront them with that "invisible" Tijuana:

> Our first idea was about the [urban] itineraries of the people who attend our parties. These are *güeyes* [guys] who come down from *La Chapu* [Chapultepec neighborhood] to Lomas de Aguacaliente, go through the Zona Río and then to *el otro lado* [the other side, the United States]. So, what we wanted to do was to show images of the city . . . but show the city that *esa raza* [those people] never see. Just for them to look at it, not for them to go to a [political] rally or make the Hipódromo or Mariscos Vallarta into sacred zones. Simply, we wanted those *morros* [kids] to look at *la 5 y 10*. Upper-middle-class people never go through *la 5 y 10* because the city is planned in such a way that every exit into San Diego is close to the high-class neighborhoods. [They drive] from the Zona Río's channel to San Diego and that's it.[28]

To this end, during Nortec City, CBrown projected a one-hour-long unedited shot of *la 5 y 10* on a giant screen behind the musicians on stage.[29]

As cultural theorist Michel de Certeau argued, the city is a space that is conditioned by those who live in it but also one that conditions the subjectivities of those individuals who transit it.[30] Among other factors, class determines the paths, trajectories, and individuals' means of transportation; therefore, different social classes experience and signify the city in different ways. Social class transforms those spaces and, at the same time, once culturally signified, those spaces help in the reproduction of the social, cultural, and economic circumstances that make them meaningful. In Tijuana, going from the residential area of Lomas de Aguacaliente to the executive offices in Pueblo Amigo implies a middle- and high-class practice of the city that is completely different from sorting out urban buses and taxis at *la 5 y 10*. The different landscapes, the individuals who populate them, and their ways of transiting them reinforce notions of class and even ethnicity that give meaning to the city and its people. This is why CBrown's images were a confrontation, because they put the marginal *5 y 10* in the international spotlight of the Nortec City party. This strategy forced those who, by their use of public spaces in Tijuana, have to or choose to avoid *la 5 y 10* into contact with a reality they refuse to see, into contact with the contradictions of their society, which, as such, intends to trigger a process that reimagines Tijuana and *tijuanenses*.

Objects in Video Are Closer Than They Appear

I walk up and down *La Revu* looking for a way to get to Playas de Tijuana, a middle-class neighborhood located in the northwestern edge of the city, on the beach, right at *el bordo*, the fence that separates the United States and Mexico. Following the advice of a man selling *tacos varios* on the street, I take a Centro-Playas taxi. The experience is fascinating as it confronts one of the most recurring stereotypes of Tijuana, the U.S.–Mexico border as "nobody's land." In fact, this neighborhood is far from being "nobody's land." It is a vibrant area where people come to enjoy the best *marlín* (swordfish) tacos in town (according to Hiperboreal) at La Terraza Vallarta—arguably the first (or last?) restaurant of Latin America, as it is located on the beach, a mere 50 meters from *el bordo*—after spending the afternoon at a bullfight in the nearby Plaza de Toros Rodolfo Gaona. Here, the myth about the border is clearly rearticulated in the people's practice and consumption of urban spaces. The young U.S. tourists who play on the beach and drink *aguas frescas* at La Flor de Michoacán, the scholars and students who work at or attend El Colegio de la Frontera Norte or the Universidad Iberoamericana and take walks along Del Pacífico street in the afternoons, and the *norteño* and *banda* musicians playing inside the many restaurants are all practices of consumption and reterritorialization that certainly dearticulate the most recurring myths about the vicious border. The same trip from Tijuana's downtown to Playas de Tijuana I have just

made is the idea behind Ángeles Moreno's video for Fussible's "Odyssea,"
another example of the Nor-tec visual artists' interest in re-signifying Tijuana through a new representation of its people, their practice of the city,
and the city itself.

Ángeles Moreno is a graphic designer from Mexico City, who moved
to Tijuana in 1998. In 1999, upon an invitation from Fritz Torres (from
Clorofila and Cha3), Moreno joined the efforts of a group of designers
interested in putting together the first exhibition of Nor-tec images as part
of an AIGA Baja conference in Ensenada.[31] The result was a long-lasting
collaboration between her and the Nortec Collective which is visible not
only in the collective's and Fussible's official Web sites but also in several
promotional flyers, CD covers (for *Odyssea* and *No One over 21*), and most
noticeably in Fussible's video for "Odyssea" [◉ **Video 3**].[32] Moreno's collaboration with Fussible and Sonic 360 in the *Odyssea* project started when
Pepe Mogt invited her to design the cover of the CD. Mogt wanted Moreno
to use the same idea she had used for the flyer of the first Toyland event
(where Fussible was featured as the main act).[33] There, Moreno had used
the image of a bus arriving at the U.S.–Mexico border with a background
fence, everything in mustard and white colors. Mogt's only request was to
change the bus into a taxi. This conceptual change would also serve as the
basis for the video of "Odyssea." Moreno recalls the invitation:

> Pepe Mogt invited me to design the cover and asked me to change the bus
> for a taxi. The "Tijuana taxi" (which Herb Alpert immortalized in his
> song) is an urban element typical of this border area. It is the city's public
> transportation system with predetermined routes. The colors were already
> there in the original design [the flyer] and they coincided with the colors
> of the taxi route to Playas de Tijuana, where Fussible has a studio, and an
> area I was very familiar with because when I lived in Tijuana I took that
> route very often. So, it was relatively easy to graphically reproduce a "vir-
> tual" trip [in the video].[34]

For the video, Moreno chose to take the Centro–Playas de Tijuana ride
as a structural skeleton upon which to introduce a wide variety of local
elements that "were already there and were obvious to my eyes as a southerner"[35] and make them all into characters in a cartoon animation. In a
way, the video works just like techno music itself, as Carol Vernallis describes the genre, "bringing elements in and out of a relatively stable mix
without establishing sharp sectional divisions."[36] Throughout the trip,
Moreno inserts a variety of stereotypical images of Tijuana (donkeys painted
as zebras, the border fence, *migra* helicopters, immigrants waiting to be
smuggled into the United States, and even DJ Tolo, the tireless Tijuana electronic music promoter, who actually mixed the track for the video, as an
unsuspecting taxi passenger) and alternates them with images of turntables,

tarola and tuba players, *norteño* musicians, imagined radio transmissions, and VCOs and synthesizers. Thus, in Moreno's work, these deteriorated taxis become characters worthy of a sci-fi *manga* (Japanese comic), proposing a new imaginary notion of Tijuana's public transportation, reevaluating the experience of traveling through the city, and metaphorically confirming Raúl Cárdenas's statement in Hans Fjellestad's documentary *Frontier Life* (2002): "Tijuana has more to do with science fiction novels than really with history books of Mexico."[37]

Fussible and Moreno's "Odyssea" ignores several music video conventions. The video has a very precise location, follows a clear narrative format, and has no place for the glorification of the music star. Many of these characteristics could be connected to the fact that Fussible's track has no lyrics, and therefore the images in the video could attempt to convey a description without the worry of overshadowing the song's story. In other words, the narrative of the images does not contradict a possible musical narrative; if anything, it sometimes punctuates some musical gestures (by using an animated *norteño tarola* player) or clarifies what the sounds in the music track represent (such as making clear that the repetitive high-pitched sound heard throughout the track actually represents a car horn). As mentioned, an important feature of the video is Tijuana as a precise action locus. As opposed to most mainstream videos, where location is left open for the listener's fantasy and imagination to construct, in "Odyssea" there is no question that the action takes place in Tijuana, a detail that is made even more evident by showing the taxi moving over an animated map of the city. Clearly, the main character in the video is the city, not Fussible or even DJ Tolo, the author of the mix. In fact, the brief appearance of a sketched Tolo inside the taxi (almost unidentifiable, in a Hitchcockian gesture) might be read as an ironic commentary on mainstream music video practices that emphasize the musician over the music. The video also articulates typical bicultural border-town practices that might be considered bizarre by outsiders, such as the common use of both U.S. and Mexican currency to conduct everyday economic transactions (observed in the customer who pays for his taxi ride with a dollar bill and receives change in U.S. quarters and Mexican pesos). Thus, the bulk of the story being told by Fussible and Moreno is the reterritorialization of the city and, particularly, of stereotypes like the Tijuana taxi, *el bordo*, tourist attractions, the running-family signs (reflected in the taxi's mirror) that inform drivers of the possibility of running illegals crossing the highway in their attempt to enter into the United States, and unique borderland cultural practices. In their animated version, Tijuana's stereotypes are acknowledged and rearticulated as colorful events that tint the everyday urban practices of *tijuanenses;* thus, they stop being the unique property of those who want to exoticize the city and become tools in a complex yet kitschy strategy to empower local individuals.

The reterritorialization of real or symbolic, virtual or actual spaces is a fundamental notion in the design of the images that accompany Nor-tec music both in actual live performances and as marketing aides. Another example of such re-signification is Wero Palma's controversial video for Hiperboreal's "Tijuana for Dummies." [● Video 1] The story of reterritorialization being told in Wero Palma's video is far more radical and politically charged than that of Fussible and Moreno's "Odyssea." As I mentioned earlier, the only lyrics in Hiperboreal's "Tijuana for Dummies" state: "This is Tijuana . . . coming." If the rhythmic ambiguities of the song already defy stereotypical assumptions of what the city might be, Wero Palma's video is a response to Hiperboreal's challenge, which results in a harsh critique aimed at the city's social inequalities and the corruption of local judicial and political institutions.

Wero Palma's "Tijuana for Dummies" shows two parallel surreal stories. The first tells the story of a sensual, young, blonde, well-dressed woman (throughout the video, the camera often runs up and down her body, focusing on her legs, buttocks, and breasts) who wakes up on a dump being harassed by a homeless man. After taking a walk around the neighborhood (we get to see the infamous *La mona* in the background), she walks toward a car and tries to sell the driver some chewing gum; the driver refuses to buy any, and she reacts by throwing the gum in his face. Next, we see the girl trying to shoplift some sweet bread from a street vendor. She is caught in the act and tries to run away from two cops who act like dogs—these are actually dogs/policemen who look human and are dressed like policemen but sit, run, and generally behave like dogs—who chase her down a street and finally stop when she enters a meat market, gets some meat, and throws it at them. The woman is finally left alone and is seen walking down the sidewalk, leaving the scene. The second story is that of a middle-aged, upper-middle-class woman (although she wears cheap clothes), who is awakened by her maid. The maid brings her breakfast in the bedroom, but when the woman realizes the meal consists only of pills, she violently pushes the maid and throws the food on the floor. Immediately after, she is seen walking down the street and encountering a variety of individuals: first, a man carrying a mirror; second, a woman reading the news while sitting on a toilet; third, two men wearing black suits, hats, and sunglasses and holding a banner. One of the guys shows the woman a bowl full of blue stones; she gets scared and proceeds to push them away but ends up falling on top of another pedestrian. The pedestrian turns out to be a hitman who, after climbing to the top of a house, starts shooting pedestrians on the street below. Injured people start falling along the woman's path; she does not seem to pay attention nor to be upset by the situation. The last person to be shot carries the *Zeta*, a local newspaper, whose headline reads "La mafia pollera [The Smugglers' Mafia]."[38] In the final sequence, the hitman aims at the woman and also shoots her.

With the exception of the dogs/cops, the men in black, and the hitman, all of the characters who appear in both stories are always blindfolded. The two stories are intertwined; the action keeps moving back and forth from the story of the young woman to that of the middle-aged woman. There are clear parallels between the two stories: both women seem to be taken out of their context (the young one dressed as a higher-middle-class woman but living almost homelessly in a low-class neighborhood, the older one dressed as a low-class woman but living in a high-class environment), they both encounter two individuals from whom they want to escape (the dogs/cops and the men in black); and everyone they come across (blindfolded) is unaware of the bizarre contradictions that surround their lives. By presenting all of the characters blindfolded with the exception of those who ultimately assault the main characters, the music video launches an attack against a society that would rather live ignorant of the events and contradictions that surround it as long as its citizens' privileges remain intact.

The mirror is a particularly important symbol throughout Wero Palma's surrealist video. The young blonde woman carries a mirror around and looks at herself whenever possible, and the middle-aged woman is confronted with a mirror as soon as she gets to the street. In fact, the very last image of the video shows the blonde woman looking at a mirror and seeing the reflection of a *norteño* musician playing the accordion. Wero Palma states that, like CBrown's shot of *la 5 y 10* at the Nortec City party, his purpose was to confront *tijuanenses* with the contradictions of their society: "everything is contradictory in the video, the beautiful young woman wearing an expensive dress who lives in a dump and has to sell chewing gum on the streets for a living, or the indifference towards the killings going on around you."[39] If the mirror works as an instrument that, in a Lacanian sense, allows the identification of the self, it also allows people to keep up appearances, disguise the self, and perform a simulacrum. In "Tijuana for Dummies," the mirror certainly plays those roles and also allows the viewer to keep track of the unlikely elements that could transform the makeup of such re-signification. The continuous reflection of *norteño* musicians in the mirrors acknowledges the existence of those elements whose everyday presence makes them invisible to the eyes of the local, the elements that "were already there and were obvious" to the eyes of an outsider like Ángeles Moreno but remain invisible to those who, metaphorically blindfolded, are insensible to their presence in the city. Thus, the mirrors in the music video work as instruments that make the local other visible and trigger its re-signification by allowing it to be part of the larger processes of identity construction that the mirrors themselves symbolize: traditional *norteño* culture, largely overlooked and neglected by young middle- and upper-class *tijuanenses* who watch the video or attend the Nor-tec party, as an ingredient for the construction of their own identity.

Furthermore, Wero Palma's video offers a unique example of Nor-tec's articulation of Tijuana's politics. By portraying policemen as dogs, the video artist not only voices a general concern among *tijuanenses* (and Mexicans in general) about the corruption that pervades that institution, but also re-signifies cops in agreement with the opinion that citizens have of them. Such an act did not go unnoticed by the right-wing government that ruled the city for several years—before it lost the city election to the former official party, PRI, in 2004. In fact, echoing the continuous acts of censorship that characterized PAN administrations throughout the country in the late 1990s and early 2000s, the city police arrested Wero Palma and his crew while they were filming the video, accusing them of mocking the authority of the city police force. The publicity generated by that event allowed the video to be largely read as a critique of corrupt government practices and made its director into a celebrity among intellectual circles in Tijuana.[40] Indeed, the detention of Wero Palma and his crew offers an insight into the anxiety that an act that appropriates the representation of a public institution creates in the very members of those institutions.

Just as the mirrors that appear in "Odyssea" and "Tijuana for Dummies" work as tools for the identification of the other and allow for its final articulation in the recognition of the self, the videos offer themselves as mirrors in which the kitschiness—"things that were already there and were obvious to my eyes as a southerner"—of such articulations is recognized. Once again, the Nor-tec aesthetic recognizes the stereotypes about Tijuana and articulates them in an attempt to reconfigure local identity in relation to both the modernity and cosmopolitanism of globalization (as exemplified in Moreno's modern reconfiguration of the Tijuana taxi) and the political specificities of their local experience (Tijuana's urban spaces and the political concerns that make them meaningful in Wero Palma's video).

"Where's the Donkey Show, Mr. Mariachi?" (Local Remix)

They confirmed to them it was the happiest place on earth. They told them about semi-nude girls walking on the eternal and unending main street. They told them about the vengeful surfer in clubs and cantinas, about the mythic drunkenness with a taste of Blue Hawaiians, Margaritas, Long Islands, Tequila, and Beer. They whispered to their ears the old gringo-

trapping donkey show legend; and they, like good children of
middle-class America—*jar heads, navy guys, white trash in
cutoffs*—believed everything and arrived thrilled in the city
after rehearsing how to order "*one* cerveza."

—Rafa Saavedra

The infamous legend of the donkey show is one of the pervasive myths that
have shaped Tijuana as an object of both desire and vilification for U.S.
tourism.[41] The strategic use of these stereotypes by young *tijuanenses*, especially members of the Nortec Collective, as exemplified in VJ CBrown's
admonition "we have to make the image of [Tijuana the] Killer City ours
and sell it [to the world],"[42] clearly responds to Slavoj Žižek's suggestion
that the quintessential question of desire is not "what do I want?" but rather
"what do others want from me?"[43] Žižek's question is indeed the issue at
stake in Nor-tec's reterritorialization and in its appropriation of sites and
discourses that support the othering of Tijuana and *tijuanense* citizenship.
The Killer City, Sin City, and the donkey show are all myths that inform
the desire of local *tijuanenses* as much as they inform the desire of American consumers. The visual and sonic appropriations of Tijuana's urban
spaces and their stereotypes of otherness that take place in the production
of Nor-tec respond to a strategy where self-identity is informed by the desire one generates in the other. However, the strategy of reterritorialization
at the core of these individuals' incorporation of such stereotypes or in the
ambiguity of their musical styles turns the tables on the workings of the
desiring machine; by adopting, appropriating, and transforming these alienating discourses, local individuals are able to profit from the libidinal economy that places them as exotic or immoral others.

     In the Nor-tec scene, reterritorialization does not only occur in the pro-
duction of sounds and images, it also takes place when *tijuanenses* imagine
themselves in the images and sounds of a reimagined Tijuana (an aesthetic
that resymbolizes discourses of class, race, and ethnic differentiation). Thus,
reterritorialization happens in the performance that allows these fans to
imagine themselves as part of the cosmopolitan imaginary articulated by
the Nor-tec scene. Nevertheless, in Tijuana's culture of ephemerality, reterritorialization works as a simulacrum, an act that reconstitutes reality
through the bits and pieces of memory that make up the myth itself as an
imaginary representation, a process that both projects and negotiates desire. The impermanence of Tijuana's original urban plat, like the discourses
of immorality challenged by the *culturosos* and the virtual *banda* in Bostich's
"Unicornio," shows us that there are no original sources of authenticity
but that the discourse of authenticity itself is a virtuality, a continuously
changing simulacrum, developed to validate the present. As Paul Ricoeur

puts it, we "have the possibility to read and re-read the places of our lives according to our ways to inhabit them."[44]

Tijuana's Nor-tec, like the city itself, built upon the technical models of First World aesthetic creeds, shows the listener that such cultural borrowings do not result in simple acts of imitation. Rather, they are points of departure for local exercises of agency, creativity, and cultural production where "authentic" sources are re-signified in continuous processes of unlimited semiosis. Here, as Michel de Certeau suggests, individuals are able to produce new cultural meaning through their practices of consumption.[45] In such a context, the contestation of hegemonic cultural practices through *relajo,* through the repossession of urban spaces, routes, and stereotypical discourses during collective and individual performances at parties and on weekly promenades, acquires an important role in the symbolic reterritorialization of the city. Thus, Nor-tec is the glocal result of a complex process of productive consumption where musicians and visual artists reterritorialize their tradition according to their desires for cosmopolitanism and modernity, while Nor-tec itself becomes an object to be consumed by fans as part of further acts of reterritorialization that momentarily but powerfully transgress the urban status quo and rearticulate their everyday place in it.

5

Producers, DJs, VJs, Fans, and the Performance of Nor-tec

My first opportunity to interview Pepe Mogt in person is in his house in Playas de Tijuana, a densely populated middle-class *tijuanense* neighborhood right at *el bordo* (the border fence). It is here, in the studio Pepe Mogt keeps in the first floor of his house, that I let the tape roll as he repeats a well-rehearsed speech about the origins of Nor-tec. His is a story I remember reading many times in newspapers, fanzines, and Web sites. Clearly, Pepe knows the speech well and wants to make sure I do not miss any of the information he wants me to remember. However, as I am interested in uncovering new information and finding out what the usual Nor-tec chroniclers have missed, I keep trying to lead Pepe away from his rehearsed answer into new, uncharted territories. Finally, Pepe responds to my insistence on learning whom he thinks defines Nor-tec by emphatically stating that Nor-tec is "nothing but the combination of *norteña* music sounds and electronic music compositional techniques."[1] This and several other answers I got from Nor-tec musicians and visual artists tells me that, for them, the unique character of Nor-tec resides in the production of the music, the graphic art, and the videos. Indeed, in the case of Nor-tec, the production of music and images proposes a unique imaginary that mediates among discourses about tradition and modernity. Nevertheless, it is consumption as a signifying practice that rearticulates and re-signifies Nor-tec beyond the processes of production emphasized by musicians and visual artists alike. Indeed, the meaning of the Nor-tec scene comes out of processes of negotiation between producers and consumers, and those who listen and

147

dance to the Nor-tec beats play a fundamental role in imagining themselves
and their world and, therefore, in defining the Nor-tec scene. As Barry
Shank suggests, "[T]he audience and the musicians together participate in
a nonverbal dialogue about the significance of music and the construction
of their selves."[2] Discourses that focus on production as the main signifying practice in Nor-tec disregard the importance of consumption, especially
through dance and the moving body, and therefore overlook the close relationships among the music, the fans who embrace it, and a wide variety
of international underground dance music scenes. Such a position ignores
the staging and the performance of Nor-tec as fundamental aspects in negotiating the identity of the scene.

This chapter discusses the performance of Nor-tec as an interactive
event and process where role playing is crucial in the staging and construction of multiple identities.[3] It focuses both on performance practice
and on its performative character as social and cultural discourse. First,
taking into account Gerard Béhague's advice for the study of performance,
I examine the musical and extramusical behavior of musicians and audiences, the codes that regulate their performance, and the social interactions
among participants in an attempt to get closer to their meaning.[4] Although
my point of departure is performance practice, my intention is not to merely
describe its performatic aspects but, as I have mentioned, to address its performative character or, as Judith Butler would put it, my intention is to
analyze "the power of discourse to reproduce effects through reiteration."[5]
In other words, in this chapter, I approach Nor-tec performances as the
collective staging of identities that produce the identities being staged. My
interest in performance is not circumscribed to the actual performance
practice of Nor-tec (the parties and events) nor its collective character; I am
also interested in interpreting the development of specific Nor-tec music
styles as effects of performance. Furthermore, I am interested in getting
closer to the meaning of performance for the individuals who participate
in it. Since music works as audiotopia, it is pertinent to consider the musicians' and dancers' actions during a given performance as embodied audiotopias. In Nor-tec, performance is the embodiment of the object of desire.

To Dance or Not to Dance I (Playas de Tijuana Mix)

> people are dancing
> all around me
> the sonic substance is repeating through the air
>
> —Claudia Algara, "Diagonales luminosas en el trópico"

A common paradox faced by many electronic-music producers is how to
reconcile their wish to make intellectually stimulating music with the fans'

request for beats that appeal to the body, music for listening versus music
for dancing.[6] The inception of early Nor-tec, with its ambiguous relation
to the dance floor, made this dilemma a central issue for many musicians in
Tijuana. José Ignacio López (El Lazo Invisible), a Tijuana-based Peruvian
electronic musician who collaborated in some of the earliest Nor-tec
events, clearly states the problem:

> [W]hen the Nor-tec boom began I produced a couple of Nor-tec tracks for
> the dance floor because those were the venues we had access to if we
> wanted to show our work . . . and obviously they requested dance music.
> But I quickly got tired of having to respond to that market, and that's
> when I asked myself the big question: "To dance or not to dance?" I ulti-
> mately decided to move away from the dance floor.[7]

The idea of pure sonic experimentation is fundamental in the mythology of
Nor-tec and in its representation as an alternative, underground endeavor.
As part of this discourse, the musicians acknowledge that many of their
first Nor-tec tracks (for example, Fussible's "Zona N" and "Ventilador,"
Bostich's "Synthakon," Hiperboreal's "Loop eterno," Clorofila's "Huata-
bampo 3 AM") were not particularly good for the dance floor as they were
driven by a desire to experiment with sound instead of pleasing the dancers.
Pepe Mogt remembers:

> [F]ans put pressure on us, I mean good pressure . . . [although] I do not
> want to say that we did it just for the fans because it was also something
> personal, but communicating with the people is always good. Once we
> played for almost 100,000 people in Mexico City, and I was with my
> tracks at 90 beats per minute [bpm] trying to play after a German DJ who
> played at 140 bpm, and all of a sudden the fans went like "Booo!!! What's
> up?!!" So, we had to react to that.[8]

Indeed, as El Lazo Invisible points out, it was the growing presence of an
underground dance scene in Tijuana that provided locations and audiences
for the exposure of the new Nor-tec sound back in 1999. However, the
scene was dominated by *punchis-punchis*, quick-paced electronic music
genres such as trance and drum'n'bass, a fact that, as Pepe Mogt states, was
determinant in the development of the more decidedly dance-floor-oriented
Nor-tec styles.

While musicians like El Lazo Invisible decided to largely withdraw
from the dance scene in response to the fans' pressure to make their music
more bodily appealing, the members of the Nortec Collective chose to
enter a process of negotiation that witnessed the fluidity of the musician-
audience relationship in the construction of musical sites of identification.
Certainly, the consumption of Nor-tec on the dance floor was critical in

shaping the cultural meaning of the overall scene. Melo further explains the process:

> At the beginning [Nor-tec] was experimental, it wasn't really dance music. Besides, before Nor-tec we didn't know how to use the instruments, we didn't know about the dynamics used by the musicians, so we had to learn. We had to go to *tocadas norteñas* [*norteña* music concerts], pay attention, and ask the musicians in order to learn about their instruments. Then we realized that if we wanted to promote the Nor-tec sound we had to play in discotheques. There were no other places to play in. But if you wanted to play in a discotheque you had to play at least at a certain number of bpm's. Thus, it became indispensable to have songs to listen to and songs to dance to. We in Fussible were the first [members of the] Nortec Collective to do that. Otherwise we wouldn't have had venues to play in; we would not have been invited to so many places. We got a lot of shit for that, some even say that Fussible is not Nor-tec. But if we had not done what we did, [the music] would have remained very abstract, and that would have alienated people.[9]

Manrico Montero (DJ Linga), a music producer from Mexico City witnessed the birth of Nor-tec from afar and offers an assessment of its development within the dominant electronica sound of the time. He recognizes that, due to the pressure of the dance floor, Nor-tec had to

> fuse, cut, and paste techniques of *norteño* samplings with house and techno styles. It became their trademark. . . . It was the time of "Odyssea 2000," very different from their early down-tempo tracks. That was when they began to collaborate with DJs to get tips about the dance floor; that's when those collaborations with DJ Tolo came out.[10]

As Melo and DJ Linga explain, it was the specific character of the EDM scene in Tijuana during the late 1990s, which lacked venues for the type of IDM and introspective electronica some members of the collective were doing, that forced them to develop a more body-engaging type of music.

With few exceptions, the members of the collective had little or no experience in making people dance. As former members of Artefakto, Pepe Mogt, Melo, and Panóptica were familiar with assembling a harsher electronic industrial sound. Being former members of Sonios certainly helped Terrestre and Plankton Man to shape their refined musical craft; however, the band's progressive jazz music was miles away from anything resembling EDM. Furthermore, the members of Clorofila (Jorge Verdín and Fritz Torres) and Hiperboreal only had experience as amateur musicians. Besides attending *tocadas norteñas* and learning about the particularities of the instruments in *norteño* and *banda* ensembles, as Melo mentions, it was necessary to seek advice from local EDM DJs, especially DJ Tolo. As DJ Linga points out, DJ Tolo's competence in the codes that make a successful

EDM performance was crucial in the development of a Nor-tec sound that would fruitfully engage the local electronica fans.

I make an appointment to interview DJ Tolo, the first local DJ to collaborate with the Nortec Collective. We agree to meet at the main entrance of Tijuana's Jai Alai building. As I wait for him, I listen to the *norteña* sounds coming out of Las Pulgas, just across the street from the Jai Alai. I walk over to the club and ask a chubby guy wearing a long moustache for the resident DJ. It turns out to be him. We chat for a little while before I ask his opinion of the Nor-tec concerts housed at the Jai Alai building. His answer is illuminating: "they produce the music across the street but I play it and make people dance here." Later on, throughout my conversation with DJ Tolo, I realize that it is indeed the disc jockey's mastery of rhythm, programming, and direction and his/her ability to communicate with the dance floor that makes the difference between ordinary and exceptional EDM experiences. DJ Tolo describes his performance strategy:

> Depending on the party sometimes I prepare sets . . . but in the end I never really follow them. Every party is different. I have some "bombs" you know, they are special tracks I play at specific moments of the party to make it explode, but there is a lot of improvisation. . . . Of course I want to build up to a climax but what gets me there is the people's responses . . . their mood, their tone of voice, the interaction[s] among themselves. . . . those things happen in a second but you learn to recognize those clues.[11]

What DJ Tolo refers to in his comment is the idea of competence. For a performance to be a successful occasion, DJs and audiences should be competent in the codes of communication that allow the collective shaping of the event's atmosphere throughout the night. Most musicians from the Nortec Collective lacked this competence not only regarding communication with the dance floor during actual performances but also in the process of production. Their collaboration with DJ Tolo in the production of the first truly Nor-tec dance recording (*The Spaced TJ Dub*) and then at dance parties gained them an awareness of the elements that make a successful dance track and helped them to recognize the ways that dancers express their desires on the dance floor. DJ Tolo explains:

> When we started doing Nor-tec I was already *muy clavado* [very involved] in dance music . . . and Pepe [Mogt] and Ramón [Bostich] needed a mediator to gain access to that scene because they had never really had to communicate with dancing people. . . . of course it is different today, after playing so many parties. Anyway, in the LP [*The Spaced TJ Dub*] you notice that the essence of "Ventilador" and "Trip to Ensenada" is the same [as that in the *Nor-tec Sampler*] but it is a dance structure. . . . When [Bostich and I] worked on "Unicornio" he gave me the finished piece, but

I felt that, although rich in textures, it was too serious. So I took some of
the sounds, made them fuller, and then added the percussive structure. In
Pepe's case it was different because he didn't have anything planned, it
was like "I have these sounds, what can we do?" So, I took his MPC and
he started playing with his synthesizers . . . and that's how "Odyssea"
came about.[12]

DJ Tolo's account shows that, in this collaborative effort, his mastery of the
dance floor was crucial in defining the early dancing groove of Nor-tec. It
also illustrates the importance of practice and familiarity with the dance
floor as the elements that allowed Bostich and Fussible to gain the necessary competence to establish fluid communication with their audiences in
performance. This was a much-needed skill if they, unlike El Lazo Invisible,
were to accept the challenges of the dance floor as the Nortec Collective's
main site for expression.

Nor-tec in Performance

Although I am well aware of the primordial aspect of performance practice
in the Nor-tec experience, it is at the Avalon in Tijuana, during one of the
parties of the 2003 Mutek Festival, that I am able to experience one of
the most amazing examples of the transforming power that performance
can offer. It is 5 December 2003. The Avalon program features Canadian
acts Egg and Deadbeat alongside local acts Murcof, Fax, and Panóptica. I
am excited to hear live Fernando Corona's alternative alter ego, Murcof.
A wonderful non–Nor-tec music project, Murcof has become one of my
favorite electronica acts. However, his performance is uneventful and even
predictable, failing to engage the Avalon's large crowd. I am somewhat dis-
appointed. But Panóptica's set is next and I have to get ready, although, to
tell the truth, I am not expecting much of it. I have all of Panóptica's CDs
and I am not particularly impressed with his music. I often find his tracks
a bit too repetitive and rather conventional. However, when he shows up
on stage, wearing a cowboy hat, I can already feel something special is in
the making. He almost immediately takes control of the evening by catch-
ing the audience's attention with rich sounds and a powerful bass that we
all feel in our stomachs. It is time to get on the dance floor! Panóptica's understanding of what the dancers want is remarkable. He takes a quick glance
at the packed dance floor and immediately knows what to do to keep and
increase the momentum of the party. With perfect timing, he throws a new
loop into the mix at just the right moment to keep the excitement and add
variety. With perfect pacing, he knows exactly when the dancers have
enough of one track and are anxious to hear the next one. Even more, as
he manipulates loops in his laptop and makes sure the balance of sound is

the best, he takes time to wave his hat like a "true" cowboy, infecting us all with the energy of his enthusiastic performance. The shaping of the party is totally under his control as he affects the fans and responds to their pleas codified as dance steps, twists, jumps, and screams. When it seems the party cannot get any better, a bass player steps on the stage and begins to play the bass line of "She Is in Fiestas," Panóptica's last track of the night. "That's the guy from Love and Rockets," I hear a fellow dancer say. Yes, it is David J! In a completely unforeseen climactic moment, the former Bauhaus bass player is there, on the stage, playing the very bass line from "She Is in Parties" that inspired Panóptica's track. They bring the house down!

Many elements influence a successful or unsuccessful performance and can change one's perception of a given artist. A musician might be tired and unable to pick up the subtle messages encoded in his audience's moves. The venue might not be the best for the type of music being played. Or, plainly, the magic of the recorded music might be impossible to reproduce in a live performance. I believe that all of these factors contributed to Murcof's unsuccessful performance that night at the Avalon. He was tired after having just flown back from London, where he had played only four days before; the fans were there to dance the night away and Murcof's IDM was not the best kind of music for that; but in the end, it was that his music is so complete and perfectly balanced in recording that sometimes it suffers when modified in a live performance. On the other hand, Panóptica's case shows that music specifically designed to be part of larger performances could never be faithfully reproduced in recording. Standing there on the dance floor amid a frenetic dancing crowd, I finally understand how the flat tracks in *Panóptica* (2001) and *The Tijuana Remixes* (2002) come to life as a result of Panóptica's keen communication with his audience. It is only through the amazing dialogic power of performance that Panóptica's tracks can be fully appreciated. It is in performance that his music makes sense; only after participating in such a fascinating event can one fully realize that, in electronica, a CD track is only the blueprint of an unpredictable experience.

A common misconception about live performances of prerecorded electronic music such as Nor-tec is that the musicians just press a button and let the computer do all the work. In fact, it does not happen like that at all. Instead, as Panóptica's performance at the Avalon shows, successful live performances of EDM require skillful improvisers. Musicians need to keep track of their audience's changing mood and respond accordingly. In a vivid recollection that illustrates the power of performance, Melo describes the technical aspect of a typical Fussible event:

> Pepe had a laptop with all the loops ready, without effects. We used a program called Live and Pepe had a mixer with which he could send or get

rid of any loop. He incorporated effects live and was also in charge of the rhythmic aspect. He had control over the duration of the song and could extend it as much as he wanted. I had all these sound modules and could incorporate any of the instruments played [in the song]. . . . many times I would play the melodies live. The good thing is that we had control over a recorded track via digital technology, which used to be impossible [before digital technology]. I remember a *tocada* [gig] when people entered into a trance with "Ventilador." That song is very slow and I remember we made it into a 45-minute-long song . . . and people did not even realize, so when we finished it they were like "*¿Qué onda? Síganle!* [What's up? Keep on going!]."[13]

As Melo states, for live performances, the members of the collective use Live, a software that gives them easy and quick access to all of the loops stored in their computers. These loops are the building blocks of the different tracks and are organized in files according to the track to which they belong. The musician selects the track he wants to play, and the software offers him a list of possible loops from which to choose. These loops have the role of musical licks, and the musician is able to play them at any given moment according to the pacing of the piece and the specific circumstances of the performance. Like with any lick, the order and possible combinations of these loops are up to the performer. He might decide to use all of the loops that make up a given track or only a couple of them. In addition to this basic software, the musicians also have extra tools that allow them to modify and transform live the loops they select to play. Besides paying attention to their audiences, musicians also need to keep in constant dialogue with video jockeys, technicians, and other musicians on stage. The multiple improvisational possibilities offered by technology make Nor-tec events into unique and unrepeatable experiences. In these types of performances, the individual music tracks are more like jazz charts; as Nicholas Cook would put it, they are scripts that loosely guide a series of social interactions among musicians and dance participants.[14] But even more, such an approach urges us to also recognize that these tracks are not musical works to be devotedly reproduced but rather frozen performances. It is in the unpredictability of performance, which gives the computer musician plenty of opportunities to improvise, that the music acquires meaning. In other words, in EDM, there is no final product; the product is always made in the ephemerality of a performance process that defines music, musicians, dancers, and audiences alike.

As Melo's compelling story illustrates, these types of multidisciplinary performances can be powerfully transforming experiences for all of those involved. Just as the dancers, fans, and observers are changed by this collective practice, the musicians and the music are also transformed. As DJ Tolo points out, time and practice on the stage made the members of the Nortec Collective more able to communicate with their fans. That knowledge in turn allowed them to conceptually refashion their performances and to make them more engaging. When the Nortec Collective started performing live in 1999, it presented a string of individual sets following one another. Thus, a typical early Nor-tec performance would have a couple of disc jockeys opening the night followed by five 30-minute-long individual sets by Clorofila, Plankton Man, Hiperboreal, Panóptica, and Terrestre, and ending with the presentations of Fussible and Bostich, each playing a 45-minute set. In this set-up, each act would play only its own tracks as part of the individual sets. Clearly the idea behind such a program is that the disc jockeys would prepare the fans for the Nor-tec performance, which would slowly build up to a climax, with the most seasoned acts of the collective, Fussible and Bostich, closing the event. This format was used for almost three years and allowed the less-experienced members of the collective not only to get familiar and comfortable with the dynamics of performance, but also to amass a repertoire large enough to eventually be able to play longer sets. At the same time, this hierarchical set-up allowed the collective to capitalize on the performance experience of Fussible and Bostich playing the most prominent Nor-tec tracks at the climactic end of the event. However, the downside of such a performance arrangement was the difficulty of controlling the flow of energy throughout the event. This happened mostly due to the continuous breaks when moving from one set to another, but also due to the uneven performance skills among the members of the collective, a situation that often translated into problems with consistently capturing the attention of the dancers throughout the night.

On 20 March 2002, the performance strategy of the collective changed when it presented a concert at Las Pulgas, Tijuana's foremost *norteña* music club. There, instead of presenting a lineup of acts following one another, all of the members of the collective shared the stage at the same time; such an arrangement changed the dynamics of the performance. In the new performance approach, each individual member has an assigned slot of time when his tracks are played. The member whose tracks are being played at a given moment controls that segment of the event; during this time slot, he is able to organize the order, sequence, and timing of the loops played and the pacing of the tracks. Often, the order of the performers controlling the specific time slots is similar to the order followed in the older format: from less- to more-experienced performers and from lesser- to better-known tracks. Although the older hierarchy remains in the new performance strategy, the innovation allows the rest of the collective to offer their input during a specific member's time slot. Hans Fjellestad, an avant-garde musician from San Diego and a friend of the collective's members, explains:

> Fussible would be doing "Casino Soul," but all the other collective members are contributing to the piece and background texture [with] peripheral material. So it all blends, the whole set is one form, one thing created [collectively], although the individual structural ideas come from the different projects. [The tracks] can be seen as charts where you actually have a piece of paper that has the progression and form and maybe a little bit of the melody and that's it. The actual length of the piece or [the decision not to] repeat one part or maybe repeat it fourteen times, is all up in the air. And how you actually voice the chords could vary. So in that way it's related to jazz composition. They're not up there playing CDs and pressing "go." They're interacting and listening.[15]

This format allows the more-experienced members of the collective to control the overall shape of the performance; it also reduces the breaks between different acts and provides a sense of continuity and coherence that was missing in the previous performance format. Regularly, only two or three Nortec Collective acts get hired to perform live; when that takes place, the musicians organize a collective set that often follows a three-part structure. The first section usually presents some of the most difficult and percussive tracks by Bostich. This section emphasizes percussion (mostly *tarola*) and isolated low brass sounds (tuba) to the detriment of melodic content. The second section introduces more melodic elements and is usually dominated by the sound of Fussible's Latin house tracks. Finally, the third section offers the better-known Nor-tec tracks. When Panóptica is on stage, one might expect him to throw looped samples of older popular Mexican (usually *norteña*) music. This frequently takes place at the beginning of the set or at important structural points in the set, e.g., when moving from section to section. At these moments, it is not rare to hear the kitschy looped fragments of Los Tigres del Norte's classic *narcocorrido* "Contrabando y traición," fragmented button accordion solos, or symphonic arrangements of mariachi music popular in Mexico during the 1970s.

These types of collective performances eventually influenced the production process of the Nortec Collective. As I mentioned in chapter 2, *Tijuana Sessions, Vol. 3*, is characterized by a more homogeneous style and less individual differences between tracks and acts. This is the product of a close collaboration that resembles the collective performance format, with all members of the collective providing their input for everyone else's tracks. Furthermore, although many members of the collective had expressed an interest in the notion of kitsch, the in-your-face references to Mexican pop culture that appear throughout the CD were obvious in performance only in Panóptica's flamboyant style. The production of *Tijuana Sessions, Vol. 3*, presents a radical conceptual change: the collective is no longer an assortment of individual projects but an actual band working collaboratively with one common musical goal, its CD. Clearly, this change was a direct result of their collective performance strategies.

In turn, this band-like collaborative approach also affected the collective's performance format, which was again transformed at the release party of *Tijuana Sessions, Vol. 3,* on 30 September 2005. Once more, the event took place at Las Pulgas. Although various acts in the collective had interacted with live musicians at different times, the second Las Pulgas concert was the first time that the collective shared the stage with an entire *banda sinaloense,* a *bajo sexto* player, and an accordionist. The idea came about mostly as a result of Hiperboreal's collaboration with various members of the Banda Aguacaliente during the composition process of "El Dandy del Sur," "Don Loope," and "El fracaso." The idea filtered into the rest of the tracks in *Tijuana Sessions, Vol. 3,* and later into the actual performances of the collective. The presence of live musicians at the release party increased the possibilities of improvisation, musical dialogue, and innovation during the performance. At the same time, such encounters in a live performance situation became an actual incarnation of the meeting of traditions that Nor-tec had represented only as audiotopia up to that moment.

The performance staged for the presentation of *Tijuana Sessions, Vol. 3,* is one of the best examples of how performances can work as performative enunciations that act out what they state. In this case, it was the negotiation of performance traditions on a stage that executed the act of negotiation between tradition and modernity at the core of Nor-tec's hybrid aesthetic. The words of Leoncio González Medina, trumpet player with Banda Aguacaliente at the release party, illustrate the moment:

> Of course we rehearse in advance, but we do it by sections because [Nor-tec] does not follow the structure of a typical *banda* song. In electronic music it is different; they take something from here and something from there and then they put the figures together. It doesn't follow the type of sequence I follow when I am playing a *banda* song; there I start at the beginning and keep going until the end. [Nor-tec] does have a beginning and an end but it is very different. . . . it even goes through a lot of tone [*sic*] and rhythm changes. So, we rehearse by sections. First the trumpets by themselves, then the trombones, then the rhythm section, and then we come here and put it together. They put [on] their tracks and we follow them. When they play trumpets we play the trumpets . . . but there are always little details that we have to improvise on the stage.[16]

As evident in González Medina's statement, the fragmentary use of acoustic samples in Nor-tec's music makes its live performance into a type of simulacrum for the traditional musician. The *banda* instrumentalists are not used to a disconnected style of music that extracts small figures out of longer music sequences and reassembles them as the performance takes place and according to the laptop musician's dialogue with the dance floor. The result is an actual act of negotiation in performance, where the traditional performance practice of the *banda* musicians is challenged but also one where the very presence of these instrumentalists reconfigures the Nortec performance and, in the end, enhances the experience of the dancing fans by powerfully contributing to the theatricality of the event.

Visuals and Music in the Performance of Nor-tec

Many electronic-music producers recognize a long-standing problem in EDM performance. For people with more traditional music backgrounds, it is difficult to reconcile their idea of what a performer should do on stage with what electronica musicians actually do. For them, musicians are entertainers and a concert should be as much a visual spectacle as a sonic experience. DJ Linga reflects on this:

> The shift from rock to electronica had terrible consequences [for] people's perception of electronica. Those coming from rock were used to the stage presence of the rock artist and could not understand the lack of stage activity in electronica performances. It was normal for most people coming from the rock scene to look down on electronica, some of them did not even consider it music.[17]

I was not able to attend any of the concerts of the Nortec Collective's first U.S. tour, but I had a chance to hear the opinion of a prominent Latin American music scholar about its concert in a large city on the East Coast. In her opinion, although the sounds were indeed interesting, she had found the concert as a performance to be extremely dull. "They were just there standing behind their laptops and nobody in the audience knew what to do," she said. Her comment shows the validity of DJ Linga's concern.

Many members of the Nortec Collective were themselves former members of the rock or electronic rock scene and, knowing the importance of the performatic aspect—its theatricality, as I mentioned above—in connecting to the public, were aware that something was needed to increase excitement in their live shows. The inclusion of visuals as a routine part of the collective's performance was the result of trying to make its shows more spectacular and appealing to the eyes as well as to the ears and the body. VJ CBrown[18] explains:

> [The visuals] were incorporated in order to have a more integrated show. It gave the stage a presence it did not have before. That's the importance of visuals . . . because these *vatos* [guys] live were kind of boring you

know. . . . they just have a laptop and a drum machine, and even though they play differently every time their performances were pretty boring. So, it was important to have visuals.[19]

For the inclusion of visuals to be successful in creating a truly "integrated" Nor-tec performance, it had to avoid the most common problem in EDM events that include visuals: the complete split between music and image. EDM producers and visual artists rarely work together in the development of a coherent aesthetic project. Frequently, VJs are hired separately from musicians, and it is not rare for them to meet only a few minutes before their collaborative performance. This results in visual shows that lack any relation to the music being played. One could be listening to a set of Latin house and be watching a series of gory images unfolding in a rhythm completely different from the music's. As I have shown in chapter 4, the visual aspect of Nor-tec attempted to translate into images the musicians' idea of articulating local elements from Tijuana via global technology. However, the images were never meant to be just visual aids to the sound; instead, they were meant as a complement to the music and became an indispensable aspect of the Nor-tec experience by consciously emphasizing a political reading of Tijuana that was intentionally avoided in the musicians' discourse.

Since images had become an intrinsic aspect of the Nor-tec aesthetic and its political overtones, it was also necessary to make them an integral part of the Nor-tec show. The live performance of the VJs is very similar to that of the musicians. They have one or two laptops and manipulate live images via software like Video Jockey. The computer is connected to a MIDI sequencer which is itself connected to a video camera and a video mixer. This technology allows the VJ to closely follow and react to the pace and rhythm of the music. VJ CBrown describes their performance method:

> Nor-tec's rhythm is in 4/4. So, what I do is to cut [and switch] images following that rhythm: one, two, three, four; one two, one, two; one, two, three, four; one, one, one, one. I cut [and switch] images like that, and when the image is ready you just have to *ponerte trucha* [be on your toes] to make it coincide [with the music] and then I *agarro un rollo* [get on a roll]. . . . I just got this really *mamona* ["bad"] mixer with an internal sequencer between the two sources . . . so, I am listening to their music, and I know they play between 126 and 133 bpm's, so I start following their beat with a combination of images from the two sources. Then I get into a rhythm and that's it. . . . Bostich always plays around 130 [bpm], Panóptica slows down a bit, and I just play around with that.[20]

Monitoring the relationship between image and sound requires a high degree of competence from the VJs. Since visual loops are created and thematically grouped together to correspond to specific musical loops and

tracks, it is important to be able to match them during live performances.
It is their knowledge of the performance codes as well as their intimacy
with the musicians' particular performing styles that allow the VJs to follow them during a performance. However, as VJ CBrown states, the necessary correspondence between visual and musical loops does not prevent VJs
from continually improvising during performances. VJ Mashaka explains
the relationships among visual loops, musical loops, and improvisation:

> There are lots of different ways to do it. Sometimes it is totally free; we
> mix as we go along, more improvised. But lately we have tried to struc-
> ture it more, with a topic for each song. [The musicians] mix live and we
> have to catch their rhythm. For example, if they play Fussible's "Col-
> orado" we need to identify it immediately and pull out the files for that
> song. . . . we usually work in couples; one pulls the files out while the
> other is mixing them. We play the images as the images are pulled out . . .
> live from the keyboard/sequencer while the other VJ controls the final
> mix. Images are designed with a certain rhythm according to the song; we
> just need to adjust the rhythm live according to the audio mix.[21]

Like everything else in Nor-tec performances, the loops are prerecorded and
preorganized. Nevertheless, within each group of loops there is plenty of
room for improvisation not only by following the musicians' spontaneous
mix, but also by selecting the order of visual loops and by deciding how they
will rhythmically relate to the pace of the music.[22] These parameters change
from performance to performance, making live Nor-tec performances less
predictable and more exciting. Just like specific tracks predetermine some
aspects of the visual show, the success of the visual shows among fans has
also altered the collective's notion of performance. Now, the musicians insist that a live VJ always be hired as part of the show; sometimes, they will
even sacrifice the presence of one of the musical acts if that allows a low-
budget organizer to cover the expenses of the VJ.

Cyberspace and digital technology have also been used to develop innovative Nor-tec performances. On 10 June 2004, during the opening ceremony for "Le mystère du kilo d'or," an arts exhibit at the Instituto de
México in Paris, the images of performance artist Héctor Falcón joined the
sounds of Terrestre and Plankton Man in a unique Nor-tec performance
entitled Plankton Man vs. Terrestre vs. Falcón. What made this a unique
event was that, although Plankton Man and Falcón were interacting in the
same hall in Paris, Terrestre was thousands of miles away manipulating his
computer in Tijuana. Falcón describes the performance process on this occasion: "Terrestre transmitted his loops from Tijuana to Paris, Plankton
Man received them and mixed them with his own music while I generated
images and mixed them in real time. Everything was live, Terrestre in Tijuana, and Plankton Man and I mixing live there [in Paris]."[23] Although

technological mediation is a common feature of Nor-tec performances, the event at the Instituto de México in Paris was not a typical Nor-tec event. Nevertheless, it was an articulation of some of the distinctive features of the Nor-tec scene and of Nor-tec performance, especially the importance of technological mediation in making the music, the visuals, and the scene possible. As Sherry Turkle suggests, the virtual world provided by computers adds a new dimension of mediated experience.[24] This is very important in simulacrum-like experiences like Nor-tec, and it is particularly meaningful in a performance like Plankton Man vs. Terrestre vs. Falcón because Terrestre's virtual presence in Paris (through his sounds via Plankton Man's mix) appeared as a metaphor for electronica's aura of nonhumanity. In this performance, technology allowed Terrestre to transcend his physical body in cyberspace and to extend it with the virtual prostheses that the Internet and the sonic and visual mediation of Plankton Man and Falcón provided. At that moment (while the performance took place), Terrestre became a posthuman cyborg capable of exerting influence over dancers thousands of miles away.[25] This type of performance adds a new layer of meaning to the process of simulacrum, one where absent performers can themselves become simulacra assembled in the fans' mental reconstitution of them through the bits and pieces of sound and image presented to them by the musician and VJ on stage.

"Something Sublime That Tastes Like Nor-tec": Partying in Tijuana III (Jai Alai Mix)

While producers, musicians, and visual artists play a very important part in the performance of Nor-tec, the role of the dancing fans in performing their personal Nor-tec audiotopias is equally significant. This is especially true when their performance is witnessed by local and foreign media for which the face of the scene is the fans' interactions on the crowded dance floors. For media that are increasingly focused on image, the attractive show put on by dancing fans is probably more important than the musicians in defining the scene. This can be witnessed in the early media coverage of the Nortec Collective, where the hybrid character of the scene could not be better expressed to those unfamiliar with northern Mexican culture than with the images of ravers wearing kitschy cowboy hats and hip "cyber ponchos." Of the three major massive events during the early Nor-tec boom—Nortec City, Maquiladora de Sueños, and Nortec Live at Las Pulgas—Nortec City was probably the most significant in generating a worldwide representation of the Nor-tec scene. And clearly, the fans were decidedly responsible for that.

On the evening of 3 March 2001, a crowd of about 2,000 dancing fans filled one of Tijuana's architectural landmarks, the old Jai Alai building on

Avenida Revolución. The reason was a multidisciplinary event called Nor-tec City that, taking as an excuse the release of the Nortec Collective's first commercial recording, *The Tijuana Sessions, Vol. 1,* presented the work of a group of installation and visual artists, filmmakers, sculptors, writers, and fashion designers produced under the unifying hybrid spirit of Nor-tec. Covered by journalists from Europe and the United States, Nortec City was the crowning moment of the long, unorthodox process of do-it-yourself underground marketing and distribution that had caught the attention and imagination of U.S. and European critics and fans alike. Before an international audience that witnessed the event as tourists, journalists, and Internet users, Nortec City became a site where musicians, artists, and dancing fans from Tijuana redefined themselves and the identity of their city through a performance that negotiated a complex web of transnational discourses, ideologies, and desires.

Ursula, a native *tijuanense,* first heard Nor-tec music during the Nortec City party and recalls her experience:

> Once I heard [the Nortec Collective] I got hooked up. . . . What happens to me is that I can't believe I am seeing people from Tijuana on the stage, creating something as real . . . something as true as this music. It is very emotional to know that finally you can touch or perceive something that is being created here in Tijuana. . . . What I like the best is to feel that we are experiencing something that does not come to us from the center [of the country], but something that is from here.[26]

The sense of local pride expressed by Ursula and many other fans—*Lo que más me gusta es que es de aquí* (what I like the best is that it is from here) is a repeated mantra I get from local fans when asked about Nor-tec—is central to the successful reception of Nor-tec in Tijuana. As I mentioned earlier, Nortec City was the first Nor-tec event that captured the attention of the international media; this would have been impossible without the energy produced by the active participation of the proud local fans who filled the Jai Alai building that night. On the evening of 3 March 2001, these *tijuanenses* were willing to play their part in the performance. Bruno Ruiz, a journalist from Tijuana, described Nortec City as a party

> where it looks like everybody is wearing sunglasses, where women are into the *onda vaquera* [cowboy trend]. Hats, jeans, boots. . . . Everybody is drinking beer. *Cerveza Tijuana.* Out there, a musician wearing a *lucha libre* [Mexican wrestling] mask plays a synthesizer. Inside, at midnight, there are stands of Nortec T-shirts and other things. *Birria* [goat stew] and *chicharrón* [fried pork skin] vendors. . . . Deeper inside [the building], there is another area where other people dance, and they dance very well. They move very well. They jump and jump because a few trumpetists play with the DJs. These trumpet players wear cowboy hats and mix [their

sound] with the [DJs'] music, making it into something sublime and perfect that tastes like Nortec.[27]

Ruiz's chronicle tells the story of the projection of the local onto the global. *Chicharrón, birria, lucha libre,* and *norteño* outfits (the *onda vaquera*) are rearticulated in the modernity of technology (synthesizers, DJs, computers, and electronic music). How is this hybrid, glocal project embodied by dancing fans? How is it that their performance "tastes like Nor-tec"?

Several American journalists also wrote about Nortec City. Among these chronicles, San Diego–based journalist Nina Garin's is especially perceptive as it recognizes the body, food, clothing, and other paraphernalia as instruments that define the scene: "Nortec is how you dress (sunglasses are very Nortec). . . . Roan Gama, 18 of Tijuana, who was dressed in a giant straw sombrero and matching poncho, . . . said he was dressed in a traditional outfit to make fun of the stereotype people have about Mexicans."[28] The choice of clothing, as Garin observes and her informant confirms, is a perfect statement that allows fans to articulate the discourses

Figure 5.1   Fan from Tijuana playing his part at the Nortec City performance. Photo by Gerardo Yépiz. Used by permission. Gerardo Yépiz/acamonchi.com

about tradition and modernity of the Nortec Collective. This way, dancing fans become the face of the scene for foreign journalists like Garin who, covering Nortec City from places as far as New York City, play a fundamental role in the global representation of the scene. By lending their bodies to this performance, the dancing fans not only make a powerful statement regarding what the scene is about (supporting the musicians' and artists' poietic discourse), but also ensure that their role as major actors in the development of the scene is recognized.

Pepe Mogt acknowledges the communitarian character of Nortec City when he points out to Garin that "the music is not even the main part of the night. This night is about bringing the community together."[29] As Pepe Mogt's statement suggests (even contradicting his own declaration about Nor-tec being "nothing but the combination of *norteña* music sounds and electronic music compositional techniques"), the collective identity of Nor-tec is what is at stake in the fans' performance. However, the dancing fans' role in the performance of Nor-tec goes well beyond simply supporting the collective's discourse about challenging hegemonic representations of their city and their culture. By dressing like *norteño* cowboys, wearing costumes such as El Chapulín Colorado,[30] or using hip sunglasses alongside unlikely ponchos, individual fans participate in processes of self-identification and self-representation that articulate modernity through a type of retro nostalgia and kitschiness. The dancing fans at Nortec City are not *norteña* music fans; their use of *norteña* clothing styles as an articulation of tradition is an act of mimicry. Both dressing as El Chapulín Colorado and the use of *norteña* music clothing styles are manifestations of nostalgia. On the one hand, it is nostalgia for the past, while on the other, it is nostalgia for that which never took place (as mentioned in chapter 2, most of these kids were never fans of *norteña* music). They are both examples of mimicry that mirror identities as building blocks for the reinvention of the self in performance. For these types of collective simulacra to be successful, each participant (dancer, musician, observer) has to speak a language that the other participants are able to recognize and interpret. In the case of the Nortec City performance and its transnational audience, the use of stereotypes worked perfectly because they could be recognized transculturally. Regardless of the different meanings they have for different people, stereotypes are unanimously recognized and thus offer a common ground to attempt a subversion of their connotations. On the dance floor, all previous meanings of a stereotype disappear in favor of a new meaning negotiated at the moment of the performance. The effectiveness of the dancing fans wearing ponchos and sombreros while dancing to the beats of EDM lies in their performance making them imaginary characters charged with a nostalgic quality who, in the end, due to the hipness of the retro aesthetic, live in the future more than they do in the past.

The *tijuanense* writer Rafa Saavedra (Rafadro) states that almost every aspect in the development of the Nor-tec scene has been recorded in one way or another. Through video recordings, written reviews and chronicles, photographic articles, and of course music recordings, the presence of both the underground and mainstream media has always been part of the Nor-tec experience.[31] Dancing fans know they are being observed continuously, and they willingly take part in the performance by adopting the heterogeneous clothing styles that I have described above, styles that betray their desire for modernity and at the same time rewrite tradition through their bodies. This performance does not take place only at the individual level; the distribution of these individual bodies on the dance floor, their interactions with the musicians and the rest of the dancers, and especially their individual awareness of being part of a larger communal performance are also fundamental. They know they are being observed and are aware that their dancing group image is the image of a Tijuana mediated by the modernity of the Nor-tec musical and visual experience. A perfect metaphor for this situation is VJ Mashaka's *El guachaman* (The Watching Man), one of the images projected onto the screen during a typical Nor-tec performance. Here, an individual filmed by the camera suddenly takes out a set of binoculars and looks back at the camera through them. *El guachaman,* the subject of our gaze, is aware that we are looking through the camera, reverses the situation, and forces us to look at ourselves as objects of his gaze as he takes an active role that emphasizes his awareness of the situation. Since the fundamental question of desire is what the other wants from us, it is clear that the gaze of those who observe these performances is a fundamental element in triggering the fantasies that inform them. Just as *El guachaman* reverses the situation by identifying the intruding gaze, Nor-tec's dancing fans, recognizing the presence of the outsider's gaze, take stereotypes of *norteña* culture and humorously rearticulate them under the light of their desire for modernity. The fans' articulation of stereotypes of what is expected from them as Mexicans is a response to this principle. Their style of dress pushes the stereotype to its limit; it makes it into a ridiculous caricature and thus momentarily subverts its negativity. Thus, the stereotype is decontextualized and recodified locally because of the validating power of the outsider's gaze, making the Nor-tec performance into a truly glocal phenomenon.

The glocal character of this re-signification is clear in the way in which the specific aspects of the Nortec City performance responded to the larger processes of globalization and the libidinal economy that fuels them.

Figure 5.2 *El guachaman,* © José Luis Martín. Used by permission

Nortec City coincided with Madonna's reinvention of herself as a cowgirl in her album *Music* (2000). This record and Jean-Baptiste Mondino's accompanying video for "Don't Tell Me" launched a worldwide cowboy vogue; this is exactly *la onda vaquera* that journalist Bruno Ruiz invokes in his chronicle of Nortec City. Fashion designer Esther Corona, Terrestre's wife, took advantage of the resonances between Nor-tec's endorsement of local *norteña* culture and Madonna's cowboy trend and created a line of stylish Nor-tec clothing that started with a celebrated piece, the "cyber poncho." She explains:

> Madonna's country fad, where she wore a *tejano* hat, had already started and the fans also began to wear hats. Fernando [Terrestre] wanted to wear a *sarape* and a sombrero, so I told him "I am going to make you a special *sarape*." I got that fabric used for windbreaker jackets and focused on the idea of the puffy coats that were in fashion. I designed it and tried different ideas and the "cyber poncho" came up. . . . you know, *al otro lado* [on the other side, the United States] they call *sarapes* ponchos. So, when Fer-

nando played *en el otro lado* the *gringos* told him "Oh! I like your cyber poncho" . . . *y pues, órale* [so, OK], the name stuck.[32]

The success of Esther Corona's clothing designs articulates desire at two different levels; at the local level, it responds to the fans' desire for a fashion fad promoted by an icon of musical cosmopolitanism like Madonna (with a striking resonance with *norteña* clothing styles at a key moment in the development of the Nor-tec scene). At the international level, Corona's designs resonate with the U.S. expectation of an exotic Mexico; the poncho decidedly lives in the U.S. imagination ("you know, *al otro lado* they call [them] ponchos"). It does not matter that a poncho is a piece of clothing from the Andes region in South America nor that its design is distinctly different from a *sarape* from the north of Mexico; what is at stake is the fulfillment of the observer's expectations, the performance of his/her desires.

To Nor-tec through Performance

As observed in the relationship between a recorded track and its different renditions in performance, like much EDM, there is no definitive Nor-tec text; its ultimate moment of collective signification is its performance. The underground circulation of a wide variety of different versions of each Nor-tec track, none of which is ever attempted to be accurately reproduced in performance, is another indication of the importance of the moment in shaping the music. Even tracks that might seem like fixed versions, such as those widely distributed in *The Tijuana Sessions, Vol. 1,* and *Tijuana Sessions, Vol. 3,* are only possible renderings of pieces whose true ideal versions live in the particularities that inform their ephemeral unfolding each time they are performed live. This is not to say that each different version might not have a particular meaning tied to the moment of its creation nor that its meaning could not be continuously transformed in consumption. However, this clearly shows that there is no definitive, authentic version of a given track; its authenticity is created in performance and consumption. Furthermore, since each of these performances is a dialogic, communal creation, where the fans, the physical space, the technology being used, and the observers play fundamental roles, it is clear that the very existence of these texts and their meanings are bound to these unrepeatable circumstances. Thus, music and context become inseparable as they continuously define each other. If the performance of Nor-tec acts as a productive fantasy that keeps both the Mexican desire for cosmopolitanism and the U.S. and European desires for difference alive (as illustrated in the complex set of glocal circumstances that determined the performance of Nortec City), then these desires become intrinsic elements for the music to exist. It is this performative character which allows the staging of the identities of the music, the musicians, the dancing fans, the observers, and the scene to produce and embody the identities being staged. Nor-tec's identity exists and is continuously shaped through the reiteration of its many performances. Nor-tec is an object of desire, one that exists as it is appropriated, as it is made to come to life in performance.

6

Dancing with Desire

¿Qué te puedo decir que no haya dicho el cuerpo?
[What can I tell you that the body has not said yet?]

—VJ Mashaka

As shown in previous chapters, the meaning of Nor-tec cannot be simply extracted from its process of production since distribution and consumption are also fundamental aspects in the negotiation of cultural meaning. According to Michel de Certeau, even individuals who are reduced to the role of consumers and who do not get a chance to be actively involved in a chain of production are able to turn their consumption into a production of cultural meaning; thus, consumption is an act of poiesis that provides the basis for identity construction and cultural regulation.[1] Since dancing is evidently an essential aspect in the Nor-tec experience, this chapter focuses on this practice as a specific type of cultural consumption. As Kai Fikentscher suggests, dance music scenes are defined by a "dynamic interaction between [the DJ] in charge of the DJ booth and the dancers who, as a collective body, are in charge of the dance floor."[2] Such a characterization is indeed true not only for the Nor-tec scene in Tijuana, but also for the diverse transnational scenes that appropriate it in cities like Los Angeles and Chicago; locally and translocally, musicians and dancers define their and each other's identity in the dynamic performance of Nor-tec.

My focus in this chapter is individual dance styles and the relationships between discourses about Latinidad and Latino bodies that inform dancing fans moving to the beat of Nor-tec. I want to show how different Nor-tec dance styles allow different communities to reconcile outside discourses of representation with their own notions of self-identity and their

169

own cosmopolitan aspirations with the commodified desires that hegemonic libidinal economies impose on them.

On 11 December 2002, as the Nor-tec craze was sweeping Tijuana, José Luis Martín (VJ Mashaka), a visual artist and a member of the Nortec Collective, posted the following sentence in his blog: "*¿Qué te puedo decir que no haya dicho el cuerpo?* [What can I tell you that the body has not said yet?]." As his question suggests, body language anticipates spoken language in communicating our desires. We are our bodies, and our bodies function as loudspeakers for our desires. In our interpersonal relations, the body speaks our most intimate needs and feelings: our anxieties, our fears, our calmness, our anger, our sexual desire. If then, in interpersonal relations, our bodies disclose the hidden, most personal feelings and hopes of our individual lives, what do our bodies reveal about our aspirations in larger social and cultural contexts? What do the bodies of dancing Nor-tec fans say? Which desires write, inform, negotiate, and are negotiated by the dancing bodies of Nor-tec fans in different translocal dance scenes?

Dancing is a form of productive consumption that actively shapes, reproduces, and contests identity roles of gender, class, ethnicity, and geographic belonging. Sally Ann Allen Ness states that body movement in dance responds to specific "embodiment[s] of history, of existential givens, of social value systems, of symbolism, and/or thought per se."[3] In other words, dance is embodied culture and, therefore, the dancing body is a site where individuals negotiate the contingencies, symbols, and desires of their everyday lives. We learn to dance in social contexts that are reproduced by our own dancing. First in the sheltered environment of our immediate family and later as part of different social crowds, dancing allows us to codify our bodies into these groups of identification. We embody family hierarchies, social relations, and ethnic and gender roles through the movements and dances allowed by our cultural contexts. Thus, dancing infuses our bodies with the ideologies that surround us while the repetition of those movements reproduces those ideological settings. However, dancing, as ideology, acts as a *point de capiton* that articulates signifiers and allows dancing individuals to use style to resolve the contradictions of their everyday lives at a semiotic level. Therefore, dancing not only reproduces existential givens, it also creates moments that give new social, economic, and ethnic meanings to the body, incorporating it as part of alternative symbolic systems. If, as Slavoj Žižek suggests, the meanings of ideology and commodification are concealed in the form,[4] then the heterogeneous dance forms of Nor-tec are manifestations of the complex reterritorialization of the body which border and multi-ideological subjects need to perform as they come into multicultural contacts. Thus, Nor-tec dances are the result of processes that reevaluate the ideologies and desires regarding tradition and modernity. They are the result of processes that write cultural significance onto the bodies of border, multicultural, and transnational individuals.

Our desires are not given a priori, they are continuously constructed as the result of the libidinal economy that surrounds and informs our every-day lives. It is desire that moves individuals to attain goals, to reach objectives, and to continuously struggle to grasp the objects of their desire. However, the objective of a libidinal economy is not to create achievable objects of desire but to reproduce desire itself, since it is the existence of desire that guarantees the reproduction of such an economy and the social and cultural system it supports. According to Žižek, it is the impossible, phantasmatic relation between the subject and the object of desire that constitutes the desiring subject; this phantasmatic site is the empty screen upon which the subject's desires are projected.[5] The importance of ap-proaching the human body in relation to libidinal economies lies in the fact that bodies are not only distinctive objects of desire—both on the individ-ual and social levels—but also desiring subjects themselves. Thus, the source and outcome of Žižek's phantom collapse into a single site, the human body. The body is at the same time a subject richly constituted by an array of symbolized desires and also an empty object upon which desires are pro-jected. The desiring/desired body is at the same time subjective and objec-tive, experiential and institutionalized, and, as Bryan Turner suggests, "it precisely indicates the weakness of the Cartesian legacy in sociology, which has almost exclusively treated the human body as *Körper* [institutional-ized body], rather than both simultaneously *Körper* and *Leib* [experiential body]."[6]

Against the mind-body dichotomy, the desiring/desired body highlights the dynamic relationship between representation and experience. As I men-tioned earlier, we are our bodies, and our minds experience their ideologi-cal environment as part of our bodies and through our bodies. Indeed, a body which desires, which experiences and lives, and is desired, which is socialized and symbolized, creates itself through those desires, thus fulfill-ing the goal of a libidinal economy; a desiring body creates new desires because a continuous experience requires the continuous renewal of desire. An emphasis on this complex process contests the essentialist, Enlighten-ment-inherited beliefs which give privilege to the mind over the body via homologizing the two entities with the notions of the "civilized" and the "savage," respectively.

When moving on the dance floor, the dancing body expresses and nav-igates a variety of discourses of representation and identification in an in-dividual as well as in a collective manner. On the dance floor, the dancing body is an individual expression of desire (both institutionalized and expe-rienced) and a member of a performance that articulates collective desires (also institutionalized and experienced). In the social context of dance music, individual and collective objects of desire are developed as responses to specific social and cultural circumstances. Different dance scenes articulate different ideological worlds and networks. Fans appropriate and consume Nor-tec according to the network of representations available to them in their own communities but also according to their desire to surpass the boundaries of their local, everyday lives. Dancing to Nor-tec is an experience that reproduces these networks of representation and desire and is also a process for the reterritorialization of the body that mediates the embodied reproduction of desire. This reproduction takes place in a body that negotiates collective and individual, social and self-reflective, experiential and institutionalized, and local and translocal objects of desire.

In an attempt to account for the multiplicity of cultural and social meanings negotiated in the consumption of Nor-tec through dance, this chapter explores and compares three different dance scenes and their appropriation of Nor-tec. Due to the particular history of American dance club scenes, Helen Thomas describes them as being "at once enthralled by the 'futuristic,' while displaying a nostalgic longing for the past 'underground house.'"[7] This complex relationship between past and future, between nostalgia and desire, between tradition and modernity, is also crucial in the consumption of Nor-tec through dance. The phantasmatic space at the intersection between imaginaries of tradition and modernity is where the collective and individual desires of dancing people from Tijuana, Los Angeles, and Chicago are projected. For these fans, Nor-tec is a fantasy that reconstitutes tradition according to present desires for a type of future modernity. It is a fantasy that ameliorates the ethnic, racial, and gender roles and class conditions that contradict these desires while at the same time contesting them, providing a site for their performative reconfiguration. The consumption of Nor-tec and the styles of dancing in each of these scenes respond to the dancers' understanding of their place within the specific social and cultural circumstances of those scenes. Dance styles developed under these conditions are, therefore, a canvas for the projection and reconfiguration (according to the meaning ascribed to the elements already present on such a canvas) of social representation and self-identification as desire. The three Nor-tec dance scenes explored in this chapter provide examples of completely different projections which necessarily respond to the objects of desire made available to the dancers in their communities. The intention is to understand these objects of desire and their implicit contradictions in order to explore their role in the reproduction of social and cultural discourses of representation and identity politics and also in the performance of alternative avenues of self-identification.

Since dance is also a subjective practice, based on individual expression, it is difficult to write about it convincingly from an objective perspective. In order to accomplish that, I have decided to base my interpretation on an analysis that traces three types of observable elements in dancing style: first, whether the dominant dancing style at a specific community is open or closed dance work, in other words, whether the dancers tend to dance holding each other or without touching their partners. Second, I look at whether the type of dancing motion is mono-centered or poly-centered. Mono-centered dancing implies a single center of body motion at a time. Poly-centered dancing suggests a variety of body centers for the production of movement. Effective poly-centered dancing stresses the equality of all body parts as synchronic centers of motion over the dominance of one center over another, while mono-centered dancing emphasizes one center over another at any one time. The third element in dancing style to which I pay attention is the presence or absence of dancing steps from specific northern Mexican traditions (*polca*, *chotís*, *quebradita*, etc.) and the presence or absence of dance steps from the international electronic rave or club scenes.

"It Lends Itself to a Few *Norteño* Dance Steps": Dancing Nor-tec I (Tijuas Mix)

At an event organized by Kimika to raise funds for the video documentary project *Que suene la calle* (Let the Street Sound), DJ Mr. Ejival, DJ Max, and former Nortec Collective musicians Plankton Man and Terrestre play at Tijuana's Centro bar, a simple, small rectangular room located in an annex of the Jai Alai building which holds around 200 people. The stage is made out of two tables and two loudspeakers located at floor level at one end of the room. On the opposite side, a bartender serves drinks and a few groups of friends await the right moment to start dancing. Around 11 o'clock, Plankton Man takes over the booth from DJ Max and introduces the Nor-tec sound with his computer and samplings of accordion, snare drums, guitars, and even the voices of street musicians. The voice of Teodoro Pacheco, a *norteño* musician sampled in Plankton Man's "Recinto portuario" compels people to take the dance floor. *Yo me llamo Teodoro Pacheco / Yo me dedico a la música desde hace cuarenta años* [My name is Teodoro Pacheco / I have dedicated myself to music for forty years] is the repeated sentence, the loop that, as the sounds of trumpets, synthesizers, drums, and vinyl scratches are incorporated, becomes more and more distorted.

The pace of Plankton Man's music starts at 138 and slowly settles into 133 beats per minute (bpm). Most people dance by themselves or as members of groups of friends whose composition and size change continuously.

There are no fixed couples, dancers do not touch each other, and they move back and forth fluidly from conversation and beer drinking to lively showings of their individual dance skills. People on the sides of the room dance and observe the action at the center of the dance floor. Two of these individual dancers are notable for the distinctive character of their movements. Pedro dances with very slow movements, eyes closed; his lowered head keeps the beat with a slight forward motion. Suddenly, he changes his dancing style; now he keeps his arms out to the sides of his body—as if trying to fly—moving according to the vigorous shift of his body from right to left, jumping on one leg while kicking with the other. A few feet away, Teresa bends her legs, lowers her body, and powerfully lifts herself into the air in jumpy, broken motions, while waving her arms above and around her head, only to return to her initial position. Swiftly, she stands up, her hands together over her head, and, keeping her upper body still, starts moving her hips in a quick, sharp, circular motion.

Improvisational open dance work—such as Pedro's and Teresa's—is all about individual expression. The dance moves embody the person's uniqueness and show the dancer's creativity as an imaginary codification of the body. Many times, however, these codifying exercises intertwine creativity and discourse in seemingly contradictory fashion. While there is an obvious personal connection between the music and the dancers expressed in the autonomy of the dancing bodies, there is also a larger communal experience that is represented in the reterritorialization of the dance floor and in the introduction of dance steps that articulate tradition and discourse in a new and novel way. The choice of clothing and paraphernalia (*tejano* hats and cowboy shirts combined with rave-style outfits) makes it clear that the dancers are aware that this is ultimately a collective performance. The movements of many of the dancers at the center of the dance floor uncover the issues at stake in their performance.

In the overcrowded center of the dance floor, the movements of Ana are particularly appealing. She heels the floor and slowly moves her body forward, making ample gestures with her arms, first the right shoulder, then the left shoulder. These movements are followed by a combination of complicated footwork based on a toe-to-heel motion in each foot; at the same time, her hands move from the front to the sides of her body as if waving a skirt. In front of her is David who, in a concealed posture, marches down the dance floor, accompanying his dance steps with sudden, jerky movements of his arms and head. Both Ana and David combine dance steps typical of ravers and clubbers in the United States or Europe with movements that seem extracted from the choreographies of traditional *norteño* dances: *polca, chotís,* redowa. While traces of the former dances appear in the general cadence of the bodies and the sharp movements "à la

Figure 6.1 Ana and David dancing to the beat of Plankton Man's
"Recinto portuario." Photo by the author

break dance," the latter tend to be reflected in the footwork—sometimes
similar to the stylized dance steps of *chotís*—and, in the case of Ana, in the
arms and shoulders. A few feet away from Ana and David, Antonio dances
by himself. He keeps his hands together in front of his body while grabbing
his belt buckle. His upper body, rather rigid, moves from right to left in a
restricted fashion while he walks forward and backward every four beats.
Antonio's movements look like a modern variation of traditional polka line
dancing and Piporro's *taconazo* style.[8] As if triggered by the snare drum rolls
in Terrestre's "El palomar," Antonio's dancing style changes. He shifts from
restricted motions to ample arm gestures. His hands leave the belt, his fingers move as if playing "air bass," and his hands play percussion on his
body. Within this heterogeneous variety, the dominant dancing style among
the fans at Centro bar could be best described as mono-centered open work.

Nor-tec fans are aware of the heterogeneous character of Nor-tec dancing and openly talk about it. "It is a sort of mix between trance and *quebradita* dance styles . . . also *zapateado* or cumbia. It is very attractive and
a lot of fun," says Daniel.[9] Alex, a younger but faithful Nor-tec follower
from Tijuana, comments on his dancing practices:

> I could not go [to a Nor-tec party] with my girlfriend because the music
> traps me. . . . I am not there to *ligar* [flirt] with anybody. . . . I always dance
> and will always dance by myself. It is a very personal thing. I do not try
> to dance in any given way, the more I get lost in the music the better.
> Sometimes, due to the rhythm, I throw in a few *norteña* or *quebradita*
> dance steps without realizing.[10]

Adriana further expands on this:

> [W]hen I was in school we used to prepare a lot of choreographies. They
> were *ranchero* style when it was for the Pancho Villa celebration, with
> your *rebozo* and your bullets. People throw those dance steps in at the
> [Nor-tec] parties. They come dressed with their boots and *tejano* hat.
> They are not actual cowboys but they do it because Nor-tec music has a
> lot to do with that. It has a certain *norteño* little sound and it lends itself
> to a few *norteño* dance steps.[11]

The improvisational open work in Ana's, David's, and Antonio's dancing
styles are good examples of the comments made by Adriana, Daniel, and
Alex. As Adriana reveals, many of the improvised steps in their dancing
styles reveal a common source: they are typical stylistic features of *ballet
folklórico* choreographies as they were taught in art classes at elementary
schools throughout Mexico up to the 1980s. My personal experience as
a kid educated in elementary schools in the northern Mexican states of
Tamaulipas and Sonora allows me to trace many of the current dance steps
to the choreographies I learned in those classes. Year after year, we spent a
few hours a week learning stylized versions of *polca* dancing (and other
danzas folklóricas) as part of large choreographies to be staged on Mother's
Day or Día de la Bandera (National Flag Day). For many years during our
childhood in Reynosa, my sister spent countless hours in *clases de baile
folclórico* (folk dance lessons), where she learned incredible embellished
choreographies of, among other dances, *chotís*—which, to my amazement,
she is able to reproduce to perfection more than 20 years later. Nevertheless, neither the stylized *polca* dance steps I learned in school nor the embellished footwork my sister mastered in dance lessons were ever present
at the parties and *carne asadas* where friends and family gathered every
other weekend. Although *norteño* music was played at these get-togethers
and the rest of the kids and I were encouraged to dance on improvised

tablados consisting of old wooden doors lying on the floor, the complicated and choreographed dance steps learned at the *clases* were never part of these weekly experiences. It was tacitly understood that these learned dance steps belonged to a different performance, one reserved for the yearly festivals at school or for the auditorium in McAllen, Texas (where my sister's class would perform), where these dances were public showcases of "tradition" and local "heritage" in the manner of a tourist attraction. It is telling that these literally learned dance steps surface in the performance of Nor-tec.[12]

The presence of these mono-centered dance steps—embodied in the bodies of northern people through cultural tradition—as part of Nor-tec dance reveals important aspects of the power of this dance scene: as individual, creative, imaginary codification and as communal, choreographic, symbolic recodification. As José E. Limón affirms, traditional *norteño* closed work dance styles place "an aesthetic value on the male ability to execute a variety of turns and swinging movements and on the female's ability to follow."[13] In contrast, the reappropriation of *norteño* dance steps in Tijuana's Nor-tec dance style creates a simulacrum-type of scenario where women have the opportunity to express themselves by reconfiguring these roles into improvisational open dance work. The submissive attitude expected from women in a macho-oriented culture like that of northern Mexico is reflected and reproduced in the dance steps of traditional *polca*, *chotís*, and redowa, where the female's role is to follow the male's lead. Moreover, this role is further reinforced in contemporary *norteño* dance genres such as *quebradita*, where the female body actually becomes an object at the service of the male's bravado dance display. This is one of the ways that tradition and heritage function as mechanisms which institutionalize the female body and make it into an object of desire.[14] However, female dancing bodies are also subjects of desire, and in Tijuana, the female desire for modernity as expressed in the Nor-tec dancing style of Ana and Teresa is a site for the subversion of the institutionalized body's desire. In the heterogeneous forms of Nor-tec dance, *tijuanense* women consume basic elements of the dancing discourse of *norteño* tradition to transform the discourse itself into imaginaries of modernity through individual experience and expression.

In Nor-tec dance, the desired bodies of these women are reconstituted into desiring bodies that demand equality and independence, desires that are enunciated in the performance itself. Just as the music of Plankton Man rearticulates ideas about modernity and tradition (*Yo me dedico a la música desde hace cuarenta años*) and validates one with the other, the Tijuana Nor-tec dancing style embodies imaginaries of modernity while performatively reconfiguring tradition in relation to an imaginary present and future. To dance Nor-tec music is to reimagine tradition and modernity through the body.

"Stick with It, 'Cuz It Keeps Everyone Together": Dancing Nor-tec II (L.A. Mix)

On the evening of 16 September 2003, the Echo, a small, underground Los Angeles dance bar (known as Nayarit in better days), houses the last concert of La Leche, an electronic music tour organized by the British label Sonic 360. On the stage, Panóptica, Pepe Mogt from Fussible, and Bostich operate their laptops and combine their sounds and talents to produce the hypnotic beats of a live Nor-tec music performance; Panóptica loops a borrowed bass line from the well-known symphonic arrangement of Rubén Fuentes' *ranchera* song "Que bonita es mi tierra" and blasts it out of the loudspeakers of the club. On the dance floor, about 20 fans, mostly Mexicans and Mexican Americans, but also some Anglos and African Americans, are intrigued by the transfiguration of the words and sounds of Fuentes' song (*Ay caray, caray / Que bonita es mi tierra, que bonita / Que linda es* [How beautiful is my land, how beautiful / How nice it is]) into modernist sounds through Panóptica's crafty computer manipulation. A down-tempo style of approximately 102 bpm steadily attracts more and more fans to the dance floor, transforming it from a talking to a dancing space. A few minutes later, the music makes a transition from the raw-sounding *tarolas* of Bostich's "Unicornio" and "Rumba" to the disco-sounding analog synthesizers of Fussible's "Allegretto per signora, Nortec Mix" and "Odyssea," and the pace of the music increases first to 107 then to 127 bpm. The dance floor is already crowded, making it almost impossible to walk among the dancers. Those standing on the sides and along the back of the dance floor watch the dancers and the musicians but avoid dancing themselves. Although among the dancers there are a few boy-girl couples and some girl-girl couples who dance holding each other, improvisational open dance work dominates. As in Tijuana, this open work informs us of a desire for modernity that is reflected in the incorporation of movements and dance steps typical of the international rave scene—jumping-while-kicking motions, movements "à la break dance," and sudden changes of style and body motion center. However, among the women, the dancing style varies from that of Tijuana fans in one basic and fundamental area: while motion among *tijuanenses* tends to be mono-centered, motion among L.A. dancing fans is mostly poly-centered.

The dancing style among L.A. female fans emphasizes a synchronic polyphony of movements that usually consist of independent-but-coordinated

hip, shoulders, and feet motions, while *tijuanenses'* dancing style highlights instead a diachronic juxtaposition of movements, each of which might emphasize different body centers. The importance of this fundamental difference at the core of Nor-tec dance styles lies in the fact that the two styles reflect different institutionalized discourses of the body and account for different desired bodies. Therefore, since these two dancing styles respond to different discourses of representation, they also inform us of different desiring subjects inasmuch as the subjects' desire triggers a negotiation between discursive and individual experiential bodies.

According to Jennifer Mañón, event coordinator for Sonic 360, the cities and venues for the La Leche tour were chosen in line with Heineken's (the sponsor) interest in reaching out to Latino consumers in the United States. The tour was presented in the American cities with larger Latino populations (New York, Chicago, Miami, Los Angeles, Houston, San Francisco), advertisement was done through major Latino radio stations, and the actual venues tended to be located in Latino neighborhoods.[15] For that reason, the majority of the attendees at the La Leche events were Latinos, and the discourses of representation reflected in their appropriation of Nor-tec are the powerful ideologies of Latino and pan-Latino identity that predominate in the United States. Mañón, a Mexican American from Wisconsin, addresses this issue in relation to Sonic 360's interest in promoting Nor-tec:

> [Sonic 360's executives] thought it was really cool to introduce [Nor-tec] to other Latinos because it's so new and people were all listening to the same old stuff, and we [Mañón and her Latino friends] were so sick of that mentality so we wanted to push it to show Latinos that there's other stuff to listen to. . . . A lot of Latinos seem stuck in their ways, and are stereotyped as wanting to keep their own ways, and radio stations are a number one way of brainwashing, saying: "stick with it, 'cuz it keeps everyone together."[16]

The stereotypes to which Mañón refers are the essentialist notions about the identity of Latin America and Latin Americans that the U.S. media has produced, reproduced, and recreated throughout the twentieth century. These are discourses that, in an attempt to create a unified Latin American other against which to identify a homogenized white U.S. identity, have themselves homogenized Latin American cultures and the diversity of Latin American experiences in the United States. "Latino" is a label that refers to a series of processes of Latinization by which individuals of Latin American descent (including Chicanos, Newyoricans, and Cuban Americans) are represented as sharing one common identity. The early ties of the Latino advertising industry to Puerto Rican and Cuban immigration to the United States in the 1950s and 1960s are clearly evident in the discourses, practices,

and materials that came to identify Latino music culture, for example, salsa, rumba, bongos, congas, maracas, carnivals, poly-centered dancing, and highly sexualized bodies. However, as Arlene Dávila states, these processes of Latinization "stem from the contrary involvement of and negotiations between dominant, imposed, and self-generated interests."[17] In fact, the adoption of this homogenizing representational discourse allows a variety of communities of different Latin American origins to access positions of power within the American political system that would otherwise be diffi-cult to achieve. Nevertheless, such representation as a performative dis-course—a performative speech, in Judith Butler's sense—enacts what it enunciates, and it is at the level of individual bodies that the consequences of this performative discourse need to be renegotiated.[18]

The dancing fans at the Echo in L.A. reflect these homogenizing dis-courses of Latinidad in their stylized moves. Nevertheless, this style is also a site for the reconciliation of these discourses and the dancers' own as-piration for individual cosmopolitan identities. The presence of couples dancing in each other's arms in male-led closed work and the prevalence of poly-centered body motion reveal that dancers at the Echo are responding in part to the embodiment of the Latino culture discourse. On the other hand, the large presence of improvisational open work suggests that the

Figure 6.2   Dancing fans at the Echo. Photo by the author

fans' appropriation of Nor-tec music also provides a site for personal expression, wherein is seen the imagination of a new relationship between the discourse of traditional Latinidad and their desire for modernity and cosmopolitanism.

On the crowded dance floor of the Echo, Diana and Leticia dance together; as Fussible's music increases the speed of its beat, they slowly start to move from the right to the left side of the dance floor. Making their way from one side of the crowded dance floor to the other, they begin to interact with other dancers who cross their path. The freedom and fluidity of these interactions are particularly patent in Diana's case. At one moment, she is dancing with Leticia; in the next moment, she seductively approaches a male dancing alone in the middle of the room. Diana's movements are slow and provocative as she nears the guy; her arms lift and her hands run through her long black hair before she reaches out toward him. They dance together for several minutes, exchange a few words, and go their separate ways without talking to each other for the rest of the night.

Diana's dance style is a site that contests her expected role in traditional Latino dancing. Not only does she not wait for the male to take the initiative, but she actually initiates the encounter, remaining in complete control of the situation and ending it when she chooses. Dancing to Nor-tec becomes for Diana an activity of gender empowerment which would not be possible in traditional Latin dancing; it is a liberating experience which allows her to express her sexuality without being institutionalized as a sexual object. By participating in the Nor-tec performance, she renegotiates for herself the problematic designation of women as desired bodies—her poly-centered dancing reveals her exposure to this discourse—and performs herself instead as a desiring subject in search of independence, power, and equality.

As Jennifer Mañón argues, Nor-tec shows these Latinos that "there is other stuff to listen to" besides the stereotypes of Latino culture emphasized by mainstream media. Thus, consuming Nor-tec provides an avenue for a performance of the self that engages the dominant discourses of Latino representation but defies their totalizing control.

"They Do Not Know How to Dance to This Music": Dancing Nor-tec III (Chi Town Mix)

Around 10 o'clock on 23 October 2003, Bostich and Fussible, beers in hand, take the stage at Chicago's Hot House. The music fills the air and an array of quickly changing modernist images of Tijuana projected by VJ CBrown rhythmically bounce on screens behind the musicians. However, while the visuals dance and provide a perfect Nor-tec counterpoint to Bostich's "Autobanda," the dance floor remains empty. Bostich tries unsuccessfully to capture the attention of the Chicago clubbers (predominantly Latinos) sitting at the tables around the dance floor. Although he increases the pace of the music from 103 to 107 bpm, throws some of the best samples of his crudest, most personal Nor-tec style, and the loud, edgy, unprocessed sound of *tarola* playing fills the room with incredible rhythmic patterns, the clubbers remain in their seats, seemingly unaffected by Bostich's virtuosic display. After 15 minutes of fruitless effort, Bostich and Pepe Mogt change their strategy; instead of the raw *norteño* sounds of *tarola*, the *cumbia* rhythms, and the fragmented *banda* brassy melodies of "Autobanda" [◉ **Track 8** and **Track 9**] and "Tijuana Bass," [◉ **Track 7** and **Track 10**] the musicians shift toward Fussible's "El sonar de mis tambores," [◉ **Track 4**] a track whose combination of sounds might be more familiar to U.S. Latinos: conga and bongo drums, in fast Latin disco and Afro-Caribbean styles that quickly reach 129 bpm. The clubbers immediately start dancing, first in the aisles, then slowly moving toward the center of the dance floor. Once the dance floor is occupied, Bostich slowly reintroduces his hardcore, *tarola*-driven Nor-tec style to a now-willing, ecstatic dancing crowd which goes crazy with the percussive sound of "Polaris," responding with loud whistles, screams, and excitement which is manifested in more energetic twists, turns, and jumps.

Most people dance in couples, many following the traditional closed work of salsa and Afro-Caribbean dance styles, where the male holds the female's hand while she turns around only to return to his arms and continue to be led by her partner. Some others show more interest in disco styles, combining closed and open work. The left corner of the dance floor has been appropriated by a group of four friends dancing in couples. One of the boys performs robot-like jerky motions with his arms, along the sides of his body, alternatively moving up and down from the elbows. His partner keeps the beat as her head shakes back and forth, her arms move freely along the sides of her body, and she moves forward and backward throughout the small area, reclaiming it with ample leg movements. The other couple holds each other, his left hand on her waist as her left hand takes his right hand up in the air; their body balance shifts from right to left and their knees remain slightly bent; suddenly, she lets herself fall back, he catches her and moves her around while keeping the right-left shifting balance going according to the beat of the music; it is a difficult movement borrowed from *quebradita* dancing. [◉ **Video 2**] This group of friends is a perfect microcosm of the dance floor: one dancer doing the Robot and performing other retro, 1980s disco movements reminiscent of Michael Jackson at his prime, another one claiming ownership of the floor through

Figure 6.3   Doing the Robot to Nor-tec music at the Hot House. Photo by the author

poly-centered dance work typical of Afro-Caribbean dancing, and a couple reinventing *norteño* dances: *polca* and *quebradita*.

   When I asked a Nor-tec fan why people would not dance as Bostich's music resounded all over the club, he plainly answered: "they do not know how to dance to this music." His answer was simple and obvious, and it forces us to observe Nor-tec as a screen upon which a cultural landscape can be reinvented and desire can be projected and rearticulated. Nor-tec is thus a site whose meaning is constructed and negotiated in practice and consumption as much as in production and distribution. Celeste Fraser Delgado and José Muñoz have stated, "Dance sets politics in motion, bringing people together in rhythmic affinity where identification takes the form of histories written on the body through gesture. The body dancing to Latin rhythms analyzes and articulates the conflicts that have crossed Latin/o American identity."[19] The heterogeneous forms and styles of Nor-tec dancing observed at the Hot House speak of the complex cultural negotiation taking place between the unbalanced powers that inform the identity of Latinos in the United States. In order to negotiate identity niches, Latinos must engage the discourses of representation on Latinidad mentioned earlier, and at the same time they must resolve the contradictions that arise when those discourses clash with larger discourses on U.S. modernity, equality, independence, opportunity, and individuality. Furthermore, Latinos need to resolve issues of identity politics within their own communities and understand their own relations to their parents' or grandparents' heritage and tradition while dealing with mainstream pressures for assimilation. As Delgado and Muñoz suggest, the dancing body is a place for Latinos to articulate and analyze these conflicts and to project their individual desires as they sort through these complex maps for themselves.

Nor-tec is a modernist cultural manifestation that engages the mainstream but is also critical of it. It is an aesthetic that rewrites tradition while confronting a variety of local and global alienating discourses, and it is a site for Latinos to resolve the conflicts they face in both of these discourses. Latino embodiment of Nor-tec through dance challenges the mainstream Latino identity discourse and exhibits its contradictions. The multiplicity of cultures embodied by individuals of Latin American descent is reflected in the variety of poly-centered and mono-centered and open and closed dancing styles. Latinos do not share one identity; the Latin American experience in the United States is multicultural, and if there is something to be shared, it is the racial and cultural discrimination embodied in a performative discourse that has attempted to erase these differences. This conflictive history of racism and cultural erasure is articulated in the Latino dancing bodies at the Hot House. However, these dancing bodies also reflect their exposure to the contradictory discourse of equality, modernity, and overall homogenization to which U.S. citizens are subjected through the media in their everyday lives. The notion of retro and kitschy aesthetics that has been pushed by the U.S. media since the late 1990s is also present in the disco and break dance steps that combine on the dance floor. Remembering Michael Jackson's dance style and combining it with Piporro's *taconazo* tell us of the desires of modernity produced and reproduced by the mainstream media, of the desire to confront conflicting ideas of tradition reproduced by Latino and American media, and of the desire to incorporate their unique experiences into the construction of a multicultural identity within an already multicultural society.

To Dance or Not to Dance II (La Estrella Mix)

I have discussed the particular features that characterize Nor-tec dancing in three different scenes. My intention has been to show that dancing bodies mediate among a variety of ideological discourses that inform the fans' everyday lives, offering a performative solution to the cultural contradictions those representations entail. I have suggested that the dancing fans are at the same time desired objects and desiring subjects whose movements reflect both the culture they have embodied and the aspirations they have imagined. Fans in all three scenes share the free, improvisational open work of disco and rave dancing, representing both a liberating potential to overcome the limitations of the institutionalized body through individual expression as well as the homogenizing danger which is inherent in globalization. However, Nor-tec provides dancers with a site for the rearticulation of local culture within a global phenomenon, thus allowing for a momentary subversion of the homogenizing nature of globalization. In this context, as Sally Ann Allen Ness states, a thorough examination of dance culture should not only focus on what dancers do, but also on what they do not do. Focusing on this "negativity of movement"[20] is crucial to recognizing the translocal limitations of many of the discourses that dancers confront and negotiate in their dance.

Different musical tastes result in different dancing practices that, in turn, reflect different discourses about the body. The difference between Nor-tec and house that prompted a Chicago fan to tell me "they do not know how to dance to this music" was pointed out by journalist Nina Garin in her review of Nortec City, when she stated that "the music wasn't easy to dance to—it does not have the ecstatic beats of house music. Nortec is more repetitive, it's more relaxed, it takes a while to feel the groove."[21] This review vis-à-vis the initial absence of dancing among Chicago fans is worth analyzing within a larger cultural context that takes into consideration dancing styles and their cultural implications.

The overall absence of poly-centered dance styles among dancing fans in Tijuana, while disregarding the extended presence of Afro-Caribbean rhythms in Nor-tec music—especially cumbia, which gives the music its "more relaxed groove," as Garin mentions in her review—reveals some of the shortcomings of the pan-Latin discourse of U.S. media. First, not all Afro-Caribbean music is able to enter this discourse—this is the reason that Garin finds it "takes a while to feel the groove." Americans are not used to cumbia because, as opposed to salsa, mambo, or cha-cha-chá, it has not yet entered the pan-Latin discourse of American media;[22] second, the discourse is unable to travel translocally. Furthermore, the middle-class *tijuanenses* who follow Nor-tec actually engage local discourses that have for decades identified cumbia and cumbia dancing with the lower classes. *Salón de baile La Estrella,* a documentary on a local cumbia club produced by Itzel Martínez del Canizo and Huicho Martín (VJ Mashaka), shows that most of the regulars of the Tijuana club are working-class individuals, especially migrants from southern cities in the country.[23] Since Nor-tec is a screen for the projection of middle-class *tijuanenses*' desire for modernity, a site for the imagination of new identities, the working-class-tinged cumbia (much like *norteño* and *banda* music and their links to older Mexican generations) can be part of these imaginary identities through a reconstitution that would liberate it from these "undesirable" cultural associations. This takes place by way of a process that views cumbia, *banda,* and *norteña* through a kitschy perspective that reterritorializes discourses about these genres from the perspective of individuals aspiring to find a place for themselves in the imagined modern global community. Therefore, the absence of poly-centered styles in Tijuana's Nor-tec dance shows us a community that embodies a complex and contradictory cultural history with respect to African-influenced cultural practices. On the one hand, it is a hegemonic culture that has, for the most part, discursively erased most African traces from everyday life; and, on the other hand, this culture embraces these manifestations when they are presented in the seductive modern clothes of the "American dream," wishing simultaneously to differentiate itself from the "lower-class" rhythms of cumbia music. Problematic issues of race and class are brought to the front of the Nor-tec dance experience when the contradictions between production (cumbia-based music) and consumption (mono-centered dance), and between presences and absences are examined.

We must also understand the absence of dance at Chicago's Hot House during the performance of Bostich's most hardcore Nor-tec music with the negative logic of this analysis. In the United States, the media play a funda-mental role in the definition of a "hip" Latino identity and in the creation of institutionalized desires for Latinos. A complex economy, disguised as a tool for identity cohesion ("stick with it, 'cuz it keeps everyone together," as Jennifer Mañón expressed), is at stake in the reproduction of these de-sires. The successful American representation of Latin America as a homo-geneous "tropical" culture resonated with the nascent Latino advertising industry in the 1950s and '60s as it became oriented toward Puerto Ricans and Cubans. The relationship between Latino and mainstream American media in the United States is a symbiotic one, as both sides feed and re-produce each other's myths and desires. For the American media, the man-ufacture of a Latino identity has been also the creation of a product of consumption. Concurrently, Latino media, by emphasizing some of the ideas that constitute this media product—the image of the *caliente* (hot) Latin lover or that "Latino women are *candela pura* [pure fire]"—reproduce the stereotypes of American media. However, this strategy allows Latino media two things: to share the benefits of the commodification of every-thing Latino and to adopt the dreams that the American media offer to Latinos. The music of Mexican Americans and northern Mexicans, which was considered unsophisticated not only by non-Mexicans but also by cen-tral and southern Mexicans, remained marginal in mainstream Latino culture until very recently.[24] The current shift being experienced in the Latino media is partly the result of the *banda* craze that swept Los Angeles in the mid-1990s, a phenomenon that forced the media to face the reality of the enormous economic power of Mexicans and Mexican Americans (who are the largest, but most underrepresented in the media, portion of Latinos in the United States).[25] Suddenly, *norteña* and *banda* were also *caliente* music, and *quebradita* dancers were *candela pura*.

Thus, Latinos are border subjects who are themselves epistemological contact zones, the ubiquitous borderline so lucidly described by Gloria Anzaldúa.[26] They are the in-between space where Latin American and American cultures interact and where the tensions between the different Latino communities are negotiated. Their bodies are the border between subjectivity and social discourses—Chicago clubbers clearly exemplify the issues at stake in their everyday negotiations of these circumstances. The fact that first they found it difficult to dance to a music dominated by the rhythms and timbres of cumbia and the loud tubas of *banda* informs us that the sources of Nor-tec music were not part of their desire for modernity. If dancing to techno music embodies a separation from the unsophisticated part of their heritage, then their first encounter with Nor-tec became a contradiction because the same sounds from which they wanted to escape were welcoming them into the party. The absence of dancing illustrated a problem, which Bostich and Pepe Mogt were able to quickly identify. Their solution, to shift away from the *norteño* toward a more Afro-Caribbean style based on salsa rather than cumbia, shows their awareness of the problems of representation among Latinos in the United States. However, Nor-tec also became that screen upon which Latinos were able to project a reevaluation of *norteño* culture through music. The musicians' reintroduction of *norteño* elements once the dance floor was occupied allowed the dancing bodies to perform themselves in relation to these elements and their desire for modernity and cosmopolitanism.

¿Qué te puedo decir que no haya dicho el cuerpo? is the sentence by VJ Mashaka that pervades this chapter; behind this enunciation lies the idea that the dancing body expresses our most inner desires and at the same time betrays the mechanism of our socialization. Dancing is an ideology inasmuch as it acts as a focal point that articulates signifiers; it is an activity that gives social, economic, and ethnic meaning to the body and incorporates it as part of particular symbolic systems. The dancing body is a site where the process of symbolization takes place in a performative manner. The dancing bodies of Nor-tec fans reveal that their desire is to be equal members in a global economy while still coming to terms with the past, rewriting traditions such as *norteño* culture and Latino representation in the process of performance. Gender roles as well as class and ethnicity

discourses are engaged, questioned, and reevaluated through the body movements of frenzied dancers in Tijuana, Los Angeles, and Chicago. This reevaluation of tradition and heritage, of representation and discourse, is reflected in the rewriting of the body that takes place when it dances to the beat of its desires. Dancing with desire reconfigures tradition in relation to an imaginary present and future and provides a site for our own reconstruction of identity.

7

Nor-tec and the Postnational Imagination

In a ceremony on 20 April 2004, a few months before my second field trip to Tijuana, Mexican president Vicente Fox joined the Spanish businessman Antonio Navalón in inaugurating Tijuana, Tercera Nación (Tijuana, Third Nation). The event, a large-scale arts project centering on the city and its border culture, was mainly sponsored by Navalón, a director of PRISA-Mexico,[1] with the private support of companies like Coca-Cola, Movistar (the cellular phone branch of the Spanish network Telefónica), and the Spanish newspaper *El País*. The most visible undertaking of Tijuana, Tercera Nación was a large-scale exhibition entitled Grito Creativo (Creative Scream), which presented gigantic prints of local art along the border fence and the walls of the Río Tijuana canal.

The exhibition featured Nor-tec visual art by Gerardo Yépiz (Aca-monchi) and Ángeles Moreno alongside works by local artists such as Tania Candiani, Iván Díaz Robledo, Max Lizárraga, and Jhoana Mora. Just as Nor-tec visual art played a vital role in Tijuana, Tercera Nación, Nor-tec music—with its hybrid character and transnational success—was also a necessary addition to the joyful project. According to Pepe Mogt, the Nor-tec Collective received an invitation to play at a concert intended to be staged near the border fence, which would allow musicians to freely move from the Mexican to the U.S. side.[2] According to the organizers, the concert, to be called Over the Border, would have featured Carlos Santana, Paco de Lucía, Julieta Venegas, Los Tigres del Norte, and the Nortec Collective, among other musicians. Although the event was finally canceled

189

Figure 7.1   Tijuana, Tercera Nación exhibition along the walls of the Río
Tijuana canal. Photo by the author

due to a series of unforeseen circumstances, the roster of musicians and the
general idea of a "transnational" concert tell us much about the ideology
behind the organization of the whole Tijuana, Tercera Nación project.
During the inaugural speech on 20 April, Navalón stated: "Tijuana offers
a model for the relationship with 'the other side'; to talk about the United
States or the *gringos* [from Mexico City], three thousand miles away implies [that we are] talking about a myth and not about an everyday reality;
that's the advantage of this society and its cultural manifestations."[3] On
the same occasion, a cheerful Mexican president Vicente Fox stated, "No
other state has advanced with Tijuana and Baja California's speed in re-
ducing crime,"[4] to which he added later at a press conference: "I see no sign
of the weakening of the [nation's] institutions."[5] Ironically, the very presence of the Mexican president validating a privately supported event which
had only a very small participation by FONCA, the governmental cultural
agency, in the decision-making process leading to its ideological design is
an important clue to the current state of affairs between the institutions of
the Mexican nation-state and the transnational private sector.[6]

   Regardless of the extensive local, national, and international media
coverage, as well as the magnificence of the event, Tijuana, Tercera Nación
generated a long-lasting polemical debate among local intellectuals and
artists from a large variety of political affiliations. At the core of this dis-

cussion were the significant center-periphery issues and the questions of representation implicit in a project that many interpreted as part of yet another centralist (and, in this case, neoliberal) political agenda. Among the most vocal critics of Navalón's project was Heriberto Yépez, one of Tijuana's most talented young writers. Soon after the inauguration of Tijuana, Tercera Nación, Yépez (who had been previously asked to grant permission for the use of his work as part of the project) requested that his work be removed from the exhibition. He argued that the reactionary ideology behind the project had only become clear at the event's opening and suggested that he (and others involved) had been taken advantage of by the organizers not disclosing the true character of the event. Yépez accused the organizers of decontextualizing the images and manipulating the artist's intentions in order to "hide the processes that are taking place in the area [and] using art as mere decoration, *cool* distraction from everything border art should do: to critically question all our bilateral processes."[7] For Yépez, Tijuana, Tercera Nación was nothing but "NAFTA art" fashioned to "validate the transnational corporate project and the hegemonic desires of the United States. . . . A dreadful message that promotes the loss of national identity and sovereignty."[8] He would later further clarify his criticism by stating:

> [M]ore than a decade after its production, we can say that the uncritical reception of the term [hybridity] has worn it out, making it an easy label to describe the border . . . [and] Tijuana as an intermediate zone, a metropolis that according to this discourse is already different from Mexican national culture. What the false metaphor of "Tijuana" as Tercera Nación hides is the asymmetries, the inequalities between the cultures that inhabit the region, the clash (and even death) produced there, the misencounters. It is not a harmless "mix." . . . Tijuana as the laboratory for a post-Mexican future. We all know that this discourse about Tijuana—a "Tijuanology"—has been excessive and very opportunistic. The border as Mexifornia, Amexico or Mexamerica? That notion does not stand. The border is not a Hegelian synthesis (or *happy meal*) of the bi-national field, [it is not] the third party which solves the problem.[9]

Julio Sueco, a *tijuanense* blogger living in Sweden, believes that Tijuana, Tercera Nación articulated a different problem of representation. For him, the pompous project was a *chilango* attempt to define the identity of Tijuana and its citizens. On 1 June 2004, he posted:

> Let these [foreign] artists come and look at this work or talk about how wonderful Tijuana is. . . . They really have romanticized it. And as always, we *tijuanenses* will stay out of the spotlight—both [from] the perspective from the "other side" and the perspective from the center [of the country]—until they leave. [But] don't come here to tell us how we are, we know that

already. In fact, this "circus" [Tijuana, Tercera Nación] is just like any other tourist in Tijuana, it will come and go, it will never stay.[10]

For others, it was Navalón's seeming lack of respect for local artists that infuriated them. Early in 2005, the Spanish businessman organized a public meeting to notify the artistic community of Tijuana that the Grito Creativo exhibition would be touring Madrid, Berlin, and Paris. In her chronicle of that meeting, Ingrid Hernández, a local photographer and one of the artists whose work was featured at the exhibit, acknowledged that most of the artists were pleased with the prospect of having their work shown in Europe. However, after the distressing experience of the first edition of Grito Creativo, Hernández confronted Navalón about the irregularities throughout the selection and curatorial processes and about the continuing decontextualization of the images for the validation of an ideological project with which most local artists did not agree. According to Hernández, Navalón replied: "I am one of those who would rather ask for forgiveness than for permission. Just imagine if sometime ago I had come to show you my plans for the event; we would have never agreed on something. It would have taken forever and maybe it would have never happened."[11] Clearly, local artists were slowly beginning to get concerned not only with the ideological context for which their pieces came to stand in Navalón's project, but also with the impresario's lack of respect toward the artists and the haziness with which the financial aspect of the project was handled. In an electronic conversation, Nor-tec collaborator Acamonchi commented: "nobody was paid anything. They screwed us all."[12]

Curiously, most critics of Tijuana, Tercera Nación point out the unnecessary presence of President Vicente Fox inaugurating a privately sponsored event that seemed to challenge the ability of the nation-state to fulfill its citizens' aspirations. Clearly, the Tijuana, Tercera Nación affair became a contested site where not only were the representation of Tijuana and the city's relation to hegemonic centers at stake, but also the perception of the Mexican government in relation to transnational corporations in a time of institutional crisis of the nation-state. Navalón's project attempted to present the border as an idealist site of "happy" encounters rather than as a problematic line of separation. In Navalón's uncritical and superficial reading of border culture, the type of mischievous cultural negotiation achieved in hybrid manifestations like Nor-tec became icons of the type of neoliberal, postnational border he wanted to portray through his project. It is intriguing that some of the critics actually returned to Nor-tec as an example of the complex issues that inform the everyday cultural negotiations of border citizens, issues overlooked in the optimism of Navalón's project. While Yépez asks how is it that "the fascinating sound of the friction between global and local culture of Nor-tec has been transformed by many into the sound of the fall of the 'old divisions,'"[13] Daniel, a local blogger, posts the following message:

> I do not agree at all with those who have tried to equate [Nor-tec] with the frivolity of Tercera Nación. What the collective does is something completely different and doesn't require an artistic Maecenas with an open checkbook. . . . They haven't received any Televisa-type support and they haven't had to prostitute their musical ideas for a contract. . . . Contracts require digested pop products and Nortec is far from being a *fast food* musical product.[14]

As Yépez and Daniel argue, and as I have shown in previous chapters, Nor-tec is not the happy meeting of two distinctly different worlds but rather a complex and ironic performative act that negotiates the contradictions of everyday life in a multi-ideological world. If indeed a postnational identity informs the borderlands' in-between culture, it is necessarily a more intricate and problematic condition than the naïve vision of a businessman who finds nothing unethical in using the work of a group of local artists to advance his own agenda.

Borders, Third Space, and Third Nation

The notion of "border" has been continuously re-signified throughout the last two centuries according to the changing relationship between selves and others, those on one side and those on the other side of the border. The term has been used to determine limits, as a line imaginarily drawn to separate cultures, peoples, and visions of the world. In the nineteenth century, the notion of "frontier" referred to "the movable landmark of the march of the civilizing mission, the line dividing civilization from barbarism."[15] Such an understanding was later replaced by the idea of the border as a separating line and eventually re-signified as a line that connects cultures. At the end of the twentieth century and the beginning of the twenty-first, the political tensions and the pressures of globalization at the U.S.–Mexico border made people ambiguously go back and forth between the notions of border as barrier and as portal.

For people living on the Mexican side, the border is *el bordo*, a term in Spanglish derived from the word "border." Curiously, Mexicans from the center of the country, including scholars unfamiliar with the particularities of border culture, have often misspelled it as *borde*, the Spanish term for "edge." This seemingly harmless phonetic confusion is in fact a perfect reflection of the desires and fears that the border generates among Mexicans from the center of the country: the border as edge, the final frontier, the periphery of national identity, a site where the *chilangos'* desire for an authentic "essence" of Mexicanidad should be defended from the advance of U.S. cultural colonialism. The central Mexican failure to account for the actual meaning of the word as locals use it could also be interpreted as a refusal to accept the cultural particularities of a region where indeed the coherence of the hegemonic national identity discourse collapses, although not necessarily replaced by a postnational identity in the cheerfully optimistic sense proposed by Navalón. Decentered subjects might imagine themselves to be cosmopolitan, but this imagining is necessarily the result of negotiating the everyday practices that violently and inevitably mark them as the unsophisticated other. In reality, the intersection between discourses of national identity and experiences of local identity, between discourses of representation and practices of self-identification, among policies of national integration, international separation, and everyday practices of economic codependence are complex sites where new notions of identity and belonging are continuously negotiated and imagined. These newly imagined notions and sites are responses to the everyday experiences of racial, ethnic, social, and economic inequality and discrimination against border citizens. Many of the cultural manifestations developed under these circumstances are necessarily informed by the shifting understanding of what a border is. The pertinence of ideas like "in-between-ness," "third nation," "third space," and postnationality—uncritically invoked by events such as Tijuana, Tercera Nación—should be examined under the light of *tijuanense* everyday life, as well as an informed understanding of what these terms stand for, under what social and historical circumstances they were developed, and what sets of values are attached to them.

Homi Bhabha uses the concept of in-between-ness to analyze diasporic communities, conceiving migration as the connecting tissue between larger hegemonic cultures. These partial cultures are both alike and different from the dominant cultures they separate and connect, they are culture's "in between."[16] Subjects living under these multi-ideological conditions experience a fragmentary reality where metanarratives collapse, leaving them unable to position themselves as part of ontologically defined groups, therefore forcing them to assume multiple identities in order to navigate and survive the complexity of dominant ideological discourses that construct them as peripheral. Chela Sandoval believes that the place where individual perception and social representation meet is a place between realities, a third site out of which "undecidable forms of being and original theories and practices for emancipation are produced."[17] The contesting character of these in-between spaces has been theorized in Homi Bhabha's notion of "third space." For Bhabha, the third space is an area where "meaning and symbols of culture have no primordial unity or fixity."[18] Against Navalón's attempt to essentialize it and inscribe it with a fixed postnational political meaning, the third space is transient, it is always in a state of becoming, and its very nature is elusive and changing. It is precisely out of this ambiguity that strategic practices can be developed.

Tijuana is a third space inasmuch as it is a site of contradictions that can only be resolved by the individuals who embody them in their everyday lives. One of the most important contradictions of Tijuana is that although many might indeed experience it as a thoroughgoing border city—with media links to both Mexico and the United States, with peoples, currencies, and cultural goods from both sides circulating intensely in Tijuana itself— we should not forget that politically, Tijuana is in fact a Mexican city. A wide variety of both Mexican and U.S. political practices remind *tijuanenses* of the Mexican-ness of their city on a daily basis: the city is in Mexican territory, there is a U.S. army patrolling the border, and there is a border wall that reminds everyone which side they belong on. Tijuana's culture makes *tijuanenses* part of a larger cultural community, but their daily political hardships and their citizenship make them the other for those actually living that cosmopolitan experience on a daily basis in cities like San Diego or Los Angeles. People from Tijuana need to be able to navigate between U.S. and Mexican ideologies, sometimes entering one, sometimes entering the other, and most of the time walking on the borderline.

The Postnational Imagination

Globalization as an economic, social, and cultural phenomenon has propagated radical changes in the lives of individuals and challenges to one of the main institutions of modernity, the nation-state. Just as the increasing speed of economic and migratory flows helps in developing social formations and human relations that show the intrinsic contradictions, inequalities, and shortcomings of the project of modernity, the political consequences of this phenomenon also provide evidence of the crisis of the nation-state. Not only do nation-states lose economic power, sovereignty, and their capability to influence events when facing the transnational corporations that control global markets, they also become inefficient in providing their citizens with a sense of security, trust, and belonging. In the United States, the increasing political influence of transnational corporations on governmental decisions and democratic practices, the impact of privatization on the social obligations of the government, and the decentralization of capital are all signs of the crisis of the nation-state. In Mexico, the increasingly unequal and unjust distribution of wealth, the growing unemployment, the slow breakdown of the legal system and the state's networks of social protection also illustrate this crisis. Furthermore, as globalization encourages transnational movement, the national identities that provide cohesion to the idea of the nation-state also come under scrutiny. Reflecting on this situation, Arjun Appadurai suggests that "as the nation-state enters a terminal crisis . . . we can certainly expect that the materials of a postnational imaginary must be around us already,"[19] while Jürgen Habermas argues that new types of decentered supranational formations are required to take over the responsibilities and raison d'être of the nation-state.[20]

However, although postnational political formations might be an option among once-colonizing countries which arguably relate to each other on a more "egalitarian" basis, such an idea might be much more problematic when dealing with countries marked by histories of power, racial, and economic imbalances like the United States and Mexico. Habermas's proposal might work for examples like the European Union, but in the case of NAFTA, these decentered supranational formations appear as cover-ups of the colonialist and interventionist policies that have historically informed the unequal relations between the United States and Latin America. The dystopian character of the postnational imagination in the case of the U.S.–Mexico border only serves to emphasize the contradictions inherent in globalization.

By focusing on the most uncritical rhetoric about globalization and postnationality, cultural projects like Antonio Navalón's Tijuana, Tercera Nación ignore the harsh and contradictory reality that savvy border artists negotiate in their work. Navalón's rhetoric overlooks the postnational third site as a space where multiple strategies for the empowerment of the other (the victims of the nation-state's crisis) occur. Particularly significant was President Fox's moral support of Navalón's project. The political and historical circumstances framing the exhibition (a right-wing administration obsessed with the privatization of the public sector, the increasing presence of a previously considered marginal northern culture in the centralized Mexican media, and a foreign private entrepreneur who embraced the postnational identity of border individuals as the perfect model for the rest of the country) could help us to interpret Fox's blessing not only as a de facto recognition of the crisis of the Mexican nation-state but also as a cynical way to relinquish its obligations. If tijuanenses have been able to develop practices that give meaning to their liminal position and have replaced obsolete and centralist discourses of identification, then the rest of the country should see their success. Such a model would eventually help nonborder Mexican citizens remedy the Mexican nation-state's increasing inability to fulfill its promises under the pressures of globalization. Fox's attitude could easily be read as a metaphor for a Mexican nation-state ready to abandon its mission in order to become a service provider for transnational capital. In appropriating Navalón's uncritical ideology, the

Mexican government refused to recognize that the nation-state's raison d'être—to protect, serve, and offer security to its citizens, particularly the most underprivileged—is very much alive along the conflictive U.S.–Mexico border.

As the experiences of many citizens at the border suggest, a post-national condition should not refer to the viability of the nation-state as a political entity but rather to its necessary restructuring according to the real needs of its citizens. Such re-signification entails recognition of the local diversity that is often homogenized by nationalist discourses. This type of reevaluation is necessary for the nation-state to be reconsidered a feasible form of political organization within the globalized postnational constellation.

Nor-tec and the Politics of Globalization

Imaginar y hacer imaginar a otros es una actividad directamente política.
[To imagine and to make others imagine is a directly political activity.]

—Jockey TJ

Late in the afternoon, after a day of working on his latest music tracks, Plankton Man opens the email.com server and enters his log-in and password. As he accesses his inbox file, a long list of messages populates the computer screen. He quickly scrolls down, glancing at the e-mails' subjects: "tracks," "hola," "THC," "Jai Alai," "fotos," "chido," "MTV News," "Nortec on Saturday," "wow," "Anti-Nortec Manifesto," "rola," "mil records"—wait a second, "Anti-Nortec Manifesto"? Intrigued, Plankton Man opens the file and finds a brazen text that ambiguously moves from joke, irony, and insult to political critique. He types a quick note and sends it to Pepe Mogt: "Have you heard about this Anti-Nortec thing? What is that all about?!"

The so-called Anti-Nortec Manifesto was put together by a group of youngsters from the border city of Mexicali and circulated briefly via e-mail and Internet sites in 2001. The manifesto's meaning is rather vague, since it is difficult to determine whether the authors were mocking or insulting the members of the Nortec Collective or if they were attempting a serious ideological critique. According to José Manuel Valenzuela Arce, the manifesto suggested that, by neglecting to engage some of the more problematic political border issues—the *bordo*, the *maquiladoras*, the Border Patrol, etc.—Nor-tec had become an instrument of globalization.[21] During my field trips to Tijuana, I interviewed many of the musicians and visual

artists who created and developed the Nor-tec aesthetic. Through these interviews, I identified a constant notion regarding their discourse about the
collective in relation to political issues: from Pepe Mogt and Bostich to
Tavo and CBrown, every member of the collective affirmed categorically
that the Nor-tec project was not a political endeavor. Nor-tec's apparent lack
of concern with political issues led some border activists to react against
the collective in the terms described by Valenzuela Arce, the same kind of
criticism aimed at Tijuana, Tercera Nación.

Curiously, while in Tijuana, I discovered a message posted by Jockey
TJ on the Internet site of the Tijuana Bloguita Front. The text was short but
powerful and thought provoking: "To imagine and to make others imagine
is a directly political activity." If performance is the site where producers
and consumers negotiate imagined constructions of identity, belonging,
gender, race, ethnicity, place, body, and cosmopolitanism, then it is also
through performance that Nor-tec consumers negotiate the power relations
that attempt to write them as liminal subjects, as marginal individuals. As
Jockey TJ's cyber-graffito suggests, it is in this intersection of production
and consumption as a confluence of imaginaries that Nor-tec functions as
an eminently political project. Nor-tec is thus an audiotopic endeavor that
transcends politics to intervene in the sphere of the political, thereby in-
forming us of the power relations and agencies that allow individuals to
respond to the ideological web that surrounds them.

Indeed, as Nor-tec became a transnational phenomenon, many politicians attempted to use the musicians' rising reputation to support their
individual political agendas. In most cases, the members of the collective
reacted in a rather pragmatic way; they accepted invitations to perform at
political rallies (and got paid for their performances) but refused to endorse
any political campaign. When I question him about Nor-tec's apparent lack
of political commitment, Pepe Mogt responds:

> Many persons ask if Nor-tec is political. All right, it could be political, it
> could even be religious. There are lots of people involved in it and some-
> times different persons give it a different tweak. But personally, I am a mu-
> sician and I believe that what could be political about Nor-tec is that we
> are showing a reality that we have personally lived in Tijuana, we try to
> paint it with music. . . . The clash of cultures between the First and the
> Third World[s] is very clear here. Tijuana is the Third World because, for
> instance, you have all these unpaved streets and the areas where people
> who have just arrived in the city go and start building their houses with
> cardboards, tires, and pieces of metal. It is a very clear Third World ex-
> perience. And then, all of a sudden, in 15 minutes you are in San Diego,
> "The Finest City in America" or whatever the slogan is, right? And it is true,

they have these freeways and everything, and when you come back here it is a disaster. So, we reflect that in our music.[22]

Pepe explains that Nor-tec's engagement with the problems and the contradictions of everyday border life is expressed in the very idea that gave origin to the music (and the visual art). Seen from this perspective, Nor-tec is not an uncritical acceptance of joyful discourses about globalization, and, as Heriberto Yépez and Daniel have argued, it should not be homologized with the naïve vision of border life projected in Tijuana, Tercera Nación. Furthermore, as I analyzed in chapter 4, the political character of Nor-tec as an iconic symbol of power struggles is even more evident in the work of the collective's visual artists.

Clearly, the political character of Nor-tec should not be understood in terms of overt "policy" but rather in the broader Foucauldian sense of power relations and, particularly in the case of Nor-tec music, as a type of audiotopia where that power struggle is temporarily somewhat resolved in the imaginations of individuals and the collective. As the cyber-graffito posted by Jockey TJ suggests, the political aspect of Nor-tec is found both in the production processes that allow musicians and visual artists to reimagine their city and its culture, and in the consumption that gives dancers and fans the possibility to reimagine themselves and their friends in the complex and contradictory binational and global culture they experience on a daily basis. Nor-tec allows them to dream in relation to the particular globalization of their living circumstances.

Center, Periphery, and Beyond

When on 25 March 2000, a friend invited me to attend a concert of EDM at Mexico City's Zócalo (main square), I was a little puzzled and did not know what to expect. A rave organized by the government of Mexico City and presented in the heart of the city's political life seemed bizarre. As it turned out, and in accordance with the history of the location, I was about to witness a true political act in the Foucauldian sense explained above. It was an event that substantiated the difficult power relations between Mexico City and the northern border of Mexico, an act that exposed and performed the complex interactions between center and periphery. The concert was the last event of the Festival Tecnogeist 2000 and presented DJs from Germany (Dr. Motte, DJ Hell, Acid Maria, and Yannick) and Mexico (DJ Linga, DJ Unknown, and Borderline from Alcachofa Sound, and Fussible and Bostich from the Nortec Collective) before an audience of 50,000 youngsters ready to dance, jump, and roll all night long. This was my first time at an event featuring Nor-tec music, and I was especially

interested in the collective since my friends considered them to be some of
the most original musicians ever to come out of Tijuana. After two German
DJs opened the concert and prepared the crowd with the powerful, hypnotic driving rhythms of typical techno music, the circumstances seemed
perfect for the presentation of Bostich. By the time the Tijuana musician
finally appeared on stage, I was excited and consumed with anticipation.
The looser rhythmic patterns, slower melodic flow, and the sounds of *güiro*
and tuba in Bostich's "Synthakon" quickly set a new pace and tempo for
the party, and suddenly, the crowd, with the exception of a few individuals
who seemed already familiar with the style, slowly stopped dancing and
began booing the musician. I was distressed by what I felt was an unfair
reception for rather interesting music, and in the days following the event
could not stop thinking about the significance of that reaction.

A few weeks after the Zócalo concert, the now-defunct cyber-magazine
Urbe 01 published a review of the Festival Tecnogeist that explained the
negative reception of Nor-tec in the following terms: "this new sound has
not been entirely digested by the electronic community in the center of the
country, they are just beginning to know it and it is certainly not an obli-
gation to please everyone."[23] Two years later, in April 2002, I returned to
Mexico City to present a paper on Nor-tec music at the International Association for the Study of Popular Music's (IASPM) Latin America conference and was surprised to see not only that my presentation was advertised
in one of Mexico's most influential newspapers as one of the "main attractions" of the conference, but also that several journalists, music critics, and
fans were eager to talk to me about the Tijuana musicians. It was evident
that the reception of Nor-tec music in Mexico City had drastically changed
in the two years since the Zócalo concert.

Although the order of the music programming might have played a
role in the reception of Nor-tec during the Tecnogeist concert, the cyber-
review is clear in noting that significant issues of identity, desire, modernity,
marginality, and center-periphery play a fundamental role in the consumption of Nor-tec music in Mexico City. The change in the reception of this
music in the capital of the country relates to a typical globalization phenomenon: the replacement of a political economy with what Slavoj Žižek
calls a libidinal economy.[24] This shift of economic concern from the production of goods to the production of desires or necessities generates a
new understanding of identity; in a society that privileges the creation of
fantasies-to-be-fulfilled over the creation of the products that fulfill those
fantasies, identity must be articulated in consumption, in an attempt to
possess the object of desire. It is in the complex intersection of desire,
consumption, identity, and modernity as defined by globalization that the
changes in the reception of Nor-tec music can be fully grasped.

For decades, modernization has been described as the goal of Mexico's political and economic policies. Such insistence has made modernity into a prime object of desire for Mexican consumers, a desire often symbolized by Mexico City itself, the central site of political and economic power and the most modern and urbanized city in the country. According to this rhetoric, the center is the source of modernization, nationality, and cohesion, while the periphery remains the area of the country to be "civilized." However, the failure of nationalistic, centralized economic policies to fulfill their promises created a large gap between the object of desire and the citizen's ability to procure at least part of it. This failure made many doubt that Mexico City and centralized power could ever deliver modernity and multicultural nationality (or cosmopolitan modern nationality) to the rest of the country. This was especially true for the northern border, where daily economic and cultural exchanges with the United States implied a continuous relationship with an industrialized, modern society and symbolized access to the objects of desire the center had failed to provide.

Its growing international recognition finally validated Nor-tec as a truly sophisticated object of consumption for Mexico City audiences. This was a group of Mexican musicians who had shared the stage with some of the most influential European and U.S. DJs, a true representation of the object of desire that so often had escaped them: modernity, cosmopolitanism, and success through technology. The migration of Nor-tec and the representational transformations that resulted from this migration forced Mexico City audiences to reevaluate their perceptions of both *norteña* culture and Nor-tec music. For Mexico City youngsters, the consumption of Nor-tec music allowed them to be part of a scene that enabled them to satisfy the desire of modernity created by a libidinal economy that did not offer any means to fulfill that desire. This attitude also contested traditional readings of center-periphery in the relations between Mexico City and Tijuana's cultural life. As I have mentioned before, the strategic position of Tijuana as a border town and its immediate access to U.S. cultural products reverses the traditional center-periphery discourse, while the consumption of Nor-tec music performs *tijuanenses* as nonmarginal subjects. Such an exercise compels residents of the former center to recognize that the margins of the nation might offer ways to satisfy their own desires for modernity and cosmopolitanism.

Irony, Nostalgia, and Memory: Nor-tec Rifa! (Grilled Meat Mix)

Globalization has not only had a strong impact on the economic and political structures of the nation-state but has also had an effect at individual levels, causing important changes in the relationship between the private and public spheres. The challenges that globalization poses on the nation-state have resulted in new ways of cultural funding; while government cultural agencies have their budgets cut as the state systematically withdraws its support of the arts, private entrepreneurs become more interested in investing in these areas. As a result of this changing scenario, the idea of culture and its political uses have also been reevaluated. George Yúdice argues that the increasing influence of private investors has slowly transformed many artistic activities into capitalist endeavors. As part of this trend, privately sponsored local cultural events and festivals seek to pave the way for investment in other areas of these regional economies.[25] Tijuana, Tercera Nación was a clear example of such a strategy. As he expressed in an article published in the Mexican magazine *Nexos,* Navalón envisioned an eventual integration of Mexico into American economics and even into its politics.[26] In order to achieve this, it would be necessary to make Mexico more attractive to foreign investment; the optimistic discourse of a harmonious Amexica provided just the right kind of transnational metaphor. The exhibition itself, once Navalón's curatorial process purged the art from its critical elements, became a strategy to "clean" the reputation of Tijuana as Sin City and make the border an attractive investment site.

As observed in chapter 4, contrary to a Navalónian vision of the border, Nor-tec does not attempt a simplistic "clearing" of Tijuana's name but rather seeks to emphasize the contradictions of border life by acknowledging the negative ideas and stereotypes about the city, humorously commenting on them, and using them to the musicians' advantage. As seen in chapter 2, Nor-tec becomes an example of border culture that provides an ironic commentary on globalization by reconfiguring memory through nostalgia and kitsch. Thus, the nostalgic and kitschy elements in Nor-tec become memories of the inequalities that optimistic discourses on globalization would rather ignore. Furthermore, the nostalgia produced in Nor-tec acts rather like a *neostalgia,* not a melancholy for an ungrieved loss but rather a nostalgia for a never-lived past. In this *neostalgia,* the past is made anew in a simulacrum-like fashion, where bits and pieces of memory are combined with present desires for cosmopolitanism and modernity in order to recreate a past that was never lived in the first place, a past that is experienced through the nostalgic memories of parents, grandparents, and other elder relatives.

"Tijuana Makes Me Happy," a puzzling song from *Tijuana Sessions, Vol. 3,* is a perfect example of the type of ironic remix quality of Nor-tec. The song was composed through a process of continuous remixes. It began as a synthesizer sequence and became an acoustic version of itself (played by accordion and *bajo sexto*); this second version was later transformed into a sample-based piece of electronica based on reworked samples from the acoustic version, then into a pop song with the addition of lyrics (borrowed from Rafa Saavedra's poignant article "Tijuana Makes Me Happy"), and finally into a kitschy pop song with the juxtaposition of corny 1970s female choruses, retro analog synthesizer sounds, and quotations from the *banda* song "Dos hojas al viento." The result is a song of extreme excesses, a type of hypertext where stereotypes of Tijuana ("the happiest place on Earth," "city of sin") are remixed through irony.[27] The power of irony in the rearticulation of tradition via the modernity of *neostalgic* retro aesthetics ("Nothing is newer than the retro," as Mexican writer Juan Villoro affirms)[28] makes "Tijuana Makes Me Happy" into a kitschy metaphor for the complex cultural processes through which *tijuanenses* reimagine their city.

The character of the border as a bicultural site, one whose citizens have historically enjoyed special economic and migration policies, makes border culture a globalized scenario *avant la lettre*. Several decades before NAFTA provided central and southern Mexico with access to their desires for modernity and cosmopolitanism, border citizens had already experienced the positive but also the negative effects of globalization. Thus, when private entrepreneurs arrived at the border carrying the banner of NAFTA, critical *tijuanense* artists were able to counterbalance their claims of democracy, egalitarianism, and a free market and to remind people of the shortcomings of globalization.

As one of these aesthetic reminders, Nor-tec allows for the performance of memory through the bodies of the dancing fans, through the style of music and visual art, and through the audiotopias created as it is consumed. Thus, the performances of Nor-tec become acts of transfer in the sense described by Diana Taylor: embodied practices that transmit knowledge and memory but also produce them.[29] In the context of the Nor-tec performance as a process of memory construction and transmission, nostalgia (understood as ungrieved loss) plays a fundamental role. Accordingly, Nor-tec music works as a kind of psychological cultural mediator for Mexican immigrants in the United States who feel trapped between the nostalgic past and the desired cosmopolitan future. At a Los Angeles Nor-tec party, I talked to Artemio, a young immigrant worker who had never heard of Nor-tec and learned about the event through word of mouth. He was fascinated with the sound of the music and told me, "it somewhat reminds me of my hometown."[30] The same type of nostalgia informs the comments of Daniel, a *tijuanense* who has recently moved to San Ysidro: "Nor-tec is helping me to adapt to living in San Ysidro. . . . everything is grunge, rock or punk here, and I do not like that. Every time I listen to Nor-tec I remember the sounds of Tijuana."[31] For them, Nor-tec plays an important audiotopic role in mediating the epistemological border crossings they face in their everyday interactions with Anglo-American culture, and nostalgia works as a catalyst to rearticulate the past in order to alleviate their present disquiet and fuel their dreams for the future.

Nor-tec is a performative enunciation that enables musicians to overcome the racially and ethnically essentialist discourse of European labels. It facilitates the negotiation of their position as individuals living in the multi-ideological context of the contested border between center and periphery. At the same time, the consumers of Nor-tec culture are able to reformulate and redefine their position as liminal individuals through a collective glocal experience. The production, distribution, and consumption of Nor-tec permit individual and collective agency by recognizing the multiplicity of ideologies and discourses that attempt to determine the existence of fans as liminal and peripheral subjects and especially by recognizing the contingency of such liminality, one that exists only in relation to the centered individuals who construct such discourses. Nor-tec is a strategy for entering and leaving the web created by the multi-ideological condition of postmodernity and postcoloniality, and as such, it shows us that individuals can also take strategic advantage of the discourses that determine their social and cultural marginality. Musicians, artists, practitioners, and promoters from the Nor-tec scene find themselves *en la línea* between subjectivity and social discourses. Such a place, marginal as it may be for the dominant culture, becomes the perfect site to launch a performative strategy that re-signifies the discourses of hegemony.

This book has been a detailed critical interpretation of the circumstances surrounding the production, consumption, and distribution of Nor-tec in order to attain a greater comprehension of the power relations that mediate the creation of discourses about modernity and tradition, hipness and unsophistication, postmodernity and postcoloniality, and center and periphery. These discourses are the discursive loops reconfigured on a daily basis by the Nor-tec experience. Such exercises of reconfiguration compel the former center to recognize that the margins of the nation might offer ways to satisfy desires for modernity and cosmopolitanism—resulting in a contrary version of the traditional saying from central Mexico, *la cultura no acaba donde empieza la carne asada* (culture does not end where grilled meat begins).

Notes

Introduction

1. Throughout this book, I follow the Nor-tec musicians' own practice and call them by their alter ego names instead of their given names. Thus, I refer to Amezcua as Bostich, to Beas as Hiperboreal, etc. Some of these alter ego names have histories behind them. I will discuss them later as appropriate.

2. Although he has abandoned the Nor-tec aesthetic, Balboa's *Plastic Judas on Fire* (2002) includes several Nor-tec tracks.

3. Kai Fikentscher, *"You Better Work!" Underground Dance Music in New York City* (Hanover, CT: Wesleyan University Press, 2000), 6.

4. Sarah Thornton, *Club Cultures: Music, Media and Subcultural Capital* (Hanover, CT: Wesleyan University Press, 1996), 5.

5. Simon Reynolds, "Prefacio," *Loops: Una historia de la música electrónica,* ed. Javier Blánquez and Omar Morera (Barcelona, Spain: Mondadori, 2002), 19. All translations from Spanish, Italian, and French throughout this book are mine unless otherwise noted.

6. Cumbia is a Colombian dance genre of African and indigenous origins that has spread throughout Latin America since the 1960s, giving birth to a large number of cumbia subgenres. An example of this phenomenon is *cumbia norteña,* which was developed in the north of Mexico and quickly entered the repertoire of both *banda sinaloenses* and *conjuntos norteños* (the musical sources of Nor-tec). See chapter 2 for a detailed description of the transnational relationships among these and other music genres, subgenres, and styles.

7. People from the north of Mexico are called *norteños* (northerners). People from Mexico City are referred to as *chilangos.*

8. For an in-depth study of the emic and the etic in ethnomusicology, see Frank Alvarez-Pereyre and Simha Arom, "Ethnomusicology and the Emic/Etic Issue," *World of Music,* vol. 35, no. 1 (1993), 7–31.

9. Akhil Gupta and James Ferguson, "Beyond 'Culture': Space, Identity and the Politics of Difference," *Cultural Anthropology,* vol. 7, no. 1 (1992), 14.

10. Pablo Vila, "Introduction: Border Ethnographies," in *Ethnography at the Border,* ed. Pablo Vila (Minneapolis: University of Minnesota Press, 2003), xxvii.

11. This is the official motto of the city government of Tijuana.

12. Stated by Krusty the clown in an episode of *The Simpsons.*

13. A traditional urban legend states that Tijuana owes its name to a mythical early eighteenth-century character named Doña Juana de la Peña y Villapuente, the *tía* Juana (aunt Juana) who allegedly had a ranch named after her near the town of Loreto, Baja California. See Olga Vicenta Díaz Castro [Sor Abeja], "La tía Juana," in *Entre la magia y la historia: Tradiciones, mitos y leyendas de la frontera,* ed. José Manuel Valenzuela Arce (Tijuana, Mexico: El Colegio de la Frontera Norte and Plaza y Valdés, 2000), 131–160.

14. The severing of the Valley of Tijuana from Alta California was a success of the Mexican diplomats who negotiated the Treaty of Guadalupe Hidalgo. They argued that, if the original limits of Alta California were to remain, the Mexican peninsula of Baja California would be disconnected from the rest of the country. See David Piñera Ramírez and Jesús Ortiz Figueroa, eds., *Historia de Tijuana 1889–1989: Edición conmemorativa del centenario de su fundación* (Tijuana, Mexico: Universidad Autónoma de Baja California, 1989), 39.

15. Humberto Félix Berúmen, *Tijuana la horrible: Entre la historia y el mito* (Tijuana, Mexico: El Colegio de la Frontera Norte, 2003), 101.

16. Homi Bhabha, "Culture's in Between," in *Questions of Cultural Identity,* ed. Stuart Hall and Paul du Gay (London: Sage, 1996), 54.

17. See "La comida del norte, lejos de la visión reduccionista de Vasconcelos," *La Jornada* (26 January 2006).

18. *Narcocorridos* (drug ballads) are songs that celebrate drug dealers and their lifestyle. The Arellano Félix brothers were for decades the most important drug lords in the Tijuana–San Diego area.

19. Roland Barthes, *Mythologies,* trans. Jonathan Cape (London: Vintage, 1993), 111–115.

20. See Slavoj Žižek, *The Sublime Object of Ideology* (New York: Verso, 1989), 87.

21. Néstor García Canclini, *Culturas híbridas: Estrategias para entrar y salir de la modernidad* (Mexico City, Mexico: Grijalbo, 1989), 301.

22. Jean Baudrillard, *Cultura y simulacro* (Barcelona, Spain: Kairós, 1978), 9–10.

23. Ibid., 30.

24. Peter Manuel, "Music as Symbol, Music as Simulacrum: Postmodern, Pre-Modern, and Modern Aesthetics in Subcultural Popular Musics," *Popular Music,* vol. 14, no. 2 (1995), 238n.

25. Veit Erlmann, *Music, Modernity, and the Global Imagination: South Africa and the West* (New York: Oxford University Press, 1999), 4–5.

26. Gilles Deleuze and Félix Guattari, *Anti-Oedipus: Capitalism and Schizophrenia*, trans. Robert Hurley, Mark Seem, and Helen R. Lane (Minneapolis: University of Minnesota Press, 1983), 26.

27. Slavoj Žižek, *Mirando al sesgo: Una introducción a Jacques Lacan a través de la cultura popular*, trans. Jorge Piatigorsky (Buenos Aires: Paidós, 2000), 20.

28. Josh Kun, *Audiotopia: Music, Race, and America* (Berkeley: University of California Press, 2005), 23.

29. Mark Slobin, *Subcultural Sounds: Micromusics of the West* (Hanover, CT: Wesleyan University Press, 1993), 23.

30. See Néstor García Canclini, *Consumers and Citizens: Globalization and Multicultural Conflicts,* trans. George Yúdice (Minneapolis: University of Minnesota Press, 2001); and Roland Robertson, "Time-Space and Homogeneity-Heterogeneity," in *Global Modernities,* ed. Mike Featherstone, Scott Lash, and Roland Robertson (London: Sage, 1995).

31. Thomas Turino, *Nationalists, Cosmopolitans, and Popular Music in Zimbabwe* (Chicago: University of Chicago Press, 2000), 7–8.

32. Anthony Giddens, *The Consequences of Modernity* (Stanford, CA: Stanford University Press, 1990), 46.

33. Fredric Jameson, "Postmodernism; or, The Cultural Logic of Late Capitalism," *New Left Review,* no. 146 (1984), 88.

34. Giddens, *Consequences of Modernity,* 51.

35. Some scholars trace it even further back in time to antiquity. See David Held, Anthony McGrew, David Goldblatt, and Jonathan Perraton, *Global Transformations: Politics, Economics and Culture* (Stanford, CA: Stanford University Press, 1999).

36. Manuel, "Music as Symbol, Music as Simulacrum," 228.

37. Chela Sandoval, *Methodology of the Oppressed* (Minneapolis: University of Minnesota Press, 2000), 27.

38. For example, Fernando Ortiz's notion of transculturation, which was later developed into a more systematic theoretical model by Ángel Rama and Mabel Moraña and eventually adopted by mainstream Anglo-Saxon intellectuals like Diana Taylor and Mary Louise Pratt. See Fernando Ortiz, *Contrapunteo cubano del tabaco y el azúcar* (Madrid, Spain: EditoCubaEspaña, 1999; first published in 1940); Ángel Rama, *Transculturación narrativa en América Latina* (Mexico City, Mexico: Siglo Veintiuno, 1982); Mabel Moraña, "Ideología de la transculturación," in *Ángel Rama y los estudios latinoamericanos,* ed. Mabel Moraña (Pittsburgh, PA: University of Pittsburgh Press, 1997); Diana Taylor, "Transculturating Transculturation," *Performing Arts Journal,* no. 38 (1991); and Mary Louise Pratt, *Imperial Eyes: Travel Writing and Transculturation* (New York: Routledge, 1992). For other Latin American cultural theories that resonate with postmodernism, see Jorge Portilla, *La fenomenología del relajo* (Mexico City, Mexico: Fondo de Cultura Económica, 1966).

39. Deleuze and Guattari, *Anti-Oedipus,* 257–258.

Chapter 1

1. The term *culturoso* or *culturosa* was coined by Tijuana artists to refer to the artistic scene of the city and its regular participants. Curiously, although the coinage of the term is an ironic self-aware commentary on the scene as a marker of elitist difference (mainly in poetry, literature, visual arts, and film), it is not restricted to highbrow cultural manifestations but also designates popular culture scenes and the leisure activities of their participants (such as the local EDM scene).

2. Pedro Gabriel Beas, "Nor-tec: Hedonismo sónico urbano," *At/Syber*, vol. 1 (2001), 8.

3. Pedro Gabriel Beas (Hiperboreal), electronic communication, 25 October 2001.

4. José Trinidad Morales (Pepe Mogt), personal interview, Tijuana, 12 May 2003.

5. Beas, "Nor-tec," 8.

6. Although in the late 1990s, several local artists were interested in developing "hybrid" visual and musical aesthetics, the use of *banda* and *norteña* music was still considered outrageous due to their cultural links to bad taste and rural and unsophisticated lifestyles. They were not deemed hip enough to be the basis of a sophisticated, cosmopolitan artistic expression. Thus, the improbability of the *norteño*-techno meeting rested on the contrastingly different claims to class, ethnicity, and cosmopolitanism that such music and dance scenes mark.

7. Olivia Ruiz, "Introducción," in *Grupos de visitantes y actividades turísticas en Tijuana*, ed. Nora L. Bringas and Jorge Carrillo V. (Tijuana, Mexico: El Colegio de la Frontera Norte, 1991), 9.

8. The legal drinking age in Mexico is 18, not 21 as it is in the United States.

9. See Eric Zolov, *Refried Elvis: The Rise of Mexican Counterculture* (Berkeley: University of California Press, 1999), 93–96.

10. See David Cortés, *El otro rock mexicano: Experiencias progresivas, sicodélicas, de fusión y experimentales* (Mexico City, Mexico: Times Editores, Opción Sónica, and Tower Records, 1999), 81–84, 109–112, and 118–123.

11. Rafa Saavedra, personal interview, Tijuana, 5 December 2003.

12. Saavedra is still prominent in his role as a music promoter in Tijuana; not only has he dutifully chronicled Tijuana's pop music scene for almost two decades, but he has also remained a driving force in the promotion of the latest European and American electronic music through *Selector de Frecuencias*, the weekly radio show he hosts at Radio Universidad.

13. "Bostich" is the title of a song featured on Yello's 1980 album, *Solid Pleasure*.

14. Mogt affirms that the idea was a practical one: "Changing the name to Artefakto with a *k* would give the band a unique identity, one that the plain word Artefacto lacks." Morales, personal interview.

15. "When I was in school in San Diego I started playing heavy metal as a way of rebelling against the classical music I had been playing since I was a kid." Jorge Ruiz (Melo), personal interview, Tijuana, 19 June 2004.

16. See Susana Asensio, "Desencanto y reencanto en la 'electrónica' mexicana," paper presented at the 2000 meeting of the International Association for the Study of Popular Music, Latin American Branch, and published electronically at http://www.hist.puc.cl/historia/iaspm/pdf/Asensio.pdf; Asensio, "Tijuana *grooves: El borde revisitado en la electronica de Nortec,*" *Arizona Journal of Hispanic Cultural Studies*, vol. 5 (2001). Asensio later amended her position and acknowledged some of the more complex glocal issues in the production of Nor-tec in "The Nortec Edge: Border Traditions and Electronica in Tijuana," in *Rockin' Las Americas: The Global Politics of Rock Music in Latin America*, ed. Deborah Pacini-Hernández, Héctor Fernandez-L'Hoeste, and Eric Zolov (Pittsburgh, PA: University of Pittsburgh Press, 2004).

17. Michel Gaillot, *Multiple Meaning: Techno: An Artistic and Political Laboratory of the Present* (Paris, France: Dis Voir, 1999), 28.

18. James A. Hodgkinson defines post-rock as "a musical attitude, a wish to go beyond the limitations of rock. . . . A 'music of the future' which came to occupy a significant, and very specific, section in the present." See Hodgkinson, "The Fanzine Discourses over Post-rock," in *Music Scenes: Local, Translocal, and Virtual*, ed. Andy Bennett and Richard A. Peterson (Nashville, TN: Vanderbilt University Press, 2004), 235.

19. See Jeff Kent, *The Rise and Fall of Rock* (Stoke-on-Trent, England: Witan, 1983), and Jeff Pike, *The Death of Rock 'n' Roll: Untimely Demises, Morbid Preoccupations, and Premature Forecasts of Doom in Pop Music* (Boston: Faber and Faber, 1993).

20. Enrique, electronic communication, 16 November 2004. I use pseudonyms for the fans in order to keep the anonymity of my informants.

21. Jorge Ruiz, personal interview.

22. Morales, personal interview.

23. Roberto Mendoza (Panóptica), personal interview, Tijuana, 13 May 2003.

24. Based on Hans Robert Jauss's notion of a "horizon of expectations," Talía Jiménez developed the idea of "frames of reception" as systems of reference that individuals bring to the understanding of any text. Jiménez states that "presumably *any* experience a given individual may have can be analyzed according to its trigger, focus, context and horizons of expectations, whereby its framework of reception could be reconstructed." Talía Jiménez, "The Framework of Reception: Reception at the Level of the Individual Receiver," paper presented at the New York University Graduate Forum, 28 March 2001. I take Jiménez's notion a step further in order to understand the development of systems of reference shared collectively at particular historical moments. As these systems allow for the meaningful collective reception, understanding, and consumption of ideas, I have called them "frames for reception."

25. Rafa Saavedra, "Once curvas de infinito," *Frontera* (12 September 1999).

26. Mogt quoted in Pedro Gabriel Beas, "Fussible," *Nitro* (1999), 29.

27. Although *raza* might translate into more than "people," the way it is most often used in Mexican *norteño* Spanish is to refer to people or groups of friends.

28. Fritz Torres, personal interview, Tijuana, 16 May 2003.

29. Morales, personal interview.

30. Raúl Cárdenas (Torolab), personal interview, Tijuana, 6 December 2003.

31. Fernando Corona (Terrestre), personal communication, 25 October 2001.

32. Pepe Mogt quoted in Josh Tyrangiel, "The New Tijuana Brass," *Time* (11 June 2001), 77.

33. James Lien, "Nortec Collective: Tijuana Sessions Vol. 1," *CMJ New Music Report*, http://www.cmj.com/articles/display_article.php?id=30163. Posted on 12 February 2001.

34. See Hodgkinson, "Fanzine Discourses."

35. Ramón Amezcua (Bostich), personal interview, Los Angeles, 17 May 2003.

36. With the exception of its official Web site (http://www.nor-tec.org), the *Nor-tec Sampler*, and a few early publications, the hyphenated version of the name is almost never used by the musicians, who prefer the nonhyphenated version.

37. Ned Seelye and Jacqueline Howell Wasiliewski, *Between Cultures: Developing Self-Identity in a World of Diversity* (Lincolnwood, IL: NTC, 1996), 56.

38. Melo quoted in "NorTec, un sonido más urbano," *LaCaja TV*, http://www.lacajatv/nrtk-press.html.

39. Torres, personal interview.

40. Morales, personal interview.

41. Mendoza, personal interview, 13 May 2003.

42. Saavedra, "Once curvas de infinito."

43. Beas, "Nor-tec."

44. Amezcua, personal interview.

Chapter 2

1. Ursula, personal interview, 14 May 2003.

2. Jorge Ruiz (Melo), personal interview, Tijuana, 19 June 2004.

3. Heriberto Yépez, http://hyepez.blogspot.com. Posted on 31 December 2002.

4. Bruno Ruiz, *Literatura aleatoria*, http://www.brunoruiz.blogspot.com/2002_12_29_brunoruiz_archive.html. Posted on 1 January 2003.

5. Alex, personal interview, 23 June 2004.

6. *Naco* is a popular Mexican term used to describe bad taste, lack of sophistication, lowbrow, etc. Many times, it is even used in a racially discriminatory fashion.

7. See Eric Hobsbawm and Terence Ranger, *The Invention of Tradition* (New York: Cambridge University Press, 1983); Barbara Kirshenblatt-Gimblett, "Theorizing Heritage," *Ethnomusicology*, vol. 39, no. 3 (1995); and Nezar AlSayyad, ed., *Consuming Tradition, Manufacturing Heritage* (New York: Routledge, 2001), among others.

8. Jean-Paul Bourdier and Nazer AlSayyad, "Dwellings, Settlements, and Tradition: A Prologue," in *Dwellings, Settlements, and Tradition*, ed. Nazer AlSayyad and J. Bourdier (Lanham, MD: University Press of America, 1989), 3. Quoted in

Nazer AlSayyad, "The End of Tradition, or the Tradition of Endings?" in *The End of Tradition?* ed. Nazer AlSayyad (New York: Routledge, 2004), 7.

9. Ibid., 6.

10. *Fara-fara* is a popular northern Mexican expression that refers to the sound of the accordion in *norteña* music. People often use this expression also to describe the music itself.

11. From the mid-1990s on, the Mexican media granted these traditions more air time and grouped them all together as parts of the same phenomenon in response to the growing influence of *norteña* culture in the country, which coincided with the signing of the North American Free Trade Agreement (NAFTA).

12. Although the term *banda* and its current instrumentation and repertoire may only date back to the nineteenth century, ensembles that used wind instruments and percussion have been ubiquitous throughout Mexico since the conquest. See Sergio Navarrete Pellicer, "Las capillas de músicas de viento y los vientos de la Reforma en Oaxaca durante el siglo 19," *Acervos: Boletín de los Archivos y Bibliotecas de Oaxaca*, vol. 6, no. 24 (2001), 4–13. I recognize that contemporary *banda* music is part of this long historical trajectory, however, my description seeks to emphasize its particular development in northwest Mexico after the transnational social, economic, and cultural transformations triggered by the industrial revolution in the nineteenth century.

13. Héctor R. Olea, *Los orígenes de la tambora* (Culiacán, Mexico: Ayuntamiento de Culiacán, 1985), 31.

14. Helena Simonett, *Banda: Mexican Musical Life across Borders* (Middletown, CT: Wesleyan University Press, 2001), 139, 149.

15. Ibid., 159.

16. Ibid., 171.

17. Ibid., 185.

18. See Helena Simonett, "Strike Up the Tambora: A Social History of Sinaloan Band Music," *Latin American Music Review*, vol. 20, no. 1 (1999), 85–86.

19. See Ramiro Burr, *The Billboard Guide to Tejano and Regional Mexican Music* (New York: Billboard Books, 1999), 60.

20. Ibid., 58.

21. Natives of the northeastern states of Nuevo León and Tamaulipas are called *neoloeneses* and *tamaulipecos*, respectively.

22. Burr, *Billboard Guide to Tejano*, 159.

23. See Manuel Peña, *The Texas-Mexican Conjunto: History of a Working-Class Music* (Austin: University of Texas Press, 1985), 20–29; and Cathy Ragland, *The Parallel Evolution and Cross Cultural Impact of Tejano Conjunto and Mexican Norteño Music* (San Antonio, TX: Guadalupe Cultural Arts Center, 1998), 3.

24. Peña, *Texas-Mexican Conjunto*, 21–22.

25. Ragland, *Parallel Evolution*, 4.

26. Burr, *Billboard Guide to Tejano*, 18.

27. Peña, *Texas-Mexican Conjunto*, 38.

28. Ragland, *Parallel Evolution*, 11.

29. Peña, *Texas-Mexican Conjunto,* 70–71. Peña argues that the withdrawal of American major labels from the U.S.–Mexico border and their loss of interest in *norteño* and *conjunto* music followed a strategy to team up with Mexican entrepreneurs like Emilio Azcárraga (owner of Mexico's influential XEW) in the more-profitable business of promoting mariachi and *rancheras,* the music of the center of the country, instead of *norteña* and *conjunto,* the music of the margins of the country, throughout Latin America and the United States.

30. Cathy Ragland, "*Ni aquí ni allá* (Neither Here nor There): *Música Norteña* and the Mexican Working-Class Diaspora," Ph.D. diss., City University of New York (2005), 148.

31. José Juan Olvera, Benito Torres, Gregorio Cruz, and César Jaime Rodríguez, *La colombia de Monterrey: Descripción de algunos elementos de la cultura colombiana en la frontera norte* (San Antonio, TX: Guadalupe Cultural Arts Center, 1996), 22.

32. See Toño Carrizosa, *La onda grupera: Historia del movimiento grupero* (Mexico City, Mexico: EDAMEX, 1997), 51–52.

33. Despite the early commercial backing of singers and groups like Los Teen Tops, Los Locos del Ritmo, César Costa, Angélica María, and bands from *La onda chicana,* Televisa (clearly a TV network monopoly at the time) refused to support rock in the 1970s and most of the 1980s in response to the conservative backlash provoked by the Avándaro Festival as well as what were considered the "immoral excesses" of U.S. rock bands like the Doors. The Avándaro Festival was a Woodstock-like rock event held in the town of Valle de Bravo on 11 September 1971. Badly organized, the chaotic event was portrayed as a "festival of drugs" by the Mexican media. See Eric Zolov, *Refried Elvis: The Rise of Mexican Counterculture* (Berkeley: University of California Press, 1999), 157 and 212–213.

34. Carrizosa, *La onda grupera,* 99–100. *Bailes sonideros* are dance events where the music is played by a DJ instead of a live band. Much cheaper than hiring a large band, group, or *conjunto, bailes sonideros* are an affordable entertainment option in poor communities of the Mexican countryside.

35. Burr, *Billboard Guide to Tejano,* 67; and Carrizosa, *La onda grupera,* 218–219.

36. See Simonett, *Banda,* 46.

37. *El Show de Johnny Canales* was a TV show locally produced in the Rio Grande Valley beginning in the early 1980s, starring *norteña* and *conjunto* music promoter Johnny Canales. In the early 1990s, the show began to be aired nationally on Univision, and its repertoire was enlarged to also include *bandas* and *gruperos.*

38. See Burr, *Billboard Guide to Tejano,* 58; Simonett, *Banda,* 57; and José Manuel Valenzuela Arce, *Jefe de jefes: Corridos y narcocultura en México* (La Habana, Cuba: Casa de las Américas, 2003), 66.

39. This concept is borrowed from Néstor García Canclini and Patricia Safa, eds., *Tijuana: La casa de toda la gente* (Mexico City, Mexico: INAH, Programa Cultural de las Fronteras, UAM-Iztapalapa, and CONACULTA, 1989).

40. See Néstor García Canclini, *Culturas híbridas: Estrategias para entrar y salir de la modernidad* (Mexico City, Mexico: Grijalbo, 1989), 293; and David G.

Gutiérrez, "Ethnic Mexicans and the Transformation of 'American' Social Space: Relations on Recent History," in *Crossings: Mexican Immigration Interdisciplinary Perspectives,* ed. Marcelo M. Suárez-Orozco (Cambridge, MA: David Rockefeller Center for Latin American Studies and Harvard University Press, 1998), 314.

41. *Jaladores* (pullers) work for local businesses and stand on the sidewalk, luring (or pulling) prospective clients into bars or strip clubs.

42. Ronald Radano and Philip V. Bohlman, "Introduction: Music and Race, Their Past, Their Presence," in *Music and the Racial Imagination,* ed. Ronald Radano and Philip V. Bohlman (Chicago: University of Chicago Press, 2000), 29.

43. Cameron McCarthy and Greg Dimitriadis, "Art and the Postcolonial Imagination: Rethinking the Institutionalization of Third World Aesthetics and Theory," *Ariel: A Review of International English Literature,* vol. 31, nos. 1–2 (2000), 240.

44. James Lien, "Nortec Collective: Tijuana Sessions Vol. 1," *CMJ New Music Report,* http://www.cmj.com/articles/display_article.php?id=30163. Posted on 12 February 2001.

45. Pedro Gabriel Beas (Hiperboreal), personal interview, Tijuana, 13 May 2003.

46. Arturo, personal interview, Los Angeles, 16 September 2003.

47. Beas, personal interview, 13 May 2003.

48. Joseph G. Schloss, *Making Beats: The Art of Sample-Based Hip-Hop* (Middletown, CT: Wesleyan University Press, 2004), 79–100.

49. Daniel Rivera (DJ Tolo), personal interview, Tijuana, 18 June 2004.

50. Stuart Hall, "Negotiating Caribbean Identities," in *New Caribbean Thought: A Reader,* ed. Brian Meeks and Folke Lindahl (Kingston, Jamaica: University of the West Indies Press, 2001), 37.

51. Mark Katz, *Capturing Sound: How Technology Has Changed Music* (Berkeley: University of California Press, 2004), 156.

52. Fernando Corona (Terrestre), personal interview, Tijuana, 14 May 2003.

53. *Cereso* stands for Centro de Rehabilitación y Reinserción Social (Rehabilitation and Social Reinsertion Center), a Mexican euphemism for "jail."

54. The vocoder is computer music software that allows one to transform a given sound into a synthesized vocal sound.

55. Alex, personal interview, 23 June 2004.

56. The title of the track, "Autobanda," not only makes reference to the type of automatic or virtual band created in Bostich's computer, but also pays homage to Kraftwerk's classic song "Autobahn."

57. Raúl Cárdenas (Torolab), personal interview, Tijuana, 6 December 2003.

58. Beas, personal interview, 13 May 2003.

59. Jorge Ruiz, personal interview.

60. José Trinidad Morales (Pepe Mogt), personal interview, Tijuana, 7 July 2004.

61. Ibid.

62. Ibid.

63. Ibid.

64. Ibid.

65. Matei Calinescu, *Five Faces of Modernity: Modernism, Avant-garde, Decadence, Kitsch, Postmodernism* (Durham, NC: Duke University Press, 1987), 242.

66. See Theodor Adorno and Max Horkheimer, *Dialectic of Enlightenment*, trans. John Cumming (New York: Seabury, 1972); and Walter Benjamin, "The Work of Art in the Age of Mechanical Reproduction," in his *Illuminations* (London: Fontana, 1970).

67. Susan Sontag, *Against Interpretation and Other Essays* (New York: Delta, 1966), 282–285.

68. Jon Perales, "Critic's Choice: New CD's," *New York Times* (25 July 2005).

69. The Mexican OTI (Ibero-American Television Organization) Song Festival was an annual pop song competition sponsored by the Televisa network and hosted by its star, Raúl Velasco. The music arrangements of Eduardo Magallanes, one of the competition's most-consistent participants, showed the typical stylistic features of the mainstream pop music supported by the network's influential TV show *Siempre en Domingo,* including the famous choruses of the Zavala Brothers, a landmark in cheesy 1970s Mexican pop music.

70. Juan Torres was a musician famous in 1970s Mexico for his corny arrangements of popular Mexican music for solo (Yamaha) electric organ. His music, marketed for the middle classes as refined versions of well-known popular tunes (like those of French pianist Richard Clayderman and, most recently, Argentinean pianist Raúl di Blassio), is a clear example of kitsch as a "failed attempt to the sublime."

71. The Almada brothers, Mario and Fernando, starred in many border-placed, low-budget Mexican action movies in the 1970s and 1980s, which often touched upon issues of illegal migration to the United States and drug-dealing culture.

72. The lyrics in "Contrabando y traición" state, *Salieron de San Ysidro / Procedentes de Tijuana / Tenían las llantas del carro / Repletas de yerba mala,* while the lyrics in "Colorado" say, "They left from San Ysidro / They were coming from Tijuana / They [went] down to Chicago in a *colorado* [red] car."

73. José Trinidad Morales (Pepe Mogt), personal interview, Tijuana, 30 September 2005.

74. Fritz Torres, personal interview, Tijuana, 16 May 2003.

75. Jorge Verdín, personal interview, Los Angeles, 17 May 2003.

76. I have not been able to verify Torres's comments about *narcochic* as a category in U.S. auction houses.

77. Celeste Olalquiaga, *Megalopolis: Contemporary Cultural Sensibilities* (Minneapolis: University of Minnesota Press, 1992), 42–43.

78. Ibid., 45.

79. Ibid., 47.

80. Ibid., 53.

81. Raúl Velasco was the host of Televisa's *Siempre en Domingo.* The show and its powerful host were responsible for the construction of mainstream popular music culture in Mexico for almost two decades.

82. David Harrington, telephone interview, 21 August 2003.

83. Ibid.

84. Ignacio Chávez Uranga (Plankton Man), personal interview, Tijuana, 10 May 2003.

85. Olalquiaga, *Megalopolis*, 54.

86. Stuart Hall, "Encoding, Decoding," in *The Cultural Studies Reader*, ed. Simon During (New York: Routledge, 1993), 91.

Chapter 3

1. José Trinidad Morales (Pepe Mogt), personal interview, Tijuana, 12 May 2003.

2. George Yúdice, "La industria de la música en la integración América Latina–Estados Unidos," in *Las industrias culturales en la integración latinoamericana*, ed. Néstor García Canclini and Carlos Juan Moneta (Mexico City, Mexico: Grijalbo, 1999), 183.

3. Ibid.

4. Morales, personal interview, 12 May 2003.

5. See Valentín Fuentes, "El triunfo de Tijuana," *Expansión*, vol. 32, no. 830 (2001), 71–72.

6. Morales, personal interview, 12 May 2003.

7. Fuentes, "El triunfo de Tijuana," 72.

8. Walter Benjamin, "The Work of Art in the Age of Mechanical Reproduction," in his *Illuminations* (London: Fontana, 1970), 220–227.

9. Ángel Quintero Rivera, *¡Salsa, sabor y control! Sociología de la música "tropical"* (La Habana, Cuba: Casa de las Américas, 1998), 11.

10. Jorge Ruiz (Melo), personal interview, Tijuana, 19 June 2004.

11. Rubén Tamayo (Fax), personal interview, Tijuana, 10 May 2003.

12. José Trinidad Morales (Pepe Mogt), quoted in "NorTec: Un sonido más urbano," *LaCaja TV*, http://www.lacajatv/nrtk-press.html.

13. Karina Paredes, "Rave: Ritual colectivo," *Frontera* (4 January 2001).

14. Ricardo Martínez de Castro (Ricky), personal interview, Tijuana, 24 June 2004.

15. Pepe Mogt speculates that "La rom u rosa" was selected because the title makes reference to the Rumorosa Sierra outside of Mexicali, the hometown of then Mexican president Ernesto Zedillo. Morales, personal interview, Tijuana, 12 May 2003.

16. Martínez de Castro, personal interview.

17. Enrique Jiménez (Ejival) states that the official number of attendees was 1,200; see Jiménez, "Chronology," in José Manuel Valenzuela Arce, *Paso del Nortec/This Is Tijuana* (Mexico City, Mexico: Trilce, 2004), 109.

18. Kim Buie quoted in Melissa Sattley, "Rock en Tijuana: The Bastard Child of Norteño and Electronica: Nortec, 'The Future of Mexican Music,'" *Austin Chronicle* (3 November 2000).

19. Roberto Mendoza (Panóptica), personal interview, Tijuana, 13 May 2003.

20. Morales, personal interview.

21. Mendoza, personal interview, 13 May 2003.

22. Roberto Mendoza (Panóptica), "Música electrónica: Latinoamérica contra el mundo," Roundtable at the 2003 Mutek Festival, Tijuana, 6 December 2003.

23. *MUTEK MX: Festival Internacional de Cultura Digital,* http://www .strobe.com.mx/mutek/index3.html. As part of this endeavor, editions of Mutek have also been presented in Brazil and Chile.

24. Alain Mongeau, "Música electrónica: Latinoamérica contra el mundo," Roundtable at the 2003 Mutek Festival, Tijuana, 6 December 2003.

25. Joanna Demers, "Dancing Machines: 'Dance Dance Revolution,' Cybernetic Dance, and Musical Taste," *Popular Music,* vol. 25, no. 3 (2006), 407.

26. These groups were founded in 2001, soon after the release of *The Tijuana Sessions, vol. 1.* The addresses are http://launch.groups.yahoo.com/group/ nortecteam/members and http://launch.groups.yahoo.com/group/norteccollective, respectively. In 2005, after being taken over by spammers, the independent group changed its URL to http://mx.groups.yahoo.com/group/NORTEC.

27. The URL of the group's main Web site is http://tijuanabloguitafront .blogspot.com.

28. The URL of the Nortec Collective's MySpace is http://www.myspace.com/ nortec.

29. An example is the following message, posted on 17 June 2005 by a fan from Playa del Carmen, a small beach town near Cancún, Mexico: "precisamente antier estabamos [*sic*] hablando de nortec. . . . Contactenme [*sic*] via email, me gustaria [*sic*] saber que onda para traerlos a playa del carmen [*sic*] [Precisely the day before yesterday we were talking about Nortec. . . . Contact me via e-mail, I would like to know what's needed to bring you to Playa del Carmen]," http://www .myspace.com/nortec. From the tone of familiarity, one could tell that the fan was under the impression of writing directly to a member of the Nortec Collective.

30. *Panóptica* was released both as a CD and as a set of four individual LPs; each LP contained two tracks and was especially designed for DJs.

31. A second, expanded version of the latter recording, entitled *Terrestre vs. Plankton Man,* was released in 2003 by the Tijuana-based label Nimboestatic.

32. Jorge Ruiz, personal interview.

33. Jennifer Mañón, personal interview, Los Angeles, 18 September 2003.

34. Aníbal Silva (DJ Aníbal), electronic communication, 23 October 2004.

35. José Trinidad Morales (Pepe Mogt), quoted in "NorTec, un sonido más urbano," *LaCaja TV,* http://www.lacajatv/nrtk-press.html.

36. Morales, personal interview, Tijuana, 12 May 2003.

37. Tomás Cookman, electronic communication, 18 October 2004.

38. Ignacio Chávez Uranga (Plankton Man), personal interview, Tijuana, 10 May 2003.

39. Morales, personal interview, Tijuana, 12 May 2003.

40. Margaret E. Dorsey, *Pachangas: Borderlands Music, U.S. Politics, and Transnational Marketing* (Austin: University of Texas Press, 2006), 51–55. In the case of Hispanics at the U.S.–Mexico border, Dorsey defines "ethnic marketing" as "advertising campaigns that focus attention on 'ethnic markets,' 'live events,' and

'brand promotion' as methods of selling products and retaining sales within un-specific 'Hispanic' communities" (51).

41. Mañón, personal interview.

42. Ibid.

43. Silvia Pedraza-Bailey, "Cuba's Exiles: Portrait of a Refugee Migration," *International Migration Review,* vol. 19, no. 4 (1985), 18.

44. James S. Olson and Judith E. Olson, *Cuban Americans: From Trauma to Triumph* (New York: Twayne, 1995), 71. It is important to note that if "black" and "white" are rather subjective terms, they are even trickier in the Caribbean; Olson and Olson's figures are most probably based on self-identification.

45. Sheila L. Croucher, *Imagining Miami: Ethnic Politics in a Postmodern World* (Charlottesville: University Press of Virginia, 1997), 107.

46. This has been recognized by the majors. The Mexican electronic duo Plastilina Mosh was first marketed as an underground band by Sony in order to take advantage of this phenomenon.

Chapter 4

1. "[En Tijuana] se tiene la sensación de que en cualquier momento todos se irán y emigrarán hacia la mitad del desierto o hacia otra frontera, incluso la zona del Río que supone ser el asiento de la modernidad tiene esa apariencia de esce-nografía, de montaje efímero, de ser una locación donde se rodarán infinidad de películas y simulacros, pero donde nada sucederá realmente porque todos son ac-tores, no por vocación o elección sino por contagio, por saberse en medio de un te-rritorio ausente de historia y de futuro, un territorio en el que todo es movimiento, flujo continuo." Guillermo Fadanelli, "Tijuana: Territorio límite," *PUB Magazine,* no. 3 (n.d.), 31.

2. I borrowed the phrase "Where is the donkey show Mr. Mariachi?" from a short story that Rafa Saavedra published electronically on 7 August 2004 in *Bukónica: Libros, cuentos, textos sueltos, b-sides, remixes and hidden tracks,* http://bukonica.blogspot.com. The story was written in a mixture of Spanish and English; this particular phrase was originally written in English.

3. *La Coahuila* is how locals refer to Coahuila Street, a street in downtown Tijuana known for its working-class bars, musicians, and prostitutes.

4. Néstor García Canclini, *Culturas híbridas: Estrategias para entrar y salir de la modernidad* (Mexico City, Mexico: Grijalbo, 1989), 304–305.

5. Pedro Gabriel Beas (Hiperboreal), personal interview, 11 May 2003.

6. "¿Ah si? A la mierda con todos ustedes. Yo nunca le voy a decir 'el foro.' Para mí jamás dejará de ser: EL JAI ALAI." *Jazzalounge,* http://www.cometouch thesun.blogspot.com. Posted on 9 March 2004.

7. Alex, personal interview, 23 June 2004.

8. *Maquilas* or *maquiladoras* are transnational factories installed along the Mexican side of the U.S.–Mexico border in order to benefit from the cheaper labor and the lax Mexican legislation in terms of workers' benefits, taxes, and toxic wastes. It is estimated, for instance, that almost 50 percent of the world's televisions

are assembled in the transnational *maquiladoras* in Tijuana. This single datum may give an idea of the importance and productivity of these manufacturing industries and their degree of "pull factor" on the Mexican workforce. See Leslie Sklar, "The Maquilas in Mexico: A Global Perspective," *Bulletin of Latin American Research*, vol. 11, no. 1 (1992).

9. The Mexican term *relajo* has been used to describe specific types of verbal challenges to social order. See Jorge Portilla, *La fenomenología del relajo* (Mexico City, Mexico: Fondo de Cultura Económica, 1966); and Roger Bartra, *The Cage of Melancholy: Identity and Metamorphosis in the Mexican Character,* trans. Christopher J. Hall (New Brunswick, NJ: Rutgers University Press). Nevertheless, I use the term in its larger, more widespread meaning: "to relax, to ease, to amuse, to divert" in order to explore the transgressive character of social amusement activities such as partying.

10. Gabriel Castillo quoted in Karina Paredes, "Rave: Ritual colectivo," *Frontera* (4 January 2001).

11. For a discussion of *relajo* in relation to Bakhtinian carnival, see José E. Limón, *Dancing with the Devil* (Madison: University of Wisconsin Press, 1994), 123–140.

12. Karla Gerardo, "Tijuana se dice Nortec City," *Frontera* (5 March 2001).

13. Jorge Verdín, personal interview, Los Angeles, 17 May 2003.

14. José Manuel Valenzuela Arce, *Paso del Nortec/This Is Tijuana* (Mexico City, Mexico: Trilce, 2004), 95.

15. Curiously, in 1999, the year he presented his first solo concert in Tijuana, the well-known Argentinean electronic musician Gustavo Cerati released a track titled "Paseo inmoral." Rafa Saavedra has confirmed that the term "Paseo inmoral" has been used in Tijuana since the early 1990s (Rafa Saavedra, electronic communication, 12 September 2007). I would like to thank Margarita Saona for letting me know about Cerati's track.

16. Rafa Saavedra, "Resúmen 2003," in *Crossfader V: 4000,* http://www .rafadro.blogspot.com. Posted on 31 December 2003.

17. Sergio Brown (VJ CBrown), personal interview, Tijuana, 23 May 2003.

18. *Ficheras* are women whom you can pay to dance with you at these clubs. The term comes from the *fichas* (tokens or chips) the customer needs to buy from the club in order to pay the women.

19. In some of the racial ideologies prevalent among Mexican northerners, southern Mexico is more backward and poor because it is more densely populated by Indians. In Tijuana, while riding in taxis and eating meals, I frequently had conversations with locals who told me stories about "poor ignorant" *oaxaquitas* (immigrant Indian women from southern Mexican states like Oaxaca), who come to the city "barely knowing how to speak Spanish" to work as maids, or about "classless" *veracruzanos* (immigrants from the state of Veracruz), whom you can recognize on the streets by their dark skin color and "because they wear plastic sandals." The desire for whiteness among Mexican northerners, and among *tijuanenses* in particular, is often evident in typically racist statements such as "she got married to

a white man to 'improve' the race," or "he was so handsome, he looked just like a Spaniard." These types of statements are also common among light-skinned Mexican Americans in the American Southwest, who identify their ethnicity as Spanish instead of Mexican in order to avoid the racism against Mexicans of Indian heritage.

20. The following slogan accompanied the images for the exhibition Tijuana, Tercera Nación: "Voltear a ver / una ciudad universal / solidaria, unida, polifacética, cercana / una ciudad que nos abraza a todos [Look back and see / a universal city / solidarian, united, polyfaceted, nearby / a city that embraces us all]."

21. Pepe Mogt, electronic communication, 19 October 2004.

22. I refer to an early, unreleased version of "Bar Infierno," not to the more polished version finally released on *Tijuana Sessions, Vol. 3* (2005).

23. Such moralist discourse permeates Mexican movies about immigration to the United States. Here, Tijuana (and the border in general), as the physical end of the nation, comes to symbolize the end of "the virtues and values" of Mexican culture. Films that reinforce this idea include classics like Alejandro Galindo's *Espaldas mojadas* (1955), comedies like Rafael Baledón and Piporro's *El bracero del año* (1963), and more recent productions like Alejandro Springall's *Santitos* (1999), plus the large amount of 1970s and 1980s border-placed action movies starring Mario and Fernando Almada. María Novaro's *El jardín del edén* (1994) offers a critique of this essentialist discourse.

24. For the sake of metric congeniality, in order to make the two loops fit together, I have notated the 4/4 loop as a 12/8 measure. Here, the speed of an eighth note in 12/8 equals that of a sixteenth note in 3/4.

25. Barbara Kirshenblatt-Gimblett, "Theorizing Heritage," *Ethnomusicology*, vol. 39, no. 3 (1995), 369.

26. In the case of VJ Mashaka and VJ Wero Palma, their alter ego names are themselves reappropriations of *norteño* cultural symbols. Mashaka is a respelling of *machaca*, a type of dry meat used in traditional *norteño* dishes such as *huevos con machaca* (*machaca* and eggs) or *caldillo de carne seca* (*machaca* stew). Wero Palma is a respelling of the nickname of Héctor "Güero" (blond) Palma, a well-known, jailed drug lord from Sinaloa whose saga has been immortalized in a series of *narcocorridos*, among them "La caída del Güero Palma" sung by *norteña* superstar band Los Tucanes de Tijuana.

27. *La mona* is a house in the shape of a standing nude woman carrying a torch, a kind of *tijuanense* Statue of Liberty. Tellingly, the house is in Tijuana's well-known working-class neighborhood Colonia Libertad. The *quinceañera* is a traditional Mexican celebration, a female rite of passage that marks a girl's presentation to society at age 15.

28. Brown, personal interview.

29. *La 5 y 10* is one of the busiest street intersections in Tijuana. A large variety of collective taxis and public transportation used by working-class individuals end and begin their routes there.

30. Michel de Certeau, *The Practice of Everyday Life*, trans. S. Rendall (Berkeley: University of California Press, 1984), 93–96.

31. AIGA stands for American Institute of Graphic Arts.

32. As of 3 October 2007, this video was available for free at http://www.fussible.com/~main/video/odyssea.html and http://www.anaimation.com/video/odyssea.html

33. Toyland is an annual electronic music event organized in Tijuana by Susan Monsalve to collect toys for homeless kids.

34. Ángeles Moreno, electronic communication, 30 September 2004.

35. Ibid. In this phrase, Moreno clearly identifies herself as an outsider (the southern *chilanga* from Mexico City) who, by that very condition, claims to be able to see many of the unique features of the city that most *tijuanenses* take for granted.

36. Carol Vernallis, *Experiencing Music Video: Aesthetic and Cultural Context* (New York: Columbia University Press, 2004), 8.

37. See Hans Fjellestad, *Frontier Life* (Zucasa Productions, 2002).

38. *Zeta* is a local Tijuana newspaper well known for its harsh and upfront criticism of local corrupt politicians and drug lords. Several *Zeta* journalists involved in these projects have been murdered since the mid-1990s.

39. Iván Díaz Robledo (VJ Wero Palma), personal interview, Tijuana, 29 June 2004.

40. See "Atentan contra la libertad de expresión," *Frontera* (1 September 2000). In the article, the video was depicted as a "video about corruption."

41. "Les confirmaron que era el lugar más feliz del mundo. Les hablaron de chicas caminando semi desnudas por la eterna e interminable acera principal. Les contaron sobre el surfing pendenciero en los clubes y cantinas, de borracheras míticas con sabor a blue hawaiians, margaritas, long islands, tequila y cerveza. Les susurraron en los oídos aquella vieja leyenda atrapa-stupid-gringos del donkey show y ellos como buenos hijos de la Middle America—jar heads, navy guys, white trash in cutoffs—se creyeron todo y emocionados llegaron a la city tras haber ensayado cómo pedir 'one cerveza.'" Rafa Saavedra, "Where's the donkey show, Mr. Mariachi?" in *Bukónica: Libros, cuentos, textos sueltos, b-sides, remixes and hidden tracks,* http://bukonica.blogspot.com. Posted on 7 August 2004.

42. Sergio Brown (VJ CBrown) quoted in Rafa Saavedra, "Tijuana Makes Me Happy," *Nexos*, vol. 26, no. 323 (2004), 63.

43. Slavoj Žižek, *El acoso de las fantasías*, trans. Clea Braunstein Saal (Mexico City, Mexico: Siglo Veintiuno, 1999), 19.

44. Paul Ricoeur, "Arquitectura y narratividad," *Arquitectonics: Mind, Land and Society,* no. 4 (2003), 28.

45. de Certeau, *Practice of Everyday Life,* xii.

Chapter 5

1. José Trinidad Morales (Pepe Mogt), personal interview, Tijuana, 12 May 2003.

2. Barry Shank, *Dissonant Identities: The Rock 'n' Roll Scene in Austin, Texas* (Hanover, CT: Wesleyan University Press, 1994), 125.

3. Richard Schechner, *Performance Theory* (New York: Routledge, 2003), x.

4. Gerard Béhague, "Introduction," in *Performance Practice: Ethnomusicological Perspectives*, ed. Gerard Béhague (Westport, CT: Greenwood, 1984), 7.

5. Judith Butler, *Bodies That Matter: On the Discursive Limits of Sex* (New York: Routledge, 1993), 20.

6. The epigraph is from Claudia Algara, "Diagonales luminosas en el trópico" (2001). This is an unpublished manuscript of bilingual poetry by the former Hiperboreal collaborator. This fragment was originally written in English.

7. José Ignacio López (El Lazo Invisible), personal interview, Tijuana, 8 July 2004.

8. Morales, personal interview, 12 May 2003.

9. Jorge Ruiz (Melo), personal interview, Tijuana, 19 June 2004.

10. Manrico Montero (DJ Linga), personal interview, Mexico City, 3 August 2004.

11. Daniel Rivera (DJ Tolo), personal interview, Tijuana, 18 June 2004.

12. Ibid.

13. Jorge Ruiz, personal interview.

14. Nicholas Cook, "Between Process and Product: Music and/as Performance," *Music Theory Online*, vol. 7, no. 2 (2001), par. 15. Available: http://www.societymusictheory.org/mto/issues/mt0.01.7.2/mt0.01.7.2.cook_frames.html.

15. Hans Fjellestad, personal interview, San Diego, 22 May 2003.

16. Leoncio González Medina, personal interview, Tijuana, 30 September 2005.

17. Montero, personal interview.

18. VJ stands for video jockey.

19. Sergio Brown (VJ CBrown), personal interview, Tijuana, 23 May 2003.

20. Ibid.

21. José Luis Martín (VJ Mashaka), personal interview, Tijuana, 15 May 2003.

22. VJ Mashaka and a group of visual artists have put together a Web site where fans can experience the art of the Nor-tec VJ. The site offers a series of musical and visual loops that can be organized and matched by the user. The computer keyboard allows the user to shift from image to image in any possible combination following the music loops' rhythm and pace. The site is called *Loops Urbanos* and can be accessed at http://www.loopsurbanos.org.

23. Héctor Falcón, personal interview, Mexico City, 3 August 2004.

24. Sherry Turkle, *Life on the Screen: Identity in the Age of the Internet* (New York: Simon & Schuster, 1995), 235.

25. Cyborgs are human beings whose physical abilities are enhanced by transforming their bodies with the incorporation of technology.

26. Ursula, personal interview, Tijuana, 14 May 2003.

27. Bruno Ruiz, "Momentos de la vida normal: Nortec," *Frontera* (9 March 2001).

28. Nina Garin, "Nortec Crosses Many Artistic Borders," *San Diego Union-Tribune* (6 March 2001).

29. Pepe Mogt quoted in ibid.

30. El Chapulín Colorado was a character created by screenwriter Roberto Gómez Bolaños (Chespirito; short for Shakespeare in Mexican Spanish) for a weekly TV show of the same title that aired on Mexican TV during the 1970s and 1980s.

31. Rafa Saavedra, personal interview, Tijuana, 5 December 2003.

32. Esther Corona, personal interview, Tijuana, 14 July 2004.

Chapter 6

1. Michel de Certeau, *The Practice of Everyday Life*, trans. Steven Rendall (Berkeley: University of California Press, 1984), xii.

2. Kai Fikentscher, *"You Better Work!" Underground Dance Music in New York City* (Hanover, CT: Wesleyan University Press, 2000), 8.

3. Sally Ann Allen Ness, "Being a Body in a Cultural Way: Understanding the Cultural in the Embodiment of Dance," in *Cultural Bodies: Ethnography and Theory*, ed. Helen Thomas and Jamilah Ahmed (Oxford: Blackwell, 2004), 124.

4. Slavoj Žižek, *The Sublime Object of Ideology* (New York: Verso, 1989), 12–21.

5. Slavoj Žižek, *Mirando al sesgo: Una introducción a Jaques Lacan a través de la cultura popular,* trans. Jorge Piatigorsky (Barcelona, Spain: Paidós, 2000), 22–25.

6. Bryan S. Turner, *Regulating Bodies: Essays in Medical Sociology* (London: Routledge, 1992), 41–42.

7. Helen Thomas, *The Body, Dance and Cultural Theory* (New York: Palgrave Macmillan, 2003), 193.

8. "El taconazo" is one of the most famous songs of the late *norteño* singer and icon Eulalio González (Piporro).

9. Daniel, personal interview, 20 June 2004.

10. Alex, personal interview, 23 June 2004.

11. Adriana, personal interview, 5 July 2004.

12. I use the term "learned" here to describe an educated and cultured practice.

13. José E. Limón, "Texas-Mexican Popular Music and Dancing: Some Notes on History and Symbolic Process," *Latin American Music Review,* vol. 4, no. 2 (1983), 234–235.

14. With this, I am not implying that women who enjoy these types of closed dance forms are victims of hegemonic culture. Undoubtedly, they find pleasure in participating in these types of closed dances, and, as Frances Aparicio and Helena Simonett have shown, there is also a space for female agency within these dances. See Frances Aparicio, *Listening to Salsa: Gender, Latin Popular Music, and Puerto Rican Cultures* (Hanover, CT: Wesleyan University Press, 1998), 96–97; and Helena Simonett, *Banda: Mexican Musical Life across Borders* (Middletown, CT: Wesleyan University Press, 2001), 281–303.

15. Jennifer Mañón, personal interview, Los Angeles, 18 September 2003.

16. Ibid.

17. Arlene Dávila, *Latinos, Inc.: The Marketing and Making of a People* (Berkeley: University of California Press, 2001), 17.

18. See Judith Butler, *Excitable Speech: A Politics of the Performative* (New York: Routledge, 1997).

19. Celeste Fraser Delgado and José Esteban Muñoz, "Rebellions of Everynight Life," in *Everynight Life: Culture and Dance in Latin/o America,* ed. C. F. Delgado and J. Muñoz (Durham, NC: Duke University Press, 1997), 9.

20. Allen Ness, "Being a Body," 135.

21. Nina Garin, "Nortec Crosses Many Artistic Borders," *San Diego Union-Tribune* (6 March 2001).

22. Nevertheless, as I explained in chapter 2, cumbia is slowly gaining more exposure in Latino media.

23. See Itzel Martínez del Canizo and Huicho Martín, *Salón de baile La Estrella* (Loops Urbanos and Bola 8 Productions, 2001).

24. Another aspect that undoubtedly played a role in the exclusion of many of these musical practices from Latino media was that the economic power of Mexican immigrants—whose predominantly illegal immigration status saddled them with the poorest paid jobs in the country—was always believed to be less than that of the largely middle- and upper-class Cuban immigrants (especially those of the 1960s, during the first decade of the Cuban revolution).

25. See Simonett, *Banda.*

26. See Gloria Anzaldúa, *Borderlands/La Frontera: The New Mestiza* (San Francisco, CA: Aunt Lute Books, 1987).

Chapter 7

1. PRISA is a rapidly expanding media conglomerate based in Spain. It owns hundreds of radio and TV stations, newspapers, and publishing houses throughout Iberoamerica, including the influential Spanish newspaper *El País,* the Bolivian newspapers *La Razón* and *El Nuevo Día,* the Mexican edition of *Rolling Stone,* the Chilean broadcast network Radio Chile, the Colombian Radio Caracol, the Mexican radio network Radiópolis (in equal partnership with the powerful Mexican TV network Televisa), and Grupo Santillana, which includes well-known publishing houses such as Alfaguara and Santillana (a leading press in the publication of education and training textbooks). As the sponsor of the Alfaguara Award, a well-respected prize among the Iberoamerican literary community, PRISA has ensured the extension of its power and influence well beyond the purely commercial and entertainment spheres.

2. José Trinidad Morales (Pepe Mogt), personal conversation, Tijuana, 14 June 2004.

3. Quoted in René Gardner, "Definen la frontera como *tercera nación,*" *Reforma* (20 April 2004).

4. "Palabras del Presidente Vicente Fox Quesada durante el evento Tijuana, la Tercera Nación, que tuvo lugar este mediodía en el Centro Cultural Tijuana, en esta ciudad," in *México: Presidencia: Actividades Presidenciales,* http://fox.presidencia .gob.mx/actividades/girasnacionales/?contenido=7964. Posted on 20 April 2004 (accessed on 3 February 2007).

5. Quoted in Ivonne Melgar, "Ofrece Presidente diálogo: Rechaza chantaje político," *Reforma* (20 April 2004).

6. According to Judith Amador Tello, FONCA contributed 10 percent of the investment required for the production of the event. See Tello, "Tijuana, la tercera nación," *Proceso,* no. 1437 (16 May 2004).

7. Heriberto Yépez, "No al arte NAFTA," *e.n.s.a.m.b.l.e.,* http://www.hyepez .blogspot.com. Posted on 29 April 2004 (accessed on 3 February 2007). The article was previously published in the local newspaper *Bitácora.*

8. Ibid.

9. Heriberto Yépez, "Arte NAFTA: Identidades artificiales," *Reforma* (23 May 2004).

10. Julio Sueco, "Tijuana: Tercera Nación," *Síndrome de Estocolmo,* http:// aztlan2.blogspot.com/2004/06/tijuana-tercera-nacin.html. Posted on 1 June 2004 (accessed on 3 February 2007).

11. Ingrid Hernández, "Tijuana: La Tercera Nación: O de cómo más vale pedir perdón que pedir permiso," *Cronika,* http://www.cronika.com/tijuana.htm (accessed on 3 February 2007).

12. Gerardo Yépiz (Acamonchi), electronic communication, 3 February 2007.

13. Yépez, "Arte NAFTA."

14. Daniel, "Sobre Tercera Nación y otras formas de esterilidad," *Eterno Retorno,* http://cunadeporqueria.blogspot.com/2005/03/sobre-tercera-nacin-y-otras-formas-de.html. Posted on 23 March 2005 (accessed on 3 February 2007).

15. Walter D. Mignolo, "Globalization, Civilization Processes, and the Relocation of Languages and Culture," in *The Cultures of Globalization,* ed. Fredric Jameson and Masao Miyoshi (Durham, NC: Duke University Press, 1998), 45.

16. Homi K. Bhabha, "Culture's in Between," in *Questions of Cultural Identity,* ed. Stuart Hall and Paul du Gay (London: Sage, 1996), 54.

17. Chela Sandoval, *Methodology of the Oppressed* (Minneapolis: University of Minnesota Press, 2000), 85.

18. Homi Bhabha, *The Location of Culture* (London: Routledge, 1994), 37.

19. Arjun Appadurai, *Modernity at Large: Cultural Dimensions of Globalization* (Minneapolis: University of Minnesota Press, 1996), 21.

20. Jürgen Habermas, *The Postnational Constellation: Political Essays* (Cambridge, MA: MIT Press, 2001), 53–57.

21. José Manuel Valenzuela Arce, personal interview, Tijuana, 13 May 2003.

22. José Trinidad Morales (Pepe Mogt), personal interview, Tijuana, 12 May 2003. "America's Finest City" is the self-proclaimed city slogan to which Mogt refers.

23. "Questo suono nuovo non è stato digerito interamente dalla comunità elettronica del centro del paese, che lo comincia a conoscere, pero non è certo obbligatorio chi piaccia a tutti." Reproduced on the Italian Web site *apt.Centauro,* http://utenti.lycos.it/aptcentauro/tecnogeist.html.

24. See Slavoj Žižek, *Mirando al sesgo: Una introducción a Jaques Lacan a través de la cultura popular* (Buenos Aires, Argentina: Paidós, 2000), 20.

25. George Yúdice, *The Expediency of Culture: Uses of Culture in the Global Era* (Durham, NC: Duke University Press, 2003), 15.

26. See Antonio Navalón, "La tercera nación," *Nexos*, no. 326 (2005).

27. For an explanation of irony as a critical weapon that adapts the discourse of the opponent to expose its flaws, see Arthur Koestler, *The Act of Creation* (New York: Macmillan, 1976), 32–38.

28. Juan Villoro, "Días de futuro pasado," in *Crines: Otras lecturas de rock*, ed. Carlos Chimal (Mexico City, Mexico: Era, 1994), 241.

29. Diana Taylor, *The Archive and the Repertoire: Performing Cultural Memory in the Americas* (Durham, NC: Duke University Press, 2003), 24–26.

30. Artemio, informal conversation, Los Angeles, 16 September 2003.

31. Daniel, personal interview, San Isidro, 20 June 2004.

Bibliography

Written Works

Adorno, Theodor, and Max Horkheimer. *Dialectic of Enlightenment,* trans. John Cumming. New York: Seabury, 1972.

Algara, Claudia. "Diagonales luminosas en el trópico." Unpublished book manuscript, 2001.

Allen Ness, Sally Ann. "Being a Body in a Cultural Way: Understanding the Cultural in the Embodiment of Dance," in *Cultural Bodies: Ethnography and Theory,* ed. H. Thomas and J. Ahmed. Oxford: Blackwell, 2004.

AlSayyad, Nezar, ed. *Consuming Tradition, Manufacturing Heritage.* New York: Routledge, 2001.

———. *The End of Tradition?* New York: Routledge, 2004.

Alvarez-Pereyre, Frank, and Simha Arom. "Ethnomusicology and the Emic/Etic Issue." *World of Music,* vol. 35, no. 1, 1993.

Anzaldúa, Gloria. *Borderlands/La Frontera: The New Mestiza.* San Francisco, CA: Aunt Lute Books, 1987.

Aparicio, Frances. *Listening to Salsa: Gender, Latin Popular Music, and Puerto Rican Cultures.* Hanover, CT: Wesleyan University Press, 1998.

Appadurai, Arjun. "Grassroots Globalization and the Research Imagination," in *Globalization,* ed. Arjun Appadurai. Durham, NC: Duke University Press, 2005.

———. *Modernity at Large: Cultural Dimensions of Globalization.* Minneapolis: University of Minnesota Press, 1996.

Appadurai, Arjun, ed. *Globalization.* Durham, NC: Duke University Press, 2005.

Asensio, Susana. "The Nortec Edge: Border Traditions and Electronica in Tijuana," in *Rockin' Las Americas: The Global Politics of Rock Music in Latin America,* ed. Deborah Pacini-Hernández, Héctor Fernandez-L'Hoeste, and Eric Zolov. Pittsburgh, PA: University of Pittsburgh Press, 2004.

————. "Tijuana *grooves:* El borde revisitado en la electronica de Nortec." *Arizona Journal of Hispanic Cultural Studies,* vol. 5, 2001.

Auslander, Philip. "Musical Personae." *TDR: The Journal of Performance Studies,* vol. 50, no. 1, 2006.

Austin, J. L. *How to Do Things with Words.* Cambridge, MA: Harvard University Press, 1962.

Avalos, David, and John C. Welchman. "Response to the Philosophical Brothel," in *Rethinking Borders,* ed. John C. Welchman. Minneapolis: University of Minnesota Press, 1996.

Bartra, Roger. *Blood, Ink, and Culture: Miseries and Splendors of the Post-Mexican Condition.* Durham, NC: Duke University Press, 2002.

Baudrillard, Jean. *Cultura y simulacro.* Barcelona, Spain: Kairós, 1978.

Beezley, William, Cheryl English Martin, and William E. French, eds. *Rituals of Rule, Rituals of Resistance: Public Celebrations and Popular Culture in Mexico.* Wilmington, DE: Scholarly Resources, 1994.

Béhague, Gerard. "Introduction," in *Performance Practice: Ethnomusicological Perspectives,* ed. Gerard Béhague. Westport, CT: Greenwood, 1984.

Béhague, Gerard, ed. *Performance Practice: Ethnomusicological Perspectives.* Westport, CT: Greenwood, 1984.

Bell, David. *An Introduction to Cybercultures.* New York: Routledge, 2001.

Benjamin, Walter. *Illuminations.* London: Fontana, 1970.

Bennet, Andy, and Richard A. Peterson, eds. *Music Scenes: Local, Translocal, and Virtual.* Nashville, TN: Vanderbilt University Press, 2004.

Beverley, John, José Oviedo, and Michael Aronna, eds. *The Postmodernist Debate in Latin America.* Durham, NC: Duke University Press, 1995.

Bhabha, Homi. "Culture's in Between," in *Questions of Cultural Identity,* ed. Stuart Hall and Paul du Gay. London: Sage, 1996.

————. *The Location of Culture.* London: Routledge, 1994.

Blánquez, Javier, and Omar Morera, eds. *Loops: Una historia de la musica electrónica.* Barcelona, Spain: Mondadori, 2002.

Blonsky, Marshall, ed. *On Signs.* Baltimore, MD: Johns Hopkins University Press, 1985.

Bringas, Nora L., and Jorge Castillo V., eds. *Grupos de visitantes y actividades turísticas en Tijuana.* Tijuana, Mexico: El Colegio de la Frontera Norte, 1991.

Burr, Ramiro. *The Billboard Guide to Tejano and Regional Mexican Music.* New York: Billboard Books, 1999.

Butler, Judith. *Bodies That Matter: On the Discursive Limits of Sex.* New York: Routledge, 1993.

Butler, Mark J. *Unlocking the Groove: Rhythm, Meter, and Musical Design in Electronic Dance Music.* Bloomington: Indiana University Press, 2006.

Calinescu, Matei. *Five Faces of Modernity: Modernism, Avant-garde, Decadence, Kitsch, Postmodernism.* Durham, NC: Duke University Press, 1987.

Carrizosa, Toño. *La onda grupera: Historia del movimiento grupero.* Mexico City, Mexico: EDAMEX, 1997.

Chimal, Carlos, ed. *Crines: Otras lecturas de rock.* Mexico City, Mexico: Era, 1994.

Clayton, Martin, Trevor Herbert, and Richard Middleton, eds. *The Cultural Study of Music: A Critical Introduction.* New York: Routledge, 2003.

Cook, Nicholas. "Between Process and Product: Music and/as Performance." *Music Theory Online,* vol. 7, no. 2, 2001. Available: http://www.societymusictheory.org/mto/issues/mt0.01.7.2/mt0.01.7.2.cook_frames.html

Corona, Ignacio, and Alejandro L. Madrid. "Ideology, Flux, and Identity in Tijuana's Nor-tec Music," in *Postnational Musical Identities: Cultural Production, Distribution and Consumption in a Globalized Scenario,* ed. Ignacio Corona and Alejandro L. Madrid. Lanham, MD: Lexington, 2007.

Corona, Ignacio, and Alejandro L. Madrid, eds. *Postnational Musical Identities: Cultural Production, Distribution and Consumption in a Globalized Scenario.* Lanham, MD: Lexington, 2007.

Cortés, David. *El otro rock mexicano: Experiencias progresivas, sicodélicas de fusión y experimentales.* Mexico City, Mexico: Times Editores, Opción Sónica, and Tower Records, 1999.

Croucher, Sheila L. *Imagining Miami: Ethnic Politics in a Postmodern World.* Charlottesville: University Press of Virginia, 1997.

Dávila, Arlene. *Latinos, Inc.: The Marketing and Making of a People.* Berkeley: University of California Press, 2001.

Davis, Mike. *Magical Urbanism: Latinos Reinvent the U.S. City.* New York: Verso, 2000.

de Certeau, Michel. *The Practice of Everyday Life,* trans. Steven Rendall. Berkeley: University of California Press, 1984.

Deleuze, Gilles, and Félix Guattari. *Anti-Oedipus: Capitalism and Schizophrenia,* trans. Robert Hurley, Mark Seem, and Helen R. Lane. Minneapolis: University of Minnesota Press, 1983.

Delgado, Celeste Fraser, and José Esteban Muñoz. "Rebellions of Everynight Life," in *Everynight Life: Culture and Dance in Latin/o America,* ed. C. F. Delgado and J. Muñoz. Durham, NC: Duke University Press, 1997.

Delgado, Celeste Fraser, and José Esteban Muñoz, eds. *Everynight Life: Culture and Dance in Latin/o America.* Durham, NC: Duke University Press, 1997.

Demers, Joanna. "Dancing Machines: 'Dance Dance Revolution,' Cybernetic Dance, and Musical Taste." *Popular Music,* vol. 25, no. 3, 2006.

Desmond, Jane C. "Embodying Difference: Issues in Dance and Cultural Studies," in *Everynight Life: Culture and Dance in Latin/o America,* ed. Celeste Fraser Delgado and José Esteban Muñoz. Durham, NC: Duke University Press, 1997.

Desmond, Jane C., ed. *Meaning in Motion: New Cultural Studies of Dance.* Durham, NC: Duke University Press, 1997.

Díaz Castro, Olga Vicenta [Sor Abeja]. "La tía Juana," in *Entre la magia y la historia: Tradiciones, mitos y leyendas de la frontera,* ed. José Manuel Valenzuela Arce. Tijuana, Mexico: El Colegio de la Frontera Norte and Plaza y Valdés, 2000.

Dorsey, Margaret E. *Pachangas: Borderlands Music, U.S. Politics, and Transnational Marketing.* Austin: University of Texas Press, 2006.

During, Simon, ed. *The Cultural Studies Reader.* New York: Routledge, 1993.

Ebare, Sean. "Digital Music and Subculture: Sharing Files, Sharing Styles." *First Monday,* vol. 9, no. 2, 2004.

Eco, Umberto. *A Theory of Semiotics.* Bloomington: Indiana University Press, 1976.

Erlmann, Veit. *Music, Modernity, and the Global Imagination: South Africa and the West.* New York: Oxford University Press, 1999.

Featherstone, Mike, Scott Lash, and Roland Robertson, eds. *Global Modernities.* London: Sage, 1995.

Félix Berúmen, Humberto. *Tijuana la horrible: Entre la historia y el mito.* Tijuana, Mexico: El Colegio de la Frontera Norte, 2003.

Fikentscher, Kai. *"You Better Work!" Underground Dance Music in New York City.* Hanover, CT: Wesleyan University Press, 2000.

Frith, Simon. "Music and Identity," in *Questions of Cultural Identity*, ed. Stuart Hall and Paul du Gay. London: Sage, 1996.

Gaillot, Michel. *Multiple Meaning: Techno: An Artistic and Political Laboratory of the Present*. Paris: Dis Voir, 1999.

García Canclini, Néstor. *Consumers and Citizens: Globalization and Multicultural Conflicts*, trans. G. Yúdice. Minneapolis: University of Minnesota Press, 2001.

———. *Culturas híbridas: Estrategias para entrar y salir de la modernidad*. Mexico City, Mexico: Grijalbo, 1989.

———. *Culturas populares en el capitalismo*. Mexico City, Mexico: Grijalbo, 2002.

———. "De-Urbanized Art, Border De-Installations," in *InSite 97: Public Time in Public Spaces*, ed. Sally Yard, trans. Sandra del Castillo. San Diego, CA: Installation Gallery, 1998.

———. *La globalización imaginada*. Buenos Aires: Paidós, 1999.

———. "Latins or Americans: Narratives of the Border." *Canadian Journal of Latin American and Caribbean Studies*, no. 23, 1988.

García Canclini, Néstor, ed. *Cultura y comunicación en la ciudad de México*. Mexico City, Mexico: Grijalbo, 1998.

García Canclini, Néstor, and Carlos Juan Moneta, eds. *Las industrias culturales en la integración latinoamericana*. Mexico City, Mexico: Grijalbo, 1999.

García Canclini, Néstor, and Patricia Safa, eds. *Tijuana: La casa de toda la gente*. Mexico City, Mexico: INAH, Programa Cultural de las Fronteras, UAM-Iztapalapa, and CONACULTA, 1989.

Giddens, Anthony. *The Consequences of Modernity*. Stanford, CA: Stanford University Press, 1990.

———. *Runaway World: How Globalization Is Reshaping Our Lives*. New York: Routledge, 2003.

Gupta, Akhil, and James Ferguson. "Beyond 'Culture': Space, Identity and the Politics of Difference." *Cultural Anthropology*, vol. 7, no. 1, 1992.

Gutiérrez, David G. "Ethnic Mexicans and the Transformation of 'American' Social Space: Relations on Recent History," in *Crossings: Mexican Immigration Interdisciplinary Perspectives*, ed. Marcelo M. Suárez-Orozco. Cambridge, MA: David Rockefeller Center for Latin American Studies and Harvard University Press, 1998.

Habermas, Jürgen. *The Postnational Constellation: Political Essays*, trans. Max Pensky. Cambridge, MA: Massachusetts Institute of Technology Press, 2001.

Hall, Stuart. "Encoding, Decoding," in *The Cultural Studies Reader*, ed. Simon During. New York: Routledge, 1993.

———. "Negotiating Caribbean Identities," in *New Caribbean Thought: A Reader*, ed. Brian Meeks and Folke Lindahl. Kingston: University of the West Indies Press, 2001.

Hall, Stuart, and Paul du Gay, eds. *Questions of Cultural Identity*. London: Sage, 1996.

Harvey, David. *The Condition of Postmodernity*. Oxford: Blackwell, 1990.

Hebdige, Dick. *Subculture: The Meaning of Style*. New York: Routledge, 1979.

Hedetoft, Ulf, and Mette Hjort, eds. *The Postnational Self: Belonging and Identity*. Minneapolis: University of Minnesota Press, 2002.

Held, David, Anthony McGrew, David Goldblatt, and Jonathan Perraton. *Global Transformations: Politics, Economics and Culture*. Stanford, CA: Stanford University Press, 1999.

Hobsbawm, Eric, and Terence Ranger. *The Invention of Tradition*. New York: Cambridge University Press, 1983.

Hodgkinson, James A. "The Fanzine Discourses over Post-rock," in *Music Scenes: Local, Translocal, and Virtual,* ed. Andy Bennett and Richard A. Peterson. Nashville, TN: Vanderbilt University Press, 2004.

Jameson, Fredric. "Postmodernism; or, The Cultural Logic of Late Capitalism." *New Left Review,* no. 146, 1984.

Jameson, Fredric, and Masao Miyoshi, eds. *The Cultures of Globalization.* Durham, NC: Duke University Press, 1998.

Jones, Steven G. "The Internet and Its Social Landscapes," in *Virtual Culture, Identity and Communication in Cybersociety,* ed. Steven H. Jones. London: Sage, 1997.

Jones, Steven G., ed. *Virtual Culture, Identity and Communication in Cybersociety.* London: Sage, 1997.

Katz, Mark. *Capturing Sound: How Technology Has Changed Music.* Berkeley: University of California Press, 2004.

Kent, Jeff. *The Rise and Fall of Rock.* Stoke-on-Trent, England: Witan, 1983.

Kirshenblatt-Gimblett, Barbara. "Theorizing Heritage." *Ethnomusicology,* vol. 39, no. 3, 1995.

Koestler, Arthur. *The Act of Creation.* New York: Macmillan, 1976.

Kun, Josh. *Audiotopia: Music, Race, and America.* Berkeley: University of California Press, 2005.

———. "File Under: Post-Mexico." *Aztlán: A Journal of Chicano Studies,* vol. 29, no. 1, 2004.

———. "They're from Where? Nortec through U.S. Ears," in José Manuel Valenzuela Arce, *Paso del Nortec/This Is Tijuana.* Mexico City, Mexico: Trilce, 2004.

Lacan, Jacques. "Sign, Symbol, Imaginary," in *On Signs,* ed. M. Blonsky. Baltimore, MD: Johns Hopkins University Press, 1985.

Lee, Steve S., and Richard A. Peterson. "Internet-based Virtual Music Scenes: The Case of P2 in Alt.Country Music," in *Music Scenes: Local, Translocal, and Virtual,* ed. Andy Bennett and Richard A. Peterson. Nashville, TN: Vanderbilt University Press, 2004.

Lepecki, André, ed. *Of the Presence of the Body: Essays on Dance and Performance Theory.* Middletown, CT: Wesleyan University Press, 2004.

Limón, José. *Dancing with the Devil: Society and Cultural Poetics in Mexican-American South Texas.* Madison: University of Wisconsin Press, 1994.

———. "Texas-Mexican Popular Music and Dancing: Some Notes on History and Symbolic Process." *Latin American Music Review,* vol. 4, no. 2, 1983.

Lipsitz, George. *Dangerous Crossroads: Popular Music, Postmodernism and the Poetics of Place.* New York: Verso, 1994.

———. "Their America and Ours: Intercultural Communications in the Context of 'Our America,'" in *José Martí's "Our America": From National to Hemispheric Cultural Studies,* ed. Jeffrey Belnap and Raúl Fernández. Durham, NC: Duke University Press, 1998.

Mackay, Hugh, ed. *Consumption and Everyday Life.* New Delhi: Sage, 1997.

Madrid, Alejandro L. "Dancing with Desire: Cultural Embodiment and Negotiation in Tijuana's Nor-tec Music and Dance." *Popular Music,* vol. 25, no. 3, 2006.

———. "Imagining Modernity, Revising Tradition: Nor-tec Music in Tijuana and Other Borders." *Popular Music and Society,* vol. 28, no. 5, 2005.

———. "Los *loops* de Nor-tec: Reflexiones sobre el trabajo de campo en la frontera México–Estados Unidos." *Boletín Música,* nos. 11–12, 2003.

———. "Navigating Ideologies in 'In-Between' Cultures: Signifying Practices in Nor-tec Music." *Latin American Music Review,* vol. 24, no. 2, 2003.

———. "Reapropiación y estética kitsch en 'Tijuana Makes Me Happy' del Colectivo Nortec." *Brújula: Revista Interdisciplinaria Sobre Estudios Latinoamericanos,* vol. 5, no. 1, 2006.

Maira, Sunaina. "TranceGlobal/Nation: Orientalism, Cosmopolitanism, and Citizenship in Youth Culture." *Journal of Popular Music Studies,* vol. 15, no. 1, 2003.

Manuel, Peter. "Music as Symbol, Music as Simulacrum: Postmodern, Pre-Modern, and Modern Aesthetics in Subcultural Popular Musics." *Popular Music,* vol. 14, no. 2, 1995.

Martin, Randy. "Dance and Its Others: Theory, State, Nation, and Socialism," in *Of the Presence of the Body: Essays on Dance and Performance Theory,* ed. André Lepecki. Middletown, CT: Wesleyan University Press, 2004.

McCarthy, Cameron, and Greg Dimitriadis. "Art and the Postcolonial Imagination: Rethinking the Institutionalization of Third World Aesthetics and Theory." *Ariel: A Review of International English Literature,* vol. 31, nos. 1–2, 2000.

McLeod, Kembrew. "Genres, Subgenres, Sub-Subgenres, and More: Musical and Social Differentiation within Electronic/Dance Music Communities." *Journal of Popular Music Studies,* vol. 13, no. 1, 2001.

Meeks, Brian, and Folke Lindahl, eds. *New Caribbean Thought: A Reader.* Kingston, Jamaica: University of the West Indies Press, 2001.

Mendoza López, Roberto A. "Electrónica en la frontera," in *Oye como va: Recuento del rock tijuanense,* ed. José Manuel Valenzuela Arce and Gloria González. Tijuana, Mexico: CONACULTA, CECUT, and Instituto Mexicano de la Juventud, 1999.

Mignolo, Walter D. "Globalization, Civilization Processes and the Relocation of Languages and Cultures," in *The Cultures of Globalization,* ed. Frederic Jameson and Masao Miyoshi. Durham, NC: Duke University Press, 1998.

Miller, Daniel. "Consumption and Its Consequences," in *Consumption and Everyday Life,* ed. Hugh Mackay. New Delhi: Sage, 1997.

Moraña, Mabel. "Ideología de la transculturación," in *Ángel Rama y los estudios latinoamericanos,* ed. Mabel Moraña. Pittsburgh, PA: University of Pittsburgh Press, 1997.

Moraña, Mabel, ed. *Ángel Rama y los estudios latinoamericanos.* Pittsburgh, PA: University of Pittsburgh Press, 1997.

Navarrete Pellicer, Sergio. "Las capillas de músicas de viento y los vientos de la Reforma en Oaxaca durante el siglo 19." *Acervos: Boletín de los Archivos y Bibliotecas de Oaxaca,* vol. 6, no. 24, 2001.

Ochoa, Ana María. "La producción grabada y la definición de lo local sonoro en México." *Heterofonía,* vol. 33, no. 124, 2001.

Olalquiaga, Celeste. *Megalopolis: Contemporary Cultural Sensibilities.* Minneapolis: University of Minnesota Press, 1992.

Olea, Héctor R. *Los orígenes de la tambora.* Culiacán, Mexico: Ayuntamiento de Culiacán, 1985.

Olson, James S., and Judith E. Olson. *Cuban Americans: From Trauma to Triumph.* New York: Twayne, 1995.

Olvera, José Juan, Benito Torres, Gregorio Cruz, and César Jaime Rodríguez. *La colombia de Monterrey: Descripción de algunos elementos de la cultura colombiana en la frontera norte.* San Antonio, TX: Guadalupe Cultural Arts Center, 1996.

Ortiz, Fernando. *Contrapunteo cubano del tabaco y el azúcar.* Madrid, Spain: EditoCubaEspaña, 1999.

Pacini-Hernández, Deborah, Héctor Fernandez-L'Hoeste, and Eric Zolov, eds. *Rockin' Las Americas: The Global Politics of Rock Music in Latin America*. Pittsburgh, PA: University of Pittsburgh Press, 2004.

Paredes, José Luis [Pacho]. "In Exotic T City," in José Manuel Valenzuela Arce, *Paso del Nortec/This Is Tijuana*. Mexico City, Mexico: Trilce, 2004.

Pedraza-Bailey, Silvia. "Cuba's Exiles: Portrait of a Refugee Migration." *International Migration Review*, vol. 19, no. 4, 1985.

Peña, Manuel. "From Ranchero to Jaitón: Ethnicity and Class in Texas-Mexican Music (Two Styles in the Form of a Pair)." *Ethnomusicology*, vol. 29, no. 1, 1985.

———. *The Texas-Mexican Conjunto: History of a Working-Class Music*. Austin: University of Texas Press, 1985.

Pike, Jeff. *The Death of Rock 'n' Roll: Untimely Demises, Morbid Preoccupations, and Premature Forecasts of Doom in Pop Music*. Boston: Faber and Faber, 1993.

Piñera Ramírez, David, and Jesús Ortiz Figueroa, eds. *Historia de Tijuana 1889–1989: Edición conmemorativa del centenario de su fundación*. Tijuana, Mexico: Universidad Autónoma de Baja California, 1989.

Portilla, Jorge. *La fenomenología del relajo*. Mexico City, Mexico: Fondo de Cultura Económica, 1966.

Pratt, Mary Louise. *Imperial Eyes: Travel Writing and Transculturation*. New York: Routledge, 1992.

Puig, Luis, and Jenaro Talens, eds. *Las culturas del rock*. Valencia, Spain: Pre-Textos, 1999.

Quintero Rivera, Ángel. *¡Salsa, sabor y control! Sociología de la música "tropical."* La Habana, Cuba: Casa de las Américas, 1998.

Racine, Étienne. *Le phénomène techno: Clubs, raves, free-parties*. Paris: Imago, 2002.

Radano, Ronald, and Philip V. Bohlman. "Introduction: Music and Race, Their Past, Their Presence," in *Music and the Racial Imagination*, ed. Ronald Radano and Philip V. Bohlman. Chicago: University of Chicago Press, 2000.

Radano, Ronald, and Philip V. Bohlman, eds. *Music and the Racial Imagination*. Chicago: University of Chicago Press, 2000.

Ragland, Cathy. "*Ni aquí ni allá* (Neither Here nor There): *Música Norteña* and the Mexican Working-Class Diaspora." Ph.D. diss., City University of New York, 2005.

———. *The Parallel Evolution and Cross Cultural Impact of Tejano Conjunto and Mexican Norteño Music*. San Antonio, TX: Guadalupe Cultural Arts Center, 1998.

Reynolds, Simon. "Androginia en el Reino Unido: Cultura rave, psicodelia y género," in *Las culturas del rock*, ed. Luis Puig and Jenaro Talens. Valencia, Spain: Pre-Textos, 1999.

———. "Prefacio," in *Loops: Una historia de la música electrónica*, ed. Javier Blánquez and Omar Morera. Barcelona, Spain: Mondadori, 2002.

Ricoeur, Paul. "Arquitectura y narratividad." *Arquitectonics: Mind, Land and Society*. no. 4, 2003.

Robertson, Roland. "Time-Space and Homogeneity-Heterogeneity," in *Global Modernities*, ed. Mike Featherstone, Scott Lash, and Roland Robertson. London: Sage, 1995.

Rojas, Manuel. *La cicatriz: El rock en la última frontera*. Mexicali, Mexico: Instituto de Cultura de Baja California, 2000.

Rojo, Luis, and Cynthia Ramírez. "El rock de Tijuana en los noventa: Lo alternativo, las nuevas corrientes: Expresiones de una generación," in *Oye como va: Recuento del rock tijuanense*, ed. José Manuel Valenzuela Arce and Gloria González.

Tijuana, Mexico: CONACULTA, CECUT, and Instituto Mexicano de la Juventud, 1999.

Roy, Ananya. "Nostalgias of the Modern," in *The End of Tradition?* ed. Nezar Al-Sayyad. New York: Routledge, 2004.

Saavedra, Rafa. *Lejos del noise.* Mexico City, Mexico: Moho, 2002.

——. "Terminal Norte: Los espacios para el rock tijuanense en los noventa," in *Oye como va: Recuento del rock tijuanense,* ed. José Manuel Valenzuela Arce and Gloria González. Tijuana, Mexico: CONACULTA, CECUT, and Instituto Mexicano de la Juventud, 1999.

Sandoval, Chela. *Methodology of the Oppressed.* Minneapolis: University of Minnesota Press, 2000.

Schaeffer, John. *New Sounds.* New York: Harper & Row, 1987.

Schechner, Richard. *Performance Theory.* New York: Routledge, 2003.

Schloss, Joseph G. *Making Beats: The Art of Sample-Based Hip-Hop.* Middletown, CT: Wesleyan University Press, 2004.

Seelye, Ned, and Jacqueline Howell Wasiliewski. *Between Cultures: Developing Self-Identity in a World of Diversity.* Lincolnwood, IL: NTC, 1996.

Shank, Barry. *Dissonant Identities: The Rock 'n' Roll Scene in Austin, Texas.* Hanover, CT: Wesleyan University Press, 1994.

Sicko, Dan. *Techno Rebels: The Renegades of Electronic Funk.* New York: Billboard Books, 1999.

Simonett, Helena. *Banda: Mexican Musical Life across Borders.* Middletown, CT: Wesleyan University Press, 2001.

——. "Strike Up the Tambora: A Social History of Sinaloan Band Music." *Latin American Music Review,* vol. 20, no. 1, 1999.

Sklar, Leslie. "The Maquilas in Mexico: A Global Perspective." *Bulletin of Latin American Research,* vol. 11, no. 1, 1992.

Slobin, Mark. *Subcultural Sounds: Micromusics of the West.* Hanover, CT: Wesleyan University Press, 1993.

Sontag, Susan. *Against Interpretation and Other Essays.* New York: Delta, 1966.

Sparke, Matthew. "Nature and Tradition at the Border: Landscaping the End of the Nation-State," in *The End of Tradition?* ed. Nezar AlSayyad. New York: Routledge, 2004.

Suárez-Orozco, Marcelo M. *Crossings: Mexican Immigration Interdisciplinary Perspectives.* Cambridge, MA: David Rockefeller Center for Latin American Studies and Harvard University Press, 1998.

Taylor, Diana. *The Archive and the Repertoire: Performing Cultural Memory in the Americas.* Durham, NC: Duke University Press, 2003.

——. "Transculturating Transculturation." *Performing Arts Journal,* no. 38, 1991.

Thomas, Helen. *The Body, Dance and Cultural Theory.* New York: Palgrave Macmillan, 2003.

Thomas, Helen, and Jamilah Ahmed, eds. *Cultural Bodies: Ethnography and Theory.* Oxford: Blackwell, 2004.

Thornton, Sarah. *Club Cultures: Music, Media and Subcultural Capital.* Hanover, CT: Wesleyan University Press, 1996.

Torres, Violeta. *Rock-Eros en concierto: Génesis e historia del Rockmex.* Mexico City, Mexico: Instituto Nacional de Antropología e Historia, 2002.

Turino, Thomas. *Nationalists, Cosmopolitans, and Popular Music in Zimbabwe.* Chicago: University of Chicago Press, 2000.

Turkle, Sherry. *Life on the Screen: Identity in the Age of the Internet.* New York: Simon and Schuster, 1995.

Turner, Bryan S. *Regulating Bodies: Essays in Medical Sociology.* London: Routledge, 1992.

Turner, Victor. *The Anthropology of Performance.* New York: PAJ, 1988.

Valenzuela Arce, José Manuel. *Jefe de jefes: Corridos y narcocultura en México.* La Habana, Cuba: Casa de las Américas, 2003.

———. *Paso del nortec/This Is Tijuana.* Mexico City, Mexico: Trilce, 2004.

———. "The Sociocultural Construction of Public Spaces," in *InSite 97: Public Time in Public Spaces,* ed. Sally Yard, trans. Sandra del Castillo. San Diego, CA: Installation Gallery, 1998.

Valenzuela Arce, José Manuel, ed. *Entre la magia y la historia: Tradiciones, mitos y leyendas de la frontera.* Tijuana, Mexico: El Colegio de la Frontera Norte and Plaza y Valdés, 2000.

Valenzuela Arce, José Manuel, and Gloria González, eds. *Oye como va: Recuento del rock tijuanense.* Tijuana, Mexico: CONACULTA, CECUT, and Instituto Mexicano de la Juventud, 1999.

Van Young, Eric. "Conclusion: The State as Vampire: Hegemonic Projects, Public Ritual, and Popular Culture in Mexico, 1600–1990," in *Rituals of Rule, Rituals of Resistance: Public Celebrations and Popular Culture in Mexico,* ed. William Beezley, Cheryl English Martin, and William E. French. Wilmington, DE: Scholarly Resources, 1994.

Verduzco Chávez, Basilio, Nora L. Bringas Rábago, and M. Basilia Valenzuela. *La ciudad compartida: Desarrollo urbano, comercio y turismo en la región Tijuana-San Diego.* Guadalajara, Mexico: Universidad de Guadalajara and El Colegio de la Frontera Norte, 1995.

Vernallis, Carol. *Experiencing Music Video: Aesthetics and Cultural Context.* New York: Columbia University Press, 2004.

Vila, Pablo. "Conclusion: The Limits of American Border Theory," in *Ethnography at the Border,* ed. Pablo Vila. Minneapolis: University of Minnesota Press, 2003.

———. "Introduction: Border Ethnographies," in *Ethnography at the Border,* ed. Pablo Vila. Minneapolis: University of Minnesota Press, 2003.

Vila, Pablo, ed. *Ethnography at the Border.* Minneapolis: University of Minnesota Press, 2003.

Villoro, Juan. "Días de futuro pasado," in *Crines: Otras lecturas de rock,* ed. Carlos Chimal. Mexico City, Mexico: Era, 1994.

Wegman, Rob C. "Historical Musicology: Is It Still Possible?" in *The Cultural Study of Music: A Critical Introduction,* ed. Martin Clayton, Trevor Herbert, and Richard Middleton. New York: Routledge, 2003.

Welchman, John C., ed. *Rethinking Borders.* Minneapolis: University of Minnesota Press, 1996.

Yard, Sally, ed. *InSite 97: Public Time in Public Spaces.* San Diego, CA: Installation Gallery, 1998.

Yúdice, George. *The Expediency of Culture: Uses of Culture in the Global Era.* Durham, NC: Duke University Press, 2003.

———. "La industria de la música en la integración América Latina–Estados Unidos," in *Las industrias culturales en la integración latinoamericana,* ed. Néstor García Canclini and Carlos Juan Moneta. Mexico City, Mexico: Grijalbo, 1999.

Žižek, Slavoj. *El acoso de las fantasías,* trans. Clea Braunstein Saal. Mexico City, Mexico: Siglo Veintiuno, 1999.

———. *Mirando al sesgo: Una introducción a Jacques Lacan a través de la cultura popular,* trans. Jorge Piatigorsky. Buenos Aires, Argentina: Paidós, 2000.

———. *The Sublime Object of Ideology.* New York: Verso, 1989.

Zolov, Eric. *Refried Elvis: The Rise of Mexican Counterculture.* Berkeley: University of California Press, 1999.

Personal Communications

Algara, Claudia. Poet and former collaborator with Hiperboreal and the Nortec Collective. Tijuana, Mexico. 17 June 2004.

Amezcua, Ramón [Bostich]. Musician, member of the Nortec Collective. Electronic communication. 6 November 2001.

———. Los Angeles, California. 17 May 2003.

Beas, Pedro Gabriel [Hiperboreal]. Musician, member of the Nortec Collective. Electronic communication. 25 October 2001.

———. Tijuana, Mexico. 11 May 2003.

———. Tijuana, Mexico. 13 May 2003.

Brown, Sergio [VJ CBrown]. Video artist, former member of the Nortec Collective, and professor at the Universidad Iberoamericana-Tijuana. Tijuana, Mexico. 23 May 2003.

Cárdenas, Raúl [Torolab]. Visual and installation artist, frequent collaborator with the Nortec Collective. Tijuana, Mexico. 6 December 2003.

Castañeda, Roberto. Musician, member of Ford Proco. Tijuana, Mexico. 6 July 2004.

Castellanos, Octavio [VJ TCR]. Video artist, member of the Nortec Collective, and professor at the Universidad Autónoma de Baja California-Tijuana. Los Angeles, California. 17 May 2003.

Chávez Uranga, Ignacio [Plankton Man and Kobol]. Musician, member of Niño Astronauta, former member of the Nortec Collective, and former member of Sonios. Tijuana, Mexico. 10 May 2003.

Cookman, Tomás. Founder of Cookman International and Fuerte Management, manager of the Nortec Collective. Electronic communication. 18 October 2004.

Corona, Esther. Fashion designer, former collaborator with the Nortec Collective. Tijuana, Mexico. 14 July 2004.

Corona, Fernando [Terrestre and Murcof]. Musician, former member of the Nortec Collective, and former member of Sonios. Electronic communication. 25 October 2001.

———. Tijuana, Mexico. 14 May 2003.

Díaz, Sebastián. Video journalist for Galatea Productions. Tijuana, Mexico. 21 May 2003.

Díaz Robledo, Iván [VJ Wero Palma and VJ Piniaman]. Video artist, former member of Nortec Collective, and founding member of Yonke Art. Tijuana, Mexico. 29 June 2004.

Falcón, Héctor. Performance artist, curator, and event organizer. Mexico City, Mexico. 3 August 2004.

Fjellestad, Hans. Musician, member of the Trummerflora Collective, documentarist, director of *Frontier Life.* San Diego, California. 22 May 2003.

Foglio, Omar. Video journalist for Galatea Productions, coordinator of Swenga, and professor at the Universidad Iberoamericana-Tijuana. Tijuana, Mexico. 21 May 2003.

García, Leslie. Graphic designer and installation artist. Tijuana, Mexico. 12 July 2004.

González, Mario [Mario Lagsbartt]. Music producer for Primo Music, EQ Studio, and Baja Sonic Music. Tijuana, Mexico. 12 July 2004.

González Medina, Leoncio. Trumpet player with Banda Aguacaliente. Tijuana, Mexico. 30 September 2005.

Harrington, David. Musician, member of Kronos Quartet. Telephone interview. 21 August 2003.

Hernández Piché, Jonathan. Visual and installation artist, head of No One over 21. Electronic communication. 10 March 2004.

Jiménez, Enrique [Mr. Ejival]. Disc jockey, music critic, and artistic director of Static Discos. Tijuana, Mexico. 16 May 2003.

Llanes, Max. Disc jockey, musician, and member of Aquadelfín. Tijuana, Mexico. 10 May 2003.

López, Alejandro. Musician and member of Ambiente. Tijuana, Mexico. 25 June 2004.

López, José Ignacio [El Lazo Invisible]. Musician and member of Miel, and disc jockey for Radio Global. Tijuana, Mexico. 8 July 2004.

Mañón, Jennifer. Event coordinator for Sonic 360 Records. Los Angeles, California. 18 September 2003.

Martín, José Luis [VJ Mashaka]. Video artist and member of Nortec Collective. Tijuana, Mexico. 15 May 2003.

Martínez de Castro, Ricardo [Ricky]. Music promoter and coordinator of Sabrosonic. Tijuana, Mexico. 24 June 2004.

Mendoza, Roberto [Panóptica and Mendoza]. Musician and member of Nortec Collective. Tijuana, Mexico. 13 May 2003.

———. Tijuana, Mexico. 6 December 2003.

Miranda, Efrén. Graphic designer, founder of *Lumbre* and *Sube Baja*, member of Radio Global. Tijuana, Mexico. 5 July 2004.

Miranda, Rubén [Tovar and Miranda]. Musician and member of Nopal Beat Collective. Tijuana, Mexico. 14 July 2004.

Monsalve, Susan. Event organizer. Tijuana, Mexico. 29 June 2004.

Montero, Manrico [DJ Linga]. Disc jockey, producer, and member of Parador Análogo Collective. Mexico City, Mexico. 3 August 2004.

Mora, Jhoana. Music promoter and local coordinator of Tijuana, Tercera Nación. Tijuana, Mexico. 19 June 2004.

Morales, José Trinidad [Pepe Mogt]. Musician; member of Fussible, Latinsizer, and Nortec Collective; music producer for Modula 3; and artistic director for Mil Records. Electronic communication. 4 November 2001.

———. Tijuana, Mexico. 12 May 2003.

———. Tijuana, Mexico, 14 June 2004.

———. Tijuana, Mexico. 7 July 2004.

———. Electronic communication. 19 October 2004.

———. Tijuana, Mexico. 30 September 2005.

Moreno, Ángeles. Graphic designer, animation artist, and frequent collaborator with Nortec Collective. Electronic communication. 30 September 2004.

Muriendas, Alfonso. Music promoter and event coordinator for Kimika. Tijuana, Mexico. 30 June 2004.

Rivera, Daniel [DJ Tolo]. Disc jockey, member of Tijuana House Club, and frequent collaborator with Nortec Collective. Tijuana, Mexico. 18 June 2004.

Rojo, Luis. Writer and coordinator of De Nortec a Sur and Flama 01. Electronic communication. 20 November 2003.

Román, Reynaldo. Graphic designer and coordinator of Ruido: Post Latin Alternative Music on the Edge. Chicago, Illinois. 14 November 2003.

Ruiz, Álvaro [Balboa and Ruisort]. Musician, member of Parador Análogo Collective, and former collaborator with Nortec Collective. Mexico City, Mexico. 19 August 2004.

Ruiz, Jorge [Melo]. Founding member of Nortec Collective and former member of Artefakto and Fussible. Tijuana, Mexico. 19 June 2004.

Saavedra, Rafa [Rafadro]. Novelist, chronicler, radio host, and disc jockey. Tijuana, Mexico. 5 December 2003.

———. Electronic communication. 12 September 2007.

Silva, Aníbal [DJ Aníbal]. Disc jockey, graphic designer, and frequent collaborator with Nortec Collective. Electronic communication. 23 October 2004.

Tamayo, Rubén [Fax]. Musician and graphic designer. Tijuana, Mexico. 10 May 2003.

Tapia, Angel, and Julio Tapia. Former disc jockeys for Radio Arte. Chicago, Illinois. 15 November 2003.

Torres, Fritz. Graphic designer, founding member of Cha3, and former member of Clorofila and Nortec Collective. Tijuana, Mexico. 16 May 2003.

Tucker, Luis. Event organizer and owner of Pueblo Café Baja. Electronic communication. 23 September 2004.

Valenzuela Arce, José Manuel. Sociologist and researcher at El Colegio de la Frontera Norte. Tijuana, Mexico. 13 May 2003.

Vázquez Ricalde, Salvador [VJ Sal]. Video artist, filmmaker, and former member of Nortec Collective. Tijuana, Mexico. 1 July 2004.

Verdín, Jorge. Graphic designer, founding member of Cha3, and member of Clorofila and Nortec Collective. Los Angeles, California. 17 May 2003.

Waizel, Uriel. Producer for Bons Records and former disc jockey for Imágen 90.5. Electronic communication. Tijuana, Mexico. 15 February 2004.

Yépiz, Gerardo [Acamonchi]. Graphic designer, visual artist, and frequent collaborator with Nortec Collective. San Diego, California. 22 May 2003.

———. Electronic communication. 3 February 2007.

Selected Internet Sites

Acamonchi: Propaganda. http://www.acamonchi.com

Anaimation. http://www.anaimation.com

AV Community: Audiovisualizers. http://community.audiovisualizers.com/mashaka

Babab. http://www.babab.com

Babylon. http://www.rockroll.gr

BLOGBLOGBLOG. http://www.blogblogblog.com

Bostich. http://www.bostich.org

Bukónica: Libros, cuentos, textos sueltos, b-sides, remixes and hidden tracks. http://bukonica.blogspot.com

Bulbo. http://www.bulbo.tv

Certificate 18. http://www.certificate18.com

CMJ: New Music First. http://www.cmj.com

Crossfader Fotopage: Blog Culture + Party + Pictures. http://rafadro.fotopages.com

Crossfader V: 4000. http://www.rafadro.blogspot.com

Daniel Norteco. http://www.danielnorteco.blogspot.com

Epitonic. http://www.epitonic.com

Fussible. http://www.fussible.com
Hear/Say. http://www.hearsay.cc
Ink Blot Magazine. http://www.inkblotmagazine.com
Ink 19. http://www.ink19.com
Jam! Showbiz. http://www.canoe.ca/Jam/home.html
Kimika. http://www.kimika.org
Loops Urbanos. http://www.loopsurbanos.org
Mil Records. http://www.milrecords.com
Murcof. http://www.murcof.com
Mutek: Music, Sound and New Technologies. http://www.mutek.ca
MySpace: Nortec Collective. http://www.myspace.com/nortec
Nacional Records. http://nacionalrecords.com
Niño Astronauta. http://www.3astronautas.com
Noarte: La presita: Panóptica, Mendoza, Desierto, Artefakto. http://www.noarte.com
Nortec Collective. http://www.nor-tec.org
Now Online Edition. http://www.nowtoronto.com
Palm Pictures. http://www.palmpictures.com
P. G. Beas: La vida después de Don Loope. http://pgbeas.blogspot.com
Plankton Man. http://www.planktonman.com
La Plume Noire. http://www.plume-noire.com
Radio Global. http://www.radioglobal.org
Sabrosonic. http://www.tijuanahouseclub.com/sabrosonic/sabrosonic.html
Sonic Boom. http://www.sonic-boom.com
Sonic 360 World. http://www.sonic360.com
Static Discos. http://www.staticdiscos.com
Supercluster: Arte y otras galaxias. http://www.supercluster.blogspot.com
Tampopo. http://www.sumodehouse.com
Tandem. http://www.tandemnews.com
Terrestre. http://terrestre.com
Tijuana Bloguita Front. http://www.tijuanabloguitafront.blogspot.com
Tijuana House Club. http://www.tijuanahouseclub.com
Torolab. http://www.torolab.com
The Unofficial Nortec Collective Fan Website. http://www.geocities.com/dannyb242
user name: octavio_castellanos password: tavo. http://www.indub.blogspot.com
Yo digo. http://mashaka.blogspot.com
Yonke Art. http://www.yonkeart.org

Newspapers, Magazines, and Fanzines

Adicción Graffiti Magazine
Artbyte Magazine
At/Syber
Austin Chronicle
La Banda Elástica
Billboard
Bitácora
BPM Magazine
Bulbo Press
Cambio

Complot
Complot Internacional: Operación Caos Cultural
DJ
Esopus
Expansión
Frontera
Fugitive Sites
Gear
Guardian
IDJ
Jockey Slut
La Jornada
LA Times
LA Weekly
Latin Pulse!
Lotus Magazine
Lumbre
Memoria
Milenio
Mix Mag
La Mosca
Mural
Muzik
New Music
Newsweek
New York Times
Nexos
Nexus
Nitro
NME
No Cover
El Norte
El Nuevo Sueño de la Gallina
Planeta X
Proceso
PUB Magazine
La Raza
Reforma
Rolling Stone
San Diego Union-Tribune
Seven
Silicon Alley
Sleazenation
Sube Baja
Time
El Universal
URB
Village Voice
Wire

Wired
Zeta
Zona de Obras

Discography

Alan Parsons, *A Valid Path*. Artemis. ATM-CD 51562. 2004.

Artefakto, *Des-construcción*. Opción Sónica. OPCD 06. 1993.

———, *Interruptor*. Opción Sónica. OPCD 55. 1997.

———, *Tierra eléctrica*. Opción Sónica. OPCD 21. 1995.

Balboa, *Plastic Judas on Fire*. Mil Records. MRCD 002. 2002.

Bostich, *Elektronische*. Opción Sónica. OPCD 11. 1994.

———, "Sería feliz, Bostich-Nortec Remix," *Mexican Divas 3*. Opción Sónica. OPJM 01. 2001.

———, *Tiempo d'Afrodita*. Noarte. NOARK7-001. 1992.

———, *Tijuana Bass Sampler*. Mil Records. No number. 2000.

Bostich and Fussible, *Bostich + Fussible: Nortec Remixes*. Mil Records. OPCCD 137. 2000.

DJ Aníbal, *Tijuana Beat Shop*. Mil Records. MRCD 003. 2002.

DJ Tolo, *The Spaced TJ Dub*. Mil Records-Tlahuila. No number. 1999.

Ford Proco, *Vértigo de lodo y miel*. Nimboestatic. NIM 005. 2000.

Fussible, "Allegretto per signora, Nortec Mix," *Ennio Morricone Remixes*, vol. 2. Compost Records. 155-2. 2003.

———, *Fono*. Opción Sónica. OPICD 108. 1999.

———, *Fussible Remixes*. Mil Records. No number. 2000.

———, *No One over 21*. Sonic 360. HACD009. 2004.

———, *Odyssea*. Sonic 360. 0 6700 36326 2 1. 2002.

Klansoff and Solariz, *Electro congal*. Nina Records. No number. 2002.

Kronos Quartet, *Nuevo*. Nonesuch. 79649-2. 2002.

———, *Nuevo: El Sinaloense Remixes*. Nonesuch. PRCD 300847. 2002.

Latinsizer, *Nómada*. Mil Records. MRV 003. 2004.

———, *Ritmo 55*. Mil Records. MRCD 006. 2004.

El Lazo Invisible, *Playas 1*. Taller Cuerda Floja. No number. 2001.

———, *Tijuana Cover Up (Calling Card Mix)*. Taller Cuerda Floja. No number. 2001.

Murcof, *Martes*. Leaf. BAY 2CD. 2002.

Niño Astronauta, *Niño Astronauta*. Nimboestatic. NIM 009. 2004.

Nona Delichas, *Aires de bocacalle*. Nimboestatic. NIM 008. 2001.

Nortec Collective, *Nortec dos*. Mil Records. MRV 002. 2000.

———, *Nortec experimental*. At/Syber. No number. 2001.

———, *Nortec/Radio Sampler*. Mil Records. No number. 2000.

———, *Nor-tec Sampler*. Mil Records. No number. 1999.

———, *Nortec uno*. Mil Records. MRV 001. 2000.

———, *The Tijuana Sessions, vol. 1*. Palm Pictures. 2045-2. 2001.

———, *Tijuana Makes Me Happy*. EMI. 094633684607. 2005.

———, *Tijuana Sessions, vol. 3*. Nacional Records. NCL 63747-2. 2005.

Octavio Hernández, *Zoosónico: Ruidos y sonidos en la frontera de dos mundos*. Insite97. 1998.

Panóptica, *Ahora yo a ti . . . Una colección de remixes por Panóptica*. Nacional Records. NCL 61290-2. 2005.

————, *Panóptica*. Certificate 18 Records. Cert18CD011. 2001.

————, *The Tijuana Remixes*. Certificate 18 Records. Cert18CD018. 2002.

Plankton Man, *4-Zeenaloas*. Bleep Records. No number. 2001.

————, *Plankton Man Sampler*. Mil Records. No number. 2000.

Plankton Man, Terrestre, and Mexicomp (n.e.a.), *Plankton Man vs. Terrestre*. Provider Recordings. PVR 33711. 2002.

Ruisort, *Acapulco Now!* Certificate 18 Records. Cert18CD015. 2002.

Sonios, *200 Fonios*. Nimboestatic. NIM 802CD. 1998.

Terrestre, *Secondary Inspection*. Static Discos. STA 008. 2004.

Terrestre and Plankton Man, *Terrestre vs. Plankton Man*. Nimboestatic. NIM 010. 2003.

Various artists, *Colores*, vol. 1. Mil Records. MRCD 004. 2003.

Various artists, *Electro-Doméstico: Mexitrónica*. At-At Records and Noise Kontrol. AT-004/CDF 005. 2004.

Various artists, *Ennio Morricone Remixes*, vol. 2. Compost Records. 155-2. 2003.

Various artists, *Escurre el cielo*. Discos Invisibles and DiJazz Studio. No number. 2003.

Various artists, *Frontier Life: Banda sonora*. Accretions. ALP031. 2002.

Various artists, *Mexican Divas 3*. Opción Sónica. OPJM 01. 2001.

Various artists, *Música maestro*. Cha3. No number. 1999.

Various artists, *Nicotina*. BMG. 828765246521. 2003.

Various artists, *Public Domain*. Esopus Magazine. CD no. 1. 2003.

Various artists, *Random*, vol. 1. Mil Records. MRCD 005. 2004.

Various artists, *Rolitas de la frontera*. Disco Bulbo. No number. 2003.

Various artists, *Stock: A Static Discos Compilation*. Static Discos. STA 004. 2003.

Films and Videos

Bostich, Sal Ricalde, and Nortec Visual Collective. *Polaris*. Palm Pictures. 2001.

Clorofila and Mario Lagsbartt. *Vivir de noche*. Cha3. 2001.

Díaz, Sebastián. *Colores*. Galatea Productions for Bulbo TV. 2003.

Fjellestad, Hans. *Frontier Life*. Zucasa Productions. 2002.

Foglio, Omar. *Bostich (El padrino de nortec)*. Galatea Productions for Bulbo TV. 2003.

————. *Memorias del Don Loope (y el Galaxy)*. Galatea Productions for Bulbo TV. 2002.

Fussible and Ángeles Moreno. *Odyssea*. Sonic 360. 2001.

Fussible and Jonathan Hernández Piché. *No One over 21*. Insite2000. 2002.

Hiperboreal and Iván Díaz Robledo. *Tijuana for Dummies*. Verdelejos/Yonke Art. 2001.

López, José Ignacio, and Huicho Martín. *La biela de oro*. Discos Invisibles and Sportic Studio. 2002.

Martínez del Canizo, Itzel, and Huicho Martín. *Salón de baile La Estrella*. Loops Urbanos and Bola 8 Productions. 2001.

Pataky, Carla. *DJ Tolo: Cooltivando un sonido*. Galatea Productions for Bulbo TV. 2002.

Plankton Man and Tu Jefa (qqbb, vj boro, vjla). *Lazer metrayeta*. Nimboestatic. 2003.

Seiffert, Annika. *Tijuana Remix*. A.M.I. Universität Hildesheim. 2002.

Terrestre and Carlos Lerma. *El trece negro*. Invisible Proyectos Gráficos. 2003.

Index

Acamonchi (Gerardo Yépiz), 5, 83, 84, 85, 123, 189, 192–193
accordion, 56, 57, 58, 211n10
Adorno, Theodor, 80
advertising, 92, 93, 124. *See also* distribution
Aguilar, Antonio, 53
Los Alegres de Terán, 58
Algara, Claudia, 5, 148, 221n6
"Allegretto per signora" (Fussible), 75, 178
Allen Ness, Sally Ann, 170, 185
Alpert, Herb, 135
Alta California, 15, 206n14
alternative music, 8, 91
ambient music, 8–9, 10
Amexica, 202
Amezcua, Ramón. *See* Bostich (Ramón Amezcua)
"And L" (Panóptica), 24, 100, 133–134, 135
Los Ángeles Negros, 53
Aníbal, DJ, 5, 102
anniversary party, 94–95
Anti-Nortec Manifesto, 197
Anzaldúa, Gloria, 187

Appadurai, Arjun, 196
appropriation, 63
architecture, 117–119
Arellano Félix brothers, 16, 206n18
art, 80; mass reproduction of, 90–91, 113; Tijuana, Tercera Nación and, 189–194, 196, 198, 199, 202, 219n20. *See also* kitsch aesthetic
Artefacto, 29, 30, 208n14
Artefakto, 30, 31, 33, 44, 208n14; dance and, 150; distribution strategy of, 89. *See also* Fussible; Pepe Mogt
Asensio, Susana, 31, 209n16
audiences, 6–7, 90, 99, 101, 163; international, 65, 94. *See also* dance; fans
audiotopia, 19, 25, 148
authenticity, 18, 23, 61–62, 65, 77, 145; in hip-hop, 66; manipulation of, 68; through sampling, 67
"Autobanda" (Bostich), 74, 182, 213n56
Avenida Revolución *(La Revu)*, 13, 63
Aviador Dro, 29
Ayala, Pedro, 57
Aztlán myth, 109

243

Baja California, 15, 206n14
balada pop tradition, 59
Balboa, 6
Banda Aguacaliente, 157
Banda El Recodo, 54–55
banda music, 4, 25, 62, 187, 205n6,
   208n6; as authentic Tijuana sound, 65;
   dissemination of, 63–64; ensemble
   lineup of, 54; as *guapachosa*, 79; history of, 54–56, 211n12; identity and,
   53; kitsch and, 80, 186; modernist
   transformation of, 68; popular dislike
   of, 50–52
"Bar Infierno" (Fussible), 77, 81, 129
bars. *See* clubs
Barthes, Roland, 17
Baudrillard, Jean, 17
Beas, Pedro Gabriel. *See* Hiperboreal
   (Pedro Gabriel Beas)
beer, 107–108, 112–113, 179
Béhague, Gerard, 148
Benjamin, Walter, 80, 90–91, 113
Bhabha, Homi, 16, 194
Blackwell, Chris, 95, 101
Bleep Records, 100
blogs, 98–99; Daniel (local blogger) and,
   193, 199; TJBF and, 98
BMG music company, 88
bodies, 187–188; body language and,
   169, 170; desired, 171–172, 179;
   female, 177, 181
Bohlman, Philip, 64
border culture, 12–13, 45, 141, 203; as
   connective, 16; contradictions of, 202;
   music access and, 27–32; Tijuana,
   Tercera Nación and, 192–193
border fence, 94, 189
borders, 3–4, 193; as "nobody's land,"
   139; Tijuana, Tercera Nación and,
   192; U.S.-Mexico, 15, 37, 79, 193,
   212n29
el bordo, 193–194
Bostich (Ramón Amezcua), 5, 48–49, 90,
   155–156, 208n13; at Chicago's Hot
   House, 181–184; in commercials, 101;
   dance and, 151–152; early career of, 6,
   29, 31; at Festival Tecnogeist 2000,
   200; international events and, 93; La
   Leche tour and, 178; on *Música maes-*

tro, 36; Nor-tec's myth of origin and,
   24, 25, 46; remixes by, 85–86, 105,
   106; style of, 9–10, 69, 72–74, 77–78.
   See also Nortec Collective
"Bostich" (Yello), 208n13
Bostich + Fussible: Nortec Remixes
   (2000), 42, 100
breakbeat tracks, 9
Bronco, 60
"Broncota" (Terrestre), 71
Brown, Sergio. *See* CBrown
Budweiser Beer, 107–108, 112–113
Buie, Kim, 95
Bulma, DJ, 33
Burr, Ramiro, 56
Butler, Judith, 148, 180

Café Tacuba, 84
Calinescu, Matei, 80
Calvo, Armando, 63
Canclini, Néstor Garcia, 17, 115
La Caravana Corona, 54
Cárdenas, Raúl (Torolab), 5, 39, 42, 74,
   141
Carrizosa, Toño, 59
"Casino Soul" (Fussible), 74, 100
Castellanos, Octavio (VJ TCR), 5, 137.
   See also Nortec Collective
Castillo, Gabriel, 92, 122
CBrown, VJ (Sergio Brown), 5, 127, 137,
   138, 145; at Chicago's Hot House,
   181–184; on performance method,
   159–160; on visuals, 158–159. *See also*
   Nortec Collective
center-periphery issues, 191, 201, 204
Centro Bar, 117
Centro-Playas de Tijuana ride, 140
Cerati, Gustavo, 218n15
"El cereso," 70–71 (Terrestre)
Certificate 18, 100
Cha3, 5, 35–36, 39, 43, 123; kitsch and,
   81; Nor-tec's myth of origin and, 25,
   26
Cha3 (fanzine), 35–37
Chau, Manu, 13, 105, 106
Chávez Uranga, Ignacio. *See* Plankton
   Man (Ignacio Chávez Uranga)
El Chavo del 8 (TV show), 84
Chicago, Illinois, 181–184

Chinese food, 62

chotís dancing, 174–175, 176, 177

city plats: Spanish, 119; of Tijuana, 118

class, 5, 60, 223n24; *la 5 y 10* and, 138–139; cumbia music and, 62, 185–186; dance and, 170, 186, 187; Kin-Klé bar and, 129; kitsch and, 80; Mexican migration and, 109, 110; *música guapachosa* and, 79; musical preference and, 51, 53, 55, 87; *paseo inmoral* and, 128; "Paseo moral" and, 127; "Tijuana for Dummies" video and, 142–144

Clorofila (Fritz Torres and Jorge Verdín), 5, 25, 101, 129, 150, 155; kitsch and, 81; style of, 10, 69. *See also* Nortec Collective

clothing of fans, 163, 174

clubs, 30–31; Centro Bar, 117; Don Loope club, 108, 117; El Dandy Del Sur, 115–117; Echo, the, 178, 180, 181; Kin-Klé bar and, 129, 130; Las Pulgas bar, 122, 155, 157; Techno Club, 33; Unicornio club, 129–132

Coachella Valley Music and Arts Festival (2001), 96

La Coahuila, 115

colonization, 124

Colosio, Luis Donaldo, 83, 85

commodification, 23, 88

communication, audience-DJ, 149, 151, 155

community, 164; on Internet, 11, 97–98, 98–99, 100

composition process, 25, 68–69, 70

computer software, 68, 74, 89, 213n54; for live performance, 153–154; Mogt and, 76; for visual art, 138; for VJs, 159

concert organizers, 45

conjunto bands, 52–53, 56, 57, 58, 205n6

consumption, 23; contradictions between production and, 186; libidinal economy and, 200; of modernization, 200–201; as partial meaning of Nor-tec, 148, 167, 169; politics and, 198. *See also* dance

"Contrabando y traición" (Los Tigres del Norte), 156, 214n72

Cook, Nicholas, 154

Cookman, Tomás, 104–105

Corona, Esther, 166–167

Corona, Fernando. *See* Terrestre (Fernando Corona)

Corona, Fernando (Murcof), 71, 152–153

Corona Beer, 107

cosmopolitanism, 31, 46, 57, 62, 101. *See also* modernity; tradition

cover songs, 28, 59

cowboys, 166

critics, 45

Cross Records, 95

Cuban Americans, 110

Cubans, 109

culture, 3, 8, 52; *tijuanense,* 13. *See also* border culture

los culturosos, 6, 90, 126–129, 132, 208n1; "Paseo moral" and, 126–128

cumbia music, 53, 59–61, 185–186; Colombian, 58, 59, 62, 205n6; as *guapachosa,* 79

cumbia norteña, 58, 59, 62

cumbia tropical, 59, 60

cyber-fieldwork, 11–12

"cyber ponchos," 161, 166–167

dance, 62, 149–150, 151–152, 164, 169–188; bodies and, 170, 171–172; in Chicago, 181–184; *chotís,* 174–175, 176, 177; closed work and, 173, 180, 182, 184, 222n14; at early Nor-tec live events, 155; Fussible and, 74; gender and, 170, 177, 178, 181, 187; improvisation and, 174, 176, 177, 178, 180, 185; in Los Angeles, 178–181; mono-centered, 173, 175, 177, 184; Monterrey, Mexico, and, 56–57; open work and, 173, 175–176, 177, 178, 180, 182, 184, 185; as partial meaning of Nor-tec, 148; *Plankton Man vs. Terrestre vs. Falcón* and, 161; *polca,* 174, 176, 177, 183; poly-centered, 173, 178, 181, 183, 184, 185, 186; *quebradita,* 55, 62, 177, 182, 183, 187; redowa, 174, 177; traditional steps and, 173–178

"Dance Dance Revolution" video game, 97

El Dandy Del Sur (club), 115–117
"El Dandy del Sur" (Hiperboreal), 81, 157
Daniel (local blogger), 193, 199
David J, 153
Dávila, Arlene, 180
de Certeau, Michel, 138–139, 146, 169
decontextualization, 66, 74, 78; Tijuana, Tercera Nación and, 192
Deleuze, Gilles, 18, 22
Delgado, Celeste Fraser, 183–184
Demers, Joanna, 97–98
Des-construcción (1993), 30
desire, 17–19, 167–168; bodies and, 171–172, 179; for cosmopolitanism and modernity, 31, 46, 57, 62, 101; libidinal economy and, 171; for originality, 35; question of, 145, 165
"Diagonales luminosas en el trópico" (Algara), 148
Díaz Robledo, Iván. See Wero Palma (Iván Díaz Robledo)
disc jockeys (DJs), 30, 45, 151, 169. See also under specific DJ
Disco Inferno (1976), 129
disco music, 7, 8, 129, 182, 184, 185
discrimination, 184, 194
distribution, 6–7, 23, 32, 49, 87–88; of flyers, 93, 124, 125, 126, 140; Mil Records and, 91–92; Nortec City party and, 162; Nor-tec's hybrid process of, 95–100, 101, 105–106, 113, 123; as partial meaning of Nor-tec, 169; technology of, 89, 104; of UDM, 9
Don Loope club, 108, 117
"Don Loope" (Hiperboreal), 81, 157
donkey show, 115, 145, 220n41
"Don't Tell Me" (Madonna) video, 166
Dorsey, Margaret, 107, 216n40
"Drama Drum" (Hernández and Mogt), 38
drum'n'bass music, 9

Echo Club, the, 178, 180, 181
economy, 58, 59; libidinal, 18, 31, 46, 165, 171, 200
EDM. See electronic dance music (EDM)
Mr. Ejival (DJ), 17, 173
Electro congal (2002), 92

electro pop music, 10
electronic dance music (EDM), 7, 33, 89; compositional principles of, 25; crisis of rock and, 45; international scene of, 30; performance of, 158–159; styles of, 8–9
electronica, 28, 32, 97
Elektronische (1994), 29
e-mail lists, 98
EMI music company, 88
Los Enanitos Verdes, 107
entertainment industry, 109
Erlmann, Veit, 18
Estrada, Erik, 60
ethnicity, 127, 170, 187
European genres, appropriation of, 61
"Evangelio's Danza" (Hernández and Mogt), 38
Expansión (magazine), 89
expansionism, 15, 20

Fadanelli, Guillermo, 114
Falcón, Héctor, 160–161
fans, 6–7, 65, 99, 101; Adriana, 176; Alex, 51, 121, 126, 176; Ana, 174–175, 176, 177; Antonio, 175, 176; Artemio, 203; Daniel, 176, 203; David, 174–175, 176; Diana, 181; dressing up for live events, 163, 174; Enrique, 32; Leticia, 181; Nor-tec Sampler (1999) and, 90; Pedro, 174; Teresa, 174, 177; Ursula, 50, 162
fanzines, 35–37, 93
Ferguson, James, 13
Fernández, César (DJ Horse), 92
Festival Tecnogeist 2000, 199–200
"FIFA 2006" video game, 101
Fikentscher, Kai, 7, 169
film music, 100–101
films, 219n23
filters, 68
First World, 198
Fjellestad, Hans, 141, 156
flyer distribution, 93, 124, 125, 126, 140
FONCA (Fonda Nacional para la Cultura y las Artes), 190, 224n6
Fono (1999), 34–35, 74, 89
El Foro, 119–121
4-Zeenaloas (2001), 100

"4 Zeenaloas" (Plankton Man), 128,
    132
Fox, Vicente, 189, 190, 196
"El fracaso" (Hiperboreal), 157
frames for reception, 33–35, 39, 43–44,
    209n24
Frontera (newspaper), 93
frontier, 193
Frontier Life (2002), 141
Fuentes, Rubén, 178
"Funky Tamazula" (Clorofila), 80–81
Fussible (Melo and Pepe Mogt), 5, 44,
    48, 155; at Chicago's Hot House, 181–
    184; in commercials, 101; distribution
    strategy of, 89; individual contract of,
    100; international events and, 93; La
    Leche Tour and, 110; DJ Matsuoka
    and, 95; Milenio and, 39; Nor-tec's
    myth of origin and, 24, 25; origins of,
    33–35, 45; style of, 10, 69, 74–77. *See
    also* Nortec Collective

Gaillot, Michel, 31
García Esquivel, Juan, 84
Garin, Nina, 163–164, 185
gender, 170, 177, 178, 181, 187
Giddens, Anthony, 20, 21
globalization, 19, 20–22, 44, 78, 195–
    197, 197–199; border communities
    and, 3; distribution and, 91, 104; elec-
    tronica and, 97; private/public spheres
    and, 201–203; U.S.-Mexico border
    and, 193
"glocal" phenomena, 19
gold rush, 15
Golden Exiles, 109
Gómez Bolaños, Roberto, 84
González, Eulalio (Piporro), 175, 184
González Medina, Leoncio, 157
government, 195, 202; Tijuana, Tercera
    Nación and, 196–197. *See also* politics
graphics, 124, 126, 159–161. *See also*
    visual artists
Grito Creativo, 189, 192
Grupo Modelo, 107
El guachaman (The Watching Man),
    165–166
El Guapachoso Vengador (the Festive
    Avenger), 122

Guattari, Félix, 18, 22
Gupta, Akhil, 13

Habermas, Jürgen, 196
Hall, Stuart, 67, 77, 86
Hannover Expo (Germany, 2000),
    93–94
Harrington, David, 83, 84–85
Heineken Beer, 107, 108, 112–113, 179
Hernández, Ingrid, 192
Hernández, Octavio, 37–39, 41, 43
Hiperboreal (Pedro Gabriel Beas), 5, 123,
    150, 155; anniversary party and, 94;
    Banda Aguacaliente and, 157; on de-
    contextualization, 66; Don Loope club
    and, 108; on impermanence, 115–117,
    120, 128–129; on Mexican reaction to
    Nortec, 65; on *Música maestro,* 36;
    Nor-tec's myth of origin and, 24–25,
    26–27, 33, 43, 48–49; previous job of,
    6; style of, 10, 69; "Sueño sur" and,
    35, 39; on Tijuana as home, 62, 63.
    See also Nortec Collective
hip-hop music, 66
Horkheimer, Max, 80
Hot House (Chicago), 181–184, 186
house music, 8, 10, 129, 185
hybridization, 124

identity, 23, 53, 92, 115, 164, 194; dance
    and, 188; as defined by performance of
    Nor-tec, 169; libidinal economy and,
    200; *norteña* music and, 52–53; pan-
    Latino, 179, 183–184; postnational,
    193; of *tijuanenses,* 191–192
IDM. *See* intelligent dance music (IDM)
La ilegal (film), 130–131
immigrants, 63, 203
immigration, 219n23
impermanence, 115–121, 128–129, 145
improvisation, 153, 157, 160; dance and,
    174, 176, 177, 178, 180, 185
in-between-ness, 194
independent music companies (indies),
    57, 88–89
industrial music, 30
"Infierno" (Fussible), 75–76
InSite (cultural institution), 37
Instituto de México in Paris, 160

intelligent dance music (IDM), 9, 10, 71, 150
International Association for the Study of Popular Music (IASPM), 200
international audiences, 65, 94
international electronic music scene, 30
Internet: blogs and, 98–99, 193, 199; community on, 11, 97–98, 98–99, 100; distribution of Nor-tec and, 7; for event promotion, 93, 94; indies and, 89; Mil Records and, 90; MySpace and, 99, 216n28; *Plankton Man vs. Terrestre vs. Falcón* and, 161
Interruptor (1997), 30
iPod, 103

Jackson, Michael, 182, 184
Jai Alai building, 95, 117, 122–123, 137; as El Foro, 119–121
Jameson, Fredric, 20
Jauss, Hans Robert, 209n24
jazz music, 154, 156
Jazzanova, 120, 121
Jiménez, Enrique (Mr. Ejival), 5, 17, 173
Jockey TJ, 197, 198, 199
Julio Sueco, 191

Katz, Mark, 68
Kazaa, 103
Kimika, 173
Kin-Klé bar, 129, 130
"Kin-Klé futurista" (Hiperboreal), 129
Kinky, 108
Kirshenblatt-Gimblett, Barbara, 136
kitsch aesthetic, 79–83, 86, 156, 184, 186, 214n70; *Música maestro* and, 35
Klansoff y Solariz, 92
KMFDM (German band), 30
Konietzko, Sascha, 30
Kronos Quartet, 83, 85–86
Kun, Josh, 19, 25

la 5 y 10, 138–139, 219n29
labels, 30, 31, 44–46, 100–102, 212n29; European, 204; Fussible and, 33; indie, 57, 88–89; major, 29, 57, 88, 217n46
labor, 21
"El lado oscuro de mi compadre" (Terrestre), 71, 95

La Leche tour (2002), 117
La Leche tour (2003), 107–113, 178–181
Latinization, 179–180
Leguizamo, John, 100
libidinal economy, 18, 31, 46, 165; consumption and, 200; objective of, 171
Lien, James, 45
Limón, José E., 177
Linga, DJ, 158
listservs, 98
Live (software), 154
live events, 92, 93–94, 158. *See also* parties; *under specific concert, festival, etc.*
loops, 154, 160
López, José Ignacio, 149
Los Angeles, California, 178–181
Love and Rockets, 153
"Lunatic Trova" (Hernández and Mogt), 38
lyrics, 203

Madonna, 166, 167
major labels, 29, 57, 88, 217n46
managers, 104–105
Mañón, Jennifer, 102, 108–109, 110, 113, 179, 181
Manuel, Peter, 18, 21
"Maquila Dub" (Hernández and Mogt), 38
Maquiladora de Sueños, 161
maquiladoras, 21, 63, 217n8
"Maraka Man" (Terrestre), 69, 71, 72
marginality, 21, 23, 44, 46, 204
mariachi music, 109
Martín, Huicho, 123
Martínez, Narciso, 57
Martínez de Castro, Ricky, 92, 93, 94, 117
Martínez del Canizo, Itzel, 123, 185
Mashaka, VJ (José Luis Martín), 5, 137, 165, 166, 185, 187, 219n26; on body language, 169, 170; on improvisation, 160. *See also* Nortec Collective
Matsuoka, DJ, 95
Max, DJ, 93, 173
media, 161, 165, 195, 223n24; attention to Nor-tec by, 90; *banda* music and, 55–56, 64; international, 162–163;

Mexican, 196, 211n11; *onda grupera* music and, 59, 60, 61; radio and, 28, 29, 53, 58, 179, 208n12; stereotypes of Latino culture in, 181, 185, 186–187; television and, 32, 58, 101, 212n33; Tijuana, Tercera Nación and, 190. *See also* Internet

Melo (Jorge Ruiz), 5, 32, 34, 50–51, 208n14; on dance, 150; on "Infierno," 76; *música guapachosa* and, 79; on naming of Nortec, 48; Nor-tec's myth of origin and, 24, 26; on Palm Pictures, 101; on promotion of Nor-tec, 91; style of, 74; in Synthesis/Artefacto/Artefakto, 29–30; on technical aspects of performance, 153–154. *See also* Nortec Collective

Mendoza, Roberto. *See* Panóptica (Roberto Mendoza)

Mexican Americans, 109–112, 186–187

Mexican War (1848), 15

Mexico, 58, 109, 195; Mexicans of Indian heritage in, 219n19. *See also* Tijuana, Mexico

Mexico City bands, 28

Miami, Florida, 108–109, 110, 111, 112

MIDI (musical instrument digital interface) technology, 28

migrants, 63, 109, 110

Mil Records, 90, 91–92, 100, 102

"Milenio" (Fussible), 34–35, 39

military bands, 54

Miller Beer, 107

mind-body dichotomy, 171

mirror in "Tijuana for Dummies" video, 142, 143–144

Modelevsky, Javier (El Bola), 29–30

modernity, 19–22, 28, 31, 79, 112–113; Bostich and, 72–74; female desire for, 177; Fussible and, 35, 74–77; international events and, 94; memory and, 86; Plankton Man and, 67–69; radicalized, 20, 21, 23; Terrestre and, 69–72; tradition and, 47, 137–139, 164, 165, 170–171, 172, 178

modernization, 23, 200–201

Mogt, Pepe. *See* Pepe Mogt (José Trinidad Morales)

Mondino, Jean-Baptiste, 166

Mongeau, Alain, 97

Montero, Manrico (DJ Linga), 150

Monterrey, Mexico, 56

Morales, José Trinidad. *See* Pepe Mogt (José Trinidad Morales)

moralism, 15–16

morality, 127–128

Moreno, Ángeles, 5, 6, 93, 140–142, 189, 220n35

La Movida Española, 28–29

mp3s, 90

Muñoz, José, 183–184

Murcof (Fernando Corona), 71, 152–153

Music (2000), 166

music industry, 7, 9, 65, 88; selling out and, 106. *See also* labels

music scholarship, 22–23

música guapachosa, 78–79

Música maestro (1999), 26, 33, 35, 36–37, 81

música tropical, 78

musician-audience relationship, 149, 151

Mutek Festival (2003), 97, 152

MySpace, 99, 216n28

"Le mystère du kilo d'or" (exhibit), 160

mythology, 17–19, 47; of origin of Nor-tec, 24–27, 33, 34, 43, 46, 48–49; of Tijuana, 14–16

Nacional Records, 99, 102

naco, 51, 210n6

NAFTA. *See* North American Free Trade Agreement (NAFTA)

Napster, 90

narcochic style, 82, 214n76

narcocorridos, 206n18

national identity, 191, 194

nation-states, 195–197

Navalón, Antonio, 189–192, 194, 196, 202

"negativity of movement," 185

neostalgia, 202, 203

"Nico y Tina" (Terrestre), 71

Nicotina (film), 71, 100

No Cover magazine anniversary party, 121

No One over 21 (2004), 100

Noche de Pasión, 107–108

"Nordic Beat" (Plankton Man), 128, 132

Nor-tec: myth of origin of, 24–27, 33, 34, 43, 46, 48–49; naming of, 46–48

Nortec City party, 95–96, 122–123, 126, 137, 161–164; CBrown and, 138; dance and, 185

Nortec Collective, 5, 47, 66, 155; Anti-Nortec Manifesto and, 197; critical responses to, 65, 197; myth of origin of, 24–27, 33, 34, 43, 46, 48–49; process of composition of, 68–69; visual art and, 137–144. *See also* Bostich (Ramon Amezcua); VJ CBrown (Sergio Brown); Clorofila (Fritz Torres and Jorge Verdín); Hiperboreal (Pedro Gabriel Beas); VJ Mashaka (José Luis Martín); Melo (Jorge Ruiz); Panóptica (Roberto Mendoza); Pepe Mogt (José Trinidad Morales); Plankton Man (Ignacio Chávez Uranga); Terrestre (Fernando Corona); VJ TCR (Octavio Castellanos)

Nortec Live at Las Pulgas, 122, 123–126, 161

Nor-tec Sampler (1999), 47, 69, 72, 81, 95, 133; distribution of, 90, 92, 93

norteña culture, 16

norteña dances, 174–178

norteña music, 4, 25, 48, 62, 208n6; as authentic Tijuana sound, 65; dissemination of, 63–64; ensemble lineup of, 57, 58; as *guapachosa*, 79; history of, 56–58; identity and, 52–53, 56; kitsch and, 80, 186; on *Música maestro*, 36–37; Nor-tec's myth of origin and, 25–26; popular dislike of, 50–52

"Norteño de Janeiro" (Terrestre), 71

North American Free Trade Agreement (NAFTA), 191, 196, 211n11

nostalgia, 203–204

Nuevo (2002), 83–84, 86

El Nuevo Sueño de la Gallina (fanzine), 26, 33, 35–37, 39, 43

Núñez, Gaby (Verdegaby), 123

Odyssea (2002), 100

"Odyssea" (Fussible), 74, 152, 178; video for, 140–142, 144

Olalquiaga, Celeste, 82, 86

Olea, Héctor, 54

Olijov, Osvaldo, 84

"Olvídela compa" (Clorofila-Panóptica), 81

onda grupera music, 51, 53, 62, 79, 80; dissemination of, 63–64; history of, 58–61

Opción Sónica, 30

"Orgánica" (Fussible), 34

originality, 35, 44

Orozco, Ricardo, 118

Ortiz, Fernando, 207n38

Over the Border (Tijuana, Tercera Nación concert), 189

Pacheco, Teodoro, 67–68, 173

Palm Pictures, 95, 96, 98, 100, 123; marketing shortcomings of, 101–104

"El palomar" (Terrestre), 71, 72, 175

PAN administration (National Action Party), 144

Panóptica (2001), 100, 153, 216n30

Panóptica (Roberto Mendoza), 5, 6, 29, 33–34, 44; dance and, 150; individual contract of, 100; La Leche tour and, 178; on Nortec City party, 95; in Nortec performance, 155–156; Nor-tec's myth of origin and, 24, 25, 46, 48–49; on Sónar Festival, 96; style of, 10, 69. *See also* Nortec Collective

"Para que no me olvides" (Santamaría), 66

Paredes, Karina, 92

Part, Ärvo, 71

parties, 92, 93–94, 121–126, 151, 158, 218n9. *See also under specific party*

paseo inmoral, 126–132

"Paseo inmoral" (Cerati), 218n15

"Paseo moral" (Clorofila), 126, 127, 132

Pedraza-Bailey, Silvia, 109

Peña, Manuel, 56–57, 212n29

Pepe Mogt (José Trinidad Morales), 5, 65, 105–106; Anti-Nortec Manifesto and, 197; Artefakto and, 30, 208n14; CD of samples collected by, 66; on community, 164; dance and, 149, 150, 151–152; early career of, 6, 29; in Fussible, 33–35; on global reception of Nor-tec, 88; on identity, 92; on labels, 44–46; La Leche tour and, 178; on lower-class bars, 129; Moreno and, 140; on Nortec City party, 95; Nortec's distribution and, 90, 96, 147; Nor-tec's myth of origin and, 24, 25, 46, 47, 49; on Nor-tec's politicality, 198–199; on Palm Pictures, 103–104; style of, 74–77, 78–79; on Tijuana Beat Shop party, 103; *Zoosónico* and, 37–38, 40–41. *See also* Nortec Collective

percussion, 4, 54, 59, 67, 73

performance, 165, 169, 203; as partial meaning of Nor-tec, 152–158, 167–168; politics and, 198; visuals in, 158–161. *See also* dance

piano, 75, 76

piracy, 91

Plankton Man (Ignacio Chávez Uranga), 5, 6, 155, 177, 216n31; Anti-Nortec Manifesto and, 197; dance and, 150; individual contract of, 100; leaving Nortec Collective, 104, 105–106, 113; Nor-tec's myth of origin and, 25; in *Plankton Man vs. Terrestre vs. Falcón*, 160–161; "El sinaloense" remix of, 85–86; style of, 10, 67–69. *See also* Nortec Collective

Plankton Man vs. Terrestre (2002), 72, 100

Plankton Man vs. Terrestre vs. Falcón (art piece), 160–161

Playas de Tijuana, 139

"Poder Beat (Politics to the Bone)" (Hernández and Mogt), 38, 40–41

"Polaris" (Bostich), 24, 25, 46, 72–73, 182

polca dancing, 174, 176, 177, 183

policemen as dogs, 142, 143, 144

political refugees, 109

politics, 142–143, 144, 159; dance and, 183–184; Nortec Collective's non-involvement in, 197–199; Tijuana, Tercera Nación and, 189–194

pop music, 214n69, 214n81

postmodernism, 19–20

postmodernity, 19–20, 21–22

post-rock music, 209n18

PRI (Institutional Revolutionary Party), 144

PRISA (media conglomerate), 189, 223n1

privatization, 195, 196, 202

production, 32, 89, 198; contradictions between consumption and, 186; as partial meaning of Nor-tec, 148, 151, 169

promotion, 89, 91, 92, 104; flyers and, 93, 124, 125, 126, 140. *See also* distribution

Provider Records, 100

Las Pulgas bar, 122, 155, 157

Las Pulgas concert (March 2002), 155

punchis-punchis (electronic music), 149

Que suene la calle (documentary), 173

quebradita dance, 55, 62, 177, 182, 183, 187

Quintero Rivera, Ángel, 91

race, 109–112, 128, 186, 217n44, 218n19

Radano, Ronald, 64

radio, 28, 29, 53, 58, 179; *Selector de Frecuencias* and, 208n12

Radio Tecnológico 88.7, 29

Ragland, Cathy, 56, 57

ranchero-style dancing, 176

rave dancing, 185

reception, 88; frames for, 33–35, 39, 43–44, 209n24

"Recinto portuario" (Plankton Man), 67, 173, 175

Red Organizada de Mutantes (R.O.M.), 29

redowa dancing, 174, 177

reterritorialization, 22, 186; dance and, 170, 172, 174; impermanence and, 115–121; Nor-tec parties and, 121–126; *paseo inmoral* and, 126–132; through imagery, 137–144; through sound, 132–136

retro aesthetic, 80, 171, 182, 184, 203

Reynolds, Simon, 8

Ricoeur, Paul, 145–146

Rigo Tovar y su Costa Azul, 53, 60

Rivera, Daniel (DJ Tolo), 5, 33, 92, 141, 150–152, 155

Robot dance, 182–183

Rock en Español movement, 29, 107–108
Rock en tu Idioma (Rock in Your
    Language), 32
rock music, 158, 212n33; class and, 53;
    crisis of, 32, 33, 45
R.O.M. *See* Red Organizada de
    Mutantes (R.O.M.)
Ruiz, Álvaro (Balboa), 5, 47
Ruiz, Bruno, 51, 162–163, 166
Ruiz, Jorge. *See* Melo (Jorge Ruiz)
Ruiz, Olivia, 27
"Rumba" (Bostich), 73, 178

Saavedra, Rafa, 98, 144–145, 165,
    208n12, 217n2; on *culturosos,*
    126–127; on donkey show, 220n41;
    on *Fono,* 34; on "Paseo inmoral,"
    218n15; on Tijuana's alternative
    culture, 28–29
Sabrosonic, 93
"Sabrosonix" (Klansoff y Solariz), 92
Salinas de Gortari, Carlos, 38
Salón de baile La Estrella (Martínez del
    Canzio and Martín), 123, 185
El Salón Vaquero (Las Pulgas room), 123
samples, 8, 67, 68, 71, 72; in "Infierno,"
    75; Mogt's CD of, 66; process of com-
    position of, 69, 70; in "Tijuana Makes
    Me Happy," 203
Sandoval, Chela, 21, 194
Santamaría, Lorenzo, 66
Schloss, Joseph G., 66
Secondary Inspection (2004), 69, 71–72
Seelye, H. Ned, 47
Selector de Frecuencias (radio show),
    208n12
selling out, 104, 106
"Sería felíz" (Bostich-Venegas), 73–74
sexuality, 181
Shadow Records, 95
Shank, Barry, 148
"She Is in Fiestas" (Panóptica), 153
El Show de Johnny Canales (TV show),
    61, 212n37
Siempre en Domingo (TV show), 214n81
Silva, Aníbal (DJ Aníbal), 5, 102
Simonett, Helena, 54
simulacrum, 17–19; of authenticity,
    61–62, 65

Sin City, 15–16
Sinaloan music, 54–55
"El sinaloense" (Kronos Quartet), 83–86
Sintonía Pop (radio show), 29
Sistema Evolutivo de Binomios, 39, 42,
    74
"Slap da Bass" (Fussible), 34
Slobin, Mark, 19
social mobility, 63
Sol Café, 94
"El sonar de mis tambores" (Fussible),
    74–75, 182
Sónar Festival (Barcelona, 2001), 96
Sonic 360, 100, 108, 110, 112, 117, 140,
    178–179
Sonios, 40, 44, 150
Sontag, Susan, 80
Sony, 88
sound-file-sharing sites, 98
Spaced TJ Dub, The (1999), 93, 151
Static Discos, 91
Subcomandante Marcos, 38
El Sueño de la Gallina, 82
"Sueño sur" (Hiperboreal), 33, 35, 39
Super Nortec (Martínez del Canizo),
    123
"Synthakon" (Bostich), 200
Synthesis, 29–30. *See also* Artefacto;
    Artefakto; Fussible
Synthesis (1988), 30
synthesizers, 68, 75

taconazo-style dancing, 175, 184
Tamayo, Rubén (Fax), 91
la tambora, 4, 54, 66
tarola rolls, 67, 73
Taylor, Diana, 203
TCR, VJ (Octavio Castellanos), 5, 137.
    See also Nortec Collective
Techno Club, 33
techno music, 8, 47
technobanda, 55, 64
technology, 4, 28, 47–48, 160–161;
    globalization and, 20; indies and, 89;
    promotion and, 89, 104; UDM and, 8
Televisa (TV network), 32, 212n33
television, 58, 101
"Tengo la voz" (Bostich), 73
"Tepache Jam" (Terrestre), 71

Terrestre (Fernando Corona), 5, 39, 42–43, 74, 95, 166, 173; dance and, 150; "El sinaloense" remix of, 85–86; leaving Nortec Collective, 104, 105–106, 113; La Leche Tour and, 111; in Nor-tec performance, 155; Nor-tec's myth of origin and, 25; *Plankton Man vs. Terrestre* and, 72, 100; in *Plankton Man vs. Terrestre vs. Falcón*, 160–161; previous job of, 6; search for originality by, 44; style of, 10, 69–72, 77. *See also* Nortec Collective

Terrestre vs. Plankton Man (2003), 216n31

"third space," 194–195

Third World, 198

Thomas, Helen, 172

Thornton, Sarah, 7

Tiempo d'Afrodita (1992), 29

Tierra eléctrica (1995), 30

Los Tigres del Norte, 58, 60, 87, 156, 214n72

Tijuana, Mexico, 136, 206n13; city plat of, 118; history and mythology of, 14–16; population growth of, 63; Zona Centro map of, 120

Tijuana, Tercera Nación, 189–194, 196, 198, 199, 202, 219n20

Tijuana arch, 115–117

"Tijuana Bass" (Bostich), 134–136, 182

Tijuana Beat Shop (2002), 102–103

Tijuana Beat Shop party, 103

Tijuana Bloguita Front (TJBF), 98

Tijuana Brass, 134–135

"Tijuana for Dummies" (Hiperboreal), 123, 132–134, 142–144

Tijuana House Club email list and listserv, 98

"Tijuana Makes Me Happy" (Fussible), 202–203

Tijuana Remixes, The (2002), 100, 153

Tijuana Sessions, Vol. 1, The (2001), 45, 48, 100, 103, 167; "And L" on, 133–134; graphics of, 81; Nortec City party and, 95, 96, 122, 162; Terrestre on, 72

Tijuana Sessions, Vol. 2, The, 102–103

Tijuana Sessions, Vol. 3 (2005), 10, 80, 167; "Bar Infierno" on, 76–77; homo-geneity of, 156–157; MySpace and, 99; as reference to *Vol. 2*, 102; "Tijuana Makes Me Happy" and, 202

Tijuana taxis, 140–141

TJBF. *See* Tijuana Bloguita Front (TJBF)

Tolo, DJ, 5, 33, 67, 92, 93, 98, 141, 150–152, 155

Torolab (Raúl Cárdenas), 5, 39, 42, 74, 141

Torres, Fritz, 5, 6, 35–36, 140; kitsch and, 81–82, 83; Nor-tec's myth of origin and, 25, 26. *See also* Cha3; Clorofila; Nortec Collective

tourism, 15–16, 27, 122, 127, 145

Tovar García, Rigoberto (Rigo Tovar), 60

tradition, 23, 51–52, 157–158; authenticity of, 62; Bostich and, 72–74; desire to break away from, 79; Fussible and, 74–77; manipulation of, 68; modernity and, 47, 137–139, 164, 165, 170–171, 172, 178; "official" Mexican music and, 54; Plankton Man and, 67–69; Terrestre and, 69–72

Trammps, the, 129

"Trance Frontera" (Hernández and Mogt), 38

trance music, 9

transculturation, 63, 207n38

transnational corporations, 195

Treaty of Guadalupe Hidalgo (1848), 15

"Trip to Ensenada" (Fussible), 151

"Trippy Boy" (Fussible), 34

Los Tucanes de Tijuana, 58

Tucker, Luis, 92, 94

Turino, Thomas, 19

Turkle, Sherry, 161

Turner, Bryan, 171

UDM. *See* underground dance music (UDM)

Undefeated (2003), 100

underdeveloped world, 21

underground dance music (UDM), 7–10, 30, 90–91

"Unicornio" (Bostich), 129–132, 145, 151–152, 178

Unicornio club, 129–132

United States, 195

U.S.-Mexico border, 15, 37, 79, 193,
212n29. *See also* borders; border
culture; border fence
Universal (label), 88
urban landscapes: celebration of, 122–
123; impermanence of, 119–121
Urbe 01 (cyber-magazine), 200

Valenzuela Arce, José Manuel, 124,
197–198
Vasconcelos, José, 16
Vázquez Ricalde, Salvador (VJ Sal), 5,
137
Velasco, Raúl, 83, 84, 214n81
Venegas, Julieta, 73, 106
"Ventilador" (Fussible), 24, 74, 89, 151
Verdín, Jorge, 5, 6, 35, 124, 126; kitsch
and, 81–82, 83; Nor-tec's myth of
origin and, 25, 26. *See also* Cha3;
Clorofila; Nortec Collective
Vernallis, Carol, 140
video, 139–144
video games, 97, 101
video jockeys (VJs), 159–160, 221n22.
See also under specific VJ
vihuela (rhythm guitar), 76
Vila, Pablo, 13
Villa, Pancho (Francisco Villa), 53

Villarreal, Bruno "El Azote," 57
visual artists, 5–6, 81, 137–144, 199,
221n22
visuals, 124, 126, 138, 158–161
vocals, 9, 203
Volstead Act (1919), 15

Warner, 88
Wasiliewski, Jaqueline Howell, 47
Web groups, 98
Web sites, 98, 140, 216n27
Wero Palma, VJ (Iván Díaz Robledo), 5,
122–123, 137, 189, 219n26; "Tijuana
for Dummies" video by, 142–144
whiteness, 128, 218n19. *See also* race
women, 177, 181

Yello, 29
Yépez, Heriberto, 51, 191, 199
Yépiz, Gerardo (Acamonchi), 5, 83, 84,
85, 123, 189, 192–193
Yúdice, George, 88, 202

Zeta (newspaper), 220n38
Žižek, Slavoj, 18, 145, 170–171, 200
Zócalo festival, 93–94
Zona Centro, 127
Zoosónico, 37–39, 40–41